Occupation: *Nazi-Hunter*

The Continuing Search
for the Perpetrators of the Holocaust

Occupation: *Nazi-Hunter*

The Continuing Search
for the Perpetrators of the Holocaust

Efraim Zuroff

Foreword by
Rabbi Marvin Hier

KTAV Publishing House, Inc.
Hoboken, New Jersey

in association with

The Simon Wiesenthal Center
Los Angeles, California

Library of Congress Cataloging-in-Publication Data

Zuroff, Efraim
    Occupation, Nazi-Hunter : the continuing search for the perpetrators of
the Holocaust / Efraim Zuroff ; with a foreword by Marvin Hier.
        p.   cm.
    Includes bibliographical references and index.
    ISBN 0-88125-489-4
    1. World War, 1939-1945—Atrocities. 2. Holocaust, Jewish
(1939–1945). 3. War criminals. 4. Criminal investigation. 5. Zuroff, Efraim.
6. United States. Dept. of Justice. Office of Special Investigatios. 7. Simon
Wiesenthal Center. I. Title.
D803.Z87 1994
364.1'38—dc20   94-20205
                                                                      CIP

Manufactured in the United States of America
KTAV Publishing House, 900 Jefferson Street, Hoboken NJ, 07030

For a horrible and terrible storm has shaken all of us and thus we are here and there and where not. We have become a generation without grandfathers and grandmothers, without fathers, without brothers and sisters . . . The decorated synagogue no longer stands, the same black benches, the white prayer shawls, and that grandfather who would pinch our cheeks. Where are the Moishes, Avrams, Yankels? Did they and we feel that in one sunset all would be destroyed and erased as if it had never existed?

And how did they die? From disease? From old age? No, not at all. It came with a horrible and terrible fury. They did not even have a chance to return their souls to their Maker, because their souls were murdered, hacked to pieces with knives and bullets; their souls were burnt and extinguished and perished as if they had never existed.

Testimony of Micah Gazit,
Yad Vashem Archives, 0-3/2205

Contents

Foreword

At the end of the Second World War, when the horrors of the Final Solution were revealed to the world, there was a general feeling among the Allies and the United Nations that something must be done to bring the perpetrators of these crimes to justice. From this notion was born the concept of the Nuremberg Trials. They were designed to show the people of the world that the Allies cared and that the perpetrators would be made to pay for their crimes.

Unfortunately, the new realities of the postwar world and the beginnings of the cold war soon set in. As a result, the Nazi trials became the Allies' final statement on bringing Nazi war criminals to justice. From this point on, those who were not brought to trial at Nuremberg were able to live out their years without fear that there was someone looking for them. Thousands of concentration camp guards and other war criminals took advantage of this climate and escaped to the West, finding safe haven in the United States, South America, Canada, England, or Australia, many of them reaching their destinations with the aid of the International Red Cross and the Vatican, which provided them with passports and identity papers. Among them were the notorious Adolf Eichmann, Josef Mengele, Franz Stangl and Walter Kutschmann, all of whom escaped to South America.

Only private individuals, such as Simon Wiesenthal, carried on the fight alone and without help either from governments or even from Jewish organizations. Indeed, it was not until the late 70s, and mainly because of the efforts of Congresswoman Elizabeth Holtzman, that the United States government created the Office of Special Investigations (OSI) that would seek to denaturalize Nazis found in the United States. Other Western governments tried to emulate the United States but without much success.

This book tells the story of Efraim Zuroff's singular determination, first on behalf of the OSI and then on behalf of the Simon Wiesenthal Center, to set the record straight and to bring some of these Nazis to justice. As Zuroff takes us through some of the most famous cases he

ix

has worked on, the reader gains an insight into his motivation and the motivation of the Simon Wiesenthal Center. Namely, that a small measure of justice is better than none, and that time must never become a refuge for crimes against humanity.

The Simon Wiesenthal Center is committed to this issue because we see it as a moral commitment to the victims of the Shoah. Zuroff's book gives credence to that commitment.

Rabbi Marvin Hier
Dean and Founder
The Simon Wiesenthal Center
January 6, 1994

Acknowledgments

Whatever has hitherto been done to bring Nazi war criminals to justice could never have been achieved without the efforts of those dedicated individuals who have spent years documenting the events of the Holocaust. Their work has enabled us not only to learn about those terrible historical realities, but also to attempt to ensure that those responsible for the implementation of the Final Solution are forced to pay for their crimes. The efforts described in this book could never have taken place, therefore, without the extensive documentation amassed and intensive research carried out over the course of the past four decades by the institutions established for this purpose, and by individual scholars and researchers.

Documentation and research do not suffice, however, unless they are accompanied by a strong sense of motivation and a determination to achieve concrete results. This was certainly true as far as the attempts to prosecute the perpetrators of the Holocaust. For years documents gathered dust and murderers grew old in peace and tranquillity. It is therefore only fitting to begin by acknowledging the role played by individuals who helped convert the international campaign to bring Nazi war criminals to justice from a private dream to a public reality.

Special thanks therefore to the leadership and staff of the Simon Wiesenthal Center in Los Angeles, primarily to Rabbi Marvin Hier, founder and Dean and to Rabbi Abraham Cooper, Associate Dean of the Center. They believed in the concept, worked with dedication to realize the goal, and provided the vehicle and the means to achieve substantial results. Rabbi Daniel Landes was a consistent source of wisdom, friendship and support. Executive Director Rabbi Meyer May and Director Dr. Gerald Margolis could always be called upon for assistance. Lydia Triantopoulis and her successor Avra Shapiro, assisted by Michele Eisman, played a vital role in our campaign as directors of public relations. Thanks also to director of media projects Rick Trank and director of research Aaron Breitbart whose help was always forthcoming. In Canada, Sol Littman was a tower of strength and he deserves much of the credit for whatever was achieved in that country. My colleagues in New

York also made a significant contribution to our efforts. Rhonda Barad provided vital assistance and could always be counted on for logistic support. She was ably assisted by Mark Weitzman and Vicky Acriche Turek. In Europe, Shimon Samuels assisted our efforts in various ways.

Last, but not least in this regard, are my staff in Jerusalem who were active participants in many of the activities described in this book. Talma Hurvitz very capably coordinated operations, while Menachem Fogel, Ettie Eisenriech and Hadassah Jacobs also contributed their share. In the early years of our campaign, Dr. Robert Rozett and Chaim Mass provided competent and significant assistance.

I am very grateful to the staff of the Yad Vashem Library who have always gone out of their way to assist me in my researh. Ora Alcalay, Klara Gini, Yitzchak Len, Efrat Weinfeld, Vered Wahlen and recently appointed director Dr. Robert Rozett are friends who have provided able assistance with a smile on practically a daily basis for the past fifteen years. Ever since I began working for the Office of Special Investigations I have made extensive use of the Yad Vashem Archives. Newly-appointed director Yaakov Lazowick, Hadassah Modlinger, Yehudit Kleinman, Moshe Band, Bella Kirschner, and Mary Ginzburg have time and again extended help which has considerably facilitated my work as a researcher.

During the past eight years I obtained considerable material from other Israeli archives, some of whose devoted workers deserve special mention. Dr. Judy Baumel, of Bar-Ilan University's Institute for Holocaust Research, was always willing to do the maximum to help our efforts and in the process became a close friend. At the Moreshet Archives, Shmuel Frankel provided not only a warm welcome but dedicated assistance during the long hours I spent there. The staffs at Beit Lohamei ha-Gettaot and especially at the Weiner Library at Tel Aviv University were also very helpful.

There were also quite a few individuals who provided particularly important assistance. Over the years, Professor Dov Levin, of Yad Vashem and the Hebrew University has played an increasingly important role in our efforts. As a former partisan and survivor of the Kovno Ghetto, he has always exhibited an active interest in the attempts to prosecute Nazi war criminals. As the world's premier expert on the fate of the Jews of Lithuania, Latvia and Estonia during the Holocaust, he has on numerous occasions made available his professional expertise. On a personal level, his warm support, friendship, and encouragement have been a unique source of motivation. Faina Kuklianskyte, of Vilnius and Netanya, has also played a very significant role in our efforts to uncover Nazi war criminals, particularly in Lithuania. The help she and her father, Professor Samuelis Kuklianskis, provided regarding the rehabilitations granted by the Lithuanian government to convicted Nazi war criminals helped us expose that scandal and paved the way for the establishment of a joint Lithuanian-Israel commission of inquiry to review all the rehabilitations. Faina greatly facilitated our work in Lithuania and I am hopeful that she will head the Center's future operations in that country.

Tel-Aviv lawyer Joseph Melamed has provided considerable expertise and resources for the efforts to expose the role played by Lithuanian Nazi collaborators in the Holocaust. He has proven to be an able and energetic partner for many of the Center's activiites. Chaya Lifshitz, of Yad Vashem, made available substantial material regarding Lithuanian Nazi war criminals, some of which led to highly significant results. Zelig Gelinsky sent me virtually inaccessible material regarding the crimes committed in Lithuania and Rachel Levin, of the Israeli Association of Lithuanian Immigrants, and Rabbi Mendy Katz also assisted me in this respect. Moshe Aronson, who recently made *aliya* from Lithuania, did a yeoman's job in translating materials from Lithuanian and Russian, and made an important contribution to our efforts. Tzila Gudrov was also very helpful in this respect. As Jews of Lithuanian origin, their assistance was, in essence, a labor of love and commemoration and their encouragement was particularly heartwarming. Dr. Shmuel Spector provided expert advice on events in the Ukraine and Dr.Mordecai Paldiel was always forthcoming with materials relating to the activities of the Righteous Among The Nations. Esther Hagar shared views and material on the fate of Latvian Jewry. Yaakov Kaplan, Shmuel Lazikin and David Slomka provided important documents and information regarding the murder of the Jews in Estonia.

No list of this sort would be complete without the name of Allan A. Ryan, Jr. who, in his capacity as director, initiated and fully supported my work in Israel on behalf of OSI. It was also a special pleasure to work with colleagues like David Marwell, whose dedication and expertise have made a significant contribution to many investigations. Among the members of the Israeli police Nazi war crimes unit, I learned a lot from Sergeant Martin Kolar, a top-notch expert with years of experience, and enjoyed working together with Lieutenant Arye Orbach.

Quite a few of my former colleagues at Yad Vashem were helpful in various ways. Besides being a source of sage professional advice, Yitzchak Mais, the director of the Yad Vashem Museum, is a close personal friend, whose support and encouragement over the years have meant a lot to me. David Silberklang was always willing to share interesting ideas and information, as he too became involved in Nazi war crimes research. Iris Berlitzky often came up with vital information. Dr. Gavriel Bar-Shaked went out of his way to facilitate my work and the staff of the education department, and especially Dr. Karen Shawn, were always ready to lend a helping hand.

Throughout the trials and tribulations which accompanied the "rebirth" of this book, I had the steadfast friendship and support of my friends and neighbors in Efrat—Rhoda and David Brandriss, Rachel and David Levmore and Tommy and Esther Lamm. Another friend who was always there for me was Dr. Seymour Adler whose assistance and expert advice have helped me both professionally and personally in more ways than I can enumerate. In recent years, I have also renewed an old friendship with Aryeh Rubin who shares my intense desire to see the perpetrators of the Holocaust brought to justice and has invested considerable resources and energy in pursuing that goal.

No list of acknowledgements would be complete without a special word of thanks to Jane Tatum who paid a heavy price for her belief in this book and what it represents. As the founder and managing director of Ashford Press Publishing, Jane initiated this project and gave it her fullest support. When her superiors in Martins Printing Group Ltd. refused to fight against the injunction barring the book's distribution obtained by a Nazi war criminal in Scotland, Jane quit in protest. Rarely does one see such steadfast devotion to principles and Jane unfortunately paid a heavy price for her ideals. The late Bernard Simon also deserves a special thanks for representing me throughout my painful dealings with Ashford Press following Jane's resignation.

Four generations of our family are involved in this endeavor. My grandfather, Samuel L. Sar, served as a model and inspiration. My parents, Rabbi Dr. Abraham and Esther Zuroff, provided me with education and support and inculcated a commitment to contribute to the community. My wife Elisheva did not have to read the manuscript. She lived through it day by day and was a full partner in the gestation process. Hopefully our children—Avigayil, Itamar, Elchanan and Ayelet—will take its contents to heart.

Introduction

In the winter of 1941, as he was being dragged out of his home in the Riga Ghetto, prior to being murdered in the mass executions carried out by the Nazis and their Latvian collaborators, the noted historian Shimon Dubnow told the Jews around him: "*Yidn farschreibt*" (Jews write down everything . . . Keep a record of it all).[1] Several hundred miles away in Kovno, the former capital of Lithuania, Jews murdered in the suburb of Slobodka (Viliampole) left a different message for their brethren. "*Yidn nekoma*" (Jews, take revenge) they scrawled on the walls of the apartment in which they were murdered by the Nazis' Lithuanian cohorts.[2]

This book lies somewhere in the middle between these two directives. Not only because it deals to a large extent with that precise geographical area and some of the perpetrators of those very crimes. It lies between the time-honored Jewish tradition of recording events and transmitting them from generation to generation to ensure their commemoration and the commandment to obliterate the proponents of evil for evil's sake, which manifested itself in recent times in the Holocaust—the most pernicious genocide in the annals of modern mankind. The attempts to prosecute the murderers on the basis of events recorded and remembered is in a sense a prosaic compromise between the two demands made by Jews on the verge of annihilation.

This book tells the story of those who were armed only with the memory of the survivors and the dedicated efforts of those who devoted themselves to preserving the tale. With this Jewish "ammunition" they attempted to undo the results of decades of apathy and inactivity, of years upon years in which the requests of those Jews who called out for action against the perpetrators remained cries in the wilderness.

This is a book about a problem which did not have to exist. Two letters which I discovered in the course of my research illustrate this point. On October 20, 1948 Simon Wiesenthal, at that time a leader of the Jewish Historical Documentation Center and a member of the American Screening Board for Persecuted Minorities in Upper Austria, wrote to Mr. Bedo, the Chief Eligibility Officer of the International Refugee Organization (IRO) in Salzburg, Austria. Wiesenthal pointed out that thousands of Nazi collaborators had obtained status as Displaced Persons and were being assisted in various ways. Some like Herbert Cukurs, one of the most notorious Latvian murderers, had already succeeded in emigrating to Brazil (where he was discovered in the course of an anti-Semitic demonstration), others would soon be leaving for Western democracies. Wiesenthal pointed out that a terrible injustice was taking place.

> The money IRO is using comes from funds of the various governments and also from the collected money and gold teeth of killed Nazi victims in concentration camps. All together, it seems, that *killed Jews are paying for the escape of their murderers through IRO. . .*I, as chairman of the Committee of former Jewish concentration camp inmates feel as my duty not only to represent the interest of the survivors, but even more of our killed parents, wives, children who were murdered by some of the present United Nations DPs. Therefore we will do everything within our possibilities to prevent this outrageous injustice.[3]

I am not certain how Mr. Bedo responded to this letter, but the unfortunate results speak for themselves.

Exactly two months later, on December 20, 1948, another survivor who was preoccupied with the issue of Nazi war criminals wrote to a committee which had been established in London to investigate Nazi war crimes in the Baltics. Rafael Schub, one of the few Latvian Jews who survived the Riga Ghetto, had emigrated to Canada and bemoaned the inexplicable apathy regarding the fate of the perpetrators of the Holocaust.

> I am living here in a small town in Canada and I am trying to enlighten the Canadian workers as to what kind of people the Latvians and Lithuanians actually are. It seems to me that most of the DPs who arrived in Canada are dangerous. I have approached Jews, MPs, charitable organizations and other officials, nobody listens to me. The things the Jews here are most interested in, are movies, sport, card games, food (plenty of good food), cars, etc. They won't listen to our grief.[4]

These two letters reflect the realities of 1948, which hardly changed in any way during the subsequent three decades. The perpetrators of the Holocaust lived in peace and tranquillity throughout the Western world, even in countries which had fought against the Nazis, and almost nothing was done to bring them to justice. Only in 1977 were the first positive steps taken by the United States government to rectify the situation, but the American Office of Special Investigations remained the only institution of its kind for quite a few years. Only in the wake of recent public pressure, the discovery of hundreds of suspected Nazi war criminals living in the West by the Wiesenthal Center and other factors, have the previously reluctant governments of Canada and Australia responded with direct measures to enable the prosecution of the perpetrators. England, which stubbornly refused for years to take any action, has finally initiated an official inquiry and hopefully will adopt similar steps to those taken by other countries.

These changes have created a veritable revolution with regard to the prosecution of Nazi war criminals. Much too little, far too late indeed, but nonetheless an important step forward for justice and historical truth. For six years I had the privilege of working for the US Office of Special Investigations and since September 1986 I have continued those efforts worldwide within the framework of the Simon Wiesenthal Center. I know quite clearly that not every Nazi alive will be brought to justice, nor will every criminal even be indicted. That battle was lost long ago. At the same time, however, I believe that very few Nazis can be certain today that their whereabouts will never be exposed and that they will never have to pay for their crimes. That is not the optimal solution, but that too—besides tens of indictments—is a tangible victory. How it was achieved is the story of this volume.

Efrat, Gush Etzion, Israel

Adar 5748/March 1988

This book was scheduled for publication on October 17, 1988. It is only appearing now because of an injunction barring its distribution which was obtained by Antony Gecas (Antanas Gecevicius), a Lithuanian Nazi war criminal currently living in Edinburgh, who is named in the book. During the past five years, I have been engaged in a twofold battle to ensure that Gecas is prosecuted for his crimes and to enable the publication of this book which tells his story among many others.

The results to date have been mixed. In June 1991, almost five years after I had initially named Gecas as one of 17 suspected Nazi war criminals living in Great Britain the British government passed a law enabling the prosecution of Nazi war criminals throughout the United Kingdom. In July 1992 Gecas lost a libel case he initiated against Scottish Television and was branded a "mass murderer" and a "Nazi war criminal" by the judge , Lord Milligan.[5] Yet despite the passage of the British War Crimes Act and the unequivocal condemnation of Gecas in his libel suit, the former Lithuanian police officer who served as a lieutenant in the notorious 12th Auxiliary Police Battalion has still not been indicted for his crimes by the Scottish authorities.

This story emphasizes the frustration of those engaged in the efforts to bring the perpetrators of the Holocaust to the bar of justice. Despite several significant successes in convincing governments to investigate the wartime crimes of suspected Nazis and, more important, pass special legislation to enable their prosecution, the struggle for justice is proving increasingly difficult as time goes by.

Perhaps the most frustrating case in this respect has been that of Ivan Demjanjuk who was put on trial in Israel for his service in the Nazi death camps. Originally convicted of being Ivan Grozny (Ivan the Terrible) the sadistic Ukrainian guard who operated the gas chambers at Treblinka, he was acquitted of that charge by the Israeli Supreme Court on July 29, 1993 due to the existence of "reasonable doubt" regarding his identification. The court, however, unequivocally verified his service as a *Wachmann* (guard) at the Trawniki SS training camp and other Nazi concentration camps and his participation in the implementation of the Final Solution.

Demjanjuk, who had been imprisoned in Israel for more than seven years, was freed due to legal technicalities. Unable to retry him for his crimes at Sobibor and Trawniki due to "double jeopardy" (those charges were included in the original indictment) and unable to convict him for those crimes because he had not originally been given ample opportunity to defend himself against those specific charges, Israel's Supreme Court ordered the release of a man they acknowledged to have been an active participant in the murder of European Jewry.[6]

More than six years ago, when this book was originally completed, I was more optimistic regarding the practical results of my efforts and of those of fellow Nazi-hunters. Buoyed by the passage of the war crimes bill in Canada and its imminent passage in Australia, and the consistent success of the U.S. government's Office of Special Investigations to denaturalize and deport Nazi war criminals living in America, I envisioned a steady stream of convictions. According to the provisions of the bill passed in Canada and its Australian counterpart, Nazi war criminals could be punished for their crimes (unlike the situation in the United States where they were being tried for immigration and naturalization violations) and given the severity of the allegations, it appeared that justice, in many cases, would finally be achieved. In Great Britain, where the Wiesenthal Center had initiated the issue by submitting a list of suspected Nazis to the authorities in October 1986, the government had at long last established a highly prestigious commission of inquiry and it too seemed at least on the path to prosecution. In Israel, Demjanjuk had been convicted by the Jerusalem District Court after the prosecution had presented what appeared to be an extremely convincing case.

It is now clear that my optimism was to a large extent unrealistic. Great Britain did eventually pass a War Crimes Act but practical, legal and political difficulties have severely plagued the prosecution of Nazi war criminals there and elsewhere. The efforts which we originally envisioned would lead to a spate of successful trials have to date not produced a single criminal conviction, although the battle is not yet over. Even worse, most Nazis today realize that despite the existence of laws enabling their prosecution, they will never be held accountable. Ironically, it is the biggest killers in most cases who are the primary beneficiaries of these problems. Those who served in murder squads such as the Lithuanian *Ypatingas burys* and 12th Auxiliary Police Battalion and the Latvian Arajs Commando, whose members can invariably only be identified by their fellow perpetrators, are the individuals most likely to escape prosecution. Whereas perpetrator testimony could occasionally be obtained from convicted murder squad members during the era of Communist rule, the chances of finding recalcitrant killers willing to help convict their former colleagues in independent Lithuania, Latvia or any of the other former Soviet republics or satellites is extremely slim.

Nowhere is this problem more acute today than in Australia where the local authorities closed down their Special Investigations Unit in June 1992 despite the presence in that country of numerous Nazi war criminals, among them quite a few members of Baltic murder squads. The high costs of the investigations coupled with legal, technical and electoral considerations led to the decision by Attorney-General Michael Duffy to close down Australia's Nazi-hunting operation, thereby in effect, granting amnesty to dozens of Hitler's worst henchmen.

Despite these setbacks, the efforts to convict the perpetrators of the Holocaust will continue as long as those who participated in the mass murder of Jews can still be brought to trial. In 1992, Josef Schwammburger, the commandant of Nazi camps in Mielec, Rozwadow and Przemysl was sentenced to life imprisonment in Germany after being extradited from Argentina, and numerous Nazi war criminals were indicted, denaturalized and/or deported from the United States.

In late summer 1993, after a lengthy and complicated research effort and political campaign conducted by the Simon Wiesenthal Center, Hallvardur Einvardsson, the Director of Public Prosecutions in Iceland announced that he had ordered the opening of an official criminal investigation for murder against Nazi collaborator Evald Mikson, who was suspected of playing an active role in the persecution and annihilation of the Jews of Estonia. If we add our partially successful efforts to date to rescind the rehabilitations unjustly granted by the Lithuanian authorities to Nazi war criminals and the recent discovery of SS Captain Erich Priebke and several other Nazi perpetrators, we see that even at this point in time important results can be achieved in this field.

These successes ostensibly justify the continuation of the attempts to seek out and prosecute the perpetrators of the Holocaust. But regardless of the results, the primary justification and motivation—our sense of obligation to the Jews who were murdered simply because they were Jews or of Jewish origin—remains as strong and valid as ever. That gives us the strength to continue what appears to be an increasingly difficult task along with the hope that despite the numerous obstacles at least a small measure of justice will ultimately be achieved.

Efrat, Gush Etzion, Israel

Sivan 5754/June 1994

Notes

1. This story is related in several sources, among them: Lucy S. Dawidowicz, *The Holocaust and the Historians*, Cambridge, 1981, p. 125.

2. Tzvi Avraham Baron and Dov Levin, *Toldoteha shel Machteret; ha-Irgun ha-Lochem shel Yehudei Kovna be-Milchemet ha-Olam ha-Shneeya*, Jerusalem 1962, photograph opposite p. 72.

3. Letter of Simon Wiesenthal to Mr. Bedo, October 20, 1948, Yad Vashem Archives, M-9/69.

4. Letter of Rafael Schub to H. Michelson, December 20, 1948, Wiener Library Archives, 539/25.

5. Opinion of Lord Milligan *in causa* Antony Gecas *Pursuer* against Scottish Television PLC *Defenders*, July 17, 1992, pp. 180-84.

6. Psak Din, Ir'ur Plili 347/68 Ivan (John) Demjanjuk neged Medinat Yisrael, Av 5753/July 1993, pp. 375-405.

1

From Holocaust Scholar to Nazi-Hunter

I never dreamt while growing up in Brooklyn that I would become a Nazi-hunter. While many Jewish children perhaps toyed with such fantasies in the immediate post-Holocaust period, I never even entertained the thought of such a possibility. The Holocaust, to the extent that I was aware that such a thing had taken place, was a term to describe events very remote and distant. Even though our family was intensely Jewish—our lives revolving primarily around our Jewish identity and observances—the Holocaust played almost no role and was relegated to the background. File under "Jewish history - suffering" would perhaps be the best way to describe my parents' attitude to those events. For them, even though (or perhaps because) they had actually lived through World War II (as young adults in the United States), the Holocaust was merely the most recent tragedy in a long series of catastrophes in Jewish history.

My first serious exposure to the Holocaust was in 1961 when Adolf Eichmann was put on trial in Jerusalem. I remember that my mother sat me down a few times to watch the television broadcasts and seemed fairly excited by the fact that Israel had apprehended him. In those days, however, the subject of the Holocaust was hardly the popular item that it has become today, and thus the Eichmann trial remained an isolated memory. It is true that as children we heard about the Holocaust, but I cannot remember it being emphasized in any special way. Even though I attended Jewish schools and summer camps and received probably as good a Jewish education as was available at that time in the United States, I never had the feeling while growing up that the subject was of unique significance, and I say so not as an indictment of my parents and teachers, but rather to describe the milieu I grew up in.

I cannot remember, for example, ever observing *Yom ha-Shoa* (Martyrs and Heroes Remembrance Day) in the 1950s or early 1960s, nor do I recall any serious attempt being made to sensitize us in a meaning-

1

ful way to the tragedy of European Jewry. Even the fact that I was named after a victim of the Holocaust, my grandfather's brother Rabbi Efraim Zar, was never stressed, nor was I in any way made to feel that I therefore had a special connection to those events, or that I bore a particular burden as a result. It was traditional Jewish practice to name children after deceased relatives, and thus there was ostensibly nothing unusual about the choice of that name. The most important fact was that he had been an *illui* (prodigy) and outstanding Torah scholar, and hopefully that might rub off on me. The fact that he had been murdered during the Holocaust was never harped upon, even though my parents had originally planned to give me a different name and switched to Efraim only at the behest of my grandfather who, in the course of a mission to Europe to assist survivors, learned of his brother's murder. As far as I was concerned, Efraim, or Efrem as I was called at school, was simply a name like any other name. A bit rare in America in those days, but there was always the popular actor Efrem Zimbalist Jr. or his famous violinist father Efrem Sr. to point to, to help explain the matter. The particulars of Efraim Zar's death were never discussed, and to the best of my knowledge were not even known by my grandfather, let alone by my parents.

The big change came in the wake of the Six Day War. Not so much the war itself, as the terrible, anxiety-filled period prior to its outbreak. Nasser had ordered the UN troops to leave the Sinai peninsula, Arab armies were gathering on Israel's borders preparing to attack, and all sorts of boasts were being made in the Arab world about throwing the Jews into the sea. The situation really looked bleak. I have a very distinct memory of sitting in my home in Brooklyn on Sunday morning June 3, 1967 reading the *New York Times* "News of the Week in Review" section. Inside there was a map of the Middle East, which included statistics on the number of troops in each of the Arab armies poised to attack Israel. My instinctive reaction upon looking at the map and the figures was "Oh my God! There's going to be another Holocaust."

That, of course, did not happen, but the specter of an imminent Jewish catastrophe of the same or similar proportions brought me a lot closer to the events of the Holocaust. It also impressed upon me in a very meaningful way the importance of the State of Israel and its unique role as the inheritor of the victims of the Holocaust and the bearer, in a sense, of Jewish destiny in the modern world. Of course the fact that Israel gained a sweeping military victory and turned what threatened to be imminent mass annihilation into a triumph of historical proportions made that linkage convenient. For what better way existed to deal with the most terrible of Jewish tragedies than through the prism of a brilliant Israeli military triumph. In the short span of less than 25 years, the Jewish people had emerged from a hopeless situation of utter impotence, to achieve independence and sovereignty. Not only had they acquired the ability and tools to defend themselves, they had even attained the status of a mini-superpower.

It was this military victory and its practical implications—primarily the liberation of Judea and Samaria but most of all the reunification of Jerusalem and the return to the Western Wall—that made it possible for an entire generation of young Jews to focus their attention for the first time on the watershed events of the Holocaust. Unencumbered by the complexes of those who had lived through that period—bystanders as well as survivors—they began to show a serious interest in the *mi-Shoa le-Tekuma* (from Holocaust to rebirth) period of Jewish history. This interest took many forms—renewed or revived Jewish identity, activities on behalf of Jews in distress—particularly those in the Soviet Union— active support for Israel—and in some cases even *aliya* (immigration to Israel)—and an awareness and desire to commemorate and study the Holocaust. This phenomenon took place all over the Jewish world from Moscow to New York, from Paris to Johannesburg and all places in between and created a new attitude towards the events of the Holocaust.

In my case there were practical implications to these developments. First and foremost, I decided to spend a year studying in Israel (which until then I had never even visited) and began reading various books on the Holocaust, primarily those written by Elie Wiesel. I also began playing an active role in the efforts on behalf of Soviet Jewry, as well as for Israel. Thus the link between Israel and the Holocaust, which was subconsciously forged in my mind during those days of anxiety and trepidation in late May and early June 1967, found practical expression and ultimately was to have a very serious influence on the turns my life was to take. In my mind those two "events" had become part of one entity which had significantly altered the destiny of the Jewish people.

This connection was further strengthened during my year of study at the Hebrew University of Jerusalem. I took a few courses in modern Jewish history which dealt directly or indirectly with the Holocaust but,

more importantly, experienced the realities of life in Israel in the immediate aftermath of the Six Day War when Jewish fate and future suddenly became popular topics. This was a very special period in Israeli
history, a period in which the country experienced profound change.
Little Israel had suddenly more than doubled its territory, had become
the focus of international attention and was basking in the glory of its
military prowess. Young Jews from all over the Western world flocked
to Israel to experience life, work and/or study in the Jewish state, drawn
by the enthusiasm and identification generated by the Six Day War.
Israel seemed to be on the brink of an exciting new era.

While in Israel, I had the feeling for the first time that I was being an
active participant in, rather than a mere observer of, the making of
Jewish history. My experiences there drew me closer to, and sparked my
interest in, the events of the Holocaust. I visited Yad Vashem, the Israeli
memorial to the six million, several times, and was very moved by the
nation-wide observance of *Yom ha-Shoa*. The fact that the entire country appeared to identify with the commemoration of the victims made
an indelible impression. The large number of survivors living in Israel
and their role in building the country also contributed to an increased
sensitivity to the manner in which the Holocaust had made an impact
on the Jewish people. At this point, however, it was modern Israel
which primarily captured my imagination rather than the tragic events
which preceded its establishment. Yet undoubtedly the link between the
two was considerably reinforced during the year I lived in Jerusalem.
Thus when I decided in the course of that year to make *aliya*, it was
basically a decision to join the people who had been the primary participants in the two major events which in my opinion had unalterably
changed the course of modern Jewish history.

In the summer of 1969 I returned to the United States to complete
my undergraduate studies at Yeshiva University and hurried back to
Israel for good in the autumn of 1970. During my last year in the
United States, I decided that I wanted to work in the field of Jewish
communal service, preferably in some capacity which would enable me
to help Jews in distress. I applied therefore to the graduate program of
the Institute of Contemporary Jewry of the Hebrew University in Jerusalem, which specialized in the history, demography and sociology of the
Jewish people in the twentieth century. At this point, however, the most
important thing as far as I was concerned was to return as quickly as

possible to Israel and the plan to study at the Hebrew University seemed to be as good a way as any.

When I arrived in Jerusalem and had an opportunity to examine the requirements and course offerings at the Institute more closely, it became clear that the program's goal was not to provide practical training for a career in Jewish communal service but rather to train scholars in the fields of Jewish history, demography and sociology. Of the various areas of specialization offered, none interested me more on a purely intellectual level than the Holocaust. There were quite a few questions regarding the historical events that had aroused my curiosity from the very beginning of my interest in the subject and for which I had hitherto been unable to find answers. Most related to the response of the Jews in the Free World and primarily in the United States. I was very curious to know what information they had had regarding the Final Solution and when that news reached them. The classic question, as I used to phrase it so often in my mind, was: What could the average Jew living in the United States have known from reading the general and/or Jewish press? The concomitant question was, of course, what could they have done to assist the Jews of Europe? There were other areas which also interested me such as: the question of resistance, the response of Orthodox leadership in occupied Europe, the degree to which Nazi leadership was sensitive to world opinion, etc. My hope was that if I could not get the practical training I needed for my chosen career, at least I might be able to obtain the answers to some nagging historical questions.

It was from these prosaic beginnings in the autumn of 1970 that I began my full-time involvement in the field of Holocaust studies. I had no idea at that time that I would ultimately devote so many years to the subject. In fact, I think if someone would have told me then that 15 years later I would be a veteran Nazi hunter, I would have probably been very surprised. In those days I was still thinking in terms of Jewish civil service, with the degree primarily a stepping stone. The truth of the matter is that had I confined myself solely to the studies at the university, it seems unlikely that I would have embarked upon my present career. As interesting as the lectures (especially those by Professor Bauer) were during my initial years at the Hebrew University, I was far more interested in contemporary Israel and world Jewry than I was in the history of the Holocaust. The plight and struggle of Soviet Jewry seemed to me to be a more pressing and important issue than whether or not there had been armed resistance in a small *shtetl* (village) in the Ukraine. The political questions which were being debated in modern-day Israel seemed more exciting than minutiae concerning the implementation of the Final Solution.

It was only after I began working full-time at Yad Vashem in the autumn of 1973 that I became more emotionally involved in the study of the Holocaust. This was a gradual process which took place over the course of several years. The daily contact with historical research in my capacity as assistant editor of *Yad Vashem Studies*, as well as with the commemorative and educational activities at the national Holocaust memorial all brought the subject that much closer to heart. The daily contact with the staff of Yad Vashem, many of whom were survivors, some of whom had been active participants in armed resistance, also left their mark. For many of them, working at Yad Vashem fulfilled an existential need. Being involved with them day in and day out made certain aspects of the Holocaust far more real for me and put the horrors of that period in a very human and immediate context, which had a far greater impact than tens of history books.

Another aspect of my job at Yad Vashem which influenced me was my role as a guide for visiting dignitaries. Initially it was primarily journalists and lower echelon politicians, but eventually I was entrusted with quite a few prominent figures—senators, governors, ministers, ambassadors, mayors—from all over the world. As their host at Yad Vashem, I became a spokesperson for Israel and the Jewish people as well as on the subject of the Holocaust, its importance and implications. My job was to expose them—via the monuments and the museum—to the scope and horror of the tragedy, its contemporary significance and how those events affected Israel and the Jewish people. These tours were a grim reminder of the horrible realities of the Holocaust. This task undoubtedly helped sensitize me and provided the emotional underpinnings for my subsequent activities in bringing Nazi criminals to justice.

My experiences while working at Yad Vashem fostered an emotional commitment to the study and commemoration of the Holocaust which complemented the intellectual component that I had acquired at the university. This was particularly important because academic research alone does not necessarily engender a sense of commitment or obligation. In fact, one of the most upsetting aspects of my work in searching for Nazi criminals was the lukewarm, and in a few cases even apathetic, response of some of my colleagues who tried very hard to confine themselves to the academic aspects of the Holocaust. It is interesting to note that at the university, and to some extent at Yad Vashem as well, there was a tendency among scholars to play down and even belittle the more emotional aspects of the commemoration of the Holocaust. The goal was to produce Holocaust historians and researchers; the attitude towards anyone who dealt with the subject in a "popular" manner was not always sympathetic unless the individual in question had the proper academic qualifications. Given the highly sensitive nature of the subject matter, this approach is perhaps understandable. However, the results were at times ludicrous: if individuals who have spent years studying the Holocaust are apathetic to issues like Nazi war criminals, then something is amiss. There is indeed at times a certain tension between the intellectual and emotional components of the subject, but each has an important role in transmitting the significance and implications of the Holocaust. In that respect my studies at the university and my work at Yad Vashem truly complemented each other, helping to create an emotional and intellectual motivation that ultimately influenced my decision to become involved in the struggle to locate and prosecute Nazi war criminals.

I worked at Yad Vashem during the years immediately after the Yom Kippur War, a traumatic experience which undoubtedly left its mark on the collective Israeli psyche. The mood in Israel turned from bravado to introspection, a development which affected the willingness of Israelis to study the Holocaust and changed their attitude to this subject. Thus while it is true that in the wake of the Six Day War Israelis, and especially the young, were willing to confront the Holocaust for the first time, their frame of reference was usually a feeling of superiority vis-à-vis the Jews of Europe—victims as well as survivors. In the Yom Kippur War, however, the Israeli army had retreated and been on the brink of defeat. As a result the Jews of Europe, who had been virtually defenseless during the Holocaust, all of a sudden did not seem all that remote. For the first time it became possible for Israelis, even the sabras or native-born, to empathize with the victims, even those who did not resist. This ongoing process, which took place at Yad Vashem, as well as at the university, was a factor in the maturation of an entire generation of scholars and professionals in the field and also had an impact on my decision to become actively involved in attempts to bring Nazis to justice.

By 1978 I had completed a master's degree at the Institute of Contemporary Jewry, as well as the course work for my Ph.D., and had already begun research on my doctoral thesis. The topic was the response of Orthodox Jewry in the United States to the Holocaust, as reflected in the activities of the *Vaad Hatzala* (rescue committee) established by the Orthodox rabbis. My master's thesis was on a related topic, but there was quite a bit of additional documentation in the United States which I needed to complete the dissertation; I therefore agreed to go to Los Angeles for two years to serve as the director of the Simon Wiesenthal Center for Holocaust Studies. I was not sure how long the research would take but assumed that two years would be sufficient time to obtain whatever documents I needed.

On my way to Los Angeles, I travelled to Poland for the first time. There I visited the sites I had learned so much about: Auschwitz, Treblinka, Majdanek and Chelmno—four of the six notorious death camps—as well as Warsaw, Cracow, Lublin and Lodz, the famous Polish cities which once had flourishing Jewish communities and now were practically without Jews at all. I cannot think of a more depressing journey, one which indelibly inscribed those horrors on the inner chambers of my heart and soul. The mountains of shoes at Majdanek, the piles of children's toys at Auschwitz, the eerie silence in the fields of Treblinka, all remained with me for months after I had left that cursed land. The trip to Poland was, in a sense, a fitting conclusion to the five years I had spent at Yad Vashem and an appropriate beginning for my new job at the Wiesenthal Center.

In retrospect, if I attempt to recount how I became involved on a practical level in the issue of Nazi war criminals, two individuals who influenced me come to mind—Simon Wiesenthal and Bill Crane. The first needs no introduction, certainly not vis-à-vis attempts to prosecute Nazis. The second worked as an investigator for the Office of Special Investigations (OSI) and was the first person from that office with whom I had personal contact. On the surface, it would be hard to imagine a more odd pair: Simon Wiesenthal, a Polish Jew from Galicia who had survived the Holocaust and had devoted his life to hunting Nazi criminals and Bill Crane, a young non-Jewish investigator for OSI who by his own admission knew practically nothing about the Holocaust until he joined the office.

I met Mr. Wiesenthal in Los Angeles in the autumn of 1978, shortly after I assumed my post as director of the Wiesenthal Center. He had come to California to appear at the world premiere of the film *The Boys from Brazil* and a benefit dinner for the Center. I had already met him in Jerusalem after agreeing to take the job in Los Angeles but this was really my first opportunity to spend some time with him. At this point he was almost 70 years old but was in good health and full of energy and vitality. We discussed various issues related to the Holocaust and specifically his relations with Professor Yehuda Bauer, with whom I had studied at the Hebrew University. The two were in the midst of a fairly bitter controversy over the question of whether or not to include the non-Jews murdered by the Nazis among the victims of the Holocaust. Should we speak only of six million Jews as Professor Bauer contended, or of six million Jews and five million others as Wiesenthal maintained? We also discussed some practical issues related to the efforts to track down and prosecute Nazis. Mr. Wiesenthal mentioned, for example, that the recent arrival in the West of large numbers of Soviet Jews might open up new opportunities for obtaining witnesses against Nazi criminals.

My second encounter with the famed Nazi-hunter was not a meeting with him personally, but rather with his myth. In the course of preparing the Center's museum, as well as various educational and publicity materials, I encountered two quotes by Mr. Wiesenthal which, in essence, sum up his personality and life's work. The first was a story that Mr. Wiesenthal used to explain his relentless dedication to the task of searching for Nazi war criminals. Frequently asked by his fellow survivors why he did not resume his work as an architect after the war (Europe after all, was in ruins and there was an enormous amount of building being done), Mr. Wiesenthal replied:

> I believe in the world to come. I am certain that after we die we will all go to Heaven, and there we will meet the victims of the Holocaust. The first question that they will ask us will be: "You were the lucky ones. You survived. You received your lives as a present. What did you do with them?" One will say "I was a businessman"; another will say "I was a lawyer"; a third will say "I was a teacher". I will say "I did not forget you."

Those five simple words "I did not forget you" struck a respondent chord. I cannot, in fact think of a more pithy and touching way to summarize the entire emotional component of our attempts to deal with the Holocaust and to express succinctly a profound sense of personal obligation and commitment. These words also shift the focus of our efforts to commemorate from ourselves—the survivors, the bystanders, their children and the coming generations—to the victims, who oddly enough sometimes seem to have been forgotten. So much of our efforts to commemorate have been self-oriented that I often felt that the victims, in essence, had been overlooked or neglected. I therefore found Mr. Wiesenthal's appeal on their behalf particularly poignant.

The second quote by Mr. Wiesenthal related to the moral aspects of the issue. He explained his intense motivation to bring Nazi murderers to trial with his categorical statement that "He who ignores the murderers of the past paves the way for the murderers of the future." This call for justice was particularly pertinent at that time in view of the fact that most efforts to prosecute the Nazi murderers living in the United States and elsewhere in the Free World had hitherto been unsuccessful. I had read Howard Blum's book *Wanted! The Search for the Nazis in America*, which had exposed the existence in the United States of Nazi war criminals and had closely followed the initial attempts by Congresswoman Elizabeth Holtzman of Brooklyn and others to force the government to deal with the problem. Like many others I was very frustrated by the lack of progress and the fact that it appeared that the Nazis were going to "get away" with their crimes. Mr. Wiesenthal's rationale for his activities was, therefore, a very persuasive argument, one which could convince even those who ostensibly had not been directly affected by the events that justice had to be achieved.

None of these ideas led to any practical results until the spring of 1979. It was then that the Office of Special Investigations was established in the framework of the Criminal Division of the US Justice Department. The office was not a new creation, but rather an expanded and improved version of the small unit established by the US Immigration and Naturalization Service in the wake of the initial revelations concerning the presence of Nazi war criminals in the United States. My initial contact with OSI came in the form of a standard request from historian Steve Rogers for any information we might possess regarding specific locations in Lithuania, Latvia and Estonia, a request which I assume was sent to numerous archives, research institutes and Holocaust centers throughout the United States.

Several days later, however, Bill Crane came to meet me at the Center and it was this visit that ultimately precipitated my active involvement. Crane had come to Los Angeles to speak to several potential witnesses but had encountered difficulties in a few cases. Several of the survivors whom he sought to interview were reluctant to speak to him, so he sought our assistance in the hope that we might be able to convince them to cooperate. At this point OSI had not yet established its credibility and was virtually unknown among the survivors, many of whom were naturally suspicious of governmental agencies. Crane hoped that if someone from a center named after Simon Wiesenthal would speak to the reluctant survivor(s), or if he came with our recommendation, it would considerably facilitate his efforts.

Needless to say, I was more than willing to be of assistance in this matter. I was also very curious about the OSI and therefore jumped at the opportunity to meet with Crane. I knew that most of the cases they were investigating involved East European collaborators—primarily from the Baltics—and I assumed, given the enormous amount of research which had been done in Israel on that particular region, I might perhaps be able to be of assistance, a prospect which very much appealed to me.

Our meeting went extremely well. Within a short time we established a rapport and by the time we finished I had the feeling that it would be a pleasure to work together. There was something about Bill Crane that I liked. Besides his pleasant personality and easygoing manner, his sincerity was obvious. I had the distinct impression that he was a person who was not simply going through the motions or doing the job because of its "exciting" aspects. He seemed genuinely upset by the fact that Nazi criminals were living in the United States. That a non-Jew, with no ostensible connection to the events, was so concerned and involved made me ask myself a pointed question: What was I—the committed Jew who was a Holocaust historian—doing about this problem? This question—accusation, which apparently had been lurking in my subconscious for quite some time, came to the fore in the course of my meeting with Bill Crane. Thus when we discussed the various difficulties that Crane had encountered in convincing survivors to be interviewed and/or testify, I volunteered our help and suggested that the Center not only persuade reluctant potential witnesses to cooperate, but also conduct an independent search for survivors, who might be able to provide information in the cases being investigated by OSI.

Crane agreed that such assistance would be very helpful and promised to provide me with a complete list of the locations of interest to OSI so that we could immediately launch our effort.

The information I received from Crane, our subsequent correspondence during the following weeks, and the initial attempts to find survivors, convinced me that a large-scale project was required. I also remembered my conversation with Simon Wiesenthal regarding the possibility of finding potential witnesses from among the recent immigrants from the Soviet Union. The result of all of the above was my decision to initiate a project to collect all the available data on the survivors living in the United States in order to facilitate the work of the OSI.

According to my original idea, we planned to collect information regarding the survivors' wartime experiences as well as their current whereabouts, all of which would be computerized. At the touch of a button we would be able to obtain all the pertinent data on the availability of witnesses from any specific geographical location. If successful, such a project would save an enormous amount of time, money and energy. (Ironically, I was to propose the same type of project—only on the criminals, not their erstwhile victims—to the Wiesenthal Center six years later and as a result would leave OSI to undertake its implementation.) It seemed such a logical, necessary and obvious thing to do that I wondered why it had never previously been undertaken (just as I was to wonder six years later why a computerized data bank on Nazi war criminals had never been established). Our efforts would ultimately provide the answer to my original question but I had no way of knowing that beforehand.

I proceeded, therefore, to launch our survivors' registry project which I assumed would require considerable work but would eventually make an important contribution to OSI's success. I began by obtaining a list of survivor organizations with which OSI was in contact and by notifying Walter Rockler, the newly-appointed director of OSI, of our plans. Rockler agreed that such an undertaking would be very useful and indicated that his office would be happy to be the beneficiaries of our efforts. With his approval in hand, we were ready to begin in earnest.

The first step I took was to issue a press release which was accompanied by an open letter to the survivors. I sensed that there were several reasons why they might feel uneasy about such a project. One was their understandable reluctance to be listed, another was the fact that the project was being launched by an organization which was not headed by survivors. I wanted to explain to them why such a project was necessary and I appealed therefore to their sense of obligation vis-à-vis the victims, writing as follows:

Dear Survivor,

Over thirty-five years have passed since the end of the Holocaust and the brutal murder of six million Jews. During that time, only a small portion of those responsible for the most heinous crimes against humanity were apprehended. Many of those who played an active role in the Final Solution are still at large, free to live out their lives. Many have already passed away due to natural causes, never having been held accountable for their crimes. Quite a few were able to escape justice and find a haven in this country.

Now for the first time a serious attempt is being made by the American judicial authorities to bring these criminals to justice. They face, however, several serious obstacles, not the least of which is the need to find witnesses who can testify against these criminals. Most of those who could have done so were, unfortunately, among the victims of the Third Reich. Those who survived, a pitiful remnant of European Jewry, are scattered the world over. To date there is no central register of survivors to which the judicial authorities—not only in the United States but throughout the world as well—can turn to for assistance in locating potential witnesses. Without witnesses, there can be no trials. Without trials these murderers will live to a ripe old age, free to laugh at the impotence of the Jewish people and the forces of justice and morality.

We owe it to those who cannot stand here and testify, to those whose lives were brutally and senselessly destroyed to come forth and stand witness in the name of our martyred brethren and the Jewish people.

The Simon Wiesenthal Center for Holocaust Studies, out of a sense of commitment and obligation, has undertaken to compile a register of all the Holocaust survivors in the Western hemisphere in an effort to facilitate the attempts to convict Nazi war criminals. We urge you to fill out the enclosed form and mail it to us and to urge your friends, relatives and acquaintances who survived the horror of the Hitler regime to do so as well.

With your assistance we hopefully will be able to achieve a certain measure of justice.

A detailed questionnaire was also prepared which asked for specific information (including approximate dates of incarceration) on each of the various ghettos, labor camps and concentration camps that the survivor(s) had been in, as well as the names and addresses of additional potential witnesses. All of the material was also prepared in Russian and specific mention was made in our press release of our interest in identifying survivors from among the recent arrivals from the Soviet Union. In late August 1979, the Jewish Telegraphic Agency (JTA) printed our release verbatim in its daily news bulletin[1] and, as a result, it appeared in numerous Jewish newspapers all over the United States. Among the communities whose local Jewish newspapers published our appeal were: New York,[2] Newark,[3] Buffalo,[4] Albany,[5] St. Louis,[6] Nashville,[7] Springfield, Massachusetts;[8] Hartford,[9] Detroit,[10] Chicago,[11] Baltimore,[12] Cincinnati,[13] etc.[14] I was pleased by the response, but was more concerned with the practical results. Expecting a deluge of requests, we got barely a trickle. This was the first concrete indication that our project might be far more difficult than originally envisioned.

Several weeks after we launched the survivors' registry, I flew to the East Coast to attend a conference on the Holocaust held in Washington, DC. I also scheduled meetings with Walter Rockler, director of OSI, and members of his staff to discuss the project and learn in greater detail about the unit's activities, plans and needs. Given the good working relationship which had been established with Bill Crane and the Center's willingness to assist the Justice Department, I looked forward to meeting Rockler in order to cement further our ties with OSI. If anything, just the opposite occurred. For some reason, which to this day is not entirely clear, Rockler appeared to indicate a lack of interest in our activities and I left his office wondering whether any Nazis living in the United States would ever be prosecuted. Under normal circumstances, recounting the contents of such a meeting would hardly be worth while. In this case, however, the discussion we conducted had an important and improbable effect on my subsequent employment by OSI.

The meeting took place at OSI on October 10, 1979. I began by outlining our project to obtain biographical information on the survivors and explained how this would facilitate the search for potential witnesses. I told Rockler about my meeting with Bill Crane and of the working relationship which had developed over the past few months between the Wiesenthal Center and OSI, and asked him a few questions about several of the cases then in litigation—Detlavs, Hazners, and others. To my surprise, Rockler did not volunteer any information or insights regarding these cases. I had the impression, in fact, that he was not fully conversant with the details of these investigations. What was even more strange, however, were some of the comments Rockler made in the course of the conversation, which were not directly related to the issue of Nazi war criminals. When I incidentally mentioned that I lived in Israel and was planning to return there in a year, Rockler said that he had never been to Israel and could see no reason on earth why anyone would want to go there. He also seemed to go out of his way to indicate that although he was a Jew, he did not feel that fact obligated him in any way.

Needless to say I was slightly taken aback by Rockler's comments. In retrospect, I think that there are several possible explanations for what happened. One is that perhaps Rockler thought it was not in OSI's best interests to work closely with Jewish organizations. It is possible that he believed that such co-operation would ultimately prove counterproductive because it would be exploited by OSI's opponents who might use it to support their claim that OSI was not sufficiently objective. On a more prosaic level perhaps he considered meetings with representatives of Jewish organizations a waste of time and wanted to do his best to reduce them to a minimum. Perhaps both factors combined to produce his reaction. In any event, I walked out of Rockler's office slightly in shock, little realizing at the time that this unpleasant meeting ultimately laid the foundation for my job as OSI's researcher in Israel.

During my visit to Washington I had an opportunity to meet with additional members of the OSI staff. Aside from Bill Crane, I spent most of the time with Deputy Directors Art Sinai and Martin Mendelsohn. The latter had headed the initial war crimes unit established in the framework of the Immigration and Naturalization Service, but had been appointed to the post of deputy director under Rockler when OSI was founded. These talks proved a stark contrast to my meeting with Rockler: both deputies were extremely friendly and welcomed the assistance offered by the Wiesenthal Center. They also appeared to be highly motivated, committed to the task of bringing to justice the Nazis living in the United States. This direct contact with them somewhat alleviated the harsh impression of my encounter with Rockler, but I nonetheless left Washington with some serious doubts about OSI's operation.

At this point, despite the establishment of OSI, it was still not clear whether the government really intended to address the issue of Nazi war criminals seriously. My meeting with Rockler was therefore particularly upsetting, because if anything it seemed to indicate the opposite. Although Rockler came highly recommended (he had been a prosecutor at Nuremberg and was a member of the prestigious Arnold and Porter law firm), I emerged from our meeting unsure whether he was the right man for the job. It seemed, at least on the surface, that he was not totally committed to the task at hand. In fact, in the course of our conversation he commented that in his opinion the real criminals had been tried at Nuremberg, whereas those presently in the United States were small fry. It was not clear to me therefore why Rockler had agreed, even temporarily, to assume the post of director of OSI. Whatever hope existed that the Nazi criminals in America would be prosecuted seemed fairly slim if these comments truly reflected his attitude. In short, I left OSI far more worried that I had been before my visit.

In early January 1980 my worries regarding OSI were considerably magnified when I learned that Rockler had fired Martin Mendelsohn. This step seemed to confirm my worst fears about OSI. It seemed quite strange that Mendelsohn, who had initiated the efforts to prosecute Nazi war criminals and appeared to be extremely committed to that goal, should be removed from his post by Rockler, who was slated to return to private practice in April 1980. Mendelsohn, moreover, had been instrumental in obtaining a certain degree of cooperation from the Soviet government and his replacement at this point might jeopardize those contacts. I therefore wrote a letter of protest to Attorney-General Benjamin Civiletti and issued a statement indicating our concern regarding these developments.

Our efforts, as well as those of numerous other concerned parties (Elizabeth Holtzman etc.), did not change the decision to remove Mendelsohn but did reflect the depth of feeling and frustration on the issue of Nazi war criminals. I also have the impression that they helped strengthen those elements in the Carter administration who agreed with us. The choice of Allan A. Ryan Jr. as Rockler's successor ultimately proved quite successful. However, since Rockler had not exactly inspired our confidence and the government's record on the issue had been so poor, I felt at this point that we had very good reasons to be wary. Our anxiety regarding this matter did not, it should be noted, in any way effect our ongoing efforts to assist OSI, primarily by finding potential witnesses via our survivors' registry.

In the meantime the project was not progressing as anticipated. When our initial press release had been published in numerous local Jewish newspapers across the country, we expected to receive at least hundreds of requests for questionnaires, but that was not the case. Our efforts, moreover, to obtain the cooperation of the various survivors' organizations were also not progressing as planned. We had been able to obtain quite a few names from various sources, but at this point only two survivors' organizations (Holocaust Survivors of Auschwitz and Labor Camps and the Society of Survivors of the Riga Ghetto) were willing to send us their mailing list or to send our questionnaires to their members. I therefore decided to issue an appeal to the survivors via the Jewish press. The idea was to have the questionnaires printed in the various local Jewish newspapers and thereby facilitate their being filled out. I wrote to every single Jewish newspaper in the United States and Canada requesting that they print our questionnaire with an accompanying letter of explanation, which included specific assurances that all information received would remain confidential. (I had been advised to stress that point in view of the reluctance of many survivors to have their names on lists.)

The response of the Jewish press left much to be desired. Only one newspaper, the *Long Island Jewish World*,[15] which was owned and edited by a personal friend, Naomi Lippman, printed the questionnaire and letter in their entirety. A few of the others published a news story or a letter to the editor about the survivors' registry[16] and one newspaper (*Dayton Jewish Chronicle*) printed an appeal by a columnist (Anne Hammerman) to fill out the questionnaires,[17] but that was all we achieved. I must have been extremely naïve to imagine that they would print the questionnaire without any recompense.

The lamentable response of the Jewish press, as well as of the survivors' organizations, made it clear that we would have to find alternative means of promoting the survivors' registry. I therefore met with Abe Bayer of the National Jewish Community Relations Advisory Council (NACRAC), an umbrella agency for the major American Jewish organizations, to enlist their assistance. Bayer agreed to participate in the project by distributing our questionnaires via the community relations councils of the local federations. In view of the fact that the organized Jewish community usually maintained contact with the survivors via the federations, this channel appeared extremely promising. In reality, however, the net result of the assistance rendered by NACRAC was minimal. I think that we received fewer than ten completed questionnaires from among those distributed by NACRAC (which bore an inscription to that effect).

The sad truth was that our project was doomed to failure because of several factors that we were not fully aware of prior to its launching. We learned the hard way about the (understandable) reluctance of survivors to fill out biographical questionnaires and allow their names to be put on lists. Our project suffered bitterly because of the internal politics within the Jewish community, particularly among the survivors' organizations. Some of the latter objected to the Wiesenthal Center's efforts because they believed that such a project could only be undertaken by survivors. Several years after our initial effort, a similar project was launched with relative success by a group of survivors in the wake of the World Gathering of Jewish Holocaust Survivors, held in Jerusalem in June 1981. One would think that the Jewish community would have learned the lesson of the high price paid for internal strife and could unite, at least temporarily, for a project of this type, but post-war Jewish organizational life continues to suffer from this infuriating time-honored ailment. Given these problems, we did not allocate sufficient resources to carry out properly a good idea whose implementation was long overdue. In the meantime we continued our efforts; it became increasingly clear, however, that it would be extremely difficult if not impossible to obtain the amount of information which we originally hoped to be able to provide for OSI. The hundreds of completed forms we received were a far cry from the thousands we anticipated when the project was launched.

In late February 1980 I was invited by CBS to appear on a television program devoted to the issue of the Nazi war criminals living in the United States, which was to be broadcast in the Los Angeles area. In the course of the preliminary discussions with the producers, I was asked to suggest the names of people knowledgeable on the subject whom it might be worthwhile to invite to appear on the program. I replied that Walter Rockler would be an interesting guest, but that I doubted whether he would agree to appear. In view of the fact that the program was scheduled to be broadcast at 6.30 a.m. and only in the Los Angeles area, I could not imagine Rockler consenting to participate. The producers thought otherwise, however, and called me a few days later to tell me "the good news." I was extremely surprised by Rockler's consent to appear on a show which would be broadcast locally at 6.30 a.m. In view of the "friendly" reception he gave me in Washington and my opposition to Martin Mendelsohn's dismissal, perhaps he felt it might be best if he presented his case personally.

I remember driving to the studio on a rainy Thursday morning. All that I could think about was the imminent confrontation with Rockler. After all, he certainly had read about our efforts on behalf of Mendelsohn. How would he respond? Would he at least be civil? If he had been almost contemptuous before that interview, who knew what he would be like in the wake of my attack on him. My greatest fear at this point, was that we would be forced to sit together for a long time before the filming of the show. Based on previous experience I knew that very often the filming ran behind schedule, and the participants in such cases usually had to sit together in a small side room until filming could get under way.

Sure enough, that was exactly what happened. Only it was far worse than I had imagined. While driving to the studio, I was afraid that I might have to spend as long as 20 to 30 minutes alone with Rockler waiting for the show to begin. As it turned out we had to wait together for more than one and a half hours. The room we were put into, moreover, was so small that there was really nowhere to "hide" and practically no way to avoid Rockler's cold gaze. The silence was getting unbearable; as there was no sign by then of the show actually getting started, I asked Rockler a few questions about several cases which OSI had recently tried. His response was not only civil but very detailed and to the point. After that auspicious beginning, a lively conversation developed regarding various aspects of OSI's activities and the survivors' registry initiated by the Center. The ensuing discussion was in stark contrast to our initial meeting in Washington. Apparently, by this point, Rockler had become convinced that the Center had a sincere interest in OSI's work and that dealing with Jewish organizations was a necessary part of his job.

There was another factor which apparently helped change Rockler's attitude towards me, one which I found extremely interesting on a personal level. In the course of our conversation, Rockler told me that he had recently visited Israel and had been extremely impressed by what he saw. It was a place, Rockler said, where people "really knew what they wanted," and that very much appealed to him. He also was apparently very taken by the dynamism and energy of the Israelis. In fact, musing out loud at one point in our conversation, he said that if he were younger he would even consider moving there and learning the language. In view of the disdain which Rockler had demonstratively expressed vis-à-vis Israel at our previous meeting, I could hardly imagine a more startling transformation. Perhaps it was his work at OSI, the daily contact with the tragedy of European Jewry which sensitized him. Perhaps it was the spark of Jewishness, said to exist in every Jew, that had finally been activated. Whatever the cause, the change wrought in Rockler set the stage for my joining OSI.

I had been toying for quite some time with an idea which up to that point did not appear practical. In the course of my numerous contacts with the staff, and particularly the historians at OSI, I realized that the office lacked two things—a researcher fluent in Hebrew and Yiddish and a full-time representative in Israel who could do the necessary research in the numerous pertinent archives. In view of the fact that Israel is one of the most important centers of Holocaust research and documentation, I was convinced that it would be extremely beneficial for OSI to have a person stationed there on a full-time basis. Since I was planning to return home to Israel that summer and was anxious to continue my involvement in this issue, I thought that such a position would be ideal.

Thus after Rockler's "speech" on the wonders of Israel, I decided to take a chance and suggested that it would be a good idea for OSI to employ a historian to do research for them in Israel.Rockler replied that a proposal to station a researcher in Germany had already been discussed, but had never materialized because OSI had been unable to find a suitable and willing candidate. My response was that Israel would be preferable due to the numerous Israeli archives which specialized in the history of the Holocaust and the large number of survivors residing there. I also added that I believed I had the necessary qualifications for the job and was in any event returning to my home in Israel in a few months. Rockler did not, of course, give me an answer on the spot, but said that he was willing to consider my application favorably. He thought, moreover, that the arrangement I proposed should definitely be tried out, if only on an experimental basis.

All of the above took place during the almost two hours we waited for the filming of the program to begin. By this point the show itself was totally anticlimactic, a fact reflected by the calm comments Rockler and

I made before the cameras. I think that we only disagreed on one or two minor points; thus if anyone were anticipating fireworks, they were undoubtedly disappointed. As far as I was concerned, I doubted whether a TV show broadcast at 6.30 a.m. could have any significant impact. In fact, I even forgot to watch it.

Nonetheless, I am not likely to forget that television program. I had previously feared that when I left the Wiesenthal Center to return to Israel, I would not be able to continue my efforts to assist in bringing Nazis to justice; now an opportunity presented itself for meaningful involvement, perhaps even for an extended period. I sensed at this point that this might indeed be the long-awaited chance to combine the intellectual and emotional components of the study of the Holocaust in the most practical manner possible.

During the spring of 1980 I went through the formal stages of applying for the job at OSI. Meanwhile our survivors' registry project continued with some modest success registered. We finally began getting replies from recent Soviet émigrés and also gained the co-operation of another large survivors' organization (Bergen-Belsen). Thus throughout my final months at the Wiesenthal Center I was in close contact with OSI.

In early August 1980 I received official confirmation that I was going to be hired by OSI on an experimental basis—initially for two months with an option for extension—and that I could begin working as soon as I arrived in Israel. At this point OSI was still uncertain as to how important the information from Israel would be, so they were unwilling to make a long-term commitment. Despite the fact that this posed a practical problem, I was convinced of the valuable nature of the documentation and testimony available in Israel, so I agreed to the proposed arrangement. I had, it should also be noted, a slightly different conception of the position proposed by OSI, but agreed nonetheless to assume the job as offered. Whereas OSI was only interested in research, I thought that OSI should have a representative in Israel who besides conducting research should also serve as a spokesperson and arouse public opinion and awareness on the issue. Knowing the Israeli scene as I did, I thought that an enormous amount could be done publicly via the media. At this point, however, I did not want to jeopardize the position by attempting to convince the leadership of OSI to change the nature of the job.

Prior to my departure, I prepared a detailed memorandum summarizing the survivors' registry project, including specific recommendations regarding the various steps which should be taken to complete the work initiated by the Wiesenthal Center. Several days before our flight home, OSI sent a special messenger to brief me on my first assignment—several Byelorussian suspects—and to give me an update on recent developments. At this point nothing beyond the initial two months had been finalized, and I had no way of knowing whether the agreement with OSI would ultimately work out. But as I listened to the briefing on the Byelorussian suspects and learned the details of their alleged crimes, I felt a strong sense of excitement and anticipation. This was a concrete opportunity to make a meaningful contribution to the attempts to achieve justice for the victims of the Holocaust rather than being confined to telling the tale, or doing research related to their tragic demise. I did not realize it then, nor did I think in those terms at the time, but my career as a Nazi-hunter had officially been launched.

Notes

1. Project Launched to Help Identify Potential Witnesses for Trials of Nazi War Criminals in the United States", *JTA Daily News Bulletin*, August 21, 1979, p. 2.

2. Project to Help Identify Potential Witnesses for Trials of Nazi War Criminals in the U.S.," *Jewish Press*, August 24, 1979; "YU Holocaust Center Seeks Witnesses," *Jewish Journal*, September 14, 1979.

3. "Survivors Are Sought as Future Witnesses," *Jewish News*, August 30, 1979.

4. "Names Sought of Accused Criminals," *Jewish Review*, September 14, 1979.

5. "Holocaust Center Organizes Witness Hunt," *Jewish World*, September 13, 1979.

6. "Holocaust Centers Compiling Registry of Survivors," *Jewish Light*, September 12, 1979.

7. "Witnesses Sought for Nazi Criminal Trials," *Observer*, September 21, 1979.

8. "Project Seeks to Identify Witnesses for Nazi Trials," *Jewish Weekly News*, September 13, 1979.

9. "Project Aims to Find Witnesses for Nazi War Criminal Trials," *Jewish Ledger*, August 23, 1979.

10. "Holocaust Center Project to Aid Nazi Trials," *Jewish News*, 24 August 1979.

11. "War Crimes Witness Search Focuses on Soviet Emigres," *Sentinel*,

August 30, 1979.

12. "Witness for Ex-Nazis' Trials Sought in U.S.," *Baltimore Jewish Times,* August 24, 1979.

13. "Identifying Nazis Is Goal in U.S.," *American Israelite,* September 6, 1979.

14. Other communities in which the local Jewish press publicized the project were: Camden, New Jersey; Houston, Texas; Dayton, Ohio; Minneapolis, Minnesota and Omaha, Nebraska.

15. *Long Island Jewish World,* January 11, 1980, p. 19.

16. *Jewish Times* (Youngstown, Ohio), January 11, 1980; *Kansas City Jewish Chronicle,* January 25, 1980; *Arizona Post* (Tucson), January 18, 1980; *Jewish Reporter* (Framingham, Mass.), January, 1980.

17. Anne Hammerman, "Survivors—Answer This Call," *Dayton Jewish Chronicle,* January 10, 1980.

2

Nazis in the Western Democracies: Who Are They? How Did They Enter?

Even before the end of the Second World War, at a time when Allied victory was not yet certain and at best a long way off, the Allies announced their intention of punishing Nazi war criminals. This goal was proclaimed publicly on several occasions and found formal expression in the establishment of the United Nations War Crimes Commission in October 1942. One of the most explicit formulations of the Allies' desire to punish Nazi war criminals was the Moscow Declaration of November 1943, issued following meetings between Roosevelt, Churchill and Stalin. The declaration expressed the Allies' commitment that those who had perpetrated atrocities, massacres and executions would be brought to trial, adding that "most assuredly the three Allied powers will pursue them to the uttermost ends of the earth and will deliver them to the accusers in order that justice may be done."[1] While there is considerable evidence to indicate that declarations such as this were issued primarily as propaganda, the fact remains that the Allies had publicly and unequivocally promised that those responsible for the heinous crimes committed by the Nazis would be brought to the bar of justice.

Post-war realities proved, however, how hollow these lofty proclamations were. Not only did the Western allies not pursue the criminals to "the uttermost ends of the earth" as they had promised, they did not pursue most of them at all. In fact they allowed something far worse to occur. They provided thousands of Nazi war criminals with a haven in their own countries, affording them an opportunity not only to escape justice but to build new lives and benefit from the Allied victory in the Second World War. How and why did the countries which had fought against the Axis powers, sacrificing tens of thousands of soldiers to defeat Nazism, grant immigration visas and later citizenship to some of Hitler's most bloodthirsty henchmen? How could a country such as the United States (and the same applies to Great Britain, Canada and Australia), which had sent its own men overseas to help make the world safe for democracy, become a haven for at least hundreds, if not thousands, of war criminals who had played an active role in the annihilation of millions of innocent men, women and children? The overwhelming majority of the criminals who emigrated to the US did so, moreover, under their own names and made no attempt to adopt false identities, a fact which makes their immigration and naturalization even more reprehensible.

A good part of the explanation for this phenomenon lies in the identity of the criminals who escaped to the West. Had the top echelon of Nazi leadership attempted to flee to the Western democracies it is very doubtful whether they would have succeeded. In fact, to the best of my knowledge, none even tried to do so. Had any such attempt been made, the individuals in question could never have possibly entered the United States under their own names and would undoubtedly have had to conceal their true identities. After all, most of the top Nazis who escaped to South America or the Middle East took the precaution of changing their names and adopting new identities.[2] Those who emigrated to the United States as well as to Great Britain, Canada, and Australia, however, were a different breed. The overwhelming majority were neither Germans nor Austrians, but rather Lithuanians, Latvians, Ukrainians, Croatians, Estonians, Volksdeutsche (ethnic Germans living in Eastern Europe) and Byelorussians. The important role that they had played in the implementation of the Final Solution was not as well known as the misdeeds of their German and Austrian counterparts. Thus while Jewish survivors from Eastern Europe were painfully aware of the critical contribution made by their former neighbors to large-scale murders, those not intimately acquainted with the details of the annihilation of the Jews usually considered those events as having been carried out almost exclusively by Germans and Austrians. This distorted view of the Holocaust played an important role in facilitating the escape of thousands of Nazi war criminals to the United States and other Western democracies.

Let us turn to the events of the Second World War and its immediate aftermath to clarify the nature and scope of the crimes committed by these collaborators and to examine how they were able to emigrate to the West. There is considerable controversy among historians of the Holocaust as to when the decision was made to launch the Final Solution,[3] but it is generally agreed that its operative implementation on a mass scale began with the Nazis' invasion of the Soviet Union on June

22, 1941. The method initially chosen by the Nazis to carry out the murders was mass shootings which were performed by units especially trained for this task. Thus accompanying the German troops which invaded the Soviet Union were Einsatzgruppen or mobile killing units whose task was to murder all the Jews and Communist officials in the areas occupied by the Wehrmacht.

The Einsatzgruppen were divided into four units labelled A,B,C and D, and they numbered a total of approximately 3,000 men. The largest was A which had 990 men, the smallest was D which numbered less than 500. These units had to cover an enormous area that stretched from the suburbs of Leningrad in the north to east of the Sea of Azov in the south, a front hundreds of miles long. Each of the four Einsatzgruppen was linked to the Wehrmacht units which operated in the same area, and there was considerable tactical and logistical cooperation between the army and the mobile killing units. The Wehrmacht supplied the Einsatzgruppen with housing, food, gasoline and communications and the mobile killing units were formally under the army's administrative control. Functional directives were issued, however, by the Reich Security Main Office (headed by Reinhard Heydrich) which was responsible for the implementation of the Final Solution.

At the time of the Nazi invasion, approximately five million Jews were living in the Soviet Union, most of them in the western areas of the country which were occupied by the Germans. The aim of the Einsatzgruppen was to carry out the murders as quickly as possible in order to ensure secrecy, prevent resistance, and limit escape. The means at their disposal to achieve this goal were in most cases solely conventional firearms—machine guns, rifles and pistols. At this point they did not have any of the more "sophisticated" means of mass murder which the Nazis subsequently employed with such staggering results (mainly in the death camps). Yet despite this limitation and the fact that the relatively small number of men in these units had to operate over such a wide geographical area, the Einsatzgruppen managed to murder approximately 900,000 Jews within 15 months.[4]

Such results could never have possibly been achieved without the active and often zealous assistance rendered by a significant proportion of the local population in the areas occupied by the Germans. The help provided by the indigenous population encompassed every phase of the murder operation. Thus, for example, Lithuanians, Latvians and Ukrainians serving in auxiliary police units carried out a significant percentage of the executions conducted under the auspices of the Einsatzgruppen. Many of these murders were carried out by special execution squads established under German aegis. Among the most notorious of these were the Latvian Arajs Commando which operated primarily in Latvia,[5] the police battalions of the Lithuanian Auxiliary Police which carried out mass murder in Lithuania and Byelorussia,[6] and the Lithuanian *Ypatingas burys* or Vilnius Sonderkommando which implemented the Final Solution of the Jews of Vilna and its environs.[7] These murder squads were responsible for the deaths of tens of thousands of Jews.

Besides those serving in police or military units, numerous locals participated in the murders of Jews which were carried out by gangs of vigilantes. In Lithuania these gangs were often referred to as "activists," "partisans" or "white-banders" because of the identifying white armbands they wore. Their members were usually "Shaulists" or Lithuanian army veterans who were extremely nationalistic.[8] In Latvia many of those who participated in the spontaneous acts of violence committed against the Jews had been members of the fascist *Perkonkrust* (Thunder Cross) movement or the *Aizsargi* who had served in the civilian guard when Latvia was independent.[9] In this context it is important to note that numerous Jews were murdered by the local population even before the arrival of the Germans or during the first days of the occupation before the Nazi administration was established. Throughout the area of the Soviet Union, but particularly in Lithuania, Latvia and the Ukraine, the local anti-Semites needed little or no encouragement from the Nazis in order to initiate persecution which resulted in the deaths of thousands of Jews.[10]

These acts of violence and the subsequent large-scale participation of Lithuanians, Latvians, Ukrainians, Volksdeutsche, etc. in mass murder were the result of several factors. One was the deep-seated traditional anti-Semitism which existed for generations in these areas. Another factor was the hatred of the Soviets by the indigenous population, an enmity which was considerably increased during the year of Soviet rule (from June 1940—June 1941) because of the wholesale deportations of the local population which were carried out by the Soviet secret police. Although numerous Jews were also deported by the Soviets, the local Jews were held responsible for these measures because of the relatively large numbers of Jews in the Communist Party and the fact that several Jewish Communists occupied prominent posts in the Soviet administration. A third factor was the belief held by many locals that the Germans would restore their independence which had been abrogated by the Russians. This line of thinking, which proved totally illusory, predicated full collaboration with the Nazis. And what better way to do so than to cooperate in the murder of the Jews who, in any event, were the object of traditional prejudice and hatred based on religious, nationalistic and economic factors. By the time local leaders realized that the Germans had no intention of restoring their independence, most of the Jews had already been murdered.[11]

The assistance which the local population provided for the Nazis came in various forms. Besides active participation in the murder of Jews, the locals carried out numerous accessory functions which enabled the Nazis to maintain their rule and implement their program of annihilation. Local police units established by the Germans maintained order and actively participated in the murder of Jews and other innocent civilians as well as in punitive operations against partisans. Local mayors ran municipal administrations composed of indigenous officials who not only provided the standard services, but also issued anti-Jewish directives and carried out the confiscation of Jewish property and the ghettoization of the local Jewish residents. Local newspapers encouraged their readers to cooperate with the Nazis and called for the murder of the Jews. Practically all the administrative mechanisms in these areas helped facilitate the implementation of the Final Solution.[12]

The assistance provided by the local population was of critical importance for the Nazis. The former, unlike the invading Germans, were intimately conversant with local conditions: they spoke the language, knew the geography, topography, and environmental hazards. They were far better acquainted than the Germans with the potential victims. Obviously if local Jews sought to hide or escape, their chances of fooling the Germans were far better than their hope of being able to outwit their neighbors or other locals who in most cases were just as anxious to see them dead. In addition, the manpower provided by the locals was extremely important due to the relatively small number of men assigned to the Einsatzgruppen. If not for the help of the numerous Lithuanians, Latvians, Ukrainians, Estonians, Byelorussians, etc. who participated in the murders, the scope of the mass annihilation would undoubtedly have been far less extensive. In this context it is important to remember one additional fact. Unlike the situation in most of Nazi-occupied Europe, the overwhelming majority of the Jews in the Soviet Union were not deported to the death camps but were murdered on the spot and thus the help provided by the local population in these areas had particularly lethal consequences.[13]

Less than six months after the Einsatzgruppen began implementing the Final Solution, the Nazis launched the second phase of their plan for the annihilation of European Jewry. On December 8, 1941, the day after the Japanese attack on Pearl Harbor, the Nazis began the operation of the first death camp—Chelmno. The term "death camp" refers specifically only to those Nazi concentration camps which had special installations or equipment to carry out mass murder. The establishment of these camps represented a significant escalation of the murder process, as they were capable of liquidating far more people in much less time and in a more efficient manner than the mobile killing units. In fact, one of the main reasons for their establishment was the numerous difficulties encountered by the Einsatzgruppen whose bloody execution methods proved problematic even for hardened Nazis.

Six death camps were built by the Nazis. All were located in Poland. The largest was the notorious Auschwitz-Birkenau complex situated in Lower Silesia near the town of Oswiecim. The others were Majdanek on the outskirts of the city of Lublin; Chelmno in the Warthgau region not far from Lodz; Treblinka midway between Warsaw and Bialystok; and two camps located in Eastern Poland, Belzec and Sobibor. These camps can be divided into two categories. Auschwitz and Majdanek were labor camps as well as death camps, whereas the other four dealt exclusively with mass annihilation. Thus those deported to Auschwitz and Majdanek usually underwent a "selection," which meant that if an individual was young and in good health he might be sent to do forced labor rather than be murdered immediately. In the other four camps, however, almost all the Jews deported there were automatically sent to be gassed. The only exceptions were those artisans, such as locksmiths and carpenters, who were kept alive as part of a small maintenance staff and those chosen to handle the clothes and belongings of the victims. Jews from all over Europe were sent to these "death factories," where more than half of the approximately six million Jews murdered by the Nazis and their collaborators were put to death.[14]

The Nazis were extremely dependent on the assistance provided by the East European collaborators, not only for the Einsatzgruppen but in the death camps as well. Here too the Germans suffered from an acute manpower shortage. They therefore recruited numerous collaborators of Baltic and Ukrainian origin to perform a wide range of tasks which were critical for the operation of the death camps.[15] Let us take Treblinka as an example. Located near the town of Malkinia, approximately 70 kilometers from Warsaw, it began operation in mid-July 1942. During the course of the approximately 15 months that it existed, at least 875,000 Jews from Poland, Germany, Austria, Czechoslovakia, Greece and Yugoslavia were murdered in the camp. Throughout its existence, Treblinka was run by a skeleton staff of 30 to 40 German SS men. They were assisted, however, by a large contingent of East European SS men, mostly Ukrainians, which numbered between 90 and 120 men, who had undergone special training at Trawniki, the SS camp where non-German personnel were prepared for their role in "Operation Reinhard," the code name for the annihilation of Polish Jewry.

The non-German SS who served at Treblinka were volunteers. Some had served in the Red Army and been captured by the Germans, others were local policemen who volunteered to assist the Nazis. The functions they performed in the camp were primarily related to security. They served as perimeter guards, manned the guard towers and supervised the prisoners at work. When transports of Jews arrived at the railway station, they guarded the area to ensure that the victims went straight to the gas chambers. There were, moreover, several Ukrainians who played an active role in the murder process. Two of the most notorious were Ivan and Nikolai who operated the gas chambers. Their job was to push the Jews inside and turn on the engine. It was important to stuff as many people as possible into the gas chambers and they did so by beating their victims with either a whip, pipe, crowbar or sword. Once all the victims were dead, they would order a team of Jewish inmates to dispose of the bodies.[16]

The functions fulfilled by the non-German SS in Treblinka were vital to the operation of the camp and undoubtedly facilitated the implementation of the Final Solution. The same situation existed in the other death camps where Volksdeutsche and volunteers of East European origin performed a myriad of tasks connected with the murder process. It should be noted that the role of the collaborators was not confined to the death camps. Numerous volunteers performed similar functions in the other concentration, labor and transit camps established by the Nazis all over Europe. While Mauthausen, to name one prominent example, was not a death camp per se, the number of persons killed there (approximately 119,000) was extremely high,[17] and there is ample evidence to indicate the participation of collaborators of East European origin in acts of persecution and murder committed there.[18] If we add the fact that Ukrainian and Latvian units, as well as numerous East European volunteers trained at Trawniki, actively participated in the concentration and deportation of Polish Jewry to the death camps (a process in the course of which thousands of Jews were murdered by the Baltic and Ukrainian collaborators), the vital role played by these criminals in the destruction process becomes crystal clear.[19] I seriously doubt whether so many Jews could have possibly been killed without the willing, active and usually zealous cooperation provided by thousands upon thousands of collaborators.

Even before the end of the war, many of the East European collaborators who had committed atrocities fled from the scene of their crimes. The Red Army was advancing from the East and the criminals knew what fate awaited them if they fell into Russian hands. The Soviets were known for their stringent policy against those who had collaborated with the "Hitlerite Fascists," as the Nazis were invariably referred to by the Communists, and it was obvious that extremely severe punishments would be meted out to those apprehended. The exact number and percentage of war criminals executed in the Soviet Union is not known, but the figure certainly considerably exceeds the number of those punished in this manner in the West. Most of those who had actively assisted the Nazis in Eastern Europe were, moreover, nationalists who were staunchly opposed to Communism on ideological grounds. They knew that they would be harassed by the Communists regardless of their activities during the war—another reason why it was only natural for them to seek to escape to the West.[20] Some retreated with their units, other travelled on their own, but almost all ended up in Germany by 1945.

In order to understand how thousands of Nazi war criminals were able to enter the United States and other Western democracies after the war, we must direct our attention to post-war Germany. Europe was in ruins, staggering from the death of tens of millions of people, devastated by the wholesale wanton destruction committed during six long years of world war. Millions were homeless, millions were on the road. Some sought to return to their former homelands in search of family, friends, property or belongings. Others wanted to escape from their homes because of pogroms and/or their desire to emigrate abroad. The country which had the largest number of refugees was Germany. This was a result of several factors, the most important of which was the enormous number of concentration camp inmates liberated by the Allies in Germany. In addition, there were hundreds of thousands of Germans who had been living in Eastern Europe and had either fled or been expelled in the wake of the Nazis' defeat.[21]

Under the chaotic conditions which existed in post-war Germany, it was not particularly difficult for Nazi collaborators of East European origin to pose as innocent refugees who had left their homelands because they did not want to live under Soviet rule. That was an entirely plausible explanation in those days and one which in fact applied to hundreds of thousands of East Europeans who ended up in Germany after the war. It also applied to a certain extent to the criminals; although they were hardly innocent refugees, it is true that almost all were nationalists who did not want to live under Communist rule. Thus the criminals had a logical and convincing alibi to account for their presence in Germany and this explanation was used to account for their emigration as well.

The overwhelming majority of the war criminals who escaped to Germany had no desire to remain there. Most sought to emigrate, preferably to the United States, Great Britain, Canada or Australia. The reasons why they preferred these countries were rather prosaic. The criminals wanted to get as far away as possible from the scene of the crimes and the threat of being tried by the Soviets. During the 1940s numerous Soviet citizens were forcibly repatriated to the Soviet Union, where many who had been prisoners-of-war were imprisoned and, in some cases, executed. The criminals knew that the Russians would eventually learn of their crimes, so it was important for those who came from the areas of the Soviet Union to avoid repatriation at all costs.[22] That would obviously be far easier overseas than in Germany. Moreover, the four preferred destinations were all countries opposed to Communism, a factor which the war criminals knew would be in their favor. In addition, the United States, Canada and Australia had suffered relatively little as a result of the war (none had been invaded or occupied by the Nazis), nor were they known to have a particularly strong sense of historical consciousness—two more factors which made them attractive to Nazi war criminals. (In this respect Great Britain, which had been severely bombed by the Nazis, was an exception.) All three were also lands of economic opportunity which had been built by immigrants and offered the prospect of financial success to newcomers willing to work hard. In fact, Australia,[23] Canada[24] and Great Britain,[25] which suffered from population shortages, actively sought European immigrants and thus were favorably inclined toward the Displaced Persons (DPs). Finally, each one of these countries already had Lithuanian, Latvian, Ukrainian, Croatian, etc. communities that were willing to help absorb the newcomers and facilitate their integration into American, Canadian, Australian or British life.

The procedures for those seeking admittance to the United States were fairly complex. Applicants had to obtain refugee status from the International Refugee Organization, classification as a Displaced Person from the US Displaced Persons Commission and a visa from the local consulate. In the course of this process the prospective immigrants were required to fill out various forms regarding their background, wartime activities, employment history, and organizational affiliations. There is no doubt that US immigration officials were aware from the very beginning of the possibility that Nazi war criminals might attempt to enter the United States. In fact at each stage of the immigration process the prospective immigrant was required to reply to several questions which, if answered accurately, would have revealed the applicant's criminal past or at least indicated the necessity of a more thorough investigation.[26] Thus, for example, the prospective immigrant was asked whether he had ever been a member of a movement hostile to the United States or had ever committed a crime involving moral turpitude, such as the persecution of civilians. Moreover, each applicant was required to present a complete record of his wartime activities. Obviously if a person indicated that he had served in the Lithuanian or Latvian police, that would have constituted a sufficient basis for his exclusion from refugee or DP status and would have prevented his entering the United States. There were, in addition, other questions which if answered truthfully would have uncovered or at least hinted at the applicant's Nazi past. Prospective immigrants were asked, for example, to list all the organizations of which they had been members.[27] If a person replied that he had been a member of the Croatian *Ustasha* or the Rumanian Iron Guard or Latvian *Perkonkrust* or any other indigenous fascist organization, that ostensibly would have prompted further inquiries. At least on paper, therefore, sufficient safeguards existed in the immigration process to weed out Nazi war criminals seeking to immigrate to the United States.

In reality, however, the screening mechanism proved woefully inadequate. Those who committed crimes brazenly lied about their pasts and were able with relative ease to fool the US officials. The latter were either unable or unwilling to properly carry out the necessary investigations which would have exposed the false information submitted by the criminals. Wolodymir Osidach, for example, who had served as the commandant of the Ukrainian police in Rawa-Ruska, which had carried out the murder of thousands of Jews, wrote on his application that during the years 1936-1944 he had been a dairy technician. Needless to say, he was granted an immigration visa.[28]

Numerous examples of this type abound. Antanas Bernotas, who played an active role in the persecution of the Jews in his capacity as an officer of the Lithuanian Security Police in Siauliai, wrote on his visa application that during the years 1941-1944 he had been a teacher.[29] Antanas Virkutis, who also actively participated in the persecution of the Jews in that city, concealed the fact that he had served as warden of the local prison and listed his occupations as "employee of the Justice Ministry" and "student."[30]

The ideal situation under those circumstances, would have been the existence of a computerized data bank on Nazi war criminals. If accurate information had been readily available to the officials processing immigration applications, perhaps the admission of thousands of Nazi war criminals to the United States and other Western democracies could have been prevented. That, unfortunately, was not the case and to this day a data bank of this sort has not yet been established. On the other hand, it should be noted that if such information had been easily accessible it is highly likely that the criminals would have changed their names and adopted new identities, which was not particularly difficult to do in Germany at that time. The fact that the overwhelming majority of the Nazi war criminals who emigrated to the United States saw no need to change their names is an indication of their sense of security. Perhaps they thought that no one would be able or willing to go to the trouble of gathering the necessary information about thousands upon thousands of crimes which took place across the length and breadth of Europe, in cities, towns, villages and farms, most of whose names meant absolutely nothing to the average American. They obviously underestimated, or failed to reckon with, the Jewish people's sense of obligation to the victims or their historical memory, both of which contributed to the fact that these criminals were ultimately exposed.

The ghastly scenes which confronted the Allied liberators of the Nazi concentration camps were given extensive coverage in the American press and left an indelible impression on the American public. The mountains of corpses and the haggard remnants which greeted American soldiers in camps such as Dachau, Mauthausen and Buchenwald impressed the horrors of the Nazi regime upon millions of Americans who had not experienced the war at first hand. Thus when the plight of the survivors, who were living in refugee and detention centers, some of which had previously served as concentration camps, was publicized, it produced an outcry. There was, therefore, a willingness on the part of certain sectors of the American public to alleviate the DP's situation by facilitating entry to the United States. These feelings of support found concrete expression in the DP Act of 1948 which authorized the immigration to the United States of 200,000 displaced persons over the course of two years.

The problem was, however, that this bill did not in practice serve the goal which inspired its formulation. On the contrary, instead of assisting the survivors, it severely curtailed their entry. To make matters worse it gave priority to Nazi collaborators who had participated in the murder of innocent men, women and children. This was achieved by the inclusion of several provisions which gave preference to various ethnic groups and professions, among whom here was a high percentage of Nazi war criminals, while limiting those categories of DPs which were predominantly Jewish. Thus, for example, the law required that 40 per cent of the visas be issued to immigrants from countries which had been "annexed by a foreign power," that is the former Baltic republics of Lithuania, Latvia and Estonia which had been incorporated into the Soviet Union following their liberation by the Red Army in 1944. The overwhelming majority of the Jewish refugees from these countries sought to emigrate to Israel, while the percentage of Nazi war criminals among the prospective Lithuanian, Latvian and Estonian applicants for emigration to the United States was particularly high. Setting aside such a large percentage of the visas for this group was tantamount to issuing an open invitation to Nazi collaborators to apply for emigration, given the grossly inadequate screening process then in operation.

The same applies to the special provision which enabled the admission of 50,000 Volksdeutsche or East Europeans of German origin.

Numerous Volksdeutsche collaborated with the Nazis, including some who actively participated in the mass murder of Jews. The Volksdeutsche were in fact not even recognized as "displaced persons" by the International Refugee Organization since they had not left their homes as a result of coercion or persecution. The US Congress nonetheless granted them special status, setting aside 50,000 visas in the framework of the DP Act. Other provisions set aside 30 per cent of the available places for farmers and stipulated that only refugees who had entered the DP camps before December 22, 1945 would be eligible for immigration. Both provisions discriminated against Jews, few of whom were farmers and most of whom had arrived in the camps after that date. To complicate matters further, the Citizen's Committee for Displaced Persons, an ecumenical group established by American Jews to enlist support for a change in the immigration laws, actively lobbied on behalf of the DPs, most of whom were not Jewish, in the hope of thereby guaranteeing enough immigration visas to the United States for the Jewish survivors of the Holocaust.

It is important to stress in this context that there were efforts to alert Congress and the public to the dangers posed by the special provisions of the DP Act. Articles in the press—Jewish and general—pointed to the absurd situation created in which it would be "easier for a former Nazi to enter the United States than for one of the Nazis' innocent victims" (*New York Times*, August 30, 1948). Abraham Duker, an expert on the crimes committed by the collaborators, attempted to persuade Congress of the injustice which was being perpetrated under the guise of a humanitarian gesture. In articles in *Der Tog* (The Day) and the *Reconstructionist*, Duker noted that the empathy engendered by the suffering of Nazism's victims was being utilized to generate propaganda on behalf of all DPs including the murderers, a policy which he termed indecent, shameful and dangerous.[31]

Duker's assessment of the practical implications of the special provisions of the DP Act proved quite accurate. Indeed, the thousands of Nazi war criminals who entered the United States constitute the ultimate proof of the accuracy of his warnings. This happened due to the inadequacy of the screening process which almost totally failed to fulfil its function. In order to understand how this took place, we must examine the mechanism more closely.

The screening process was carried out in two stages. The first was under the aegis of the International Refugee Organization (IRO) which was responsible for granting classification as a refugee. According to IRO regulations, war criminals were denied that status, as was anyone who had voluntarily assisted the Axis powers or participated in the persecution of civilians. The problem was, however, that the IRO made no serious effort to examine the wartime activities of the applicants. There were actually several cases in which Nazi collaborators were hired to do that job and instead of screening out war criminals, they assisted them. Thus numerous ex-Nazis were granted refugee status, which ultimately facilitated their emigration to the United States.

On a practical level the ineffectiveness of the IRO screening process meant that the only hope of identifying the Nazi war criminals among the prospective immigrants was in the second stage; this was carried out by the Counter Intelligence Corps (CIC) of the US Army under the auspices of the Displaced Persons Commission. The latter had been created by a provision of the DP Act for the express purpose of screening out undesirable applicants. (The undesirables in question were Communists as well as Nazis.) The CIC carried out its investigations by examining wartime records and the files of the Berlin Document Center. They also checked documentation related to the applicant's behavior during the period he or she was in Germany. The problem was, however, that none of the sources consulted had the pertinent information. The Berlin Document Center had comprehensive files on members of the Nazi Party, as well as SS personnel records, but neither included information on Baltic or Ukrainian collaborators. Thus a Lithuanian could have been a member of the infamous Vilnius Sonderkommando which carried out the murder of thousands of Jews, but it is unlikely that a screening team would have discovered that fact. Unfortunately no reliable information of the sort required was readily available and thus the screening process did not fulfil its function.

In 1950 Congress finally cancelled most of the provisions of the DP Act which had facilitated the entry of Nazi war criminals to the United States. A stipulation was added, moreover, that anyone who had participated in the persecution of civilians would be barred but by this time considerable damage had already been done. Allan A. Ryan Jr., who headed the Office of Special Investigations during the years 1980-3, estimated the number of Nazi war criminals who immigrated to the United States at about 10,000. His estimate is based on the following statistics. Among the 393,000 immigrants admitted to the US under the DP Act, approximately 169,000 were from the high-risk categories of Lithuanians, Latvians and Estonians (68,000), Ukrainians (48,000) and Volksdeutsche (3,000). Ryan estimates that about 5 per cent of those admitted engaged in persecution and thus arrives at the figure of 10,000 cited above, after adding 1,550 more for those nationalities not included in the calculation (Croatians, Rumanians, etc.).[32] The problem, as Ryan admits, is that such figures are hardly scientific. The truth of the matter is that it is practically impossible to collect the names of all those who participated in persecution; thus to arrive at exact figures is extremely difficult. Ryan's hypothesis that 5 per cent of the DPs in the high risk categories who entered the US were war criminals cannot be checked and can only be regarded as an educated guess. In fact, based on recently acquired documentation from archives in the former Soviet Union, it might even be a bit low. Regardless of the figures, the overall picture remains unequivocally clear: thousands of Nazi war criminals who lied on their immigration forms were admitted to the United States in the framework of the DP Act of 1948. As far as the other countries are concerned, they also relied for the most part on the same ineffective agencies as the Americans. The limited screening procedures they instituted on their own were similarly totally inadequate.[33]

With the above description of the historical events as background, we can attempt to categorize the Nazi war criminals who emigrated to Western democracies. It should be pointed out, however, that there are two other categories of perpetrators whose stories are quite different from the above scenario. The first group to consider are those known as initiators, high-ranking officials who made decisions regarding the implementation of the Final Solution which influenced the fate of thousands of Jews. These individuals occupied prominent positions and were therefore relatively well-known. They obviously could not enter the United States under their own names and thus were forced to adopt false identities.

The most famous of these criminals was Andrija Artukovic who served as Minister of the Interior in Croatia, a state established by the Nazis in part of Yugoslavia following the occupation of that country in April 1941. The Germans entrusted the administration of Croatia to the *Ustasha*, the indigenous fascist movement which was infamous due to the cruelty and barbarism of its members. In his capacity as Minister of the Interior, Artukovic was in charge of dealing with the country's minorities—primarily Serbs, with whom the Croats had feuded for years, and Jews. The results of his policies were horrifying. Hundreds of thousands of Serbs and approximately 20,000 Jews were murdered in Croatia during the three year rule of the *Ustasha*. Many of the victims were killed in the concentration camps established by Artukovic (the most famous of which was Jasenovac), while others were slaughtered by roving bands of *Ustasha*. In Croatia, as in areas of the Soviet Union, many of the Jews were murdered locally and the role of the indigenous population was particularly significant.[34]

Given his wartime record, Artukovic could not apply for immigration to the US under his own name. After fleeing to Austria, Switzerland and Ireland, he obtained a tourist visa for the US under the name of Alois Anich and arrived in New York on July 16, 1948. Unlike the cases of the overwhelming majority of the Nazis who entered the United States, various attempts were made to extradite or deport Artukovic as early as 1949. The extradition request submitted by the Yugoslav government was turned down, however, because of various legal technicalities and the contention that he would be subject to physical persecution in Yugoslavia.[35] As a result, Artukovic was able to continue living in the United States as a free man until 1986 when the OSI finally succeeded in deporting him to Yugoslavia.[36] Artukovic was put on trial in Zagreb and was sentenced to death,[37] but the implementation of the verdict was postponed due to ill health. He died in January 1988 in prison in Zagreb at the age of 88.[38]

In terms of the crimes he committed, Artukovic is the highest-ranking Nazi war criminal to have entered the United States. He is, moreover, the only person in his category, the only true initiator. There are several other Nazi collaborators who immigrated to the United States who held the equivalent of Cabinet posts in their countries of origin, but they were invariably figureheads, members of governments which existed on paper but not in reality. The most prominent among them was Radislav Ostrowski who headed the Byelorussian Central Council, a Nazi puppet organization which ostensibly constituted the representative body of the Byelorussian people. While Ostrowski and his cohorts supported the annihilation of the Jews, they had relatively little involvement in carrying out the mass murders. Their major contribution to the German war effort—the recruitment of Byelorussians for the SS—was made in 1944, long after the Jews had already been killed.[39]

There is one other category of criminals whose background and wartime activities do not fit the description presented above—the German scientists who were brought to the United States after the Second World

War. Their story differed from that of the other Nazi criminals described above in two respects—their national origin and the fact that they did not have to lie about their wartime activities to obtain entry. On the contrary, the American authorities invested considerable effort to bring them to the United States precisely because they knew all about the scientific projects they worked on during the war. The scientists were sought-after immigrants for whom the American authorities had prepared a special role, and special efforts were invested in bringing them to the United States lest they fall into the wrong (i.e. Soviet) hands.

The story of the German scientists began in a base at Peenemunde on the Baltic Sea, where leading Nazi rocket specialists began working on the secret weapons which Hitler hoped would win the war for Germany. The major projects were the V-l and V-2 rockets, the latter of which carried a one-ton warhead. During the course of the war, the Allies learned of the existence of Peenemunde and the research being conducted there and tried to destroy the base in August 1943. The project was therefore transferred to Germany and installed in a massive factory in the Dora-Mittelbau concentration camp. One of the reasons for this choice of locale was that the inmates of the camp provided a convenient pool of slave labor which could be utilized as needed. The prisoners constructed the enormous underground tunnels built to house the factories (and protect them from Allied bombers) and they were put to work building the rockets. The combination of particularly harsh physical conditions in the camp and the long, back-breaking work shifts were practically tantamount to a death sentence. Indeed, the life expectancy of those who worked in the rocket factories at Dora was approximately six months. At least one-third of the first 60,000 inmates who were transferred from the nearby Buchenwald concentration camp to work at the rocket factories in Dora died before the end of the war.

Those in charge of the construction of the rockets at Dora were Nazi scientists. Under normal circumstances their involvement in this project together with the harsh treatment and punishments they meted out to prisoners under their supervision, would have made them prime candidates for prosecution after the war. In the realities of post-war Europe, however, the exact opposite occurred. Instead of being apprehended and brought to justice, Nazi scientists were sought by the American, British and Soviet intelligence services for a totally different reason. Even before the war ended it was obvious that the Anglo-American-Soviet partnership would not continue and that those who had hitherto been allies against the Nazis would henceforth be rivals for world hegemony. Thus each side sought to capture as many of the leading Nazi scientists as possible and thereby ensure that their expertise did not fall into the hands of their opponents. Instead of prosecuting the Nazi scientists, the victors of the Second World War awarded them free entry, citizenship, and fascinating and lucrative jobs. The competition for the services of the Nazi scientists was so intense that each side invested considerable manpower and resources to capture them. These Nazis subsequently played a leading role in the space programs on both sides of the Iron Curtain,[40] proving Simon Wiesenthal's contention that the Nazi war criminals who escaped justice were in fact "the real winners of the Cold War."[41]

The scientists who came to the United States were put to work on various important projects, among them the American space program. Many settled in Huntsville, Alabama, where they were engaged in military research. Needless to say, they were not harassed by the US authorities or put on trial for their crimes. It was only after the OSI was established that initial efforts were made in that direction. The first person against whom legal steps were taken was Arthur Rudolph, who had been director of production for V-2 missiles at the Dora concentration camp. Rudolph was alleged to have participated in the persecution of inmates from the camp who were employed under inhumane conditions. He agreed to relinquish his American citizenship and returned to Germany in March 1984 after reaching an agreement with OSI, according to which the US government would refrain from filing charges against him for his wartime activities.[42] To date, he is the only German scientist against whom any concrete action has been taken, although others involved in similar activities were under investigation.

While the Nazi scientists did not use the classic methods of murder associated with the horrors of the Final Solution (gas chambers, killing squads), the crimes they committed were extremely serious. Working people to death is perhaps less shocking than murdering them in gas chambers, but the ultimate result is exactly the same. German scientists were involved in a wide range of scientific experiments in which concentration camp inmates were used as guinea pigs and often died as a result. These experiments were designed to determine, for example, how much cold the human body can stand (to help Luftwaffe pilots shot down over the North Sea) or examine immunity to various contagious diseases. Almost invariably the subjects died in the course of the experiments.[43] The fact that learned professors willingly adopted the ethical norms of the Third Reich is one of the most appalling and frightening features of that regime of horror. The efforts to prosecute these individuals consequently assumed a special dimension with important moral and educational significance.

Another category of Nazi war criminal whose immigration to the West was purposely facilitated by governmental agencies, was those recruited as prospective intelligence operatives. The individuals in question came from the areas which had been occupied by the Soviet Union during the course of World War II and were chosen for their knowledge of the local conditions, language, etc. and their anti-communist political orientation. Intelligence agencies in the United States and Great Britain planned to send them back to their native countries to serve as spies and organize resistance to the communist regime. Although such schemes invariably failed, they did facilitate the immigration to the West of at least several dozen Nazi war criminals whose entry would otherwise, at least in theory, have been barred.[44]

With the exception of the initiators, the scientists and intelligence operatives, the rest of the criminals more or less fit the background described above. The overwhelming majority were of East European origin and entered the United States under the DP Act. They were the ones who provided the massive local assistance that facilitated the implementation of the Nazis' evil plans. The help rendered by tens of thousands of Lithuanians, Latvian, Ukrainians, Croatians, Rumanians, Byelorussians, etc. came in various forms and encompassed the entire spectrum of collaborationist activities. Not all were equally culpable, not all personally committed the most severe crimes. It is therefore important to attempt to classify the criminals presently living in the United States and other western democracies.

These perpetrators of the Holocaust can be divided into two major categories. The first consists of those who personally committed murder or actively assisted in an act of execution. The second consists of those who participated in persecution but were not actively involved in actual murder. The first category must be divided into several subdivisions to distinguish between mass murderers and minor killers. The former are individuals who had the means of mass annihilation at their disposal, such as commanders of concentration camps or those who operated the gas chambers, and the members of the special murder squads which operated in a wide geographical area over a considerable length of time, and were responsible for the deaths of tens of thousands of victims. The minor killers are those who were involved in the murder of Jews during a limited time period and only in a specific geographical location. This distinction separates those whose primary function was mass liquidation from those who committed a limited number of murders, usually in the course of their duties as local policemen or soldiers. Also included in this category of minor killers are those who carried out spontaneous pogroms which took place even before the German occupation and those who participated in the murders without fulfilling any official function. The bands of Lithuanian and Latvian nationalists who carried out the murder of numerous Jews during the initial weeks following the invasion of the Soviet Union are a prime example.

Those who did not actually commit murder can also be divided into several subcategories. One consists of officials of quisling regimes which carried out German directives and facilitated German rule. The individuals in question were not involved in police measures against Jews but were part of a collaborative mechanism which facilitated such activities. A second category is of administrators on various levels who played an active role in promulgating and implementing anti-Jewish directives but did not participate in actual murder. They were actively involved in every stage of persecution—definition, discrimination, confiscation of property and ghettoization—except annihilation. The final subcategory consists of propagandists who ostensibly did not play any role in actual murder but contributed to that result by urging the local population to support the Nazi occupation and participate in anti-Jewish persecution.

The following examples will help to clarify the various categories. There are relatively few Nazi war criminals who lived in the United States who belong in the first category of murderers—those who operated the mechanisms of mass annihilation. Karl Linnas, an Estonian, was a commander of a concentration camp in Tartu, Estonia. In 1962 he was sentenced to death in absentia in the Soviet Union, where he was charged with the murder of 12,000 inmates.[45] Another individual who was initially convicted on charges which would have put him into this category was Ivan Demjanjuk, a Ukrainian accused of being the infamous "Ivan Groszny" who ran the gas chambers at Treblinka and was alleged to have carried out the murder of hundreds of thousands of Jews.[46] (By comparison, the atomic bomb dropped on Hiroshima claimed the lives of some 200,000 victims. Needless to say, this comparison is made to compare the quantitative scope of the events and in no way implies, or even suggests, that the acts were similar or equivalent with the exception of their ultimate result.) Linnas lived in Greenlawn, NY, Demjanjuk in Seven Hills, Ohio, a suburb of Cleveland. Both were ordered deported to the Soviet Union but in Demjanjuk's case an Israeli extradition request was given precedence. He was put on trial in Jerusalem,[47] where he was subsequently acquitted due to the existence of "reasonable doubt" regarding his identity,[48] while Linnas was sent to the Soviet Union where he died in jail several weeks after his arrival.[49]

The "shooters" who employed conventional means of murder include mass murderers as well as those whose activities were on a far more limited scale. Jurgis Juodis, a Lithuanian, is an example of those in the former category. He was an officer (Oberlieutenant) of the 12th battalion of the Lithuanian Schutzmannschaft or auxiliary police, a unit whose major function was mass murder. It carried out the execution of Jews in Kaunas (Fort IX), Lithuania, as well as in Slutzk, Koidanov and Minsk, Byelorussia, and also participated in the murder of Soviet prisoners of war in Rudensk. A conservative estimate of the number of victims murdered by this unit is 15,000.[50] Juodis was one of numerous members, including officers, of the unit who escaped to the United States. Many others emigrated to England,[51] as well as to Canada, Australia and New Zealand.[52] There were two other murder squads which fulfilled similar functions in areas which were for many years parts of the Soviet Union. One was the *Ypatingas burys* ("the special ones"), otherwise known as the Vilnius Sonderkommando, which murdered tens of thousands of Jews from the city of Vilnius (Vilna) and its environs. The other was the Arajs Commando, a Latvian unit named after its commander, Viktor Arajs, which carried out the mass murder of the Jews of Riga and later played an active role in similar operations elsewhere in Latvia and Byelorussia. Members of all three murder squads escaped to the West and they constitute, among those who implemented the Final Solution using conventional weapons, the majority of the mass murderers.

Those classified as minor killers are persons whose activities were chronologically and geographically, and hence quantitatively, limited. Their involvement in murder was confined to a specific area, usually their own town, city and/or its environs and was generally carried out in the course of their assigned duties. This fact in no way mitigates the horror of their crimes or their culpability. The categorization, therefore, relates primarily to the quantitative aspects of the crime and not to the nature of the acts committed. There are numerous examples of individuals in this category who emigrated to the United States: Ukrainian policemen such as Wolodymir Osidach of Rawa-Ruska; Volksdeutsche such as Alexander Lehmann of Zaporozhe who also served in the Ukrainian police; officers of the Lithuanian Auxiliary Police such as Mecis Paskevicius of Ukmerge; officers of the Latvian Security Police such as Boleslavs Maikovskis of Rezekne;[53] and concentration camp personnel such as Stefan Leili (Mauthausen).[54] The common denominator was participation in the murder of innocent civilians. Most played an active role in the actual implementation, serving as executioners, others did everything possible to facilitate the operation. The assistance provided by these "minor shooters" was enormous. Across the length and breadth of Eastern Europe they carried out the "small" local murders whose victims constituted a significant percentage of the overall total of those murdered by the Nazis. Without their assistance the annihilation could never have reached the dimensions that it did.

No consideration of those responsible for the Holocaust can ignore the criminals in the next category. Although they did not physically murder anyone, they bear an important share of the responsibility for the fate which befell the Jews. They were the administrators, the support staff that issued and implemented the anti-Jewish decrees and directives. Kazys Palciauskas, the mayor of Kaunas, Lithuania, for example, supervised the confiscation of Jewish property and issued the order for the establishment of the local ghetto.[55] Vanya Awdziej, the Byelorussian mayor of Stolpce was similarly involved in the initial stages of the persecution of the Jewish community in his town.[56]

The final category concerns those who were involved in the war of words. They did not run a gas chamber, serve in a murder squad or even order Jews into a ghetto, but their contribution to the Jews' ultimate fate was important. They were the propagandists who prepared the local population for the anti-Semitic measures taken by the Nazis and their collaborators. They poisoned the minds of the local residents by inciting them against the Jews and assisted the Nazis by urging their readers to support the occupation authorities and join the local police or SS units. They wrote in glowing terms of the "Thousand Year Reich" to be established under Hitler's aegis and served as willing, compliant tools of their Nazi masters.

The most famous of the criminals in this category are the Rumanian Archbishop Valerian Trifa and the Russian journalist, later professor Vladimir Sokolov-Samarin. The former edited *Libertate*, the publication of the fascist Rumanian Iron Guard, while the latter was an editor of the Nazi-sponsored newspapers *Rech* (Orel, USSR) and *Yola Naroda* (Berlin). In his capacity as leader of the Iron Guard students, Trifa also played an active role in fomenting the large-scale pogrom which took place in Bucharest in January 1941. In his articles Sokolov advocated the complete annihilation of the Jews and supported the institution of Nazi rule the world over. Unlike the overwhelming majority of the criminals who reached the US, both achieved a degree of prominence in their adopted homeland. Trifa became the head of the Rumanian Orthodox Church in the United States and Sokolov was appointed a professor at Yale. Both, however, lost their posts as a result of the revelation of their wartime activities and/or legal action taken by OSI.[57]

The above classification encompasses practically all the Nazi war criminals who entered the United States. There are, of course, several exceptions such as Otto Von Bolschwing, a German who served as head of the SD (Security Service) in Rumania and as one of Eichmann's advisers on Jewish affairs.[58] His background was obviously different than that of the collaborators of East European origin. His wartime activities, moreover, put him into a separate category in between the initiators and the administrators. In the course of current research it is likely that additional cases will be uncovered whose stories are different from those presented above and for whom the categories listed do not exactly fit, but the overall picture will undoubtedly remain the same.

The overwhelming majority of the thousands of Nazi war criminals who entered the United States were collaborators of East European origin—mostly Lithuanians, Latvians and Ukrainians—who immigrated under the DP Act. Their crimes during the war cover the entire spectrum of active assistance provided for the Nazis by the local population from mass murder to propaganda. In numerical terms most of the criminals were murderers, the overwhelming majority of whom committed their crimes on a limited scale, that is in a specific geographical area over a limited time-period usually in the course of their duties as policemen or militia. Since the data on this subject is incomplete—additional war criminals who emigrated to the United States are being discovered almost daily—the final statistics will have to wait. From the information presently available, however, the following tentative summary can be presented. The preponderant majority of those revealed living in America were members of the local police and security forces who carried out the persecution, incarceration and murder of thousands of Jews in countless small, middle and large-sized villages, towns and cities all over Eastern Europe. Practically anonymous men who carried out heinous crimes in the service of a regime which loathed them as well (though not as much as they loathed the victims), motivated by anti-Semitism, jealousy and greed. Men who fled to the West posing as victims, who concealed their perpetrator past. Men who thought that they could escape justice in a world governed by self-interest and threatened by the cold war. Men who assumed that they would never be caught because they failed to reckon with the almost obsessive memory of a few committed Jews and the guilty conscience of the countries which mistakenly gave them refuge.

Notes

1. Tom Bower, *Blind Eye to Murder; Britain, America and the Purging of Nazi Germany—A Pledge Betrayed*, London, 1983, pp. 69-70. Bower presents the background to the various steps taken by the Allies during the Second World War regarding Nazi war criminals and indicates the serious opposition these measures encountered in various quarters, such as the British Foreign Offfice, prior to their adoption.

2. The best-known examples are Adolf Eichmann who was living in Buenos Aires under the name of Ricardo Klement, and Dr. Josef Mengele who used various aliases (Helmut Gregor, Peter Hochbichler, etc.). There was a period, however, in which the Auschwitz doctor lived in Argentina under his own name. Gerald L. Posner and John Ware, *Mengele: The Complete Story*, New York, 1986, pp. 90-91,133-47, 162-65.

3. For a summary of the various views see Christopher R. Browning, "The Decision Concerning the Final Solution," *Fateful Months: Essays on the Emergence of the Final Solution*, New York, 1985, pp. 8-38.

4. Raul Hilberg, *The Destruction of the European Jews*, Chicago, 1961, pp. 171-256. See also Helmut Krausnick and Hans-Heinrich Wilhelm, *Die Truppe des Weltanschauungskrieges: Die Einsatzgruppen der Sicherheitspolizei und das SD 1938-1942*, Stuttgart, 1981; Heinz Hohne, *The Order of the Death's Head: The Story of Hitler's SS*, New York, 1970, pp. 354-73; Alfred Streim, "The Tasks of the SS Einsatzgruppen," *Simon Wiesenthal Center Annual*, Vol . 4, New York, 1987, pp. 309-28.

5. See the trial records of Viktor Arajs who was sentenced to life imprison-

ment in Hamburg, West Germany in 1979, Yad Vashem Archives (hereafter, YVA), TR-10/994, 1140; M-21/476; "Report on Riga Ghetto Case," Wiener Library Archives (hereafter, WLA), file 539/22; Andrew Ezergailis, "Who Killed the Jews of Latvia?," lecture at conference on "Anti-Semitism in Times of Crisis," April 10, 1986, Cornell University, Ithaca, New York.

6. See, for example, the report of Carl, Gebietskommissar of Slutzk to General-kommissar, Minsk, October 30, 1941, Nuremberg document PS-1104; *Nazi Conspiracy and Aggression*, Vol. III, Washington, 1946, pp. 785-89; Other pertinent documents and witness testimonies are listed in "Plaintiff's Responses to Defendant's First Set of Interrogatories and Requests for Production of Documents" submitted to the district court of the middle district of Florida in the case of Jurgis Juodis, civil action No. 81 - 1013-CIC-T-H, pp. 11-18.

7. For the results of the activities of this unit which functioned as a detachment of Einsatzkommando 3 see the report by Karl Jaegar (commander of Einsatzkommando 3), December 1, 1941 in which he lists the number of victims murdered in Vilnius and its environs, YVA, 0-18/245, reproduced in Raul Hilberg, *Documents of Destruction; Germany and Jewry 1933-1945*, Chicago, 1971, pp. 53-54, see also the material from the trials of Martin Wiess and August Hering who served as German liaison officers to the Vilnius Sonderkommando, YVA, M-21/12; TR-10/381.

8. See the accounts of the events in the provincial Jewish communities of Lithuania, *Yahadut Lita*, Vol. IV, Tel Aviv, 1984, pp. 234-373. See also Leib Garfunkel, "Cheshboneinu im ha-Lita'im," ibid., pp. 48-60; Sara Neshamit, "Bein Shituf Pe'ula le-Meri," *Dappim le Cheker-ha-Shoa ve-ha-Mered*, Sidra Shniya, Me'asef Aleph, Tel Aviv, 1970, pp.152-77. Azriel Schochet, "Chelkam shel ha-Lita'im be-Hashmadat Yehudei Lita," *Dappim le-Cheker Tekufat ha-Shoa*, Measef Aleph, Tel Aviv, 1979, pp. 77-95.

9. Ereignismeldung, No. 24, July 16, 1941, Nuremberg document, No. 2938, YVA; Dov Levin, *Im ha-Gav el ha-Kir; Lechimat Yehudei Latvia ba-Nazim*,- Jerusalem, 1978, pp. 148.

10. On the events in Lithuania see, for example, Yitzhak Arad, "The 'Final Solution' in Lithuania in the Light of German Documentation," *Yad Vashem Studies*, Vol. XI, Jerusalem, 1976, p. 240; *Yahadut Lita*, Vol. IV, pp. 48-60, 234-73; Neshamit, pp. 152-77, Schochet, pp. 77-95. On the role of the Latvians see *Im ha-Gav el ha-Kir*, pp. 144-51; Max Kaufman, *Churbn Lettland*, Munich, 1947, pp. 45-63; YVA, TR-10/1140; Nuremberg document NO-2938; on the initiative of Ukrainians in the persecution of Jews see, for example, the entries on Stanislawow and Stary Sambor in *Pinkas ha-Kehillot*, Polin, Vol. II, Galitzya ha-Mizrachit, Jerusalem, 1980, pp. 369, 379. In his summary report on the mass annihilation in the areas in which the forces under his orders operated, Franz Stahlecker, commander of Einsatzgruppe A claims credit for organizing pogroms in Kovno and Riga, but this does not explain the numerous outbreaks

of violence against the Jews elsewhere in the same area. It is likely that Stahlecker sought to convince his superiors that he was responsible for anti-Jewish violence which he did not in fact initiate. Summary Report by Stahlecker, October 15, 1941, Nuremberg document, L-180. Philip Friedman "Ukrainian-Jewish Relations During the Nazi Occupation," *Roads to Extinction*, New York, 1980, pp. 183-85.

11. This pattern repeated itself in all the areas which came under Soviet rule in 1939-40 and were invaded by the Nazis in June 1941. See, for example, Garfunkel, *Yahadut Lita*, Vol. IV, pp. 48-60, who analyzes the situation in Lithuania. *Im ha-Gav el ha-Kir*, pp. 149-50. In the Ukraine, political differences during the inter-war period were also a factor which contributed to the hostility of the local population against the Jews. *Pinkas ha-Kehillot*, Polin, Vol. II, p. 24.

12. Among the Nazi war criminals indicted by the Office of Special Investigations and convicted by the US courts were individuals in each of the above categories. The various cases investigated by OSI confirm the extensive collaboration of the local population in the Baltic states, Byelorussia and the Ukraine in the implementation of the Final Solution.

13. According to Hilberg, the number of Jews murdered in these areas was approximately 1,000,000. *The Destruction of the European Jews*, p. 256.

14. According to Eichmann, by August 1944 four million Jews had been murdered in camps. While this figure cannot be accurately ascertained (the death camps did not record statistics), it reflects the reality in which most of the Jews murdered during the Holocaust were executed in the death camps. Ibid., p. 631, 555-77.

15. Ibid., pp. 576-77. Gitta Sereny, *Into that Darkness; From Mercy Killing to Mass Murder*, New York, 1974, p. 155.

16. Yitzhak Arad, *Treblinka; Ovdan ve-Mered*, Tel Aviv, 1983, pp. 32-39, 55.

17. Binyamin Eckstein, *Mauthausen; Machane Rikuz ve-Kilayon*, Jerusalem, 1984, p. 326.

18. Several Mauthausen guards of East European origin, such as Martin Bartesch, Stefan Leili, Johann Leprich and Josef Wieland, have been denaturalized and/or deported by OSI during the past several years.

19. Numerous testimonies note the role of these units in the concentration and deportation of Polish Jewry to the death camps. See, for example, the testimony of Aharon Grynspan who notes the cruelty of the Ukrainian and Latvian units in the round-ups in the Warsaw Ghetto. "The Ukrainians and Latvians were cruel as animals, they beat, tortured, shot and murdered anyone in their path." Bar Ilan University Institute for Holocaust Research, testimony Gimmel-43, pp. 13, 16. Chaim Frimer also notes the brutality of the Latvian and Ukrainian units in the Warsaw Ghetto, Bar-Ilan University, testimony pay-41. See also "Przemysl," *Pinkas ha-Kehillot*, Polin, Vol. II, p. 439. On

the role of East European volunteers trained in Trawniki in the roundup and murder of Polish Jews see Christopher Browning, *Ordinary Men; Reserve Battalion 101 and the Final Solution in Poland*, New York, 1992.

20. Many of the collaborators came from the ranks of the indigenous fascist movements: *Perkonkrust* in Latvia, Iron Wolf in Lithuania, Iron Guard in Rumania, *Ustasha* in Croatia. Others had been members of various nationalistic veterans, military, or paramilitary associations such as the Shaulists in Lithuania and the *Aizsargi* in Latvia.

21. Yehuda Bauer, *Flight and Rescue: Brichah*, New York, 1970, pp. 75-76. Leonard Dinnerstein, *America and the Survivors of the Holocaust*, New York, 1982, pp. 9-24.

22. Ibid., p. 19.

23. Upon the initiative of Arthur Calwell, the Minister of Immigration, Australia signed an agreement with the International Refugee Organization on July 21, 1947 to resettle displaced persons in Australia. Under the terms of that agreement 170,695 refugees immigrated to Australia. See "Review of Material Relating to the Entry of Suspected War Criminals into Australia" (hereafter, Menzies Report), submitted to the Australian government November 28, 1986, p. 34.

24. Canada, which had initially been reluctant to admit increased numbers after the Second World War, changed its policy in 1947 and began to facilitate the entry of European Displaced Persons. Irving Abella and Harold Troper, *None Is Too Many: Canada and the Jews of Europe 1933-1948*, Toronto, 1982, pp. 238-47.

25. In the late forties, the British actively recruited Baltic immigrants, including those who had served in the Waffen-SS, to work in the coal and other industries. David Cesarani, *Justice Delayed; How Britain Became a Refuge for Nazi War Criminals*, London, 1992, pp. 85-100.

26. Allan A. Ryan Jr., *Quiet Neighbors; Prosecuting Nazi War Criminals in America*, San Diego, 1984, pp. 19-26.

27. See, for example, "Plaintiff's Proposed Findings of Fact and Conclusions of Law," United States of America vs. Bohdan Koziy, case no. 79-6640 CIV JCP, United States District Court, Southern District of Florida, pp. 5-7.

28. *Quiet Neighbors*, p. 7.

29. Antanas Bernotas file, Simon Wiesenthal Center Archives (hereafter, SWCA).

30. United States of America vs. Antanas Virkutis, Complaint, submitted to United States District Court for the Northern District of Illinois Eastern Division, February 18, 1983, p. 4.

31. *America and the Survivors of the Holocaust*, pp. 39-50, 163-79; *Quiet Neighbors*, pp. 12-19.

32. Ibid., pp. 20-27.

33. Regarding Great Britain see *Justice Delayed*, pp. 1-161; on Australia see "Review of material relating to the entry of suspected war criminals in Australia" (Menzies Report), November 28, 1986; regarding Canada see Jules Deschenes, *Commission of Inquiry on War Criminals*, Ottawa, 1986.

34. Testimony of Alexander Arnon (secretary of the Jewish community in Zagreb during the Second World War), *Mishpat Eichmann; Eiduyot* (Testimonies from the Eichmann Trial), Vol. II, Jerusalem, 1974, pp. 646-57; Menachem Shelach, "Retzach Yehudei Kroatya al yeddei ha-Germanim ve-Ozreihem be-Milchemet ha-Olam ha-Shneeya," Ph.D. dissertation, Tel Aviv University, January 1980, pp. 67-135.

35. *Quiet Neighbors*, pp. 150-90; Henry Friedlander and Earlean M. McCarrick, "The Extradition of Nazi Criminals: Ryan, Artukovic and Demjanjuk," *Simon Wiesenthal Center Annual*, Vol. 4, 1987, pp. 70-73.

36. John Kendall, "Artukovic Extradited to Yugoslavia for Trial," *Los Angeles Times*, February 13, 1986, pp. 1, 3.

37. Nesho Djuric, "Artukovic," United Press International, May 14, 1986.

38. Ivan Stefanovic, "Andrija Artukovic, 'Butcher of the Balkans,' Dead at 88," Associated Press, January 18, 1988.

39. The Byelorussian collaborators played a less influential role in determining the fate of the Jews in Byelorussia than did their counterparts elsewhere in Lithuania, Latvia and the Ukraine. Several prominent Byelorussian collaborators who immigrated to the United States after the Second World War were under investigation by OSI, but to date none has been indicted. Those accused of the most active participation in the murder of Jews died before they could be brought to trial. (Emmanuel Jasiuk, the mayor of Kletzk; Franz Kushel, a leader of the Byelorussian police; and Stanislaw Stankevich, mayor of Borisov.) The only study of Byelorussian collaboration with the Nazis is the controversial work by John Loftus, *The Belarus Secret*, New York, 1982. See Charles R. Allen Jr.'s review of this book in *Jewish Currents*, April 1984, pp. 5-9, 19-21.

40. For full details on "Operation Paperclip," the code name for the project to bring German scientists to the United States, see Tom Bower, *The Paperclip Conspiracy: The Battle for the Spoils and Secrets of Nazi Germany*, London, 1987; Michael Bar-Zohar, *The Hunt for German Scientists*, London, 1967.

41. Mr. Wiesenthal has expressed this opinion on numerous occasions. Several years after the war he closed down his office since he believed that the consequences of the cold war had made his work almost impossible. Simon Wiesenthal, *The Murderers Among Us*, London, 1967, p. 87.

42. Statement of US Justice Department, October 17, 1984.

43. Nuremberg document PS-2428, *Nazi Conspiracy and Aggression*, Supplement A, Washington 1947, pp. 414-22; Nuremberg document PS-3249, ibid., Vol. III, Washington, 1946, pp. 949-55; Alexander Mitscherlich and Fred Mielke, *Doctors of Infamy: The Story of the Nazi Medical Crimes*, New York,

1949, pp. 20-33, 42-55; *German Medical War Crimes: A Summary of Information,* London, n.d., pp. 1-15.

44. Christopher Simpson, Blowback; *America's Recruitment of Nazis and its Effect on the Cold War,* New York, 1988; Tom Bower, *Red Web; MI6 and KGB Master Coup,* London, 1989.

45. "Memorandum of Decision and Order," United States of America against Karl Linnas, July 30, 1981, 79 C 2966; "L.I. Man Fails In Court Bid On Nazi Link," *New York Times,* October 5, 1982.

46. "Memorandum of Decision and Order," United States of America vs. John Demjanjuk, June 23, 1982, C 77-923.

47. Indictment, State of Israel versus Ivan (John), son of Nicholai, Demjanjuk, September 29, 1986; James Vinicini, "Court-Nazi," Reuters, December 16, 1985; Howard Goller, "Israel To Stage First Nazi Trial Since Eichmann," Reuters News Service, February 12, 1987.

48. Ir'ur Plili 347/88, Ivan (John) Demjanjuk neged Medinat Yisrael, Av 5753/July 1993.

49. Carol J. Williams, "Condemned War Criminal Dies in Leningrad Clinic," Associated Press, July 2, 1987.

50. This figure, which appears in a document prepared by the Office of Special Investigations, was recently confirmed by Natalya Kolesnikova, the Soviet Procurator-General, during a visit to London in early 1988. David Healy, "Soviets Hand Over Gecas Dossier," *Daily Record,* January 29, 1988.

51. Antanas Gecevicius, who subsequently changed his last name to Gecas, is presently living in Edinburgh, Scotland. He served as a junior lieutenant in the same unit. For further details on this case, see below.

52. Several cases of suspects from this unit whose names were submitted by the Wiesenthal Center to the governments of the countries in which they reside are currently under investigation.

53. For details on these cases see *Quiet Neighbors,* pp. 353-61.

54. Alfonso A. Narvaez, "A Court Strips Ex-Nazi Guard of Citizenship," *New York Times,* December 31, 1986.

55. "Final Judgment," United States of America vs. Kazys Palciauskas, March 23, 1983, Case No. 81-547 CIV-T-GC.

56. Awdziej participated in the registration of the Jewish residents of Stolpce and their internment under inhumane conditions in ghettos. During his tenure as mayor virtually all the Jews in the area were murdered. Statement by Department of Justice, October 19, 1984.

57. "Brief for the United States," filed in the Court of Appeals for the Sixth Circuit, May 1981, p. 3; Joan Radovich, "Portugal Takes Fascist Prelate," *Los Angeles Times,* August 1984, p. 1; "Affidavit of Good Cause in Support of Complaint," United States of America vs. Vladimir Sokolov, December 14, 1981, pp. 1-2; Frank Szivos and Jack Dolan, "Action against Nazi Suspect First for

U.S.," *The Telegram* (Bridgeport, Conn.), January 29, 1982, p. 21.

58. "Statement of Allan A. Ryan, Jr." regarding Otto Albrecht Alfred von Bolschwing, released by US Justice Department, December 22, 1981.

3

The Process of Investigation:
Three Cases—The "Student," the
"Bookkeeper" and the "Office Clerk"

The investigation of Nazi war criminals is in most cases a lengthy, painstaking, and arduous process. Despite the aura of adventure and drama which is associated with attempts to bring Nazis to justice, the work involved is usually far from exciting. On the contrary, the meticulous, detailed research which forms the basis for the prosecution can at times be extremely tedious and boring. Yet it is precisely this very prosaic and often monotonous work which yields positive and, at times, spectacular results.

The work of Nazi war crimes researchers is ostensibly very similar to that of criminal investigators. Both seek to obtain evidence regarding specific crimes in order to bring the guilty party to the bar of justice. Both rely on documents and eyewitness testimony. There are, however, several important differences. One is that while the criminal investigator focuses on a crime that he or she will try to solve by finding the perpetrator, researchers of Nazi war crimes usually work in the opposite direction. In most cases they begin with a suspect and an allegation, which they then attempt to corroborate, rather than starting with the crime committed and then seeking out the perpetrators. The reason for this mode of operation is quite simple. Given the advanced age of the suspects and the extremely large number of criminals who remain unprosecuted, the most logical approach is initially to handle those cases in which a specific individual has already been identified as the person responsible for the crime.

Another significant difference stems from the nature of the crimes being investigated. The fact that Nazi war crimes researchers are investigating atrocities that were committed approximately 50 years ago presents specific problems which regular criminal investigators do not usually face. The manner in which the crimes were committed during the Holocaust also poses severe difficulties for those investigating these criminals. The paucity of witnesses from many locations, the practically anonymous means of mass murder employed by the Nazis and their collaborators, and the difficulty in determining the ultimate responsibility at the various levels of collaboration in the murder process, constitute several of the special problems faced by those seeking to obtain evidence to prosecute Nazi war criminals. There are also very complicated legal and technical difficulties which have had a pronounced effect on these investigations. The authenticity of Soviet-held documentation, the legal ramifications of eyewitness testimony presented in Soviet courts, the validity of testimony by perpetrators and the value of recorded oral history, are all issues which ultimately have had a significant impact on the research process.

Although the search for evidence has taken lawyers and historians practically all over the world, most of the research for the cases of the Nazi war criminals tried in the United States has been carried out in the United States, (West) Germany and Israel. Each of these countries has major repositories of documentation related to the Holocaust period, which have proven invaluable in researching the events of the Second World War and its aftermath. The United States has extensive collections of captured German documentation, as well as the immigration files which document the entry of post-war immigrants and which have played such a critical role in legal proceedings against Nazi criminals living in the US. Documentation of interest has also been found in the Hoover Institute, YIVO Institute for Jewish Research, and other American research institutes. Numerous survivors currently reside in the United States and they have proven an excellent source of eyewitness testimony and background information.

Various archives in West Germany have also been consulted extensively. The documentation culled from West German sources relates primarily to the functioning of the Nazi regime and the implementation of the Final Solution. The material comes in two forms—original documentation from Nazi sources and trial records of the criminals prosecuted in West Germany. In view of the fact that more Nazi criminals have been brought to trial in that country than anywhere else in the Western World[1] the material provided by the West German judicial authorities has proven to be particularly valuable. The existence of the *Zentrale Stelle der Landesjustizverwaltungen zur Aufklarung nationalsozialistischer Verbrechen* (Central Office of the Judicial Authorities for the Investigation of National-Socialist Crimes), a special government agency established for the specific purpose of investigating Nazi war crimes,[2] made West Germany an important link in the research process. The Berlin Document Center, with its extensive files on members of the Nazi Party and the SS, has also provided extremely valuable documentation in numerous cases.

The third center of research carried out during the past decade regarding Nazi war crimes is Israel. This is only natural in view of the large number of survivors absorbed by the Jewish state and the resources invested by government and private and semi-official agencies in documenting the tragedy of European Jewry. During the immediate aftermath of the Second World War, Israel absorbed tens of thousands of survivors[3] and many others arrived in the 1970s after the gates of the Soviet Union opened for Jewish immigration.[4] From its establishment Israel has viewed the commemoration and documentation of the Holocaust as a sacred obligation and has created the world-renowned Yad Vashem Martyrs and Heroes Remembrance Authority to carry out this task.[5] Extensive efforts have been invested to collect available documentation and record the testimony of the survivors. The establishment of additional private and semi-official agencies dedicated to these goals, such as *Beit Lohamei ha Gettaot* (Ghetto Fighters' Kibbutz) and the Moreshet Archives, as well as university research institutes, has enhanced Israel's role as a center of Holocaust documentation.

No list of the countries with abundant archival resources on the history of the Holocaust would be complete without mention of the former Soviet Union. Many of the documents and witnesses presented at the trials of the Nazi criminals prosecuted in the United States have come from the Soviet Union. There is a major difference, however, between the material which emanated from that country and the documentation found elsewhere. Documents obtained in and/or from the Soviet Union were not researched by OSI in the classical sense, because they were chosen by Soviet experts and were not the product of historical research by OSI historians. The fact that they emanated from a totalitarian regime, whose archives were closed to Western researchers and whose judicial system was known to have convicted innocent defendants on political grounds, created various juridical, technical and moral problems, and had, as we shall see, a distinct effect on our research efforts elsewhere. I did not, therefore, include the Soviet Union on the list of countries in which most of the research was carried out, even though we were the beneficiaries of considerable material from

Soviet archives as well as numerous Soviet witnesses. In the wake of the dismemberment of the Soviet Union, various archives in the former republics have granted access to researchers from the West for the first time. While the documents in these repositories are of exceptional potential for Nazi war crimes research, it is still not clear to what extent they will be utilized by OSI and other prosecution agencies.

Conducting a Nazi war crimes investigation is similar to putting together an extremely large and complicated jigsaw puzzle. The task of obtaining information from numerous—and at times contradictory—sources, some of which are in relatively obscure languages, regarding events that took place decades ago and turning this into a comprehensible, cohesive and convincing legal case is quite difficult. It is usually the combined effort of historians, criminal investigators and lawyers, all of whom are links in a chain, the sum result of which is an indictment. Success is predicated on the thoroughness and ingenuity of the research, the ability to find all the available documents and witnesses (assuming such exist), and the validity of the legal arguments which form the basis of the charges. Ultimate responsibility lies with the leadership, but each member of the team must perform his or her duties effectively if the operation is to succeed.

As OSI researcher in Israel for six years (1980-86), I was one of the links in the chain described above. My task was to find all documentation, witnesses, and background material that could be of assistance to OSI in the prosecution of the Nazi criminals living in the United States. As the individual responsible for the historical research carried out in Israel, I was able to obtain a considerable amount of data which played a role in the prosecution of quite a few criminals. This was not a solo effort since the material from Israel was only part of the documentation presented to the courts by the OSI attorneys. What we learned from years of research and investigations was that no one country could provide all the necessary evidence to convict a Nazi war criminal living in the US. Thus of necessity OSI's efforts spanned the globe. Israel, it should be noted, played an important role in OSI's research due to the large number of collections of Holocaust documentation and the numerous survivors living there. For those reasons OSI decided—initially as an experiment but later on a permanent basis—to employ a full-time researcher in Israel, a step later taken by other prosecution agencies.

The research carried out in Israel for OSI during the years 1980-86 represents a microcosm of the work being carried out the world over to prosecute Nazi war criminals. While some of the results achieved stem from factors intrinsically Israeli, the research nonetheless affords a penetrating insight into the processes and problematics involved in such efforts. These can best be illustrated by concrete examples, so let us examine the following three cases in which considerable research was carried out in Israel in the course of the investigations.

The "Student"

Bohdan Koziy was a Ukrainian policeman in Lysiec, a small town in Eastern Galicia, not far from the district center of Stanislawow. This area had been part of Poland during the interwar period, but was occupied by the Red Army in the autumn of 1939. In the summer of 1941, following the invasion of the Soviet Union by the Nazis and their allies and several weeks of occupation by Hungarian troops, the entire area was taken over by the Germans. Before the war about 150 Jews had lived in the town, comprising approximately 7.5 per cent of the local population. In this region, as elsewhere in the areas that were part of the Soviet Union, the Germans relied heavily on the assistance of local collaborators to enforce their rule and carry out their anti-Jewish policies. Thus the Ukrainian police played an active role in the persecution and murder of Jews throughout the Stanislawow district.

The measures against the Jews in Lysiec were carried out step by step. In the summer of 1941 Jews in the Stanislawow district were forced to wear identifying armbands and had their property confiscated. During the autumn and winter of 1941 the first large-scale shootings took place in Stanislawow and a ghetto was established in that city. In the summer of 1942 the Jews of Lysiec and other neighboring towns were rounded up by the Ukrainian police and forcibly deported to the ghetto of Stanislawow, where they suffered from extremely difficult living conditions—forced labor, famine and disease. Many were murdered in the mass executions carried out during this period. Others were deported to the Belzec death camp. The ghetto was liquidated by the Nazis in February 1943 when the remaining Jews were shot. Throughout this period, in addition to implementing the anti-Jewish measures outlined above, the Ukrainian police played an active role in locating and murdering those Jews who had gone into hiding in Lysiec and its environs.

Bohdan Koziy was a native of this area. Born in Pukasiwci, Poland, on February 23, 1923, he was living with his parents in that town when the Nazis invaded the Soviet Union. Koziy had been enrolled in a trade school in Stanislawow, but on April 1, 1942 he joined the Ukrainian police in the Stanislawow district. He was initially assigned to the Lysiec area, which included the town and its environs, in which there were approximately ten villages. Among the duties performed by his unit were the arrest and murder of the Jews caught hiding in the Lysiec area. Most of the local Jews had been rounded up during the summer of 1942 and deported to the Stanislawow Ghetto, but some had eluded capture and remained behind in hiding. Koziy was accused of personally murdering 14 Jews whom he caught in various places in the area and of arresting the Poles who had helped these people.[6]

By the time I was asked to do research on Koziy in early July 1981, a considerable amount of evidence had already been uncovered and the case had been filed. In fact, a trial date had been set for September 15, 1981. The problem was, however, that all the prosecution witnesses were individuals who were living in the Soviet Union and none of them were Jewish survivors. OSI turned to me in the hope that I might be able to find Jews living in Israel or elsewhere in the West who could identify Koziy or at least testify regarding the crimes committed in that area. This request highlighted one of the most serious problems which plagued OSI practically throughout its existence, that in numerous cases the crimes being investigated had been committed in small towns and villages from which there were no survivors. In such instances our ability to prosecute was contingent on finding other individuals who could testify regarding the crimes perpetrated by the suspect. The only persons who could do so were bystanders or fellow perpetrators, both usually difficult to find. This problem existed in many of the cases of crimes committed in areas which were part of the Soviet Union, and meant that OSI was more or less totally dependent on the Soviet authorities to find the evidence. This dependence made OSI vulnerable to charges by émigré groups who claimed that Soviet documents and witnesses were unreliable and that the evidence was fabricated in order to implicate innocent Lithuanians, Latvians, etc. for their anti-Communist activities and/or views. OSI always preferred therefore to have witnesses who were the victims of persecution and were currently living in the West, with first preference—for reasons of economy and efficiency—for those living in the United States.

The first place I began my search was of course Yad Vashem, the official Israeli remembrance authority. Founded in Jerusalem in 1953 by a special law of the Knesset, it is the world's premier repository of Holocaust documentation, testimony and information. Since its establishment, Yad Vashem has invested enormous resources in collecting all available data regarding the destruction of European Jewry. The Yad Vashem archives contain millions of documents covering every aspect of the persecution and murder of the Jews of Europe, including tens of thousands of testimonies of survivors. The Yad Vashem Library, which has over 100,000 volumes, is the largest collection of its kind in the world.[7] It is in fact practically impossible today to conduct any major research on the Holocaust period without making use of Yad Vashem's extensive holdings. Thus it was the most logical place to begin the search for material on Lysiec, Koziy and the Ukrainian police in the Stanislawow district of Galicia.

Over the course of the past three decades, Yad Vashem has developed detailed guides and bibliographical aids to assist researchers and has published numerous monographs, anthologies, source books, and the proceedings of international academic conferences. These materials have considerably advanced Holocaust research and in many cases we know far more today about the events of the Final Solution in various locations than we did 20 and even ten years ago. This was certainly true in the case under investigation. I was able, for example, to find detailed summaries in encyclopaedic form of the events which occurred during the Holocaust in Stanislawow and a few of the other towns and villages in the Lysiec area, in one of the volumes of the *Pinkas Ha-Kehillot* (Encyclopaedia of Jewish Communities) series published by Yad Vashem.

This series recounts the history of the various Jewish communities of Europe from their establishment until the aftermath of the Second World War. Luckily, the volume on Eastern Galicia had already been published so I was able to obtain the material I needed. The problem, however, was that while an attempt had been made to document the persecution and murder of the Jews in each and every community, there was no precise information on the events in Lysiec, and a few of the other nearby towns. The entry on Lysiec related, for example, that

We have no information on the annals of this small Jewish community during World War II. It can be assumed that it was liquidated by the Nazis in September or October 1942. The local Jews were apparently deported to the Stanislawow Ghetto (it is likely that some of them were murdered on the spot during this *Aktion*), where they were murdered with the rest of the Jews concentrated in the area of Rudolph's Mill or were deported to the Belzec death camp.[8]

The paucity of information was not that surprising. Lysiec, after all, was not exactly a bustling metropolis, but it did not augur well for the investigation.

Faced with this problem, I tried to find additional material on Stanislawow where many of the Jews of Lysiec and its environs had been murdered. This search proved fairly productive since the amount of material on this community was quite extensive. Of particular note was a recently-published memoir by Dr. Avraham Liebesman, a survivor of the Stanislawow Ghetto, who remained in the city throughout the entire existence of the ghetto. Liebesman recounted the fate of the Jews of Stanislawow in great detail and even provided some information on the murder of the Jews from the surrounding towns. He also recorded the testimony of an individual who had personally witnessed the murder of the Jews of Halycz, a town in the area of Lysiec. The problem was, however, that the person in question had subsequently perished in the ghetto and Liebesman himself had died several months before his book was published.[9] If his memoir was any indication, he would have been a superb background witness, but that of course was now obviously impossible.

Having perused the available historical research background material, I proceeded to the next step—the documentary evidence. If one had to wade through all the documentation in the Yad Vashem Archives for each and every case, the task would obviously be impossible. Consequently, special guides were published by Yad Vashem and the Institute of Contemporary Jewry of the Hebrew University to facilitate research at Yad Vashem (and other) archives. The guides are arranged according to geographical area and indicate what information is available in the archives on a wide range of topics. Years in preparation, the guides are invaluable research tools for historians and students of the Holocaust period.[10] With their help it is relatively easy to determine in a matter of minutes whether or not there is archival material on a particular subject. Obviously the documentation must be examined to determine its value but, without these guides, research at

Yad Vashem would be infinitely harder. The guides do have one pitfall, however: human error. The researcher is completely dependent on the information which appears in the guide, since he has no way of knowing if there is additional material in the archives on his subject which was not listed because it was, for example, inadvertently omitted. This happened in a different case, as we shall see, and almost had serious consequences. The guides, moreover, only cover the material which arrived at Yad Vashem prior to 1979, and not all the documents which were obtained subsequently are cataloged, another problem which must be kept in mind.

A quick perusal of the guides indicated that there was considerable material on Stanislawow, as well as several items on some of the other towns in the Lysiec area, but none on Lysiec itself. Most of the documentation was from the 0-3 collection of testimony recorded by a special department of Yad Vashem established for that purpose. In the course of the three decades after the end of the war, Yad Vashem had interviewed thousands upon thousands of survivors whose testimonies have added much important information on numerous aspects of the Holocaust, aspects which were not reflected in official documentation. This was especially true vis-à-vis the response of the Jews under Nazi rule and more specifically on topics such as the various forms of Jewish resistance, the activities of the Jewish councils (*Judenrate*), the role of the Jewish police, etc. Each of the testimonies recorded by Yad Vashem had a cover page with the survivor's name, address and date and place of birth, as well as a summary in Hebrew of the contents. It was also usually supplemented by a list of all the names of persons and places mentioned in the testimony. This information made the work of the researcher considerably easier in view of the fact that the testimonies are not always in languages that the historian can read. This was one of the advantages of the testimonies recorded by Yad Vashem. Another positive aspect was that in almost every case the survivor's address was recorded, which was particularly significant especially in those instances in which we wanted to find the person in question. By comparison, the testimony recorded in the DP camps was much more problematic because there was no indication where the survivor ultimately emigrated.

The guide to the Yad Vashem Archives listed 18 testimonies regarding Stanislawow and the other sites I was researching, but none even mentioned Lysiec. The overwhelming majority dealt primarily with the events in the Stanislawow Ghetto, but nonetheless I was still hopeful that some of the survivors might be able to provide valuable information. My optimism was based on the fact that many of those interviewed were not originally from Stanislawow but rather from the surrounding villages, and might perhaps be able to provide details on Koziy's unit. In theory they might also have been able to identify him but the chances of that were very slim. This was one of the major problems faced by OSI. In many of the cases investigated, the killers were not locals, but rather members of special units which travelled from place to place to murder Jews, spending only a day or two in each location. In cases such as these, the chances of the suspect being identified by a survivor were close to zero. If, on the other hand, the perpetrator committed the crimes in his home town and over the course of an extended period, the chances of his being recognized by one of the survivors were obviously greater. A killer from the Arajs Commando, or the Lithuanian police battalions had a lot less cause for anxiety than someone who had been a police chief or a commander of a ghetto or even a guard in a concentration camp, where daily contact increased the chances of identification. Koziy was a case somewhere in the middle between the two extremes. If there were survivors from Lysiec they might remember him because he had married the mayor's daughter, but the chances of his being identified by someone from another village did not appear to be too good.

The usual procedure I had to follow in such investigations was that when the names (and addresses) of individuals who might be able to provide valuable information had been found, they were sent to Washington. OSI evaluated the material and, having decided which survivors they wanted to interview, sent those names to the Nazi war crimes unit of the Israeli police. I would have preferred to be able to interview the survivors myself, but according to Israeli law testimony in such cases could only be taken by lawyers or police officers, so I had to confine my official duties to historical research. I did, however, have an opportunity to participate in the interviewing of witnesses when lawyers from OSI came to Israel to do so.

By the end of July 1981 I had already sent OSI the names of 17 potential witnesses, for 14 of whom we had addresses in Israel. I had also transmitted all the available background material I could find on the events in the area of Stanislawow—articles, memoirs, encyclopaedia entries, etc. This was not a bad start, but the problem was time since the date for Koziy's trial was rapidly approaching and the discovery stage of the proceedings had to be completed by August 11. OSI therefore asked me to determine whether the police would agree to allow me to interview the survivors and by early August I had begun to track down the individuals whose testimonies I had found at Yad Vashem. This was the first time I had an opportunity to do a little detective work besides the usual scholarly research. Equipped with an extensive list of precise questions supplied by Jovi Tenev of OSI I proceeded to attempt to find the various survivors, hoping that perhaps at least one of them might be able to provide the testimony that we were missing.

On a certain level, my conversations with the survivors were a bit of a relief. People, live individuals, instead of paper documents. A welcome change, after months of dealing exclusively with objects. There was also a certain sense of satisfaction which I derived from my conversations with the survivors. Almost invariably they would ask me whether I or any members of my family were from this region. Perhaps they assumed that only someone with some kind of personal connection would take the trouble to attempt to find evidence against a murderer from Lysiec. When I explained to them that I had no direct links to this area, had been born after the war, and was involved in this issue because I considered it important, many expressed support and encouragement. These warm feelings which were obviously heartfelt gave me increased motivation and were a timely reminder that while others might be apathetic, there were many people who believed that our campaign was very much their fight. They were in my opinion, the silent majority, those whose voices were often not being heard by those in power. They also represented the hope that I might be able personally to discover some valuable information or an important witness who could clinch the case.

After determining the phone numbers of the survivors, I began to call them one by one, and call by call my frustration grew. If I had approached the task with a certain degree of optimism, I soon realized that our chances of finding a survivor from Lysiec were not very good. Initially, I could not find a single person who had lived in Lysiec under the Nazi occupation. The closest I got were a Mrs. Hamburger from Haifa and a Yitzhak Mandelbaum, both of whom were indeed from Lysiec but had left the town prior to the arrival of the Germans. Neither of them had ever been interviewed, so finding them was an achievement of sorts. In practical terms, however, it did not bring us any closer to our goal. The encouraging aspect was that each call usually yielded new leads regarding persons from the area whose names were unknown because they had neither submitted testimony nor written memoirs or been interviewed by Yad Vashem or any of the other research institutes. Time after time I was disappointed, however, as the individuals in question had not been in the places that Koziy had been or had been there at different times. Some appeared to be quite knowledgeable about the Ukrainian police and had a good recall of the events, but the critical element was missing.

This is best illustrated by a story that Mrs. Hamburger related. She had left Lysiec on June 30, 1941 and had returned to the area after the war. Her family had been murdered in Lysiec and she attempted to determine exactly how they and the other Jews of the town had been killed. As a result of her inquiries, she learned that one of the members of the Kandler family, which had owned the local flour mill, had survived the war and was living in the United States. The rest of his family had been murdered in Lysiec after being betrayed while in hiding with a local Ukrainian family. As it turned out it was Koziy who had personally committed that murder,[11] but Mrs. Hamburger did not know that. Her information, moreover, was based not on her own witnessing of the events but on the testimony of others. Had she been there and seen the crimes I have no doubt that her testimony could have been conclusive, but unfortunately that was not the case. We eventually found Munya Kandler, the sole survivor of the family, who was living in the United States. He, however, had been in the Stanislawow Ghetto when his family was murdered and thus did not witness that crime. The terrible irony which emerged at the trial was that the same country which had offered him a haven after the war had also opened its gates to the person who had inflicted upon him the worst iniquity.

To further complicate matters, there were the false leads—incorrect information which resulted in countless wasted hours, frayed nerves and frustration. This was usually the result of the ominous combination of good intentions and faulty memories. People wanted to help and tried hard to dredge up facts from the distant painful past. Unfortunately the information was not always accurate. Those individuals who had supposedly been in Lysiec during the war had either left long before or had been in the Soviet Union during the Nazi occupation. One such case stands out in my mind. Several days before the trial, OSI asked me to track down a survivor of Lysiec living in Bat-Yam. All they knew about him was that he sold lottery tickets there, but it was imperative to find him. I doubt whether anyone at OSI was aware of the fact that Bat-Yam was a city of over 100,000 inhabitants with *Mifal ha-Payis* lottery booths on practically every other corner, and that lottery salesmen were not registered according to their Second World War experiences. The person in question was eventually found, but it took some doing. The information, as it turned out, proved to be inaccurate. There was indeed a lottery ticket salesman from Lysiec living in Bat Yam, but he had left the town in 1934 and had shortly thereafter made *aliya* to Palestine. The story does not end there, however, because he gave me a lead on a survivor from Lysiec who, as far as he knew, was living in Israel and was ostensibly in a position to help us. The person in question was suspected of collaborating with the Nazis, according to the testimony of Poles from Lysiec who had come to Palestine as soldiers with the Anders Army. In terms of his knowledge of the events, this made him potentially invaluable. On the other hand, if the accusation was true, who in his right mind would agree to testify and thereby possibly expose himself as a traitor? The issue proved to be purely academic when we discovered that the person in question had passed away three years previously taking whatever knowledge he possessed with him to the grave.

The Koziy trial began in West Palm Beach, Florida, on Tuesday, September 15, 1981, without our having found any Jewish survivors who had lived in Lysiec under the Nazi occupation. The most important evidence against Koziy were various documents proving his membership in the Ukrainian police and the testimony of several witnesses from the Soviet Union. As it turned out, these ultimately proved sufficient. Koziy was not only convicted of lying on his immigration and naturalization applications but was actually branded a murderer by US District Judge James C. Paine.[12] In retrospect, the successful outcome of the trial was achieved because of two major factors—the conclusive nature of the testimony provided by the Soviet witnesses and the willingness of the judge to accept their statements. We were not always that lucky in these two respects. There were cases, as we shall see, in which US judges refused to accept the testimony of Soviet witnesses and as a result OSI, at least initially, lost the cases.

In that respect Lysiec became, at least for me, a symbol of countless towns and villages throughout Eastern Europe, whose Jewish communities were destroyed without leaving a trace. Forty years after the events, there was no one to tell the tale from among the erstwhile victims. Only those Jews who had had the foresight to immigrate or escape to the Soviet interior could testify to the existence of a once-vibrant Jewish community. Only a few bystanders who had by chance witnessed the atrocities could point an accusing finger at the murderers. None but the killers themselves knew the full scope of their crimes.

Even if Lysiec had been an isolated case, its fate was obviously tragic. Lysiec, however, was only one virtually anonymous town among thousands of such places which had been wiped out without a trace. I recall in the course of the investigation attending a memorial service for the Jews of the Stanislawow area who had been murdered during the Holocaust. It was held on the fortieth anniversary of the first large-scale *Aktion* conducted in the city during which approximately 10,000 Jews had been murdered.[13] I was allowed to address the large crowd and appealed for their help in finding the survivors of Lysiec. Their response was one of pleasant surprise. I think that they were astonished that anyone would take an interest in that small town, let alone someone with no ostensible connection. People who came over invariably asked, are you from there? Are you from Galicia? When I replied that I had no direct connection with the area, they found it relatively hard to believe. The fact, moreover, that someone of my age was trying to investigate Nazi war criminals seemed almost incongruous. After all, even they had to some extent allowed the memories to recede as time went by. How many of their children showed an active, or for that matter any, interest whatsoever in the history of their hometown? How few indeed had come to the memorial assembly.

These phenomena repeated themselves in numerous encounters with survivors. I did not find any survivors from Lysiec as a result of my speech at the memorial assembly, but by this point in the investigation I was hardly surprised. The experience was illuminating, however, since it reinforced my sense that there was a large public whose silence on the issue was not an indication of apathy but rather of their inability to muster the energy necessary to revitalize a long dormant cause. If they could not do so, there were younger people who were willing to try. That appeared to me to be a very practical, concrete means not only of remembering but of effectively commemorating those so cruelly murdered.

Koziy's citizenship was revoked in March 1982 by Judge Paine and in October of the same year OSI submitted for deportation.[14] After lengthy legal proceedings Koziy was finally ordered deported to the Soviet Union in April 1985, but before he could be sent back to the scene of his crimes he fled to Costa Rica, where he established residence on a farm in the northern province of Alajuela.[15]

Koziy would never have been able to escape to Costa Rica, if U. S. efforts to have him prosecuted in Germany had been successful. In August 1986, the World Jewish Congress revealed that as early as 1983, the United States had attempted to have Koziy extradited to stand trial in West Germany, but the Germans had refused to prosecute him. According to the West German authorities, Koziy was only guilty of "manslaughter," a crime for which he could no longer be prosecuted due to the statute of limitations. Only individuals who had committed "murder," which was officially classified as killing which involved "cruelty, iniquity, lust for murder and base motives" could still be tried in West Germany for crimes which had been committed several decades previously. The West German Foreign Office explained in its reponse, that "cruelty would only exist if the perpetrator, beyond the purpose of executing the killings, had imposed special pain or torture on the victims out of a mentality entirely devoid of feeling or mercy " and "the fact that one of the victims was a four-year-old child in itself does not suffice to establish a determination of a cruel or underhand killing."[16] Given the fact that Koziy was personally involved in the murder of several individuals, among them women and children, one wonders what a criminal has to do to be labelled cruel by the Germans, but this was only an added element of injustice in the case of a murderer who lived for three decades in peace and tranquillity in the United States.

Following Koziy's escape to Costa Rica, several attempts were made to bring him to justice. In March 1986 the Soviet Union submitted an official request for his extradition to put him on trial for the murders he committed in Lysiec. The request was initially rejected by the Costa Rican authorities, but a year later the Superior Penal Court overturned the initial decision, paving the way for Koziy's extradition to the Soviet Union. The court stipulated, however, that the extradition would only be carried out if the Soviet authorities guaranteed that Koziy would receive a fair trial and be spared the death penalty (which had been abolished in Costa Rica years ago). Three months later, in March 1987, the Costa Rican Foreign Ministry told Criminal Court Judge Ligia Maria

Gonzalez that it could not guarantee what would happen to Koziy if he were extradited to the Soviet Union and as a result the judge overturned the extradition order, allowing Koziy to remain in Costa Rica.[17]

Three months later, on September 11, 1987, the Costa Rican government announced that it had granted Bogdan Koziy and his wife temporary visas "subject to renewal based on periodic reports on the Ukrainians behavior during their stay in the country." According to Interior Minister Ronaldo Ramirez, insufficient evidence had been presented to warrant his extradition and "his supposed authorship of crimes against Jews had not been demonstrated."[18] Thus the Costa Rican government was added to the list of those who had assisted the former Ukrainian policeman in his efforts to elude justice.

Despite the incomprehensible actions of the Costa Rican government, concerned Costa Ricans such as Bernardo Baruch, a Jewish lawyer from San Jose, and others continued their efforts to force Koziy to leave the country or have him extradited to stand trial.[19] To date, however, these activities have proven unsuccessful and the murderer from Lysiec continues to reside in Costa Rica.

On July 30, 1993, the Simon Wiesenthal Center listed him as one of fifteen Nazi war criminals likely to be prosecuted within the next two or three years[20] and has accorded the case high priority, but it remains to be seen whether this new campaign will succeed. Given Koziy's relatively young age (he was born in 1923) and the particularly cruel nature of his crimes (specifically the murder of a four-year-old girl) I believe that there is a reasonable chance that justice will be achieved. In the meantime, however, his denaturalization and forced departure from the United States remain the primary price he has been forced to pay for his crimes.

The Koziy case was typical of the investigations of the murderers, usually policemen, who operated in a specific, limited geographical area and committed crimes in the course of carrying out their duties. The major problem which OSI usually faced in such investigations was the lack of survivor witnesses. The Jewish community of Lysiec, like that of so many other small towns, had been wiped out without trace. Not a single survivor could be found who could identify the criminals who murdered the local Jews. Luckily, there were others who were able and willing to do so and their testimony ultimately decided the case. If not for their testimony, I have no doubt that Koziy would still be living in Fort Lauderdale, Florida to this day. All our efforts in Israel, however, proved fruitless and we could not come up with a single document or witness who could provide conclusive proof of Koziy's crimes. It is true that much valuable background material was provided, but the research and the survivors found in Israel were insufficient to convict the suspect. The efforts in the Koziy investigation highlighted the problematic nature of any attempt made at this relatively late date to bring the murderers to justice. Nevertheless the Koziy case remained a partial, if incomplete, victory, although the type of difficulties met with were endemic to my efforts in Israel on behalf of OSI.

The "Bookkeeper"

Another case in which I encountered similar problems and which provides insight into the specific nature of the research conducted in Israel was that of Juozas Kungys. A former student at a theological seminary, Kungys was alleged to have been the leader of a gang of Lithuanian nationalists that murdered the Jews of Kedainiai (Keydan) Lithuania in the summer of 1941.[21] Kedainiai, the center of a district by the same name, was located some 30 miles north of the Lithuanian capital of Kovno (Kaunas), and had a Jewish population of approximately 3,000 before the Second World War. Immediately after the Wehrmacht invaded the Soviet Union on June 22, 1941, local Lithuanian nationalists organized gangs of so-called "partisans" or "activists" who initiated anti-Jewish decrees which included forcing Jews to wear the yellow star and forbidding them to walk on the pavement. In the meantime, Lithuanian activists were allowed free rein to take measures against the local Jews who were drafted into forced labor, often to carry out extremely dangerous tasks. Thus, for example, the Jews were forced to remove bombs left by the Soviets in the Kedainiai airport. Several Jews were killed when some of these bombs exploded. On July 23, 1941 Lithuanian nationalists rounded up approximately 200 Jews, ostensibly to take them for forced labor. They never returned. It was only after bribes had been paid to a Lithuanian that the local Jews learned the truth about their fate. They had been taken to the Babences forest, eight kilometers from town, where the Lithuanians murdered them.

Shortly afterwards, Povilius, the Lithuanian mayor of Kedainiai, ordered that all the Jews should be rounded up and concentrated near Smilgos Street. The area was surrounded by barbed wire and approximately 3,700 Jews from Kedainiai and the nearby towns of Zeimiai and Seta were thus incarcerated in a ghetto where living conditions were extremely harsh. This was only a temporary measure, however. On August 15, 1941 all the Jews were deported to a stable at the Zirginas horse farm where they remained under heavy guard for 13 days. On August 28, 1941 the mass murders began. Initially all the young and strong men were taken out of the stable in groups of 60 and were shot by the Lithuanians behind the Catholic cemetery on the road to Dotnuva. Here they were buried in a long pit which had previously been prepared by Soviet POWs. After all the men had been murdered, women and older children were taken to the pit in groups of 40 and shot in the same manner. Elderly and sick women were then brought by truck to the site and thrown alive into the grave. The massacre was concluded by the murder of babies and very young children, which was carried out in the most brutal manner by Lithuanians who threw the children in the air and caught them on their bayonets. A total of 2,076 men, women and children were murdered by the Lithuanians on that fateful day of August 28, 1941.[22]

Kungys was accused of having played a leading role in the ghettoization and mass murder of the Jews of Kedainiai and its environs. He had been born in Reistra, Lithuania on September 21, 1915 and had studied at a theological seminary in Telsiai as a young man. He subsequently moved to Kedainiai, where he was employed at a local bank before the outbreak of war. When the Germans invaded the Soviet Union, he played a leading role in organizing the local nationalist gang which carried out the murder of the Jews. Shortly after these atrocities took place, Kungys apparently left Kedainiai for Kaunas where he claims he worked at a government printing plant for a year and later as a bookkeeper for a brush manufacturer.[23]

Towards the end of the war Kungys fled Lithuania and found refuge in Germany, where he was granted status as a Displaced Person. In early 1947 he applied in Stuttgart for immigration to the United States, and on April 29, 1948 arrived in New York aboard the boat *Marine Flasher* with a quota visa. Less than six years later he was granted American citizenship. When our investigations were launched, he was working as a dental technician for his dentist wife and was living in anonymity and tranquillity in Clifton, New Jersey, a suburb of Passaic.

Throughout the entire process of his immigration and naturalization, Kungys never alluded to his role in the events in Kedainiai. When asked to list his activities during previous years he wrote "student, dental technician, farm and forestry work." When asked to list his places of residence he wrote that he had lived in Telsiai from 1940 to 1942. In fact, based on the statements Kungys submitted to the American authorities regarding his wartime whereabouts and activities, one would never have known that he had even been in Kedainiai during that period, let alone that he had actively assisted the Germans in the implementation of the Final Solution. Given the severity of the allegations against him, that is hardly surprising. As we shall see, OSI investigators eventually reached the conclusion that Kungys had made a special effort to change all his pertinent data including even his date and place of birth.

The Kungys case was one of the investigations which OSI had inherited upon its establishment in 1979. In fact, the US Immigration and Naturalization Service had interviewed Kungys regarding his wartime activities as early as 1975 and had in its possession since September 1977 the statements of 15 witnesses who identified Kungys as an active participant in the murders in Kedainiai. The most important testimonies had been submitted by fellow perpetrators who stated that Kungys had issued orders to shoot Jews and/or had personally murdered Jews by shooting.[24] The problems we encountered in this case were similar to those we faced in the Koziy investigation, with one major difference. In the latter case, the Soviet witnesses had been uninvolved bystanders whose testimony was ostensibly objective. In this case, however, those recounting the events were fellow perpetrators who could hardly be considered paradigms of virtue and might be suspect due to their own involvement. This made it even more important to be able to find Jewish survivors who could corroborate the charges against Kungys.

I received a request for information regarding the events in Kedainiai very shortly after I began working for OSI. As usual, my first step was to examine the background material at Yad Vashem. In this respect it was far easier to determine the course of events in Kedainiai than to research what had transpired in Lysiec. Not only was there a fairly detailed summary of the persecution and murder of the Jews of that community but there was an entire *sefer yiskor* (memorial book) devoted to its annals. The material in this volume outlined the events, and clearly indicated the problematic aspects of the case. According to the accounts in the *sefer yizkor*, there were only three Jews who had survived the 1941 massacres. Chaim Ronder and Shmuel Smolsky had escaped from the stable at the Zirginas farm, while Ben-Zion Berger had run away while the Jews were being forced into the ghetto. The latter later married a Lithuanian woman and lived throughout the war in a forest outside of Kedainiai. He had witnessed the mass murder of the Jews, and in theory might personally have seen the crimes allegedly committed by Kungys. The problem was, however, that as far as I could tell from the material, Ronder and Berger were still in the Soviet Union and there was no indication as to Smolsky's whereabouts.[25] Thus I continued my search for material, especially for any information which might lead me to live survivors from Kedainiai.

One of the most important sources which I discovered during this period was volume IV of the *Yahadut Lita* series published to commemorate Lithuanian Jewry, which included inter alia encyclopaedic entries on the fate of almost every Jewish community in that country during the Holocaust. This volume, which had been years in preparation by the Association of Lithuanian Immigrants in Israel, had still not been published at this time because of a variety of the usual technical and financial problems which so often plague projects of this sort. With the assistance of Moshe Barak, who played a major role in preparing the book, I was granted access to the material prior to its publication. The information on the small communities, for example, was particularly valuable and saved me countless hours of research. In this particular case the entry on Kedainiai corroborated most of the information contained in the *sefer yizkor* and added a few important details. About this time I also learned of the existence of another extensive collection on the small Jewish communities of Lithuania, which potentially seemed to be very valuable. It consisted of testimonies and documents collected in Lithuania and the DP camps during the years 1945–49 by Leib Kunichowsky, a survivor of the Kovno Ghetto. Despite an inordinate effort on my part to obtain permission to peruse this material, that collection remained inaccessible to OSI researchers until many years later.

In March 1981 the research on Kungys started branching out in new directions in the wake of the discovery of several testimonies at the Oral History Division of the Institute of Contemporary Jewry at the Hebrew University. This department was one of the pioneers in interviewing Holocaust survivors. Under the direction of Dr. Geoffrey Wigoder and the guidance of Professor Yehuda Bauer, it had amassed a fairly large collection of testimonies, among them a considerable number by Holocaust survivors from Lithuania and Latvia, areas which were of particular interest to OSI. From the testimonies at the Institute, I learned that several Jews from the Kovno Ghetto had been deported to a labor camp in Kedainiai in 1943 and that various Lithuanian Jews had actively sought out Lithuanian collaborators after the war.[26] These facts ostensibly opened up entirely new avenues of research and gave me hope of being able to find survivors who could testify against Kungys. As it turned out, neither of these facts yielded any definitive results. The Jews who arrived in Kedainiai did so at a relatively late date long after Kungys had left, a piece of information which OSI had somehow neglected to tell me. The post-war angle also failed to yield results because none of the avengers had attempted to punish or prosecute collaborators in Kedainiai, and the information in their possession was in any event invariably hearsay or second hand.

It is interesting to note that most of the testimonies recorded by the Institute's Oral History Division were far less valuable from the point of view of the research conducted on behalf of OSI than they could and should have been. This was because of the orientation of the interviewers and the research topics dealt with at the Institute. The projects in question dealt almost exclusively with armed Jewish resistance and almost completely ignored the issue of Nazi war criminals. There are many extremely complex reasons for this phenomenon, which deserves detailed analysis. The most important in my opinion is the desire of Israeli researchers to prove that European Jewry did not all go to their deaths like sheep to the slaughter. An inordinate amount of attention was therefore devoted to questions such as who smuggled the first gun into the various ghettos, whereas the survivors were rarely asked who were the Lithuanian, Latvian, Byelorussian or Ukrainian collaborators who carried out the murders. Nonetheless, the material in this collection led us to numerous survivors whose testimony was potentially valuable, although we could usually not determine to what extent they could be helpful for our purposes from the text of the interviews.

The Kungys investigation also afforded some interesting experiences. The first communal memorial assembly I ever attended was held to mark the fortieth anniversary of the murder of the Jews of Kedainiai and its environs. I learned about this event purely by accident. One day while browsing through the obituary notices in the Israeli daily *Ma'ariv*, I happened to notice an announcement that a memorial assembly of Kedainiai survivors was scheduled to take place in three days.[27] The first thought that came to mind was the potential in terms of finding witnesses, although initially I was a little hesitant about utilizing the opportunity. Never having attended such an event, I had no idea what to expect. The thought of wasting almost an entire day in the hot muggy Tel Aviv suburb of Holon was hardly appealing, but on the other hand there was always the chance that I might be able to find a survivor or a good lead. Perhaps Smolsky, the Polish refugee who had survived and whose whereabouts were not known, would show up. Perhaps someone at the meeting might know where to find him or at least whether he was alive, and if so where he was living.

The first step was to call the organizer of the event to enquire whether I could address the assembly at some point. Given the sensitivity of the survivors, the fact that I was calling so late and the unfortunate reality that at this point OSI was virtually unknown in Israel, I was ready to settle for an announcement by the moderator. As it turned out, Mr. Glatstein was very accommodating and agreed to make an appeal in the course of the assembly. Prior to the meeting I spoke to Jovi Tenev, the OSI attorney in charge of the case, and we went over all the pertinent data regarding Kungys and his activities in Kedainiai, so that if I did find a survivor we would know immediately whether he had serious witness potential or not. Tenev informed me that Kungys had apparently left Kedainiai shortly after the mass murder so the only hope we had of locating any witnesses was to find someone who had been in the city from the beginning.

On Sunday September 6, 1981 I travelled to the new cemetery at Holon with hardly a clue as to what to expect. I was, in fact, a bit apprehensive. Although I had countless speaking engagements to my credit, I always felt a bit uncomfortable speaking to survivors. First of all, it was difficult for someone born after the war to talk about those terrible events to the very people who had suffered through them. Another factor was that some survivors had a tendency to universalize their own experiences and conclude that if something had happened to them, then it had been the norm throughout occupied Europe. This was obviously not the case, but the resulting differences of opinion had on a few occasions led to heated interchanges which, given the subject matter, were extremely unpleasant. In addition, there was the uncertainty. I had no idea what to expect. Would they be helpful? Perhaps they might be hostile, perhaps apathetic. What also bothered me was my fear that I would probably be the only young person there and would stick out like a sore thumb. All these thoughts crossed my mind as I sought out the members of the Kedainiai *Landsmannschaft* (association). Needless to say, it was not very difficult to find them. They were after all, a unique group, one which stood out among the hundreds of people milling about attending the several funerals simultaneously being held in different parts of the cemetery. This group was composed entirely of middle-aged and elderly people, all of Eastern European origin. In fact, they looked amazingly similar in dress, manners, etc. I found Mr. Glatstein, who told me that he was not that optimistic about my chances and we began walking slowly towards the site of the memorial.

The Holon cemetery is relatively new; consequently there is very little that is of particular interest or of any unique artistic or historical value, with the exception of a small section of memorial monuments dedicated to the Jewish communities destroyed during the Holocaust. Since most of the victims were either buried in unmarked mass graves or cremated, relatives and survivors have attempted to create a physical site of memorial and pilgrimage to replace the graves which either did not exist or were until recently practically inaccessible because they were located in what was once the Soviet Union. Thus the custom of building special monuments for communities destroyed during the Holocaust has become fairly popular, especially during the past decade as survivors became older and more anxious to commemorate on the one hand and more affluent and able to do so on the other. The Kedainiai memorial was located in a row of such tombstone-memorials, most of which were dedicated to Polish communities. There appeared to be no ostensible order or meaning to its geographical location in the cemetery. Apparently it was only a question of first come first served, and financial means.

The Kedainiai memorial was being dedicated in conjunction with the fortieth anniversary of the massacre of the Jews of Kedainiai and its environs which had taken place on the 5th of Elul 5701 (August 28, 1941). Since that date in the Hebrew calendar came out on a Friday, the ceremony was held on the subsequent Sunday. About 50 people participated, almost all of whom were at least middle aged and from "there." No young children or even teenagers, perhaps one or two people my age or a little older. As I suspected I seemed a bit out of place, but of course by this point that was not the problem. I must admit, however, that I did feel somewhat uncomfortable. The speeches on this occasion were more or less exactly what I anticipated: *Landsmannschaft* business, praise for those who had contributed to the memorial, references to the fact that there were fewer people attending the memorial assembly each year, and mention of those who had recently passed away. The main speech provided a very good indication of the problematics of our investigation. One of the younger men spoke of the bravery of several Jews who had tried to attack the Nazis and stop the massacre.[28] The story is well-known and very moving. The narrator, however, was not an eyewitness. He had been in the Soviet Union during the war and had only heard about the events upon his return to Kedainiai after the war. There was, in fact, only one person present who had actually lived under the Nazi occupation in Kedainiai, and that, from my vantage point, was the proverbial "bottom line."

At the end of the assembly, an announcement was made that the US Justice Department was looking for witnesses from Kedainiai in conjunction with an investigation against Lithuanian collaborators living in the United States and that anyone with information should approach me. A few people did come over, but none had been in Kedainiai at the right time. One woman had been deported there from the Kovno Ghetto after Kungys had already left. Another was from the town of Raseiniai but was curious to know whether one of the criminals from her town was living in the United States. A third person made a similar enquiry about another criminal from Kedainiai who was known for his particularly cruel behavior towards children. The first person did, however, give me the name of Yehuda Ronder, originally from Kedainiai and presently living in Kaunas, who was considered an expert on Lithuanian collaborators. In addition, he was a relative of Chaim Ronder, a survivor—eyewitness who had passed away a few years previously in the Soviet Union. Yehuda Ronder was living in Soviet Lithuania, but my informant promised to write to him immediately to enquire whether he could be of assistance. In short, the results were precisely what could be expected in an investigation regarding the destruction of a relatively small Jewish community in an area that was once part of the Soviet Union.

The next step in the investigation process was to interview potential witnesses in Israel. Jovi Tenev of OSI realized that our chances of finding survivor eyewitnesses were close to zero, but a new development in the case made even those who were not eyewitnesses to the murders in Kedainiai potentially valuable, if they had firsthand knowledge of other events in the town during the Nazi occupation. This was because the chief defence witness on Kungys' behalf was Walter Janson (the former

Vladas Jancauskas) who was an employee of the Kedainiai district administration from 1942 to 1944. Janson was in charge of administering and maintaining the district's buildings and roads and thus any involvement of his agency in persecution of Jews suddenly became important. The new information regarding the labor camp established in Kedainiai after the massacres had taken place suddenly assumed significance, even though Kungys was in no way connected to the events which took place there.

In January 1982 a team of three OSI lawyers headed by deputy director Neal Sher came to Israel to interview a long list of potential witnesses in various investigations. Among them were a few persons with knowledge of the events in Kedainiai, several of whom had been discovered by myself in the course of the previous six months. Yet even though the scope of the investigation had been somewhat expanded, thereby increasing our chances of finding witnesses, the results were meager. Hearsay, hearsay, hearsay. This is not intended to impugn in any way the integrity of the individuals interviewed but merely to evaluate the practical value of their testimony. Most had not lived in Kedainiai during the time of the massacres, and those who had been there later were unable to shed significant light on those aspects of the persecution in which the collaborationist Lithuanians were involved. The others were natives of Kedainiai who had escaped to the Soviet Union and returned to their hometown after the war. It was only then that they learned what had happened to their relatives and friends.

Shortly thereafter I was contacted by Zev Ronder, a nephew of Yehuda Ronder, who had been recommended to me as an expert on the Lithuanians who had played an active role in the murder of the Jews of Kedainiai. Zev had attended the memorial assembly, where he learned of the investigation being conducted against Kungys. Like his uncle Yehuda, he had escaped to the Soviet interior when the Nazis invaded and had fought with the Lithuanian Division of the Red Army, a unit composed to a large extent of Lithuanian Jews. He had just received an article from his uncle on the Lithuanian collaborators in Kedainiai and wanted to give it to me. I already had the article in question but, while discussing the possibility of finding witnesses, Zev Ronder gave me an important piece of information. He related that he had seen Smolsky, one of the two Jews who had survived the murders, after the war, which meant that there was at least a chance that he was alive. This was the first confirmation that Smolsky had indeed survived the war, a fact which we for some reason assumed to be true but which had never been confirmed. Ronder thought, moreover, that there was a good chance that he had gone to Israel. At this point we still did not know Smolsky's first name, so I sent Sergeant Kolar of the Israeli police a list of all the Smolskys in the telephone book and a request that an attempt be made to find him. His investigation did not yield any results and thus, despite considerable effort, we found ourselves in the unenviable position of being dependent on Soviet witnesses who were perpetrators of the crimes Kungys was alleged to have committed.

In subsequent months I continued to send additional information to OSI, looking for new avenues of research which might advance our investigation. In April 1982 I sent the names of additional survivors of the Kedainiai labor camp, as well as the names and addresses of the local Lithuanians who had rescued them.[29] This was a bit of a long shot because there was every reason to believe that the rescuers were still living behind the Iron Curtain. I thought, however, that it would be preferable to obtain the testimony of a Righteous Gentile as opposed to that of a perpetrator. The problem was that as far as Soviet witnesses were concerned, OSI was totally dependent on the Communist authorities. If they wanted to make a certain witness available they did so; if not then all the good research in the world was worthless.

The Soviets, for example, very rarely made Jewish witnesses available to testify against Nazi war criminals. On the surface there was a very prosaic reason for this policy, namely that there were very few Jewish survivors in the Soviet Union. On the other hand, I always suspected that this phenomenon was primarily a result of an ideological stance which consistently refused to recognize the uniqueness of Jewish martyrdom during the Holocaust. Soviet publications on the war, of which there are an enormous number, write mainly of the fate of "Soviet citizens" and the monuments which mark the mass graves of Jews in Lithuania, Latvia and the Ukraine commemorate the fate of the "victims of fascism."[30] Very rarely does one find a direct reference to Jewish victims in Soviet secondary sources or on monuments to commemorate the memory of those slaughtered by the Nazis and their collaborators. And while there are inscriptions in Yiddish on many of these memorials, Hebrew is almost nowhere to be found.[31]

Regardless of the above, we had to try to obtain the best witnesses available and therefore every possible lead was checked out. The results, however, were not always in direct proportion to the efforts invested. Regardless of how much work we invested in a particular case, or how innovative our research was, we could never guarantee success. Thus, in the Kungys investigation all of our efforts did not lead to any concrete results.

In early April 1983 Kungys' denaturalization trial began in Newark, NJ. OSI presented evidence to prove that he had obtained entry to the US and American citizenship by misrepresenting his past, and that during the Second World War he had engaged in "acts contrary to civilization and human decency."[32] The latter charge was based primarily on the testimony of the Soviet perpetrator witnesses. This fact played a critical role in the decision of Federal Judge Dickinson R. Debevoise, who on September 28, 1983 decided against OSI. Debevoise, unlike the judges in twelve previous litigations in which OSI presented testimony from the Soviet Union, refused to accept evidence gathered with the assistance of Soviet judicial authorities. According to the judge, such evidence was tainted because the witnesses had testified under duress. He ruled therefore that there was insufficient evidence to prove that Kungys had committed atrocities, although on his immigration and naturalization applications he had indeed lied about his date and place of birth, and thus his citizenship had not been illegally procured.[33] Needless to say, this decision was a tremendous blow to OSI, which was dependent in so many cases on evidence from the Soviet Union. Luckily, however, Debevoise's decision did not have an influence on other judges, who continued to decide in OSI's favor, even in cases in which extensive use was made of evidence which emanated from the Soviet Union.

OSI appealed against the decision by Judge Debevoise in a federal Court of Appeals and subsequently won the case. On June 20, 1986 a three judge panel overturned the initial ruling and stripped Juozas Kungys of his American citizenship for making "material misrepresentations" regarding his past when he immigrated in 1948 and obtained citizenship in 1954. "Truthful statements by Kungys would have led to an investigation, which in all probability would have revealed the disqualifying fact that the defendant had not been a victim of Nazi persecution and therefore would not have been eligible for a visa," explained Judge Mansmann. The court, however, did not relate to the exclusion of the Soviet evidence, nor did it rule on whether Kungys had actually committed the crimes which the government accused him of committing.[34]

The ruling byDebevoise and the failure of the Court of Appeals to rule on Kungys' participation in acts of persecution highlight the problematics of OSI's efforts to prosecute Nazi war criminals. Time and again the Justice Department found itself dependent on evidence and/or witnesses from the Soviet Union.[35] This dependence on sources from behind the Iron Curtain exposed OSI to bitter attacks by its major opponents—émigré groups in the United States and staunch anti-Communists of conservative leanings. It should be noted that every document submitted by OSI to the courts has been thoroughly examined and there has never been a case of a document from a Soviet archive being proven a forgery. Yet due to the nature of the Soviet regime, doubts persist and these are exploited by OSI's opponents. The same applies to the use of witnesses from the Soviet Union. The claim is made that the information is not authentic since witnesses who live in a totalitarian state can be forced to testify in accordance with the dictates of the authorities. Although this has never proven to be the case, these allegations cast a pall over the proceedings. Thus OSI always made a special effort to find as much documentation and as many witnesses as possible in the West in order to be able to avoid such charges. Unfortunately, such evidence was not always available outside the areas where the crimes were committed, as is evident from the two cases described above.

In the summer of 1986 Kungys appealed his denaturalization to the Supreme Court on the grounds that he denied participation in atrocities and that the false information about his date and place of birth which he submitted to the immigration authorities should not have had any bearing on his admission to the United States. The Supreme Court agreed to hear the case on November 10, 1986[36] and on May 2, 1988 reversed the decision to strip Kungys of his citizenship, sending the case back to a lower court to further clarify the evidence regarding his participation in the murders in Kedainiai.[37] Six months later, on November 22, 1988, OSI revealed that it had signed an agreement with Kungys whereby he confirmed that he had submitted "false testimony" to the U. S. authorities and therefore his American citizenship would be revoked but the Justice Department would not seek his deportation from the United States. When asked why the Justice Department had agreed to allow Kungys to remain in the country despite the serious charges levelled against him, OSI director Neal Sher explained that it was doubtful whether the courts would have ordered him deported,[38] thereby emphasizing the obstacles faced by Nazi-hunters in cases in which the only available witnesses are fellow perpetrtators living in a country under communist rule.

The Koziy and Kungys investigations are typical cases of East European collaborators from relatively small towns in areas which were once part of the Soviet Union, who committed their crimes in a limited geographical area over a defined period of time. In investigations such as these, the material available in Israel was rarely sufficient to prepare an indictment, and the witnesses who were so badly needed did not always exist. The assistance I was able to provide was primarily background material, second-hand accounts of the events, and various leads which only on occasion yielded results. This was not the case, however, in the investigation of criminals who committed crimes in the large Jewish communities. In cases such as these, the extensive efforts invested by Yad Vashem and other Israeli research institutes yielded impressive results and we were usually able to find important documentation and numerous witnesses. A case which clearly demonstrates the difference between the two types of investigations—in terms of the Israeli contribution to OSI's efforts—is that of Kazys Palciauskas, the mayor of Kovno.

The "Office Clerk"

Kovno (or Kaunas) was the capital of Lithuania during the interwar period and the home of a Jewish community of approximately 30,000 persons. The city was occupied by the Nazis on June 25, 1941 and approximately at that time Palciauskas, then aged 34 and a prominent member of the Lithuanian Activist Front which advocated collaboration with the Germans, was appointed mayor. Even before the Germans entered the city, Lithuanian nationalists had murdered numerous Jews and large-scale pogroms were also carried out immediately following the Nazis' entry. In late July approximately 800 Jews were killed in the Kovno suburb of Slobodka (Viliampole) and several thousand were murdered shortly thereafter in the Seventh Fort (part of a series of fortifications built many years previously outside the city).[39] Within the initial weeks of the occupation, Palciauskas, in his capacity as mayor, ordered the Jews, by August 15, 1941, to move into a ghetto in the Viliampole district, the most run-down section of the city and to wear the Jewish star on their clothing. He also issued additional directives which forbade Jews from walking on pavements and supervised the massive confiscation of Jewish property throughout the city.[40]

During and after the establishment of the ghetto, the large-scale murders of Jews by the Lithuanians continued. In August more than 900 Jewish men picked up at random were put to death and in mid-August over 500 intellectuals who had volunteered for work in the municipal archives were murdered. These killings culminated in the large-scale *Aktion* which took place on October 28, 1941. All the Jews of Kovno were forced to appear at Democracy Square early in the morning. A *Selektion* was carried out by the Germans and their Lithuanian collaborators in the course of which approximately 10,000 Jews, more than one-third of the inhabitants of the ghetto, were brutally murdered by Lithuanian auxiliary police forces. Those remaining in the ghetto were subjected to pitifully hard conditions. They were taken for forced labor and had to subsist on inadequate rations. Housing and sanitary conditions in the ghetto were so bad that epidemics were a constant danger.[41]

Palciauskas served as mayor of Kovno until May 1942 when he resigned and went to work as an official of the Sodbya dairy co-operative. Throughout his tenure he was the leading figure in the local municipal administration, which was responsible for the establishment and administration of the ghetto. In addition, he and his staff carried out the confiscation of the valuables and property of the Jews of Kovno. While he apparently was not involved in the persecution of Jews after his resignation as mayor, there is no doubt that he occupied a prominent position during a critical period. Like so many of his fellow Lithuanian collaborators, Palciauskas escaped from Lithuania towards the end of the war and went to Germany, where he posed as a refugee and received DP status.

In questionnaires filled out during that period, Palciauskas never even intimated at his "illustrious" past. In the Personal Data Forms which he filed with UNRRA (United Nations Relief and Rehabilitation Agency) in 1946 and 1947 he listed his employment as office worker and his occupation as office clerk. In addition, he wrote that he had never voluntarily assisted any country at war with the Allies nor had he ever been a member of any political party. On an International Refugee Organization (IRO) Resettlement Registration Form which he filled out in 1949, Palciauskas stated that from August 1940 until September 1941 he had worked as a clerk in the Meat and Milk Ministry and that from September 1941 until February 1943 he had been the manager of the Union of Cooperatives. With such sterling credentials, Palciauskas, needless to say, was able to obtain an immigrant's visa to the United States from the American Consulate in Munich and he arrived in Boston on April 19, 1949.[42] For many years he lived in Chicago but following retirement moved to St. Petersburg Beach, Florida.[43]

Palciauskas was named as one of the Nazi war criminals living in the United States long before OSI was established. As early as 1963 his name appeared on a list compiled by journalist Charles Allen, one of the first people to focus public attention on the existence of Nazi war criminals in the United States, and he was subsequently mentioned in various publications.[45] The book *Documents Accuse* published in Vilnius in English in 1970, for example, notes Palciauskas' role as the mayor of Kovno and includes documentation regarding his activities in the ghettoization of the Jews. The book's "Index of Select Names" notes that "After the war he found refuge in the USA."[45] This information obviously became known to the American authorities. Palciauskas was investigated by the Immigration and Naturalization Service (INS) as early as 1973, and he was personally interviewed by INS investigators on several occasions starting in 1975. Throughout the questioning, Palciauskas denied any wrongdoing, claiming that he was merely a figurehead and that whatever edicts were issued in his name were actually written by the Gestapo. In his first interview he claimed that neither he nor any other Lithuanians were in any way connected to the establishment of the ghetto. In a subsequent session he admitted his connection to the events, but claimed that they had been determined by the Germans. Palciauskas claimed, moreover, that he had attempted—unsuccessfully—to limit and later alleviate the transfer of the Jews. He noted that he had asked to be relieved of his post, a request which led to accusations that he was pro-Jewish and in fact endangered his life.[46]

Given the above background, it was obvious that our research would focus primarily on the Kovno municipal administration. The fact that Palciauskas had been the mayor of Kovno was important, but the major question was what role did he and his administration actually play in the implementation of the Final Solution in the erstwhile Lithuanian capital. The task at hand, which was one of my first assignments at OSI, was very different than the research carried out in the two investigations described above. Unlike the cases of the crimes com-

mitted in Lysiec and Kedainiai, there was an enormous amount of documentation of all sorts regarding the events which had transpired in
Kovno during the Holocaust. Besides the original documentation,
which was of unique importance as we shall see, quite a few books and
articles had been written about the fate of that Jewish community,[47]
one of the most famous in Europe. The number of survivors of the
Kovno Ghetto was, moreover, relatively large and thus by OSI standards
there was a significant number of testimonies available to researchers.
The investigation ostensibly appeared as if it was going to be relatively
easy. In reality, however, it presented us with quite a few serious difficulties.

The major problem in researching this case was the paucity of pertinent material. The documentation which dealt with the Lithuanian
administration was in inverse proportion to the abundant material on
Kovno, most of which virtually ignored the subject. Invariably almost
all the material in Israel focused on the killers (Germans as well as
Lithuanians) and the actual and potential victims. There was no shortage of books, articles and testimonies on the large scale *Aktion* of October 28, 1941, life in the ghetto, and especially on the Jewish resistance.
There was relatively little on the local bureaucracy which did so much
to make those terrible events possible. In short, the problem in this case
was the exact opposite of those we confronted in the Koziy and Kungys
investigations.

I began my research at Yad Vashem by going over some of the books
and background material on Kovno. Of particular interest were the
memoirs of Leib Garfunkel who served as a member of the Judenrat
(Jewish Council), which was in close contact withPalciauskas during
the period in which the ghetto was established. Garfunkel specifically
mentions the mayor, his functions and/or activities three times in his
book, but oddly enough omits his name.[48] The book, however, did lead
me to four people whom I thought might be able to provide valuable
testimony. The first two were members of the Judenrat—Zvi Levin and
Yaakov Goldberg. My thinking was that if any Jews knew the Lithuanian mayor, it most probably was those who came into contact with
him as representatives of the community. Since both Dr. Elkes, the head
of the Judenrat, and Garfunkel, his deputy, had already passed away,
the other members of the Jewish Council seemed to be our best bet.
After doing some preliminary investigative work, I discovered that Levin
and Goldberg were the only surviving members of the Judenrat. Levin

lived in Tel Aviv and Goldberg resided in Johannesburg. The problem was that by the time OSI contacted them, the former had passed away and the latter was so old that he could not testify.

That left us with the Judenrat staff and officials. My research showed that at least two individuals living in Israel might be able to testify regarding Kovno's Lithuanian mayor. The first was Avraham Tory, a well-known Tel Aviv attorney who had served as the secretary of the Judenrat. The second was Lucia Lavon, the widow of Israeli Defence Minister Pinchas Lavon, who had worked as a typist in the offices of the Judenrat. Tory indeed knew Palciauskas because he had served on the joint Lithuanian-Jewish committee established to oversee the ghettoization of the Jews. Lavon, as it turned out, was also helpful. Although she did not know Palciauskas personally, she had typed documents concerning the mayor's activities and his role in the anti-Jewish measures. Both were alive and well and both later travelled to the United States to testify at the trial.

While these witnesses were able to provide helpful information, their role in this investigation was secondary to that of the original documentation regarding the Kovno Ghetto which I found in the Yad Vashem Archives. This was a unique collection which played a significant role in illuminating the functions and activities of the mayor of Kovno and ultimately made an important contribution to his conviction. Finding the documents in the Yad Vashem Archives was relatively easy thanks to the special guides prepared to assist researchers. The story behind the documents and how they arrived in Israel, however, is quite fascinating and reveals much about the Jews' determination to record their own history.

The documents in question constituted an attempt by the leaders of the Jewish community of Kovno to document their tragic fate. Despite the trials and tribulations of life under the German occupation, inhabitants of the ghetto attempted to collect all the documentation relating to their persecution by the Nazis and their Lithuanian collaborators. It is not entirely clear whether those involved in this task as early as 1941 actually had a premonition vis-à-vis the ominous nature of the Germans' plans for the Jews and therefore sought to collect evidence to ensure that this tragedy would be recorded for posterity. In any event, great pains were taken to collect the documentation decree by decree, minutes by minutes, protocol by protocol. The collection included documents which dealt with the process of ghettoization, the supply of food to the ghetto and the use of Jews for forced labor. It was hidden by the Judenrat throughout the entire existence of the Kovno Ghetto (which was officially turned into a concentration camp in 1943) until the Jews were deported to Germany in June 1944. Prior to the deportation, the documents were smuggled out of the ghetto and given to a trustworthy Lithuanian who was asked to hide them until the end of the war, at which time he was to turn them over to someone from the Jewish community. That is precisely what happened.

Many of the Jews evacuated from the Kovno Ghetto survived the war and some returned to Lithuania to find family members and/or to recover property and valuables. The collection was retrieved and turned over to Jewish hands. The problem was, however, that Lithuania was once again part of the Soviet Union, a country known for its repression of Jewish identity, religion and culture. Most of the survivors of Kovno were by this time living in Israel and they thought that the most appropriate place for the collection was Yad Vashem. Once again the collection had to be smuggled, this time from Soviet Lithuania to Israel. This was achieved and documents were deposited at Yad Vashem—this time hopefully for ever.

The importance of these documents in the Palciauskas investigation was obvious since they dealt specifically with ghettoization, a process in which the municipal administration played a highly significant role. Palciauskas' name, moreover, appeared on at least one document which dealt with the transfer of the Jews to the ghetto, a fact which confirmed his own personal involvement in that process.[49] When I found this particular document I remember that I felt like jumping for joy. I had already been working for OSI for several months and this was the first case in which I had actually found a document mentioning a suspect by name. I had until then spent most of my time researching several Byelorussian cases, but without finding a single document which had specifically named the suspects I was investigating. Thus, discovering this document was a very special occasion.

I sent copies of the entire collection to Washington, where the staff at OSI were busy preparing the indictment. Once they had reviewed the material it became imperative to determine exactly how the documents had originated and how they had arrived in Israel in order to be able to present them to the court. That story, told above, was finally obtained by investigators of the Israeli Police Nazi war crimes unit from Avraham Tory, who had played an important role in collecting the documents and had brought them to Yad Vashem. Once that information had been determined, the last step was to authenticate the documents which is standard procedure for all materials introduced into evidence. The Yad Vashem Archives issued an authorization that the documents in question were authentic copies of originals in its possession and then a special seal or apostil was affixed to each document by the Foreign Ministry.

The documentation was sent to OSI via the American Embassy in late October 1982, well in advance of the trial which was scheduled to begin in December. As it turned out, however, something went wrong with the mail and I began getting frantic cables from Washington asking me where the documents were. Rather than take any chances, I decided to transmit a second set via the good offices of US Ambassador Samuel Lewis who personally brought them to Washington, one of the unknown services that he performed during the course of his long tour of duty in Tel Aviv.

The documents arrived in time and were admitted into evidence at the trial,[50] which began on December 6, 1982 in Tampa, Florida. In the course of the trial, Palciauskas frequently invoked the Fifth Amendment, refusing to answer numerous questions related to his immigration. This fact made a very strong impression on federal judge Robert Morgan who noted that Palciauskas' professed poor memory obviously reflected a lack of honesty which seemed "strange, strange indeed. I find it very difficult to understand how this defendant who needs help with the English language in a proceeding that involves his naturalization cannot remember steps he took to get into this country."[51]

Judge Morgan found it "beyond dispute" that Palciauskas had participated in the establishment and administration of the Kovno Ghetto in which all the Jews of the city were forced to live behind barbed wire under terrible conditions. The judge also noted the role played by the Palciauskas administration in the confiscation of Jewish property outside the ghetto and in the redistribution of Jewish homes to non-Jewish Lithuanians following the mass executions of the city's Jews in the summer and fall of 1941. On March 23, 1983, Morgan concluded therefore that Palciauskas "lacked the good moral character required for citizenship" and ordered him stripped of his citizenship.[52]

Several months later, Palciauskas appealed the verdict, but Judge Morgan's decision was affirmed unanimously by the U.S. Court of Appeals for the 11th Circuit. Palciauskas subsequently asked the

Supreme Court to review the case, but his petition was denied.[53] OSI
submitted for his deportation, but the former mayor of Kovno died of a
stroke on January 7, 1992 at the age of 84 in St. Petersburg Beach,
Florida before he could be expelled from the United States.[54]

Throughout the entire period that the case was in the courts I continued to search for documents and/or witnesses that might assist in Palciauskas' conviction. The results of that search which continued on and
off for practically six years are very illuminating vis-à-vis the possibilities for research in Israel on Nazi war criminals. In this respect, Kovno,
the site of Palciauskas' crimes, had enormous research potential. First
of all, because of its size. The chances of finding survivors from a particular city, town or village are usually in direct proportion to the number
of Jewish inhabitants. Kovno was one of the larger Jewish communities
in the Baltic region (third after Vilna and Riga) and had approximately
30,000 Jewish residents.

Size alone, however, does not always ensure a large survivor population. Another critical factor is the history of the particular community.
Since the Kovno Ghetto existed practically until the end of the war, the
number of survivors was proportionally much larger than in other
communities which were liquidated during the initial stage of the war.
By the time the Jews of Kovno were deported to Germany, the Second
World War was nearly over and consequently many were able to survive. The fact that they were deported to concentration camps rather
than death camps also increased their chances of survival.[55]

A third factor relates to the level of Jewish communal life and identification. The more intense Jewish life was in the community, and the
stronger the sense of Jewish identification, the higher the degree of
active and passive resistance. Since recording the events and the acts of
persecution was considered an important form of opposition to Nazi
oppression, this type of activity was fairly widespread in the major centers of Jewish life in Eastern Europe. In this context, the attempts of the
Kovno Judenrat to preserve the documentation concerning the persecution and annihilation are hardly exceptional. Similar efforts were carried out in an organized manner in other large Jewish communities
such as Warsaw and Lublin.[56] Another related factor concerns efforts
by individuals to record their wartime experiences. The more educated
the members of the community, the larger the number of individuals
who maintained diaries during the war and the higher the number of
survivors who wrote their memoirs after the war.

These sources invariably prove extremely helpful to researchers. In this respect, although Kovno did not produce an Emmanuel Ringelblum or even an Anne Frank who recorded their daily experiences throughout the war, quite a few survivors wrote afterwards about life in the ghetto. In addition to all the above, it should be noted that the extent of the research on a specific locale is also usually dependent on the history of that community and the extent to which it engaged in resistance. Thus the more active a community was, the greater the chances are that its fate will be researched. This is particularly true in Israel where research on resistance, and particularly armed resistance, was something of a national obsession during the initial 25 years of Holocaust research. This applied in the case of Kovno, which had an active Jewish underground, and which was the subject of a major monograph by Dov Levin and Avraham Tzvi Baron.[57]

The Israeli obsession with resistance, however, was in this case a double-edged sword. While it led to increased research and generated numerous testimonies in Israeli archives, the material in question totally ignored most other aspects of the life and fate of the Jews of the community and shed almost no light on the activities of the collaborators. In that context I jokingly used to tell my colleagues at Yad Vashem that if I had a dollar for every testimony I read in which the survivor was asked when the first gun was smuggled into the Kovno (or for that matter any other) ghetto, I would be wealthy. If, however, I would get paid only for the testimonies in which the survivor was asked who the local collaborationist mayor was, I would undoubtedly be reduced to poverty. On the other hand, the testimonies regarding resistance activities did have a positive aspect because they identified and helped us find numerous survivors. If not for their testimony on the resistance, there is no guarantee that we would have ever known of their existence.

Besides the above points, I think it is important to note that I was able to benefit from a few new research tools, as well as to utilize materials which had hereto not been used for the investigation of Nazi war criminals. One of the best potential leads I found was a German engineer named Herbert Haardt who had worked for the Wehrmacht in an administrative capacity in Kovno during the war. He and his wife Maria had rescued three Jews from the ghetto and were honored by Yad Vashem for their noble deeds. Their story appeared in the files of the Department for the Righteous Among the Nations, a resource which had, to the best of my knowledge, never been utilized before in investigations of this sort. The importance of the material in these files was that it helped us uncover individuals who had a unique vantage point to view the events, since they were able to move about freely and were not subject to the various restrictions imposed upon the Jews. These files also included the names of numerous survivors, many of whom had never submitted testimony to any archives. The problem in this case was that many of the Righteous were still living in Lithuania and consequently were neither readily available for questioning nor able to appear as witnesses. For this reason the German Righteous who were in Lithuania during the war were particularly valuable because of the likelihood of their being able to cooperate in this investigation.[58] In addition to Haardt, there was another German who helped the Jews in the Kovno ghetto. SA *Obersturmführer* Gustav Hormann, who headed the ghetto's labor office, assisted the Jews on numerous occasions.[59] Unfortunately both he and Haardt had died before OSI began investigating Palciauskas and thus could not provide information regarding his activities.

In terms of new material, one of the most helpful tools in our research has been the registration files of the World Gathering of Holocaust Survivors held in Jerusalem in June 1981. Approximately 10,000 survivors came to Israel to celebrate their survival and to dedicate their efforts to commemorate the victims of the Holocaust. Each participant filled out a registration form regarding his or her wartime experiences, thereby creating an extremely valuable repository of data. This information was sent to Yad Vashem,[60] where I was able to use it to discover the current whereabouts of tens of survivors of Kovno. The most important advantage of the information culled from these forms was the fact that the data were up to date. Those survivors who participated in the Gathering could be found immediately, unlike those whose names were discovered through the use of testimonies submitted years before, when the individual in question might have been living at a different address and in some cases even had a different name. The disadvantage of these forms was that there was no indication as to the relative value of the testimony. The only fact recorded was that the survivor had been in a certain place at a specific time. In order to determine whether he or she was a potentially valuable witness, each person had to be interviewed. If we had been suffering from an acute shortage of witnesses, that would not have been so terrible, but that was certainly not the case in this investigation.

In retrospect, if I have to evaluate the material found in Israel regarding Palciauskas I think that the effort invested was worthwhile. The collection of documents from the Kovno Ghetto was admitted as evidence at the trial and two witnesses were identified who were invited to the United States to testify on behalf of OSI. At the same time the research in this case highlights the problematics of our work—both in terms of original documentation and witnesses. The fact that the overwhelming majority of OSI's suspects were collaborators of Eastern European origin complicated the search for evidence. Even though these individuals played a significant role in the persecution and murder of the Jews, their contribution and participation is not always fully and accurately reflected in the documentation. In this case, for example, even though we were able to find an entire collection regarding the persecution of the Jews, we were only able to find one document which Palciauskas had personally signed. This is a serious problem which we encountered numerous times in the cases of other officials. I know, for example, of several individuals, currently living in the United States, who served as mayors or high officials in cities in Eastern Europe and who apparently played a significant role in the persecution of the local Jews, but against whom there is insufficient documentary evidence and as a result they have yet to be indicted. (Most of the places in question are located in areas which were formerly part of the Soviet Union; this undoubtedly complicated the research effort.)

These difficulties also exist vis-à-vis the search for witnesses, as is evident from the Palciauskas case. During the course of the investigation I found the names of well over 200 survivors of Kovno and read the testimonies of at least several dozen. Palciauskas was not mentioned in a single testimony! The most I could elicit from the material was whether an individual could have possibly known him and/or have witnessed his participation in persecution. As a result, an extraordinary amount of work had to be invested in order to determine whether the survivors I found had the information we were looking for. This was to a large extent due to the origin of the testimonies and the nature of the research carried out in Israel, where the primary focus was Jewish resistance and Jewish life under the Nazi occupation. Whatever curiosity existed vis-à-vis the killers was directed primarily at the Germans and Austrians who were considered the major villains. Even though the extensive collaboration and participation of the local population were legendary, very little effort was made by Israeli researchers to identify the perpetrators, hence the lacunae in the research. Even today, after international attention has been focused on the collaborators, insufficient attention and resources are allocated for this critical field of research.

Despite the various difficulties faced by its historians, OSI was able in the three cases above to find sufficient evidence to submit an indictment. In that respect, the cases are typical of the tens of cases OSI has brought to court. These cases, however, are to a certain extent only the tip of the iceberg, a small percentage of the cases investigated by OSI. In numerous investigations no practical results were achieved, unfortunately, since the problems cited above proved insurmountable. Thus various individuals who committed serious crimes were not brought to justice because we lacked either the documents or the witnesses. In addition, there are those against whom a case could perhaps have been brought but who were spared that fate—either because they died before OSI was able to prosecute them or because the witness who could help convict them passed away before they could be brought to trial. While the question of the prosecution of Nazi war criminals is undoubtedly an issue of morality and justice, the prosaic mechanics of that process as demonstrated above are such today that even given the best intentions of governments, the percentage of criminals who will ultimately pay for their crimes is infinitesimally small.

Notes

1. According to statistics prepared by the Deschenes Commission, 6,842 Nazis were convicted in West Germany prior to 1985. See "Commission of Inquiry on War Criminals Report," Part I (hereafter, Deschenes Commission Report), p. 31.

2. Adalbert, Rückerl, *The Investigation of Nazi Crimes: A Documentation*, Heidelberg and Karlsruhe, 1979, pp. 48-52.

3. During the years 1945-48 approximately 115,000 Jews were brought to Palestine (some had attempted to immigrate illegally, were caught by the British and interned in Cyprus), most of whom were survivors. Abraham Sacher, *The Redemption of the Unwanted: From the Liberation of the Death Camps to the Founding of Israel*, New York, 1983, p. 189. After the establishment of the State of Israel, numerous survivors immigrated to the Jewish state primarily from the DP camps in Central Europe. During the period from May 14, 1948 until March 31, 1951, 271,188 Jews of Eastern European origin came to live in Israel, among them a high percentage of Holocaust survivors. The source of the immigration figures is: Tom Segev, *1949 ha-Yisraelim ha-Rishonim*, Jerusa-

lem, 1984, p. 105.

4. There are no exact figures on the number of Holocaust survivors among the recent Soviet Jewish immigrants to Israel. From personal experience, I know that many of the potential witnesses interviewed by OSI regarding crimes committed in areas that were part of the Soviet Union, especially Lithuania and Latvia, immigrated to Israel from the Soviet Union after 1969.

5. See the Martyrs and Heroes Remembrance (Yad Vashem) Law passed by the Knesset on August 19, 1953, and published as law on August 28, 1953. *Yad Vashem*, Jerusalem, 1976, pp. 7-9.

6. "Plaintiffs Proposed Findings of Fact and Conclusions of Law," United States of America vs. Bohdan Koziy, submitted to US District Court Southern District of Florida, October 22, 1981, case no. 79-6640 CIV JCP, pp. 1-4.

7. For details on Yad Vashem's documentary resources see *Yad Vashem*, Jerusalem, 1976, pp. 45-57.

8. "Lysiec," *Pinkas ha-Kehillot: Polin*, Vol. II, Galitziya ha-Mizrachit, pp. 301-302.

9. Abraham Liebesman, *Im Yehudei Stanislavov be-Yimei Kilya*, Tel Aviv, 1981, pp. 70-72.

10. *Guide To Unpublished Materials of the Holocaust Period*, Vols 1-6, Jerusalem, 1970-81.

11. See note 6, p. 3.

12. "Order and Judgement," United States of America vs. Bohdan Koziy, March 29, 1982, pp. 7-8, 12-13.

13. For details on the large-scale massacre which took place on October 12, 1941 see "Stanislawow" in *Pinkas ha-Kehillot: Polin*, vol. II, pp. 370-71.

14. Statement of US Justice Department, October 21, 1982.

15. Oldemar Ramirez, "Koziy Ordered Released, Not Deported to Soviet Union," Associated Press, June 11, 1987.

16. Arthur Spiegelman, "West Germany Refused Request to Take Alleged War Criminal," Reuters, August 25, 1986; Mary Thornton, "West Germany Rejected Wartime Cases," *Washington Post*, August 26, 1986.

17. Oldemar Ramirez, "Koziy Ordered Released, Not Deported to Soviet Union," Associated Press, June 11, 1987.

18. "Alleged Ukrainian War Criminal Receives Costa Rican Visa," Reuters, September 11, 1987.

19. As a result of Baruch's efforts, for example, the Ninth International Congress of the Association of Jewish Lawyers and Jurists held in Jerusalem and Tiberias, December 28, 1992—January 1, 1993 passed a resolution calling for Koziy's extradition to the Ukraine or prosecution in Costa Rica. See "Resolutions of the Ninth International Congress," *Newsletter* (of the Association), No. 8, 1993, pp. 21-22.

20. See, for example, David Horovitz, "After Demjanjuk is the Hunt for Nazis

Over?" *Jerusalem Report*, August 12, 1992, p. 31.

21. "Complaint," United States of America vs. Juozas Kungys, US District Court for the District of New Jersey, June 27, 1981, p. 9.

22. Keydan," *Yahadut Lita*, Vol. IV, Tel Aviv, 1984, pp. 345-47.

23. Juozas Kungys file, SWCA; Vytautas Zeimantas, *A Call for Justice*, Vilnius, 1986, pp. 103-12; idem, *Gimtasis Krastas*, No. 26 (1008), June 26, 1986.

24. Juozas Kungys file, SWCA; see note 17, pp. 20-22; YVA, files of International Tracing Service, microfilm, K-333, YVA.

25. David Volfa, "Churban Keydan" and Yehuda Ronder, "Ha-Getto, ha-Hitnagdut ve-Ovdan Yehudei Keydan," Yosef Krust (ed.), *Sefer Keydan*, Tel Aviv, 1977, pp. 229-33, 235-36.

26. See the testimonies of Shmuel Chalusin (12/92), Dr. Gershon Faktor (12/86) Yaakov and Lyova Reuveni (12/113), regarding attempts to bring Lithuanian collaborators to justice after the war and of Abraham Wiener (12/96) regarding the Jews deported to the Kedainiai labor camp from the Kovno Ghetto, Oral History Division—Institute of Contemporary Jewry, Hebrew University of Jerusalem.

27. *Ma'ariv*, September 3, 1981, p. 15.

28. Tzadok Shalpoversky, who was among the Jews taken to be murdered on August 28, 1941, killed one of the Lithuanian collaborators and shot at the German commandant on the edge of the murder pit. He was then murdered by the Lithuanians. "Keydan," *Yahadut Lita*, p. 346.

29. The survivors were rescued by Jonas Antanaitis and Veronika Petrulaitiene, both of whom were recognized by Yad Vashem for their noble deeds. See files 1459 and 1798, Department for the Righteous Among the Nations, Yad Vashem.

30. For example, the monument at Rumbuli, the site of the mass murder of the Jews of Riga (November, 30, December 7, 1941) is dedicated to "Di Korbonos Phun Fashism" (the victims of fascism). Even this inscription in Yiddish was considered a concession by the Soviet authorities. See Yoseph Mendelevitch, *Mivtza Chatuna*, Jerusalem, 1985, p. 23.

31. See the photographs of the monuments erected in various Jewish communities in Lithuania, *Yahadut Lita*, in between pp. 304-5 and 368-9. Among the few exceptions to this rule are the monuments in Rumsiskes and the monument honoring the Jews of Anyksciai, whose remains were transferred to the Jewish cemetery in Vilna.

32. Tom Rosenthal, "Citizenship Trial of Alleged Nazi Collaborator Begins," Associated Press, April 6, 1983.

33. Tom Rosenthal, "Prosecutors Concerned by War Criminal Evidence Decision," Associated Press, November 7, 1983.

34. Pete Brown, "Man Accused of War Crimes Ordered Stripped of Citizenship," Associated Press, June 21, 1986.

35. Among the cases in which documentation from Soviet archives and/or witnesses from the Soviet Union were utilized: Henrikas Benkunskas, Antanas Bernotas, Ivan Demjanjuk, Vytautas Gudauskas, Jurgis Juodis, Talivaldis Karklins, Juozas Kisielaitis, Bohdan Koziy, Alexander Lehmann, Boleslavs Maikovskis and many others.

36. George Andreassi, "Lithuanian Émigré Pleased Supreme Court to Hear Case," United Press International, November 10, 1986.

37. Stuart Taylor Jr., "Court Delays Effort to Deport a Man Accused of Nazi War Crimes," *New York Times*, May 3, 1988.

38. Robert Cohen, "Citizenship Revoked in Jersey Nazi Case," *Newark Star-Ledger*, November 23, 1988.

39. Garfunkel, pp. 51-52.

40. Complaint, United States of America vs. Kazys Palciauskas, US District Court For the Middle District of Florida, June 5, 1981, p. 2.

41. Leib Garfunkel, "Ha-Eeru'im ha-Chashuvim be-Yoter ba-Ghetto," *Yahadut Lita*, Vol. IV, pp. 63-67; see also in the same volume by the same author "Te'na'ai ha-Chayim ba-Ghetto," pp. 73-78 and Dr. Eliyahu Segal, "Ha-Irgun ha-Refu'i ba-Ghetto," pp. 119-24.

42. See note 34, pp. 3-4.

43. Marilyn Kalfus, "Man, 75, Faces Nazi Collaboration Charge," *Tampa Tribune*, December 6, 1982.

44. For details on Allen's activities and his initial lists of Nazi war criminals in the United States, see Rochelle G. Saidel, *The Outraged Conscience: Seekers of Justice for Nazi War Criminals in America*, Albany, 1984, pp. 47-77.

45. *Documents Accuse*, Vilnius, 1970, pp. 136-69, 293.

46. Kazys Palciauskas file, SWCA.

47. Three of the best-known works on the Kovno Ghetto are Leib Garfunkel, *Kovna ha Yehudit be-Churbana*, Jerusalem, 1959; Tzvi Avraham Baron and Dov Levin, *Toldoteha Shel Machteret*, Jerusalem, 1962; Yosef Gar, *Umkum Phun der Yiddischer Kovna*, Munich, 1948.

48. *Kovna ha-Yehudit be Churbana*, pp. 30, 42, 46.

49. Letter of General-Major Pohl to the mayor, July 16, 1941, YVA, 0-48/12-4.

50. "Memorandum of Decision," United States of America vs. Kazys Palciauskas, U. S. District Court, Middle District of Florida, Tampa Division, March 23, 1982, case no. 81-547 CIV-T GC, p. 4.

51. "Government Rests Case against Lithuanian," Associated Press, December 8, 1982; Marilyn Kalfus, "Lithuanian's Testimony Called Strange," *Tampa Tribune*, December 8, 1982.

52. "Memorandum of Decision," United States of America vs. Kazys Palciauskas, US District Court, Middle District of Florida, Tampa Division, March 23, 1982, case no. 81-547 CIV-T GC, pp. 2-18.

53. "The Campaign against the U. S. Justice Department's Prosecution of Suspected Nazi War Criminals," ADL Special Report, June 1985, p. 17.

54. "Kazys Palciauskas," *Orlando Sentinel Tribune,* January 10, 1992.

55. For the history of the Kovno Ghetto from its establishment until the deportation of the Jews to concentration camps see note 41.

56. For the documentation collected clandestinely in the Warsaw Ghetto see "Oneg Shabbat," the underground archives directed by Emmanuel Ringelblum. Over the past four decades parts of this important archive have been published in Israel, for example: Emmanuel Ringelblum, *Polish-Jewish Relations During the Second World War,* Jerusalem, 1974; Shimon Huberband; *Kiddush ha-Shem,* Tel Aviv, 1969. Some of the documentation preserved from Lublin was published in Nachman Blumental, *Teudot mi-Ghetto Lublin; Yudenrat le-Lo Derech,* Jerusalem, 1967.

57. See Note 41. By the early 1960s when Baron and Levin's book was published tens of accounts of life in the Kovno Ghetto had already appeared in print. See the bibliography in their book, pp. 403-8.

58. File of Herbert and Maria Haardt, Department for the Righteous Among the Nations, Yad Vashem, file 2132.

59. Testimony of Gustav Hormann, Yad Vashem Archives, M-l/E-694/585. See also *Kovna ha-Yehudit be-Churbana,* pp. 221-22.

60. Yad Vashem Archives, 0-37/A-Z.

4

Of Human Errors, Caprices and Failings

One of the major obstacles in the efforts to prosecute Nazi war criminals is the lack of sufficient documentary evidence or witnesses. Indeed, in quite a few cases allegations could not be proven and consequently the suspects were not indicted. For every Koziy, Kungys and Palciauskas brought to trial there are far more others against whom similar allegations had been made, but in whose cases sufficient documentation or testimony could not be produced. Such investigations proved extremely frustrating for the historians at OSI; this was a problem which plagued our work from the very beginning. Yet as problematic as these cases were, imagine how much more frustrating it was to deal with cases in which the material existed but was unavailable because of factors beyond our control, factors which derived from human errors and/or what could best be termed human weaknesses. Cases such as these ultimately proved to be the most difficult to cope with emotionally, and that pain was multiplied many times over when the inaccessible material in question held the key to the prosecution not of one Nazi criminal but of many.

Three incidents related to the search for documentation and witnesses illuminate this problem; they indicate to what a great extent we were dependent on others, and how we were often the victims of human errors, whims and caprices. In one case a mistake was overcome by a strange set of circumstances, which could almost be classified as miraculous. In another case we do not know to this day how much important evidence was destroyed by well-meaning but uninformed individuals. In the third case we were unable for many years to obtain access to a collection of testimonies which could have considerably facilitated the prosecution of numerous Nazi war criminals.

Let us begin with our success story. One of my first assignments for OSI was to find evidence concerning the police chief of Skaudville, Lithuania, a small town in the Taurage district, about 35 kilometers (22 miles) from the German border. Before the war approximately

1,000 Jews lived in Skaudville, a typical middle-sized Lithuanian Jewish community. The Jews of Skaudville, like those in all the provincial towns and villages throughout Lithuania, were murdered during the initial months of the war by the Nazis and their Lithuanian collaborators,[1] who in numerous instances carried out most of the murders themselves. Indeed, the assistance provided by the local population played a significant role in the extremely high percentage of Lithuanian Jews murdered during the Holocaust (over 95 per cent of those who lived there during the Nazi occupation, a figure which was even higher in the provincial communities).[2] I therefore approached this assignment with a certain degree of pessimism, doubting whether any documents, and especially witnesses, could be found. At this point all I knew was that 300 male Jews from Skaudville had been murdered in the nearby village of Puzai in the summer of 1941 by German soldiers, local policemen and Lithuanian "partisans," and that these same groups had killed more than 100 Jewish women and children a month later near the village of Batakiai, a few kilometers south of Skaudville.

My first step was to check the pertinent files at Yad Vashem and the other Israeli archives for material on the events in Skaudville, Puzai and Batakiai. The only material listed which related to the events in the three locations were two testimonies on Skaudville from the Yad Vashem Archives.[3] Normally, finding two testimonies on the murder of the Jews of a provincial town in Lithuania would be considered a fairly promising start. That was not the case in this instance, however, since the material, which had been recorded in the Displaced Persons camps in Germany after the Second World War, proved problematic for two major reasons. The first was that it was not clear from the testimonies whether the survivors had actually experienced the events or had heard about them after the war. The second was that even if they had lived in Skaudville under the Nazi occupation, there was no indication as to their present whereabouts. We had no idea whatsoever where they were currently living or, even more important, whether they were presently alive. One was a woman, who might possibly have subsequently married and changed her name. There was also the possibility that these survivors had come to Israel and Hebraized their names, so our situation was hardly encouraging. Various other avenues of research were explored and a few insignificant secondary sources were found, but we relatively rapidly reached a deadend.

Having exhausted all the local sources I stopped looking for material in the autumn of 1980, convinced that unless someone could come up with documentation outside Israel our chances of indicting the police chief of Skaudville were exceedingly slim. I more or less forgot about the matter, returning to it only briefly in January 1982 when a team of OSI lawyers headed by Neal Sher came to Israel to interview potential witnesses. I participated in many of the interviews, often serving as a translator from Hebrew to English and vice versa. Among the survivors we interviewed was a woman from Herziliya who had lived in Skaudville during the war and had survived by hiding in the nearby forests. Her recollections of the police chief were, however, rather hazy, hardly the convincing type of testimony which could lead to an indictment. This was quite disappointing in view of the dearth of documentary evidence.

What made the situation even more frustrating was that the very same witness had testified five years previously and had clearly recalled the police chief and his involvement in the persecution of the Jews. Our chances of being able to bring him to court looked extremely bleak therefore until one summer day in late July 1983, when I unexpectedly revealed a potentially invaluable source of information at the Moreshet Archives. Moreshet, which is located at the Givat Chaviva Seminar Center of the Kibbutz Artzi movement near Hadera, is a repository of Holocaust documentation dedicated to the memory of Mordechai Anielewicz, commander of the Warsaw Ghetto Revolt. It specializes in the history of the *Ha-Shomer ha-Tzair* socialist Zionist youth movement during the Holocaust, but also has extensive documentation on many other aspects of the annihilation of European Jewry.[4]

I spent considerable time at the Moreshet Archives and on numerous occasions found material of value. On this particular trip, I was looking for documentary evidence and testimony regarding the Vilnius Sonderkommando, a unit of Lithuanians which carried out the mass murder of the Jews of Vilna and later were sent from town to town throughout the Vilna area to implement the Final Solution. I had therefore ordered a large number of testimonies regarding the events in Vilna from the Moreshet Archives catalogue. The first testimony I began reading looked as if it would not be of any value. Apparently it had been listed in the catalogue under Vilna because the survivor in question had been in a Jewish orphanage in Vilna *after* the war. Since he had not been in Vilna or its environs during the Nazi occupation, he

obviously could not supply any information on the activities of the
Vilnius Sonderkommando. I was going to put it aside, but instead
checked the catalogue listing again, to see if I had perhaps written
down the wrong number. Something in the brief description of the testimony caught my eye. According to the catalogue, the survivor,
Yoseph Ben-Yaakov (Yankelewitz) had been "hidden by the Lithuanians
during the Nazi occupation,"[5] that is he had survived in Lithuania
throughout the course of the war. That information immediately put
this testimony into a special category because the number of individuals who had survived in hiding in the provincial areas of Lithuania was
extremely small. The thought which immediately crossed my mind was
that perhaps he was from one of the other places in Lithuania which
we were investigating. (At that time I was engaged in research on quite
a few Lithuanian cities and towns.)

I therefore began reading the testimony very carefully, hoping that I
might have inadvertently discovered something of value. The initial segment dashed my hopes. Ben-Yaakov was from Kraziai, a town near
Kelme that was not on my list of Lithuanian locales that had to be
investigated. He had, moreover, been born in 1931 so he was extremely
young at the time that the crimes had been committed. There was
something about his testimony, however, which I personally found fascinating and which induced me to continue reading, despite the fact
that it could not ostensibly contain any information of value for my
purposes.

The part of the testimony which intrigued me concerned the local
rabbi. After the initial *Aktion* in which all the males over the age of 14
had been murdered, he was left together with 60 children and a hand-
ful of other adults in a barn guarded by local collaborators. The day
after the *Aktion*, local women came to the barn to take the children of
their friends home with them and related that the children's parents
had already been murdered. The rabbi, however, refused to allow them
to do so. Two weeks later, Lithuanian women kidnapped about 15 of
the children in order to convert them, or, in Ben-Yaakov's words, "perhaps out of mercy." The rabbi made sure to get back every single one of
them with the exception of two sisters who for some reason were not
returned. In other words, he rescued them from the friendly Lithuanians and the peril of conversion, little realizing that he was thereby
inadvertently facilitating their murder. The story was extremely heart-
rending, especially the rabbi's particular role (perhaps as the son of a

rabbi I empathized with the dilemma which he faced). At the same time I was very curious to learn how Ben-Yaakov survived and therefore continued reading the testimony, even though it did not apparently relate to the areas I was investigating.

Ben-Yaakov sensed that something was about to happen when Lithuanian guards were suddenly stationed around the silo where the remaining Jews of Kraziai were concentrated and security was tightened. As he recounted in his memoirs: "All of a sudden there were guards again. Two days later security was reinforced. We were guarded by Lithuanian partisans. . .I understood that something bad was about to happen. We will share the same fate as our parents, I thought." Ben-Yaakov, acting on his own healthy instincts, escaped, hiding in a pile of hay in the attic of a nearby barn. He remained there for three days and three nights during which time the remaining Jews were taken out and murdered. Yoseph eventually left the barn after all the Lithuanians who had participated in the murder had gone away, and he went to the home of a Lithuanian friend of his father who gave him food, money and clothes. Yoseph had hoped to remain with him, but the friend was afraid to hide him lest he be discovered by the police or his anti-Semitic neighbors, and thus Yoseph was forced to set out on his own. The continuation of the story proved to be fascinating and, as it turned out, extremely important. Ben-Yaakov related:

> I saw that the situation was desperate. I decided to go to a relative who lived about 40 kilometers away. I walked for a day and arrived there. All the way I had terrible stomach aches since I ate so much after not eating for three days. My stomach hurt. I was writhing in pain.
>
> I reached a point not far from where my relatives lived and I asked a farmer about the Jews of the town. The farmer, who saw that I was wearing the clothes of a non-Jew and that I spoke fluent Lithuanian, assumed I was a Gentile and explained that they [the local Jews] were in a camp near Batakiai.

Imagine my astonishment when I read the last sentence. How was it possible that he had been in Batakiai? After all, Batakiai was not listed in the Hebrew-language catalogue or in Volume VI of the *Guide to the Unpublished Materials of the Holocaust Period*. Obviously a mistake had been made, but of course the critical questions remained: Had Yoseph been there when the Jews had been concentrated and murdered? Had he personally witnessed the crimes? Most importantly, could he identify the perpetrators and specifically our suspect? I continued reading with bated breath, hoping against hope that he had indeed been there and had personally witnessed the atrocities.

I arrived there the same evening. I found only my aunt, her daughter, and a young son. All the males under fourteen [*sic*—he obviously meant the opposite—all the males *over* age fourteen] were no longer alive. In the beginning I did not relate what had happened in my town of Krozh [Kraziai]. I only said that there was famine and that was the reason that I had run away from there. After I had been there two days, I told my cousin the truth about my town. He told his mother and she told the other women and thus it became known to everyone in the camp. People panicked and were very afraid. The women were naive and had not imagined that the men had been killed.

They were so angry at me that one woman wanted to inform on me, to tell the authorities that I was not a local. They thought that I was a liar who was needlessly spreading tall tales and arousing panic.

I pleaded with them and my aunt intervened and thus that step was prevented. I was there for about 10 days. One evening the Lithuanian guards informed us that before the winter we would all be sent to a camp near Adakawai, another small town, where we would remain until the end of the war, when we would all be sent to Palestine. Thus they calmed us all down and fooled everyone, preparing the atmosphere. Instead of taking us to Adakawai, they led [the Jews] to the forest and shot all of them. I escaped from there, from out of the pit. This is how it happened. When they seated us in the vehicle [to take them to the site of the murder], I told my cousin who was a year older "Let's escape. They will kill us all. I know."

I proposed that we return to my town and hide in the home of a non-Jewish acquaintance. "Better to be killed a Jew than to live as a non-Jew," he replied. He convinced me and I too remained in the vehicle and went with all of them. We reached the forest. There was a path in the forest and on the side of the path a long pit about 20 meters long. Five German SS men in black uniforms stood near the pit taking photographs. . .They were armed. There were many Lithuanian partisans there, some had sticks and some held crowbars. One of the Lithuanians sat on the vehicle and brutally pushed everyone out with the butt of his rifle. Children, women, everyone. He kicked whoever could not hop off the vehicle and rolled them off, especially the women. The Lithuanians attacked the women and children and ordered them to go to the other side of the road. They had to undress and thus they were pushed and beaten with crowbars and rifle butts to the pit, where they were shot.

I stood up to get undressed. I started to unbutton my shirt. At that instant I thought of escaping. No one stood near me. I leaped into the trees, and ran in a zig-zag as fast as I could. I got further and further away and thus I escaped.[6]

There it was. Black on white, he had been there—an eyewitness. I was so excited I could barely control my emotions. I hurried to point out the error of omission to the director of the archive, but at this point I was so happy that I could hardly be upset. There were, at this point, two critical questions which remained to be answered. Was Yoseph Ben-Yaakov (Yankelewitz) alive? And if so, where was he living? At the time of the interview, he had been living in Holon, a suburb of Tel Aviv, but that was several years ago and who knew what had happened since?

With no small degree of trepidation, I checked the Tel Aviv area phone directory. I was hoping against hope that he was alive and well and willing to testify, but in these matters one can never be sure of anything. Even though I assumed that there was an excellent chance of his being alive because he was so young at the time of the war (according to the date of birth recorded on the interview, he should have been 52-years old when I found his testimony, an incredibly young age for a survivor), I still felt that I had to prepare myself for every eventuality.

There were two Yoseph Ben-Yaakovs living in Holon listed in the phone directory. That was already a good sign. I called the first one, who was living at the address recorded on the testimony in the Moreshet Archives. The person who answered was not Yoseph Ben-Yaakov, but rather his tenant who told me that Ben-Yaakov was alive and well and living at the other address listed in the phone book, so I knew that we had hit the jackpot. I immediately called Ben-Yaakov and told him about my search for evidence and witnesses regarding the events which took place in Batakiai. He responded by inviting me to his home to hear his story.

A few days later, I went to Holon to meet Ben-Yaakov and spent a fascinating afternoon listening to him relate the incredible story I had read in his testimony. Based on what I heard from Ben-Yaakov, as well as what I read in his testimony at the Moreshet Archives, there was no question that he was a prime potential witness. I did not mention the suspect's name nor did I ask any specific questions about him since that might jeopardize our efforts. (In a previous case, a judge had accused the Nazi war crimes unit of the Israeli police of prompting witnesses[7] so we had to be extremely careful regarding this point.) It appeared obvious, however, that if anyone might be able to testify against the police chief from Skaudville, it would be Yoseph Ben-Yaakov.

There was an ironic postscript to this story. Yoseph and his son walked me to the bus and while we waited, Yoseph related that he had already been interviewed by the Nazi war crimes unit of the Israeli police. I was slightly surprised because I knew that there were no other potential witnesses in this case (besides the above-mentioned woman from Herziliya) and if he had been interviewed, OSI should have been aware of his existence. Ben-Yaakov explained that he had been questioned regarding Bronius Kaminskas, a Lithuanian who had participated in the murder of Jews in Kraziai, Ben-Yaakov's home town, and was presently living in the United States. The investigators, however, had not questioned Yoseph about what had happened to him after leaving Kraziai. They therefore had no idea that he had ended up in Batakiai and that he had seen the Jews being brought to the pits to be murdered. If not for the story related above, OSI would have never known about a superb potential witness for this case.

Yoseph asked me about the status of the Kaminskas case and I told him that Kaminskas had been declared unfit to stand trial and had thus escaped prosecution.[8] Yoseph, and especially his son, were particularly perturbed and asked me all the standard questions that are usually raised in such situations: Why can't we just go in there and assassinate him? How do we know that he's not faking? I explained that he was periodically examined by court-appointed doctors, but I have the distinct feeling that my reply hardly satisfied them. After reading Yoseph's testimony, it is not hard to understand why.

The Ben-Yaakov story was an eye-opener. As a result of several seemingly innocuous human errors, a situation was created in which it was extremely likely that Ben-Yaakov's experiences would never have been discovered and no one would have been aware of the fact that a prime potential eyewitness existed in this case. If not for the strange set of circumstances described above, who knows if anyone would have revealed the fact that he had been at Batakiai and had witnessed part of the atrocities?

As it turned out, however, this discovery did not lead to any practical results. In the meantime, the Skaudville police chief had become too ill to be prosecuted. Perhaps if Ben-Yaakov's existence had been known earlier, this Lithuanian criminal could have been brought to justice. In view of the serious difficulties we encountered in our attempts to find documents and especially witnesses, this episode emphasized the need for professional expertise and the utmost precision in research on the Holocaust and the extent to which we were dependent on the efforts of those working in this field. Those are precisely the lessons to be learned from the second story as well.

This episode relates to a collection of several hundred testimonies of survivors housed in one of Israel's better known universities. Unlike many of the survivors' testimonies in Israeli archives, the documents in question were not recorded by professional interviewers. They were prepared by university students and therein lay the crux of the problem.

One of the first individuals to teach courses on the Holocaust at university level was Dr. Marc Dworzecki, a survivor of the Vilna Ghetto, who devoted his life to documenting the persecution and annihilation of European Jewry, and especially of the Jews of his hometown.[9] During his lengthy teaching career, Dr. Dworzecki taught the history of the Holocaust to hundreds of students, each one of whom had to interview a survivor as one of the requirements for the course. Over the years, Dr. Dworzecki collected these testimonies and they were incorporated into his personal archives, which were turned over to the university where he taught following his demise in 1974.

The archives remained untouched for quite some time, but a few years ago the university decided to grant access to the material, including the interviews submitted by Dr. Dworzecki's students. Prior to doing so the testimonies were reviewed by a team of researchers. To their amazement, they discovered that some of the interviews appeared to be fabrications. Students being students, some had apparently taken the liberty of either "inventing" survivors or of copying the work submitted by others. The staff decided therefore to review each and every one of the testimonies in order to verify their authenticity. The method of verification, which was related to me by one of the individuals who participated in the process, was as follows. Each testimony which bore the signature of the survivor was considered authentic. Those testimonies that were not signed were carefully read and checked. In parenthesis I should add that I failed to understand why the signatures were automatically accepted as proof of authenticity. After all, if a student was willing to fabricate the Holocaust experiences of a survivor, why should he or she refrain from signing as well? This criterion was hardly foolproof, but at least it was not harmful since as a result those testimonies, even ones of dubious origin, remained in the collection and could be perused by researchers. In this manner we had, if nothing else, an opportunity to review the material and determine (and continue to investigate if necessary) whether the testimonies were authentic and/or of historical value. The problem was that other material, which might have proved valuable, was destroyed.

The materials in question were the testimonies without a signature. They were reviewed by the staff of the university's Institute for Research on the Diaspora. The problem was, however, that the individuals to whom the task was entrusted were not experts on the history of the Holocaust. This became clear to me when I came across the testimony of one of the most famous survivors of the Holocaust—Yankel Wiernik. Wiernik had spent almost a year in the infamous Treblinka death camp and had participated in the armed revolt by Jewish prisoners on August 2, 1943. Even before the war ended, Wiernik recounted his experiences and the horrors of the death camp in a pamphlet entitled *Rok w Treblince* which was published in 1944 by the Polish underground. (The pamphlet was subsequently translated into English and appeared under the title *A Year in Treblinka*.[10]) Following his arrival in Israel after the war, he built a model of the death camp, which is on now display at the museum of Kibbutz Beit Lohamei ha-Gettaot (Ghetto Fighters' Kibbutz). He was, moreover, one of the most important witnesses who testified at the Eichmann trial.[11] The researchers who reviewed the various testimonies had apparently never heard of him because scrawled across the front page of his devastating testimony was the phrase "*nir'eh amin*," or "appears to be credible."[12]

If those testimonies which did not appear to be credible had been kept on file, the researchers' ignorance and lack of expertise would not have proven so potentially disastrous, but that, unfortunately, was not the case. Those testimonies which did not appear to be authentic were thrown out. Who knows how many good witnesses were lost in the process? I shudder to think that perhaps among the rejected testimonies were those of survivors who could have provided key testimony in cases where we lacked the necessary witnesses and/or documentation to prepare an indictment. Several years after this took place, I spoke about it with one of the participants. She subsequently completed a Ph.D. and has become an expert on the history of the Holocaust. We joked about the treasures that were probably thrown out, but both of us realized only too well that the best of black humor is only a defence mechanism which we use to try and deal with tragedies of this sort.

We will never know exactly what was destroyed in that university's archives. We can nevertheless console ourselves by saying that perhaps the material discarded was worthless or would not have made any difference to the various investigations being conducted by OSI. We cannot do so in the case of our third story, an episode about an important documentary collection whose value is unquestioned.

I learned about the existence of the Kunichowsky collection in the autumn of 1980 shortly after I began working for OSI. From the very beginning of my OSI assignment, I was in close contact with Chaya Lifshitz of Yad Vashem. She had been born, raised and educated in Lithuania and was very knowledgeable regarding the fate of Lithuanian Jewry during the Holocaust. I had often sought her advice in investigations concerning Lithuanian criminals and it was she who told me the fascinating but tragic story of Leib Kunichowsky's collection. She also urged me to take whatever steps necessary to obtain access to this extremely valuable source of information. The story of how the collection was created was initially related to me by Chaya Lifshitz and later corroborated by Kunichowsky himself as well as by others.

Leib Kunichowsky, an engineer by profession, was born and raised in Lithuania. During the Second World War he was incarcerated in the Kovno Ghetto, where he suffered the trials and tribulations which befell the Jews of the erstwhile Lithuanian capital. Immediately after the war, initially in Lithuania and later in the DP camps in Germany, Kunichowsky collected information and testimonies on the recent history of numerous Lithuanian Jewish communities (according to Lithuania's pre-1939 boundaries). The materials he collected related primarily to the Holocaust period but also included information on Jewish communal activities in Lithuania prior to the Second World War. Kunichowsky's collection not only told the tale of the tragic fate of Lithuanian Jewry but also of the flourishing Jewish life which existed in the Baltic republic during the interwar period and which was so brutally and senselessly destroyed by the Nazis and their Lithuanian collaborators.

Kunichowsky had spent four years searching for materials and survivors and had devoted an enormous amount of time and energy to this task. The results he achieved were indeed formidable. When I initially heard about the collection from Chaya Lifshitz, I did not realize how large it was. She told me that it included material on practically every small and middle-sized Jewish community in Lithuania and that fact alone was enough to arouse my interest. This appeared to be precisely the material that I was desperately looking for, since it was so difficult to find solid evidence on the crimes committed in the provincial towns and villages of Lithuania.

The problem was, however, that Kunichowsky was not willing to allow anyone to use his material. The reason for his refusal to grant access to his collection was that for years he had attempted to publish it as a book, but had hereto not succeeded. He therefore was adamant that no one use or benefit from the material in any way. The story of Kunichowsky's efforts to arrange for the publication of his collection is quite complex. Suffice it to say that he was always in the wrong place at the wrong time. According to the version I heard, Kunichowsky had initially sought to sell his collection, but at that time either no one had the necessary funds or perhaps the interest in the subject was not at the level it is today. In later years Kunichowsky no longer demanded any money for the material, but maintained his insistence that it be published in toto. Thus the material remained in two old leather briefcases in Leib Kunichowsky's possession, awaiting its publication, off-limits to anyone and everyone.

On October 28, 1980 I began my efforts to arrange for OSI to gain access to the material. I cabled Allan A. Ryan Jr., director of OSI, to inform him of the existence of an extensive collection of documentation on the destruction of the Jews in Lithuania, which included material on many of the communities then under investigation by OSI. I inquired whether the attorneys and historians at OSI knew of the collection and whether he wanted me to take any steps towards obtaining access. About two weeks later Ryan replied that OSI was not aware of the material in question and instructed me to estimate the total volume of the relevant materials and the cost of reproducing them. While that, indeed, would have been a positive initial step, it was no longer possible at that point since in the meantime Kunichowsky had left Israel, taking his two briefcases (and all the material) with him. I wrote to Ryan that Kunichowsky was in Miami Beach and that he should try to contact him, but apparently that was never done.

In June 1981 Allan Ryan came to Israel to participate in the international gathering of Holocaust survivors held in Jerusalem and the Kunichowsky collection was one of the topics we discussed. Aside from exchanging ideas on possible approaches, no real progress was made because OSI had nothing to offer Kunichowsky, and Ryan, while interested in the material, seemed at a loss as to how to approach him. Shortly thereafter, Chaya Lifshitz told me that Kunichowsky had returned to Israel and encouraged me to speak to him. I therefore called him, told him about my work for OSI, and asked whether I could see the material. Kunichowsky agreed to meet but it was quite clear that it was going to be very difficult to negotiate with him. I began by briefly explaining my duties as OSI's researcher in Israel and he countered by telling me about how he had toiled for four years to collect his material, running from place to place to track down potential witnesses, even stopping boats or trains (I forget which one it was) to get hold of survivors about to emigrate so that he could obtain the material in their possession and record their stories. Kunichowsky's discourse on the efforts he had invested in his project was merely an introduction to the bottom line, that he would not allow anyone to use his material in any way, for any purpose, under any circumstances, until he was certain that it would be published as a book.

I expressed my admiration for his efforts and explained that we had no intention of plagiarizing the material. We simply wanted to use it for a very specific, limited and important purpose—the prosecution of Nazi war criminals. I explained that I had been the director of the Simon Wiesenthal Center in Los Angeles, and that they might be interested in publishing material of this sort. Kunichowsky then took me to another room and showed me a few pages taken from two battered leather briefcases. All the material was in Yiddish and was written in a neat longhand script. I was not, however, able to go over it carefully because he quickly took it away and put it back in the briefcase. It seemed rather obvious that Kunichowsky was loath to trust anyone with his most prized possession. When we later discussed the possibility of reproducing part of the material in order to send it to Los Angeles for perusal, he insisted that the xeroxing be done in his home, as he feared that if it were done elsewhere the documentation might be lost or damaged.

At this point I felt that I still had to try at least once more to obtain access for OSI regardless of whether the Wiesenthal Center would agree to publish the collection. I tried to appeal to Kunichowsky's Jewish conscience to make the material available, as it might be our only chance of prosecuting many Lithuanian collaborators. His response was: "I did it for the *kedoshim*" (holy martyrs). In utter desperation I replied: "But those who turned them into *kedoshim* are walking around free and there is every chance that they will die in peace and tranquillity if we cannot have access to your material." But it was all to no avail. I left Bat-Yam frustrated and emotionally spent, but retained a bit of optimism regarding our chances of obtaining Kunichowsky's material. Little did I realize that four years later we would still be in the exact same position.

Shortly afterwards I tried once again to interest OSI in the Kunichowsky collection. The background to this attempt was a similar case, that of a film producer who possessed potentially valuable material on the murder of the Jews in Lithuania and Latvia. Someone in OSI had read about Misha Lubetzki's collection of films in a newsletter published by an organization of survivors, and I was instructed to contact him and determine its contents. Neal Sher, then deputy director of OSI, was about to visit Israel and if need be, wanted to meet Lubetzki to arrange for access to his material. I visited him in his home in Jerusalem and heard about the films and other documents he had collected to prepare a documentary on the annihilation of the Jews of the Baltic states, primarily those of Lithuania. The materials he described sounded as if they might be potentially valuable, particularly a film of the mass executions carried out by Einsatzgruppe (mobile killing unit) A, which played a major role in the murder of the Jews in Lithuania and Latvia.

During the course of the visit Lubetzki also told me his own personal story which to some extent paralleled Kunichowsky's. A journalist by profession, Lubetzki had been born and raised in Lithuania. Prior to the Nazi invasion he escaped to the Soviet interior where he worked in his chosen field and closely followed, to whatever extent was then possible, the events in his native land. Immediately following the liberation of Lithuania, he returned home and began collecting material on the destruction of Lithuanian Jewry. He had, however, no realistic hope of ever being able to produce a film on that topic in the Soviet Union, so he waited until he came to Israel (also the fulfillment of what then seemed to be an impossible dream). Lubetzki left Russia during the large-scale Jewish emigration of the early 1970s and succeeded in bringing his material with him, an achievement which entailed a certain degree of risk. Following his arrival he set out to make his film, motivated by personal obligation (he lost many members of his family in the Holocaust) and ideological commitment, as well as by professional ambition.

Lubetzki enlisted the assistance of Yad Vashem, which provided him with funds to enable him to continue his research in various archives in Europe and the United States where he obtained valuable documentary material. The problem was, however, that Lubetzki ran out of money before he completed his research and he could not find a source which would allocate the necessary funds. When I met him the problem had reached an impasse. To complicate matters, he was in bad health and had ruined his relations with Yad Vashem because following his trip abroad he had not turned over to them as agreed the material he had collected.

Under these circumstances it was fairly difficult to reach any agreement with Lubetzki which would have assured us access to his material. I therefore merely tried to obtain as much information as possible about the contents of his collection and told him about our work at OSI. The maximum we could ostensibly hope for was a sudden change of heart or a large grant which would enable him to complete the film, both of which seemed unlikely. Nonetheless, I felt that we had some hope in this case because Lubetzki, unlike Kunichowsky, seemed at least willing to discuss the possibility of limited access or the exchange of OSI documents for his film footage. In this respect we were lucky that he had still not completed the film and were in a position to bargain with him.

Following my meeting with Lubetzki, I immediately reported to Neal Sher about the collection, noting that he had a film of the murders by Einsatzgruppe A. At the same time, I also reminded him, in view of his forthcoming visit to Israel, about the Kunichowsky collection. He appeared to be excited by the prospect of obtaining these materials and I know that he spoke to Allan Ryan regarding the matter. Ryan encouraged him to take whatever steps were necessary to obtain the material but refused to approve their purchase.

Shortly thereafter, I wrote to my former boss, Rabbi Marvin Hier, Dean of the Simon Wiesenthal Center in Los Angeles, in the hope that he might be willing to provide the funds to publish Kunichowsky's book and complete Lubetzki's film. Simultaneously, I turned to Member of Knesset Avraham Melamed of the National-Religious Party, a survivor of the Kovno Ghetto, who was also a leading member of the Knesset Finance Committee and a member of the Executive Committee of Yad Vashem. I appealed to him to become involved in this matter, noting that while I empathized with Kunichowsky who had expended so much time and energy in collecting the material, it was simply unthinkable that his stubbornness should prevent the prosecution of Nazi murderers. Melamed apparently agreed, because shortly afterwards he invited me to meet him at the Knesset to discuss the matter.

Our meeting turned out to be quite interesting, not only because the possibility of a solution emerged, but for personal reasons as well. Melamed, it turned out, had known my late grandfather Samuel L. Sar, and was personally acquainted with his activities on behalf of the survivors in DP camps in Germany. My grandfather had been sent from the United States to assist in their rehabilitation and had headed the Central Orthodox Committee, which was established to care for their religious needs. In his capacity as a leader of the Orthodox Zionist youth in occupied Germany at that time, Melamed had had frequent contact with him. He spoke very warmly about my grandfather and that undoubtedly made my task that much easier. I explained the problem to him and after a relatively brief discussion he said that he would make an effort to solve the matter. In the meantime he wanted me to find out exactly how much it would cost to publish Kunichowsky's collection and to attempt to involve other interested groups. If all else failed, he appeared ready to assume responsibility for the project and that was the only good news on the subject when Neal Sher arrived in Israel in mid-January 1982.

Despite the fact that Sher had planned to meet with both Kunichowsky and Lubetzki during the course of his visit, neither meeting worked out. Lubetzki was scheduled to meet with him, but he called in sick and the meeting never took place. Kunichowsky, for some reason unknown to me, was not included on the agenda prepared by the Nazi war crimes unit of the Israeli Police. I urged Neal nonetheless to take some action on this issue while in Israel, and he therefore called Kunichowsky prior to his departure. Their conversation turned out to be a classic Kunichowsky dialogue, complete with an open invitation to see the material but, of course, without any guarantee of unhampered access. Since Neal was about to return to the States and did not read

Yiddish, it was agreed that Lieutenant Aryeh Orbach of the Nazi war crimes unit of the Israeli police and a survivor of the Vilna Ghetto would peruse the collection and report to OSI on its contents. Orbach subsequently visited Kunichowsky and was duly impressed by the material, but unfortunately he soon suffered a severe heart attack which incapacitated him for several months. I cabled Neal about the results of Orbach's visit and in the meantime continued my efforts via other avenues such as MK Melamed, to whom I sent the figures on the projected cost of publishing Kunichowsky's magnum opus (387,468 old shekels, or approxiamtely $22,090, as of February 1982).

By April no progress had been made, and I was getting increasingly frustrated. I therefore called Yosef Achimei'er, a well-known journalist at *Ma'ariv*, who was also the son-in-law of Zelda Hayit, a survivor from Latvia who had testified in OSI cases and had always been particularly helpful. I explained the problem to him and suggested that his newspaper publish an expose on Kunichowsky in conjunction with the forthcoming observance of *Yom ha-Shoa* (Martyrs and Heroes Remembrance Day). Achimei'er promised to do his best, and I hopefully awaited the results. By this point, I should have known better.

The outcome was, to put it mildly, absolutely exasperating. Since Achimei'er did not read Yiddish, he turned the assignment over to Nurit Dovrat. She visited Kunichowsky but instead of being upset by his apparent stubbornness and its tragic implications, as I supposed she would have been, she came away convinced that he was right. In a feature article entitled "153 Files," which appeared in a special supplement published on Martyrs and Heroes Remembrance Day 1982, she wrote sympathetically of his predicament. Imagine my sense of frustration as I read Dovrat's description of the situation:

> Leib Kunichowsky has no intention of turning over the hundreds of testimonies and photographs to any old institution so that they can gather dust in basements. He wants his work to be recognized and to be useful both in searching for and in prosecuting war criminals and in helping survivors determine details about their families. Today, apathetic, alienated with a trace of pain and anger in his resolute voice, he asks, "Whom does this interest anyway? The Holocaust is over, forgotten."[13]

I tried to use the article to interest various politicians and journalists in the issue but to no avail. Deputy Minister Dov Shilansky, a survivor

from Lithuania whom I had previously turned to, reiterated his refusal
to become involved in an active manner and referred me to Yad
Vashem and the Ministry of Education. Several journalists were interested, but nothing came of it, and MK Melamed did not answer my letters. I even tried to utilize Nurit Dovrat's article by writing an acerbic
response to the "Letters to the Editor" column of *Ma'ariv* in which I
noted that it now appeared as if

> many Lithuanian war criminals would have "the last laugh" knowing
> that only the stubbornness of an old Jew on the one hand and the stu-
> pidity of the Jewish organizations which deal with the subject [of the
> Holocaust] on the other, prevented their being brought to the bar of
> justice and enabled them to live out their lives in peace and tranquil-
> lity.

To add insult to injury, *Ma'ariv* refused to publish the letter "for lack
of space." They did, however, send me Nurit Dovrat's response, which I
thought illuminating. It seems that the journalist had the distinct
impression that "the old Jew" (as I had described him) was not holding
out because of insufficient publicity but rather because he was

> a realistic man who knows that the numerous documents which he
> collected at great risk and with great effort and devotion will collect
> dust in the warehouses of Yad Vashem and will not receive the proper
> treatment which requires the appropriate sum of money and proper
> attitude.

In the meantime I again spoke to Kunichowsky who continued to
maintain his original position. His adamant refusal to cooperate coupled with Dovrat's response brought me to boiling-point. I was so frustrated and infuriated by what had happened that I decided to make at
least one last attempt to straighten matters out. On the chance that she
might not have understood the situation as I saw it, and in the hope
that perhaps something constructive might still be salvaged, I wrote to
Nurit Dovrat and recounted the entire story from the very beginning. I
pointed out that I had initiated the article and related the content of my
most recent conversation with Kunichowsky. I tried to muster all my
powers of persuasion, noting that it would be extremely unfortunate if
we were to lose a concrete opportunity to bring to trial those who had
murdered the Jews of Lithuania because we had been unable to obtain
access to Kunichowsky's material. There were already far too many

objective obstacles to the prosecution of Nazi war criminals 40 years after the events for Jews to add additional difficulties. I concluded the letter by offering to supply her with additional details regarding OSI, and noted that Kunichowsky was not unique and that there were other Jews in Israel who were withholding material of importance, thereby hampering the investigation of Nazi war criminals. I was hoping that Nurit Dovrat's curiosity in the issue would be aroused further and that perhaps she might deal with both Kunichowsky and Lubetzki in one article, but that was not the case.

The practical implications of our inability to obtain access to Kunichowsky's material became even clearer when I obtained a document from Yad Vashem which contained precise details on the contents of his collection. It had been prepared by Yad Vashem during the course of the negotiations they had conducted with Kunichowsky and noted the exact number of testimonies (and number of pages), photographs and maps from each one of the Lithuanian communities on which Kunichowsky had found material. The figures were indeed staggering—a veritable gold mine of information: 11 testimonies (197 pages) from the Alytus district; 15 testimonies (197 pages) from the Taurage district; 6 testimonies (97 pages) from the Telsiai district; 14 testimonies (145 pages) from the Raseiniai district, etc.[14] I sent OSI the document and practically begged Allan Ryan to do something in view of the enormous potential of the material. I suggested that perhaps Kunichowsky could be invited to the United States and wrote to Neal Sher and Steve Rogers, the historian in charge of the Lithuanian cases, to enlist their aid in convincing OSI to take action in this matter.

The response was almost immediate. Peter Black, a historian, and Kathleen Coleman, an attorney, were just about to leave for Israel to interview potential witnesses for the Trifa case and were instructed to attempt to make progress on "the Kunichowsky affair." I arranged for Chaya Lifshitz of Yad Vashem to brief them on the significance of the collection and Lieutenant-Colonel Russek of the Israeli police was to set up a meeting for Kathleen with Kunichowsky. At this point, however, the situation became more complicated. Until then, I had been the only person who had attempted to negotiate on OSI's behalf with Kunichowsky. Once Allan Ryan asked Kathleen and Peter to speak to him in Israel, it meant that the Nazi war crimes unit of the Israeli police, which handled all the arrangements for OSI staff from Washington who were on working visits in Israel, would become involved. Since this project was being undertaken upon my initiative, I had the distinct impression that they did not exhibit their usual cooperation. The reasons behind this negative attitude are discussed elsewhere in this book, but the fact remains that Lt. Col. Russek was far from enthusiastic about our efforts to obtain the collection. Throughout the visit by Peter and Kathleen, whenever the Kunichowsky material was mentioned, Russek appeared to belittle its importance and I had the impression that he only begrudgingly took care of the technical details which had to be arranged. In fact, at one point he told Kathleen that it would be a problem to review the material because no one on his staff spoke Yiddish, which was patently ridiculous. Yiddish was the mother tongue of several members of his staff and quite possibly of Russek as well.

I was very glad, therefore, that Allan Ryan cabled Kathleen and Peter in the course of their visit to make every effort to meet personally with Kunichowsky and obtain access to his material. Thanks to Allan Ryan's efforts, the meeting finally took place the day before Kathleen left Israel.

Kunichowsky was a gracious host and patiently explained the nature of the collection to Kathleen and even invited her to be his guest. Unfortunately, when it came to practical results his position remained the same, although at one point he did indicate that he might allow the material to be reproduced if a xerox machine were brought to his house. No agreement to this effect could be reached, however, and thus the situation remained stalemated. I cabled Allan Ryan and asked him to speak to Kunichowsky personally, but that never happened. To add insult to injury, about a week later I received a cable from Steve Rogers, the historian whose aid I had tried to enlist in convincing OSI to make an effort to obtain the Kunichowsky collection, indicating that he was busy preparing a "comprehensive request for information located in the Kunichowsky collection."

OSI did not relent, however, and a month and a half later Allan Ryan cabled me that Ruth Winter, an Israeli who had worked for the office in Washington for two years and had considerable experience in dealing with survivors, was returning to Israel. He hoped that with my assistance, she might be able "to get through to Kunichowsky." The problem was, however, that OSI either had nothing to offer or was not willing to offer anything of substance. Since Kunichowsky wanted something concrete, it was inevitable that under those circumstances our efforts would fail. I therefore cabled Ryan that the only possible way to succeed with Kunichowsky was to offer him something tangible, such as a trip to the United States in the course of which he could meet with publishers and attempt to arrange for the publication of his book. Ryan concurred but unfortunately did not consider the prospect of a tangible offer as likely at that point.

During the next few months the matter lay dormant. I attempted to persuade the Israeli media to do a major story on Kunichowsky, but despite initial interest on their part, nothing came of it. In 1984, the Kunichowsky affair ostensibly came to an end—at least as far as I was concerned. Plagued by bad health, Kunichowsky, returned to the United States briefcases in hand. I notified OSI and suggested that he be invited to Washington but once again it did not work out. About a year later I again suggested direct contact but again no positive results were achieved. More than seven years after I learned of the existence of the Kunichowsky collection, it still remained off-limits to researchers.

This situation suddenly changed in late 1989 in the wake of persistent efforts by Professor Dov Levin to persuade Kunichowsky to donate his collection to the Yad Vashem Archives. Undaunted by the repeated refusals of the Lithuanian survivor to cooperate with other agencies, Levin (himself a survivor of the Kovno Ghetto, a former partisan and leading historian on the fate of Lithuanian Jewry during the Holocaust) continued his attempts to persuade him to deposit the testimonies at Israel's premier repository of Holocaust documentation. These efforts suddenly bore fruit in September 1989 when Kunichowsky acceded to Levin's request. According to media reports, he did so because he was gettintg old and wanted to make sure that he fulfilled his pledge to commemorate the fate of the victims. In his words, "They yelled, 'Brothers and sisters, Yidden, please remember us! Take revenge for our poor blood!' And I didn't forget even for a minute of my life."[15]

By this point I was no longer working for OSI, but as the coordinator of Nazi war crimes research for the Simon Wiesenthal Center I was, needless to say, extremely excited when Dov Levin called to tell me that the Kunichowsky collection had at long last arrived in Jerusalem. Even more important was his assessment, based on an initial review of several of the testimonies, that the material had superb potential for war crimes research. He urged me therefore to make every effort to review all the material as quickly as possible. This task was entrusted to my father Rabbi Dr. Abraham N. Zuroff, who has a superb command of "Lithuanian"Yiddish, and carried out the project quickly and efficiently.

Together we compiled a master-list of the criminals mentioned in the collection. Only after doing so, did we realize just how valuable Kunichowsky's material actually was. Unlike the majority of those who interviewd Holocaust survivors, Kunichowsky made a special effort to record the names of all the local collaborators who participated in the murders, and the results of his efforts were indeed exceptional. A total of 1,284 local participants in the persecution and murder of the Jews in 171 Lithuanian communites are named in the 160 files (1,684 pages) of the Kunichowsky collection, a veritable gold mine of data on the criminals. Given the fact that we previously possessed information on only 163 of the perpetrators named by the witnesses interviewed by Kunichowsky, the importance of his collection becomes evident. Kunichowsky, it should be noted, was meticulous in his research and had each page of testimony (all recorded in Yiddish in his neat longhand script) signed by the survivor and the testimonies authorized by the local historical commission to ensure their authenticity.

In short, the collection was invaluable and should have been accessible decades ago. Indeed our investigation of the names mentioned in the testimonies led to the by this point hardly surprising discovery that hundreds of the perpetrators had escaped at the end of the war to Germany and from there had emigrated to the United States, Canada, Australia and other western countries. Their names were submitted by the Wiesenthal Center to the governments in question, but the precious years lost during which the Kunichowsky collection was inaccessible to Nazi-hunters, irreparably harmed the chances of bringing these criminals to justice.

The stories related above reflect on an integral part of the daily work of Nazi-hunting. Day in and day out those engaged in this type of research find themselves dependent not only on the existence of evidence but also on the work invested in preparing it for use, as well as on the whims and caprices of those who possess valuable documentation. In this field it is difficult to countenance human errors, even those committed inadvertently, because of their tragic implications. It is even more difficult to understand how Jews, and especially survivors, can for their own reasons impede the prosecution of the murderers of their brethren. As hard as it might be to believe, both types of cases are a common occurrence in this profession.

Notes

1. "Skaudville," *Yahadut Lita*, Vol. IV, p. 372.

2. Approximately 150,000 Jews lived in Lithuania prior to the Second World War. After the outbreak of the war approximately 95,000 additional Jews were added to the total—80,000 from the area of Vilnius which was incorporated into Lithuania and 15,000 Polish refugees, seeking to flee the German or Soviet occupation. From this number about 25,000 must be deducted, 15,000 of whom succeeded in escaping to the Soviet Union prior to the Nazi takeover. In addition approximately 7,000 Jews were deported by the Communists to the Soviet interior in June 1941, and several thousand, primarily Polish refugees, managed to emigrate from Lithuania during the year of Soviet rule before the Nazi occupation.

3. Of the approximately 220,000 Jews who remained in Lithuania under Nazi rule, only 8,000 survived, very few from the provincial towns who hid with the assistance of Lithuanians. The majority of the survivors were from the ghettos of Vilna, Kovno and Shavli, many of whom were deported to German concentration camps in 1944. Arad—*Yad Vashem Studies*, pp. 234, 272; Garfunkel, *Yahadut Lita*, pp. 48-60; Dov Levin, "Lithuania," *Encyclopedia of the Holocaust*, New York, 1990, Vol. III, pp. 895-899.

4. Testimony of Ella Kagan, YVA, M-l/E-1235/1201; testimony of E. Skaudviller, YVA, M-l/E-1390/1341.

5. The holdings of the Moreshet Archives are outlined in detail in Yehuda Bauer (ed.), *Guide to the Unpublished Materials of the Holocaust Period*, Vol. VI, Jerusalem, 1981.

6. The catalogue consulted was the Hebrew edition, which was published two years before its English-language counterpart. Shmuel Krakowski (ed.), *Madrich le-Archiyon Moreshet be-Givat Chaviva*, Jerusalem, 1979, p. 79.

7. Testimony of Yoseph Ben-Yaakov, Moreshet Archives, A. 401.

8. Rob Warden and Margaret Roberts, "The Walus Prosecution—A Review," *Chicago Lawyer*, Vol. 4, No. 1 (January 1981), p. 8.

9. *Quiet Neighbors*, p. 356.

10. Among his more notable works were: *Yerushalayim de-Lita be-Meri u-ba-Shoa*, Tel Aviv, 1958; *Machanot ha-Yehudim be-Estonia*, Jerusalem, 1970. The first recounts the history of the Jews of Vilna during the Holocaust; the second tells of the camps in Estonia to which many Jews from the Vilna Ghetto were deported in the latter stages of the war.

11. Jankiel Wiernik, *Rok w Treblince*, Warsaw, 1944; Yankel Wiernik, *A Year in Treblinka*, New York, n.d.; Wiernik's book was also published in Hebrew (*Pinkas Katan-Shana be-Treblinka; (Mi-Pi Eid Re'eyah)*, Tel Aviv, 1944) and Yiddish (*A Yahr in Treblinke*, New York, 1944).

12. Testimony of Yankel Wiernik, *Mishpat Eichman; Eiduyot*, Vol . II, 1084-

88.

13. Testimony of Yaakov Wiernik, Institute for Holocaust Research, Bar-Ilan University, testimony vav-7.

14. Nurit Dovrat, "153 Tikkim," *Ma'ariv,* April 20, 1982, p. 21.

15. Document in possession of the author.

16. Elinor J. Brecher, "A 45-year Crusade to Fulfill a Vow," *Miami Herald,* December 22, 1989; Elli Wohlgelernter, "A List of 1,300 War Criminals Comes to Light after 44 Years," *JTA Daily News Bulletin,* December 21, 1989.

5

The Mengele Case—
The Evolution of a Rumor

Of the numerous cases I investigated in the course of the six years I worked for OSI, none was more intriguing but at the same time more frustrating than the Mengele investigation. Accustomed to searching for documents and witnesses to substantiate crimes committed, I suddenly found myself trying to determine whether an arrest had taken place and whether the prisoner had subsequently been released. Trained to investigate the atrocities committed during the Holocaust, I spent months searching for details on an event which paled in significance to those horrors and ultimately proved to be no more than a rumor.

The background to this investigation is particularly illuminating vis-à-vis the search for Nazi war criminals and the efforts to bring them to justice. By the time this project had been completed, three governments had spent hundreds of thousands, if not millions, of dollars to apprehend the infamous "Angel of Death." The truth of the matter is, however, that if not for a seemingly innocuous letter sent by the Simon Wiesenthal Center to the US government archives in late 1984, the massive manhunt which ultimately led to the discovery of his remains would never have been launched.

On October 25, 1984 the Wiesenthal Center wrote to the National Archives requesting all available documentation on Josef Mengele and all his known aliases.[1] This request was not based on any knowledge of specific documentation in the archives, but was simply an intuitive guess regarding an avenue of research which the Center thought should be investigated. The results of that hunch are perhaps the ultimate proof that in this field every possible lead should be thoroughly examined. Among the documents which the Wiesenthal Center received was a letter dated April 26, 1947 by Benjamin Gorby, an American intelligence officer of the 970th Counter Intelligence Corps (CIC) of the US Army in occupied Germany. According to Gorby, his office had received information from a CIC agent that Dr. Mengele had been arrested and subsequently released by the American authorities in Vienna.[2]

The Wiesenthal Center, undoubtedly surprised by the revelations in the documentation, immediately mounted a campaign for a full-scale investigation of American involvement in the Mengele case. This effort, combined with the impact of the public hearings held at Yad Vashem by the CANDLES organization (the victims of Mengele's pseudoscientific experiments at Auschwitz) regarding Mengele's heinous crimes led to the decision by the United States government, announced on February 6, 1985 by Attorney-General William French Smith, to conduct a full-scale investigation of the Mengele case. The American inquiry was to examine three questions: whether Mengele had indeed been arrested and released by the American authorities in 1946; whether he had ever entered the United States; and most important, his present whereabouts. The task of determining the answers to the first two questions was entrusted to the Office of Special Investigations, while the search for the war criminal was assigned to the US Marshals Service.[3]

The American decision to launch a full-scale search for the infamous Auschwitz doctor was undoubtedly a turning-point in the decades-long effort to apprehend the "Angel of Death." What had been reduced during the previous 20 years to a totally unsuccessful competition between private Nazi-hunters suddenly became a multi-government effort when West Germany and Israel, encouraged and/or embarrassed by the American efforts, joined forces with the United States to launch an exhaustive search for the person who had become the most notorious Nazi criminal thought to be alive. It seems fairly obvious, therefore, that if not for the American involvement, the world would still believe today that Mengele was alive and in hiding in Paraguay. The case proves, in fact, why governments are best-equipped to take action against Nazi war criminals. The problem, however, is that governments invariably refuse or are reluctant to become involved until prodded or forced into action by private agencies and/or public opinion. The Mengele case provides an excellent example of how these forces can be successfully combined. Unfortunately, that has not always been the case.

Shortly after the Attorney-General's announcement, OSI began to investigate whether Mengele had been arrested and released by the American authorities, an investigation that would last for months and prove to be nearly as baffling as Mengele's whereabouts had been over the years. On April 16, 1985 OSI historian David Marwell, who was my liaison with the office and also in charge of the historical research on the Mengele investigation, gave me my first assignment on the case. He asked me to look for mention of Mengele's arrest during the immediate post-war period and told me a little bit about the material that OSI had already found. According to Marwell, the office had uncovered evidence that testimony regarding Mengele's crimes had been collected by a Jewish committee in Eggenfelden, Germany and that the Poles had sought to extradite the Auschwitz physician. At this point, however, there was no conclusive evidence of the arrest. It was not known exactly where he had been arrested, by whom, and if so where he had been held. The rumors regarding Mengele's arrest had circulated from December 1946 until March 1947, but that too was not absolutely certain. The entire story seemed unclear, to put it mildly.

I began my research at the Yad Vashem Archives by checking the information regarding Eggenfelden, where testimony had supposedly been collected regarding Mengele's crimes. That turned out to be a good starting point because those documents helped explain why testimony had been collected, and provided some leads regarding the supposed arrest.[4] I subsequently learned that in early 1947 the Central Committee of Liberated Jews in Germany had asked its committees in the various DP camps and other communities to establish local, legal committees to collect evidence and testimony from survivors.[5] This step was designed to facilitate the work of the Legal Department established by the Central Committee to play an active role in the prosecution of Nazi war criminals. A legal committee was established in Eggenfelden in March 1947, and one of its first activities was to collect testimony against "Dr. Mengele who was arrested in Vienna."[6] This was the first concrete evidence I found which indicated that such an arrest had indeed taken place. Moreover, it noted the site of the arrest, Vienna, another valuable piece of information. It also led me to the most important institution involved at that time in attempts by survivors to bring Nazis to justice—the abovementioned Legal Department of the Central Committee, an agency which ostensibly should have been able to provide a conclusive answer to our queries regarding Mengele. Luckily, the Central Committee's archives were at Yad Vashem, so our chances of unearthing the facts appeared fairly promising.

I reported my initial findings to David Marwell who shared my optimism and enthusiasm. I also suggested that efforts be made to interview the individuals who worked for the Legal Department in Munich, one of whom—Joseph Riwosch or Riwash—was at that time living in Montreal. At the same time I proposed that it might be worthwhile to look in an entirely different direction and interview those individuals who were involved in revenge attempts after the war, as Mengele was probably high on their list of potential targets. Based on my initial research regarding their activities,[7] I thought that they might be able to provide information concerning Mengele's postwar whereabouts and whether or not he had been arrested and released in 1946. Most of those who had played an active role in these efforts were alive and living in Israel and it would therefore be relatively easy for me to interview them.

OSI agreed with the proposal, but not with the tactics, and insisted that the interviews be conducted by someone from Washington. In the meantime, therefore, I continued my search in the Yad Vashem Archives, after sending them a list of names and addresses of the individuals living in Israel whom I thought should be interviewed. Among the persons I suggested were: Abba Kovner, Vilna partisan leader and poet, who played a key role in the plans for mass revenge against the Germans after the war; Asher Ben Natan, the Israeli diplomat who was in charge of the Jewish Agency office in Vienna for two years and under whose auspices the efforts to capture Nazi criminals were conducted, as well as less well-known "avengers" such as Manus Diament, Dov Ben-Yaakov and Eli Tanzi.

Meanwhile my research at Yad Vashem was progressing very rapidly. On the day after I cabled OSI with my suggestion about the avengers, I discovered additional evidence regarding the arrest. The documents which I found indicated that the legal committee in Eggenfelden was not the only one collecting testimony against Mengele. In fact, committees in five additional DP camps and/ or survivor communities (Moosburg, Wasseralfingen, Bad Reichenhall, Haustein and Vilseck) were engaged in the same activity.[8] Most importantly, the documentation revealed the basis for this widespread activity—reports in three different newspapers published by survivors that Dr. Mengele had been arrested. The newspapers in question were: *Moment* (March 24, 1947);[9] *Undzer Weg* (March 21, 1947);[10] and *Undzer Wort* (March 28, 1947).[11]

I immediately began searching for these newspapers, hoping to be able to find additional details regarding the arrest. Luckily, Yad Vashem has an excellent collection of publications published in the DP camps and within a relatively short time I was able to obtain the original articles in *Undzer Weg* and *Undzer Wort*. The content of these articles proved quite surprising because they clearly indicated that the Mengele of 1985, who had become a symbol of evil and the personification of the perversion of science, did not enjoy the same notoriety in 1947. The information regarding Mengele appeared on the back page in each of the newspapers (the wording of the articles was identical) among various notices published at the request of the Legal Department of the Central Committee. And while Mengele did merit a subheading with an exclamation mark in *Undzer Wort* ("Mengele is arrested!"), the notice in *Undzer Weg* was published under the caption "Inmate from Auschwitz" in a notice calling upon survivors of that camp to testify against Georg Deffner of the SS and Mengele in that order. According to the notice, Mengele had been arrested in Vienna. Those with any knowledge of his crimes were asked to either write to, or appear in person at, the Munich offices of the Legal Department of the Central Committee.

There were several interesting things about the notice published in these newspapers. First of all, it contained several factual mistakes. Mengele was referred to as "*SS-Obersturmfuhrer* (Lieutenant) *Hauptarzt* (chief doctor) *phun KZ lager Auschwitz*," when in effect he had attained the rank of *Hauptsturmführer* (Captain), but was not the chief doctor of the camp. (Dr. Eduard Wirths was the chief physician, Mengele was the senior doctor at the women's camp in Birkenau.[12]) Moreover, from the wording of the notice and the place it appeared in the newspapers, it was obvious that Mengele was not considered a very high-ranking criminal, nor was his supposed arrest regarded as an event of exceptional significance. Had that been the case, the DP press would obviously have accorded the news and the request for witnesses far more prominence. I do not know who Georg Deffner is, but, if he had recently been caught at the same time as Mengele, I find it hard to imagine him getting equal billing.

This notice was, in effect, the first indication that the status of the infamous "Angel of Death" had grown by leaps and bounds over the years. This feeling was significantly reinforced in the course of a lengthy meeting I had in early May 1985 at Yad Vashem with Joseph Riwash, who had headed the Legal Department of the Central Committee for several years after the war.[13] The Legal Department had issued the call for witnesses against Mengele, yet Riwash, who has an excellent memory, did not remember Mengele being arrested or his office dealing with the case. This was a clearcut indication to me that the person we were looking for was, in a certain sense, not the same person who was simultaneously being hunted in South America. Ultimately, this factor was to play a very important role in our historical investigation.

The questions raised by these notices and my meeting with Riwash did not in any way affect the investigation. I continued my research at Yad Vashem, finding valuable new material practically every day. Sometimes it was another newspaper which carried the news of Mengele's arrest and a call for witnesses, sometimes a testimony of a survivor of Auschwitz. By early May 1985 I had already found six different publications that had publicized news of Mengele's arrest.[14] Unfortunately, none added any new details. In fact, the wording of each item was practically identical. All were published at approximately the same time and probably stemmed from the same source. Although we seemed to be making progress, we hardly had found any specific details of the arrest. All we knew was that Mengele had apparently been arrested in Vienna, that as early as March 1947 news to that effect and a call for witnesses had been publicized by the Legal Department of the Central Committee in various Jewish newspapers in Germany, and that as a result of that appeal survivors in various places began to submit testimony regarding the crimes he had committed in Auschwitz. We still did not know who had arrested him, when he had been apprehended, where he had been held, where he was to be tried, and by whom.

In the meantime OSI was quite busy attempting to find additional parts of this historical jigsaw puzzle. On May 10, 1985 David Marwell notified me that he had found someone named Daniel or Danielski Mordka whose name had been linked to the news of Mengele's arrest and who probably knew the details. I immediately realized that David, who was not fluent in Hebrew or Yiddish, had obviously mixed up the person's first and last names. (Indeed, David eventually found Mordechai Danielski or Milton Daniels in Chicago.) This was, in effect, the first serious lead regarding the origin of the news concerning Mengele's arrest. At the same time, David also asked me to find a newspaper named *Der Mahnruf* which appeared in Vienna and which might have published information on the events in question.

This lead led to another breakthrough because *Der Mahnruf* was one of the first newspapers to publish news of Mengele's arrest. In its January 31, 1947 issue, the magazine, published by the Austrian victims of

Fascism, publicized the fact that Mengele had been arrested and called for witnesses to submit testimony. Unlike the notices which appeared in the Jewish press, this item was highlighted and appeared in the form of a quarter-page spread (on page 24) in which Mengele was described as "one of the most important war criminals . . . who sent hundreds of thousands to the gas chambers"[15] It was obvious from the details in *Der Mahnruf* that the supposed arrest had taken place at least six to eight weeks before the news to that effect was published in the DP press. We therefore returned to the archives looking for material in a slightly different time framework, but still fairly convinced that the events in question had indeed taken place.

About two weeks later, in late May 1985, I thought I made a significant and very surprising breakthrough. While searching in the Yad Vashem Archives for additional information regarding the arrest, I came across the files of the Jewish Historical Documentation Center which had operated in Vienna during the late 1940s. The archives of this organization, which had played an active role in post war efforts to prosecute Nazi war criminals, appeared to be a potential gold mine for the type of documentation we were seeking. As it turned out, I was not mistaken. I found numerous documents in the archives which referred specifically to the arrest, shed new light on the events and raised some fascinating new possibilities. Ironically, the most interesting document in the collection was written by an individual whom I have known for years. As I was sitting in the Yad Vashem Library perusing the documents, he was in his office right across the hall, intensively engaged (as he has been for the past 40 years) in Holocaust research. The documents from Vienna related the following story.

On June 19, 1947 the Jewish Historical Documentation Centre of Vienna wrote to the Central Jewish Historical Commission of Lodz, Poland, to inquire whether Dr. Mengele was in custody in Poland. The basis for the inquiry was that the Center had testimony regarding Mengele's crimes and wanted, if need be, to send it to Poland.[16] The Lodz Commission replied, in a letter dated July 30, 1947 from Dr. Joseph Kermish (secretary-general) and Nachman Blumental (manager) that

> Dr. Mengele, the former chief doctor of Auschwitz, was extradited to Poland in the first group of German war criminals who were active in Auschwitz. The investigation is continuing. A trial date has still not been set. The trial will not take place in Auschwitz as originally

planned, but rather—for technical reasons—in Cracow and we therefore ask you to send us the material in your possession as quickly as
possible.[17]

One can imagine how shocked I was when I had this document
translated from Polish by one of the workers at Yad Vashem. I had to
restrain myself from exhibiting my intense excitement in view of the
confidential nature of the investigation.

This was not the only document in the files of the Vienna Documentation Center which related to Mengele's arrest. The archives contained
numerous documents written in the summer of 1947 in which the best
means of transferring the evidence from Vienna to Lodz were discussed,
which indicates that throughout that period the people in Vienna operated on the assumption that the Auschwitz doctor had indeed been
arrested and extradited.[18] Apparently I had uncovered a new direction
in the investigation. To add to my excitement, Dr. Joseph Kermish, the
man who ostensibly held the key to the mystery, one of the two individuals who had written the letter to Vienna informing the Jewish Historical Documentation Center that Mengele was in Poland awaiting trial
was a personal acquaintance whom I had known for many years and
whom I saw practically every day at Yad Vashem. The answer to our
questions appeared to have been literally almost within reach all along,
without our having realized that that was the case.

Under those circumstances the most natural reaction would have
been to drop everything and run to Dr. Kermish's office and show him
the document. For some reason, however, I held back. I knew that my
super-circumspect bosses in Washington would not appreciate my alac-
rity in this matter, so in the meantime I relished my discovery and hurried to Tel Aviv to cable OSI. In retrospect, I think that there was
something else besides the constraints of confidentiality which
restrained me from immediately asking Dr. Kermish about the letter. I
sensed that there was something strange about the whole story. Was it
possible that Mengele had been extradited to stand trial in Poland and
had escaped? Obviously such a development could not have been kept a
secret and there was no mention of any such incident in any of the
accounts of Mengele's life. Could he possibly have been released by the
Poles? That was also highly unlikely. I therefore sensed that perhaps the
Polish scenario had never actually taken place, in which case we were
back to where we started from. I think that was the reason I held back.

I simply wanted to enjoy the satisfaction, however temporary, of having uncovered *the* document which ostensibly solved the mystery.

Besides the letter by Kermish and Blumental, there were numerous documents of interest in the archives of the Vienna Documentation Center. There was a letter, for example, which referred to Mordechai Danielski, the mysterious informant now living in Chicago. According to the letter, the Jewish community of Vienna had asked Danielski where Mengele was being held but he had not yet replied. This document confirmed my suspicion that David had mixed up Danielski's first and last names. It also confirmed the information we possessed regarding his role. Interestingly, a copy of this letter was sent to "Mr. Arthur,"[19] or Asher Ben-Natan who headed the Jewish Agency's office in Vienna, which was involved in some of the operations against Nazi war criminals. This letter reinforced my initial suggestion to David Marwell that we interview Ben-Natan who, after serving abroad for many years as Israeli ambassador to France and Germany, was alive and well in Israel.

The Vienna collection also contained a fairly large number of statements by survivors which enabled me to draw several important conclusions. One was that the news regarding Mengele's arrest had been publicized as early as December 1946. Another conclusion was that the news had been reported not only in Germany and Austria but in Rumania, Hungary and Holland as well. We also learned the names of at least four additional newspapers which publicized the story.[20]

This information was supplemented by additional reports regarding Mengele's arrest which I found in early June 1985 at the Israeli National Library on the campus of the Hebrew University. Two stories which appeared in Palestinian dailies added to the data in our possession and ostensibly confirmed the information in the files of the Vienna Jewish Historical Documentation Center. The first story appeared on January 24, 1947 in the Revisionist Zionist daily *Ha-Mashkif*. Entitled "The Arrest of the Monster from Auschwitz," the article, which was based on a Jewish Telegraphic Agency release from Bucharest, related that the Poles had already demanded Mengele's extradition and that the news of his arrest and possible extradition had aroused considerable excitement among the Jews of Transylvania "many of whom were victimized by him and only thanks to a miracle were rescued from his clutches." The article added that *Igipssag*, the Jewish weekly in Cluj, Rumania, was collecting evidence regarding Mengele's crimes and that a group of Auschwitz survivors had already asked the government for permission to attend the trial which was to take place shortly in Warsaw.[21] The second article, which appeared on May 30, 1947 in the Socialist Zionist daily *Davar*, confirmed the Polish extradition request and added an important piece of new information. According to *Davar*, the Polish request had been submitted to "the American authorities in Germany."[22] This was the first evidence that Mengele had indeed been arrested by the Americans. It now appeared as if we were on the right track and what remained to be done was to find proof that the events reported in the press had actually transpired. These reports confirmed that the Polish angle had to be thoroughly investigated and reinforced my original suggestion to David Marwell that an effort be made to interview Israeli professor Marian Mushkat, who had served in Germany as an officer with the Polish Military War Crimes Commission during the period in question.

The story of Mengele's death by drowning in Brazil had been publicized in the meantime, and OSI director Neal Sher went to Sao Paulo to participate in the investigation. The news came as a total shock. Even though I never had participated in the search for Mengele, I always assumed that he was alive and that the problem was "merely" to find and apprehend him. With three governments engaged in the search and more than three million dollars offered as prize money, the situation appeared for the first time to be fairly promising.[23] Perhaps that is why I was initially skeptical about the news of Mengele's death, as were many of my colleagues at Yad Vashem. For years, moreover, we had been fed a steady diet of Mengele "sightings" and were justifiably convinced of the deviousness of the doctor and his helpers, all of which combined to strengthen the doubts regarding the story which emanated from Brazil. We anxiously awaited word from Sao Paulo that the entire episode was another hoax perpetrated by the former Nazis and their sympathizers.

These developments did not affect our historical investigation which proceeded apace. If anything, the pressure on us was reduced because if the story regarding Mengele were true, we would have more time to complete our investigation, the element of urgency having been eliminated. As the forensic experts examined the remains exhumed from the cemetery in Embu outside Sao Paulo, OSI continued its efforts to corroborate events which had occurred 40 years earlier.

These efforts soon bore fruit in Israel. Shortly after the news of Mengele's death in Brazil was publicized, I found additional evidence indicating American involvement in Mengele's arrest. This time it was in the form of a report published by the Jewish Telegraphic Agency in its daily news bulletin of January 5, 1947. Datelined January 3 Warsaw, the report clearly indicated that Mengele was being held by the Americans. It also noted that he had recently been "captured near Berlin" and that it was expected that "the American authorities will accede to the Polish request for his extradition since most of the witnesses who can testify on his activities reside in Poland."[24] This assertion was historically questionable (numerous Hungarian Jews had also suffered at Mengele's hands), but that hardly mattered vis-à-vis our investigation. In addition, I found the source of the article which had appeared in *Ha-Mashkif* on January 24, 1947 and discovered that an important fact had been omitted. While the Revisionist daily had indeed noted that the Poles had submitted an extradition request for Mengele, it neglected to mention to whom that request had been directed. The JTA report of January 23, 1947, which was the source on which the *Ha-Mashkif* article had been based, stated specifically that the Poles' request had been submitted to "the American occupation authorities in Germany,"[25] further proof of US involvement in the arrest of the Auschwitz physician.

Several days later, on June 11, 1985, David Marwell told me that he had obtained copies of the Hungarian newspapers that had publicized Mengele's arrest. According to Marwell, one of the reports specifically stated that Mordechai Danielski and D. Freimann had sent information regarding Mengele's arrest in the American-occupied zone of Germany to Dr. Otto Wolkan, the editor of *Neue Weg* and the head of the Vienna organization of Jewish former concentration camp inmates. That meant that those three individuals held the key to our investigation. Wolkan, however, had already passed away so we were left with two major leads, one of whom had been unable or unwilling to help us. Danielski had told David Marwell that he did not remember anything concerning an arrest of Mengele, so our hopes now centered on D. Freimann. My major objective became to find out whatever information I could about him, a task which appeared to me after two months of intensive research on the case to be practically hopeless. In the course of our phone conversation, Marwell also related that there was no indication in the records of the Polish war crimes commission of any request for the extradition of Dr. Mengele, a finding which cast serious doubt on the evidence we had so far uncovered. I suggested that perhaps Mengele had been arrested, but was either released or had escaped before a formal extradition request could be filed. Marwell agreed that such a scenario was a possibility, but it was obvious to both of us that we needed more substantive evidence before we could draw conclusions with any degree of certainty.

In the meantime the reports out of Brazil and Austria in late June seemed to indicate that perhaps our historical investigation, as well as the search for Mengele, had been in vain. The pathologists in Brazil seemed to concur that the remains exhumed in Embu were almost certainly those of Mengele and the Austrian weekly *Bunte* published an in-depth account of Mengele's postwar life which indicated that there was no evidence that he had been arrested under his own name by the Americans in late 1946. According to *Bunte*, he had been arrested under a different name immediately after the end of the war and had also been jailed by the Italians prior to his departure for South America, but there was no confirmation of the story heard by Benjamin Gorby.[26] The *Bunte* report confirmed our research but, given the severity of Mengele's crimes and the public uproar in the wake of the Gorby letter, we wanted to be absolutely certain of our conclusions. Since we had by that time been unable to find any documents to corroborate Mengele's arrest, the only remaining avenue of investigation was to speak to the participants themselves. On July 1, 1985 Neal Sher informed me that he would be coming to Israel shortly for that purpose and I prepared a list of eight persons who I thought might be able to provide useful information. Among them were "avengers" (Abba Kovner and Asher Ben-Natan) as well as individuals who played an active role in the efforts to prosecute Nazi war criminals (Dr. Marian Mushkat and Mr. Blumstein of the Legal Department of the Central Committee of Liberated Jews). At the same time, I also cabled OSI the names of all those who had worked at the various offices in Vienna which dealt with Jewish relief and rehabilitation work, historical documentation, and the prosecution of Nazi war criminals in case OSI would want to have them interviewed as well. (I assumed that the majority, if alive, were living in Israel.)

The first person we spoke to was the noted Israeli poet Abba Kovner who had been one of the leaders of a group which planned mass revenge against the Germans after the war. We hoped that he might be able to provide us with information on the efforts to apprehend Mengele, the assumption being that had the "Angel of Death" been arrested, the avengers would have known about it. Unfortunately, Kovner did not provide us with any new information. Although he was obviously anxious to help, and warmly encouraged us to continue our efforts, he knew nothing about Mengele's arrest. The Auschwitz doctor, in fact, had not even been one of his high-priority targets.[27]

The next day we met with Asher Ben-Natan who for two years had headed the Jewish Agency's office in Vienna and Professor Marian Mushkat, who had headed the Polish Military War Crimes Commission. Ben-Natan did not have any information regarding Mengele whose capture had not been a priority for the representatives of the Jewish Agency. Ben-Natan spent most of his time in Vienna organizing the *Bricha*, the mass escape of Jewish survivors from Eastern Europe to DP camps in occupied Germany and Italy, from whence they hoped to emigrate to Eretz Yisrael (Palestine). His efforts vis-à-vis Nazi war criminals focused primarily on Adolf Eichmann and his lieutenants. According to Ben Natan, the Americans had indeed arrested and released a high-ranking Nazi criminal, but the person in question was Alois Brunner, one of Eichmann's top aides (presently living in Syria), not Mengele. Ben-Natan noted, moreover, that Brunner had been released even though he had been identified and separated from the rest of the prisoners as a result of Ben-Natan's efforts. That information, while undoubtedly of historical significance, did not assist us in our investigation. If anything, it provided the basis for an additional inquiry regarding America's failure to apprehend and prosecute numerous prominent Nazi war criminals.

By the time we met with Professor Mushkat late that afternoon, we were already beginning to doubt seriously whether the interviews would be any more illuminating than the documents had been. So far no one seemed to know anything about Mengele's arrest and nearly everyone seemed to confirm that during those years the Auschwitz doctor had not been ranked very high on the list of Nazi war criminals at large. Yet just when it appeared as if our efforts had been for naught, we finally found a plausible explanation regarding Mengele's supposed arrest by the American authorities.

In his capacity as head of the Polish Military Mission in Germany after the Second World War, Professor Mushkat attempted to persuade the Allies to extradite Nazi war criminals to Poland. During the interrogation of one of the high-ranking defendants in the Auschwitz trial—

Mushkat thinks that it was Hans Aumeier, one of the commanders of Auschwitz I—he was told that Mengele had been arrested by the Americans. Without further investigation, Mushkat immediately submitted an extradition request to the American authorities in Germany. In addition, he subsequently publicized the request at a press conference,[29] and in this manner the news of Mengele's "arrest" spread throughout Europe. There it was! For the first time we had a logical explanation of how everyone seemed to know that Mengele had been arrested when in fact there was no evidence whatsoever that such an arrest had ever taken place. We had finally arrived at the scenario which for so long had managed to elude us.

The rest of the interviews we conducted did not shed any new light on the events or in any way reflect on the developments described by Mushkat. According to Manus Diament, Mengele was approximately number ten on the list of war criminals whom the "avengers" were looking for, but he knew nothing about his arrest.[30]

During the next few weeks I checked out a few additional leads and loose ends. One important conversation was conducted with Dr. Kermish. As I initially suspected, he did not remember anything about Mengele's supposed arrest and extradition to Poland. When I showed him the letter he and Blumental had written to Tuvia Friedman in Vienna he was practically speechless. The only explanation that he could offer was that at the time he apparently really thought that Mengele had been arrested and extradited. Dr. Kermish did confirm, however, that the scenario presented by Mushkat was feasible and I think that he was a bit relieved when I told him about Mushkat's press conference, as it provided him with an explanation for his letter to Friedman. During this period I also investigated whether Mengele's name had appeared on various lists of Nazi war criminals prepared during and immediately after the war. It did not appear on the lists compiled by the Jewish Agency, but it was on the wanted lists issued by the United Nations War Crimes Commission—list no. 8—May 1945, criminal no. 240.[31]

By late July 1985 I had concluded the research conducted in Israel in connection with the Mengele investigation. Based on the findings, it seemed fairly certain that Mengele had not been arrested and that all the reports to that effect, including the news of his extradition to Poland, were in reality no more than rumors, fuelled perhaps by a good dose of wishful thinking. In this case our own preconceived notions were one of the biggest obstacles in the investigation. Having been raised on decades of conspiracy stories about Mengele, his postwar escape to South America and his ability to elude his pursuers, it seemed only natural to suppose that he had been arrested by the Americans and somehow managed to escape. In reality there was no conclusive evidence that the arrest had ever taken place and we had to overcome our inclination to view the story as an integral part of the "reality" presented for countless years by enterprising journalists and eager Nazi-hunters.

Another aspect which proved problematic was that the person whom we were searching for—the Mengele of 1946-47—was far less notorious than the fugitive sought by the US marshals. The Auschwitz doctor had, in the interim, become a symbol of Nazi evil and the perversion of science. This was one of the keys to our investigation. Had Mengele in 1946 been the notorious criminal that he ultimately became, I am certain that the events would have been fully clarified at that time. Under those circumstances it would have been impossible for such a rumor to exist for such a long time.

At this point I thought that I had completed my role in the Mengele investigation. However, on August 9, 1985 David Marwell called and asked me to try to find David Freimann who, along with Danielski, had been one of the informants regarding Mengele's arrest. Since Marwell had not succeeded in obtaining any information from Danielski, Freimann represented our last hope of possibly determining what had actually happened from the participants themselves. In the interim Marwell had uncovered several facts about Freimann which he hoped might prove helpful. According to David, Freimann had been an inmate clerk at the Hygiene Institute in Auschwitz and as of September 1946 was living at Wiesenhutten Street in Frankfurt am Main, Germany. My first step in searching for Freimann was to go to the Israeli population registry to check whether any persons with that name were living in Israel. Although the lists are computerized, using them is very difficult because they do not include or indicate name changes. Thus if someone arrived in Israel as David Freimann and subsequently changed his name to David Ben-Chorin (the Hebrew equivalent of Freimann) there would be no indication that a person named David Freimann had ever lived in Israel. The same applied to name changes as a result of marriage, but thank God, it was a male we were looking for in this case. It was obvious that there were no short cuts available and that the search would probably prove quite difficult, with absolutely no guarantee of success. Given the fact that we had no proof whatsoever that Freimann was living, or had ever lived, in Israel, this investigation did not appear particularly promising. Despite the abovementioned difficulties, the initial results of the search in the population registry were not entirely negative. According to my calculations, Freimann had to have been born in Europe prior to 1925 at the latest, and to have immigrated to Israel after the Second World War. Our most promising candidate was a David Freimann of Kfar Sava who had been born in Poland in 1908 and had arrived in Israel in 1950. Less likely was a David Freimann who had been born in England in 1901 and had been living in Haifa. Since the latter had just passed away several months previously, it was extremely important that he not be the Freimann in question.

As it turned out, neither of the individuals whose names were found in the population registry were the Freimann I was looking for. The more promising candidate had been in the Soviet Union during the war and thus had obviously not been in Auschwitz. Since our second candidate had also not been there, we were back to stage one. At this point, I reached the conclusion that in order to findFreimann I would have to use some fairly unorthodox research methods and be willing to do an enormous amount of the kind of boring, mechanical work which at times made me regret that I had ever begun searching for Nazis. I began checking every possible list of survivors and/or next of kin that I could find in Israel. The number and the scope of such lists was fairly large, but the results were negative. I also examined the lists of the participants of the World Gathering of Jewish Holocaust Survivors held in Jerusalem in June 1981, hoping that Freimann had perhaps attended. I even recorded the name and address of every Freimann, Freeman or variation thereof who had participated, in case any was a relative of the elusive David. All to no avail.

By this time it was already December, and it looked as if our investigation had reached an impasse. Shortly thereafter, however, I met Shmuel Gorr, a former colleague from Yad Vashem, who gave me some information which opened up a new avenue of research. Gorr had been working for the past few years as a Jewish genealogist and had recently completed a project in which all the name changes that had been made in Palestine during the British Mandate (1920-48) were put on computer. This information, which had previously been scattered in numerous publications, was critical for his work and its computerization considerably facilitated his research. I told Gorr about my search for David Freimann and he immediately volunteered as a first step to check his list. The problem was that the Mandate had ended on May 14, 1948, so if my Freimann were to be found on that list he had to have come to Israel and changed his name prior to that date which was not necessarily the case. Shmuel Gorr checked his list and, as expected, did not find anything, but it was his idea which led me to the next logical step: checking the name changes that had been made since Israel's establishment. Gorr told me that they were published in *Reshumot*, the official government bulletin, and were available for perusal in the National Library. Under normal circumstances the task of checking all the David Freimanns who had changed their names during the past 35 years appeared relatively simple. In reality, however, the task proved enormous. First of all, tens of thousands of Israelis had Hebraized their names over the course of nearly four decades. (There was governmental and social pressure to do so during the early years of the State of Israel.) Moreover, the lists were arranged in such a manner as to make the task a veritable nightmare. Instead of publicizing one annual alphabetical list of the name changes that had been made during the course of the past year, separate lists were published several times a year by each of the district offices of the Ministry of the Interior and therefore numerous lists had to be reviewed for each year, in all a total of hundreds of lists.

By this point I was so determined to find David Freimann that I was ready to try practically anything. I therefore spent several hours daily for the next two weeks at the National Library going over all the name changes made in the history of the State of Israel. To say that such a task is exasperating is, of course, a gross understatement, but the search did yield results. I found four possible candidates from among the David Freimanns who had changed their names during the period from 1948 to 1970. (The most popular choices to replace Freimann, which means a free man in Yiddish, were Ben-Chorin, Dror or Drori, all of which are approximate Hebrew equivalents.)

In the meantime I met with Neal Sher and David Marwell in Israel in mid-December and suggested the possibility of publishing an advertisement in the Israeli press. Other proposals were that OSI examine the files of the International Tracing Service (ITS) at Arolson, West Germany, as well as the applications submitted to the Claims Conference for reparations. At about the same time I discovered several lists of survivors which contained important information. The first list was in the form of a two-volume set entitled *Register of Jewish Survivors*, published in 1945 by the Jewish Agency Search Bureau for Missing Relatives. Sure enough, there was a David Freimann, or to be precise, a Dawid Frajman listed who was a Polish survivor of Buchenwald, originally from Lodz, and who had been born in 1912.[32] This data was important because we hoped to use it to obtain additional facts from Arolson or other sources which had hitherto been inaccessible.

I continued searching for lists of survivors and began checking the Freimanns in Israel who had changed their names. The first four individuals were checked via the population registry, but none matched the description of our informant. Before I could be truly disappointed over the lack of success using this method, I found an additional list of Polish survivors in the Yad Vashem Archives, with four David Freimanns listed, at least two of whom seemed to fit the description of the man we were looking for. The list, moreover, included such important data as year of birth, postwar address and, in one case, even the names of parents.[33] Soon afterwards I also found a list of Buchenwald survivors which included the David Freimann from Lodz who had been born in 1912,[34] but *his* name did not appear on the list I found at Yad Vashem. At this point we had three definite possibilities, for each one of whom we possessed some, though not all, the pertinent biographical information. When I subsequently found a list of survivors published by the Jerusalem office of the Joint Distribution Committee,[35] we learned the precise date of birth—October 25, 1912—of the David Freimann from Lodz. This piece of information soon became highly significant. In the course of a discussion with David Silberklang of Yad Vashem regarding the trials and tribulations of our search for Freimann, he suggested that I consult the Arolson (International Tracing Service) records in the Yad Vashem Archives. Initially I was a bit taken aback by this suggestion since during the five or more years that I had been doing research at Yad Vashem on Nazi war criminals I had never used that material, and had quite forgotten that those documents were available in Jerusalem. Little did I realize then that the search in the Arolson records for a Jewish survivor would lead to the discovery of hundreds of suspected Nazi war criminals.

I began searching for Freimann in the alphabetized list of Displaced Persons and victims, and found 17 different individuals named David (or Dawid) Freimann (or Freiman, Frajman or Fraiman) in the Arolson files who had lived in the areas under Nazi occupation during the Second World War. After examining all the available data on these individuals, I reached the conclusion that the David Freimann we were looking for was the one who had been born in Lodz in 1912. The evidence which proved most conclusive was his postwar address: Wiesenhuttenstrasse 11, Frankfurt am Main, which matched the documentation in David Marwell's possession. The information on his whereabouts during the war also matched what we knew about Freimann's life. We were able, on the basis of the Arolson records, to compile a fairly detailed summary of his wartime experiences, including even the dates on which he had been deported to various concentration camps and his prisoner numbers.

David Freimann, elusive informant, was born on October 25, 1912 in Lodz, Poland to Israel and Blima née Leiserowicz Freimann. He was deported to Buchenwald for the first time shortly after the outbreak of the Second World War and arrived there on October 15, 1939. During the course of his stay at Buchenwald, he was assigned prisoner numbers 2832 and 2215. On October 16, 1942 Freimann was deported to Auschwitz. He arrived there three days later and was assigned inmate number 68439. While in Auschwitz, he lived in block 7a and was in the camp hospital either from January 11-23, 1943 or March 11-23, 1943 or both. Freimann was subsequently (apparently in January 1945) deported to Gross-Rosen and from there was sent to Buchenwald, arriving February 9 (or 10), 1945. He lived in block 3 and was assigned prisoner number 129837. He remained in Buchenwald until the liberation of the camp.

After the war Freimann lived in the Zeilsheim DP camp near Frankfurt at West Hoechst 23, and later moved to Wiesenhuttenstrasse 11 in Frankfurt am Main. His DP registration number was G 21722808. The Arolson information also included the names of all those who had enquired regarding Freimann's fate and/ or whereabouts—a cousin, an uncle or nephew, the Polish consul in Frankfurt, some of whom might possibly be able to assist us in finding him if all else failed.[36] I immediately cabled the information to David Marwell, who was very excited about the data I had uncovered, especially in view of the fact that it usually took Arolson a minimum of several months to reply to OSI's requests for information. It finally appeared as if we would be able to find Freimann and hopefully determine once and for all whether Mengele had indeed been arrested and released by the American authorities in 1946. The search for Freimann marked the end of my involvement in the Mengele investigation. What had started out as an eager, enthusiastic search for historical evidence concerning the possible arrest and release by the Americans of one of the world's arch Nazi criminals had by this time lost a lot of its excitement. The discovery of the remains at Embu outside Sao Paulo and the findings of the pathologists had considerably dampened my enthusiasm, but there was another very important factor involved. While I was spending the best part of nearly six months on the Mengele case, time was rapidly running out on literally hundreds of cases of Nazi war criminals who were living in relative tranquillity in various countries in the Free World. As time went on and our investigation continued, this fact increasingly bothered me. I often found myself wondering why I was spending so much time investigating an event which might have transpired in 1946, when that time could have been spent far more constructively doing research on Nazi criminals who had committed very serious crimes and had still not been brought to justice in 1985.

I received an answer to my question in the form of a discovery which I made while searching for David Freimann in the Arolson records at Yad Vashem. In the course of this seemingly useless task I discovered the documentation which helped reveal the emigration to the West of hundreds of Nazi war criminals. In fact, if not for the research on Freimann, we most likely would never have realized that the Arolson files held the key to uncovering the postwar escape of thousands of East European Nazi collaborators. It was this discovery which convinced me that I had to leave OSI and launch a last-ditch effort to ensure that as many Nazi criminals living in the West as possible would be brought to justice. On the basis of this material I was able to convince the Simon Wiesenthal Center to lead this world-wide campaign. That story is the subject of the next chapter.

Before relating those events, there are two postscripts to the Mengele investigation. Using the information I had uncovered in the Arolson archives, David Marwell finally found David Freimann or to be more accurate, traces thereof. The David Freimann we were looking for was indeed the one who had been interned in Buchenwald and Auschwitz. He had emigrated to the United States after the war, but subsequently returned to Germany. The problem was, however, that he had passed away on April 14, 1976, taking his secret with him to the grave.

On October 8, 1992 the U. S. Department of Justice published "In the Matter of Josef Mengele; A Report to the Attorney-General of the United States," confirming that the remains found in Embu, Brazil in 1985 were indeed those of Josef Mengele. In addition the report made clear that Mengele had not been arrested and released by the American authorities in late 1946, thereby confirming that the information cited by CIC officer Benjamin Gorby in 1947 was only a rumor. In fact, in 1945 Mengele was held briefly in two prisoner-of-war camps in Germany but was released because the U. S. Army never learned his true identity.

The report whose publication was witheld for several years at the request of the Israeli and West German governments, appeared following the completion of a DNA-typing investigation carried out in early 1992. Its findings confirmed "beyond reasonable doubt" that the remains were those of Josef Mengele, paving the way for official acknowledgement by all three governments which had engaged in the search for the Angel of Death of Auschwitz that he was no longer alive.[37]

Notes

1. Letter of Rabbi Abraham Cooper (Simon Wiesenthal Center) to US Army Records Center, October 25, 1984, SWCA. Identical requests were sent by Rabbi Cooper to other archives.

2. Letter of Ben J. M. Gorby to Commanding Officer, Hgs. 430th CIC (Vienna Detachment), April 26, 1947, SWCA.

3. *Mengele: The Complete Story,* pp. 305-7.

4. YVA, M-21/III/38.

5. "Farfolgt di murder!," *Undzer Moment,* January 27, 1947, p. 5.

6. "Bericht fun der tetigkajt fun Referat fun naci-un krigsfarbrecher far der cajt biz 10.4.47," Jewish community of Eggenfelden, April 20, 1947, YVA, M-21 /III/38.

7. Michael Bar Zohar, *Ha-Nokmim,* Tel Aviv, n.d.; Michael Elkins, *Forged in Fury,* New York, 1971.

8. YVA, M-21/3-75.

9. This source was quoted in a letter from the Eggenfelden committee to the Legal Department in Munich, April 3, 1947, YVA, M-21/3-75.

10. "Mir Zuchn Ejdus Kegn Nazi-un Krigsfarbrecher, Kaczetlr phun Oishvitz!," *Undzer Weg,* March 21, 1947, p. 8.

11. "Mir Zuchn Ejdus Kegn Nazi-un Krigsfarbrecher! Mengele arestirt!," *Undzer Wort,* March 28, 1947, p. 8.

12. *Mengele: The Complete Story,* p. 24.

13. For details on his activities in that capacity see Joseph Riwash, *Resistance and Revenge 1939-1949,* Montreal, 1981, pp. 89-146.

14. The others which published the news were: *Jidisze Cajtung,* March 21, 1947; *Ibergang,* March 30, 1947; *Bafreiung,* April 4, 1947.

15. *Der Mahnruf,* January 31, 1947, p. 24.

16. Unsigned letter from the Jewish Historical Documentation Center of Vienna to Director Blumental of the Central Historical Commission of Lodz, Poland, June 19, 1947, YVA, 0-5/4.

17. Letter of J. Kermisz and N. Blumental to the International Committee for Jewish Concentration Camp Inmates and Refugees in Vienna, June 30, 1947, YVA, 0-5/5.

18. Letters of Wilhelm Krell, Jewish Community of Vienna, to Tuvia Friedman, Jewish Historical Documentation Center, Vienna, August 4 and 14, 1947; letter from *Der Mahnruf* to Tuvia Friedman, August 29, 1947, YVA, 0-5/11.

19. Letter of Lewit and Krell to Dr. Schmorak of the Polish-Jewish Committee, April 8, 1947, YVA, 0-5/11.

20. The testimonies arrived from Jews in such places as: Targu Mares, Rumania; Budapest and Kisvarda, Hungary; Amsterdam, Holland, etc. Among the newspapers which publicized the news regarding Mengele were *Villagossag, Igazsag, Der Neue Weg,* and *Neuen Weg,* YVA, 0-5/39.

21. "Ma'asar ha-Mifletzet me-Oshvintzim," *Ha-Mashkif,* January 24, 1947, p. 1.

22. "Rotzchim she-Hitchamku me-Onesh," *Davar,* May 30, 1947, p. 2.

23. *Mengele: The Complete Story,* pp. 308-25.

24. "Nazi Doctors Who Sent Jews to Gas Chambers to be Tried in Poland," JTA, January 5, 1947, p. 4.

25. "Transylvanian Jews Eager to Testify at Trial of Former Chief Physician of Auschwitz Death Camp," JTA, January 23, 1947, p. 2.

26. Based on conversation with David Marwell, June 26, 1985.

27. Interview with Abba Kovner, July 17, 1985, Tel Aviv.

28. Interview with Asher Ben-Natan, July 18, 1985, Tel Aviv.

29. Interview with Prof. Marian Mushkat, July 18, 1985, Tel Aviv.

30. Interview with Manus Diament, July 19, 1985, Tel Aviv.

31. United Nations War Crimes Commission, Lists of War Criminals, Suspects and Witnesses (Germans), Part 1, Eighth List of War Criminals (Germans), criminal no. 240 Joseph Mengele, p. 27.

32. "List of Polish Jewish Survivors at the Buchenwald Camp," *Register of Jewish Survivors: List of Jews Rescued In Different European Countries,* Vol. I, Jerusalem, 1945, p. 111.

33. "Wykas Alfabetyczny Zydow Polskich," list of Polish Jews published by

the Central Committee of Polish Jews (Warsaw), January 1947, list no. 3, letter F, YVA, O-37.

34. "Second list of names of Jews liberated in Buchenwald," published by the Jewish Agency for Palestine, YVA, O-37/O-817(6).

35. "Reshimat Nitzolim," published by the Jerusalem office of the American Jewish Joint Distribution Committee, YVA, O-37, p. 13.

36. YVA, ITS files, microfilm, F-101.

37. "In the Matter of Josef Mengele; A Report to the Attorney General of the United States," October, 1992.

6

Widening the Net:
Research and Development

One of the questions which I frequently asked myself and which others asked me was how much longer this work would continue. By definition, this was a time-ended assignment. The criminals were elderly men, the youngest already in their sixties, most of the others in their seventies and eighties if not even older, so the day would soon come when our efforts would ostensibly no longer be needed. The inevitable biological solution would solve all the outstanding problems and thereby forever seal this chapter of history.

If OSI and the various special prosecution agencies continued to exist until that time, we would know that the maximum effort had been made to prosecute the Nazi war criminals living in the United States and other Western democracies. Another possibility existed, however, one which I found extremely perturbing: that these units might be closed down long before they finished their task. It was with no small degree of reluctance and only as a result of public pressure that such agencies had been created. Throughout its existence OSI, for example, encountered considerable opposition not only from émigré groups but from prominent conservative politicians as well. Its activities, moreover, had on several occasions caused the American government considerable embarrassment by exposing past mistakes which otherwise would have probably never been revealed. It was true that OSI was ridding the United States of undesirable individuals who never should never have been admitted in the first place, but the concomitant complications led many people to wonder whether the price being paid was worth the results achieved.

The fear existed, therefore, that if it appeared that the work was near completion, OSI and other agencies would be disbanded and whatever remained to be done would be turned over to local prosecutors. The claim would be made that there was no longer a need for a special office to handle litigation of this sort and the investigation and prosecution of Nazi war criminals living in the United States and elsewhere would, for all practical purposes, come to an end.

The most convincing argument to marshal against the above scenario was to find the maximum number of cases. The leadership of OSI therefore decided in the initial half of 1984, several years after OSI's establishment, to launch a search for Nazis who had entered the United States. Until that point, the office had been relatively passive. Most of the cases under investigation had been brought to its attention by outside sources or had resulted from ongoing investigations. For the first time a serious attempt would be made to determine whether additional criminals, besides those already known to OSI, had entered the United States. The manner in which this was done was by checking the names of known criminals against the US immigration files. OSI therefore began seeking lists and data regarding all Nazi criminals whose current whereabouts were unknown, including those in whose cases there was no evidence whatsoever that they were living in the United States.

The primary initiators of this new development were OSI director Neal Sher and historian David Marwell. Sher assumed his post in 1983 after Allan A. Ryan Jr. left the office following his investigation of the Barbie affair. Both Sher and Marwell had been with OSI from the very beginning and were extremely devoted to its task. Both believed that this effort would yield numerous additional suspects and thereby contribute to OSI's success and future.

I began research on this project in August 1984 at Yad Vashem whose extensive holdings made it the natural place to start any such investigation. At first I concentrated on the card-index of Nazi war criminals in the Yad Vashem Archives. This list contained the names of thousands upon thousands of criminals as well as, when available, pertinent biographical information, details regarding the crime, and a listing of the sources of the allegations. My primary focus during the initial stage was on criminals of Eastern European origin—primarily Lithuanians, Latvians, and Ukrainians—who constituted the overwhelming majority of the Nazi criminals who had immigrated to the United States.

While the Yad Vashem index had considerable potential for this type of research, it soon became clear that several complicated problems existed. The material had not been updated since the mid-1960s, so we could not benefit from the considerable research regarding Nazi war crimes that had been carried out during the previous two decades. This was particularly unfortunate because only recently had sufficient attention been focused on the role of collaborators; the index had been compiled at a time when relatively little effort had been made to identify the Lithuanian, Latvian, Ukrainian, Estonian, Croatian and Byelorussian criminals and thus the number of these Nazis listed was relatively small.

Another problem resulted from a careless oversight on my part. I did not realize that there were geographical indices for the criminals and began going over all the cards from A to Z. It turned out, however, that my mistake was in the long run worthwhile because the geographical indices did not cover all the pertinent cases. The cards listed under Lithuania, for example, related only to the site of the crime committed and not to the nationality of the perpetrator. In order to find all the Lithuanians listed I had to peruse all the cards since quite a few Lithuanians had committed crimes outside Lithuania. The same applied for other nationalities, so I ended up scanning many thousands of cards even though these non-Germans constituted only a small percentage of the criminals listed in the index. I decided, moreover, that it would be a good idea to record the names of all the Germans who had committed crimes in these areas since the documents on their crimes might prove helpful in the investigation of the collaborators. I therefore had no choice but to review the entire index, a task for which the adjectives tedious and boring would be gross understatements. Had this information been computerized it would have spared us a considerable number of headaches.

A third problem which I encountered in going over the index was that many of the entries were incomplete. The biggest problem in that respect was the lack of first names. For example, only 37 per cent of the entries for criminals who committed crimes in Lithuania had complete names. This posed a serious difficulty since such cases could not be checked by the American immigration authorities. Whatever hopes we had of uncovering a large number of additional criminals in the United States were dependent to a certain extent on our ability to find those names.

By mid-September 1984 I had already transmitted a total of 273 names to Washington, with the longest lists being a miscellaneous list and the list of Ukrainians. The former requires clarification. In the course of reviewing the entire Yad Vashem index, I came across quite a few entries which related to cases under investigation by OSI or of criminals who committed crimes in Eastern Europe but were not members of any of the nationalities for whom I had compiled a separate list. The result was a miscellaneous list under which all names which might be potentially valuable were included. Among those sent to OSI were Russians and Hungarians, for example, as well as quite a few guards from the Wiener-Neudorf concentration camp and individuals who had served in the *Selbstschutz* (a local militia established in Lublin), both of which were under investigation by OSI.

The lists of Lithuanians and Latvians were surprisingly small because of technical problems. I had previously sent OSI two extensive lists of Lithuanian collaborators that had been compiled by survivors immediately after the war.[1] Those names constituted the overwhelming majority of the Lithuanian criminals listed in the Yad Vashem index. Of 310 entries on individuals who committed crimes in Lithuania only 40 (22 of which were lacking first names) were sent to OSI. The others were either Germans or Lithuanians whose names had already been sent to Washington. As far as the Latvians were concerned, the large majority of the criminals listed in the index were Germans and thus the initial list had only 18 names.

Under these circumstances the focus of the investigation soon shifted to the search for first names. This was particularly true in the case of the Lithuanians, since the lists compiled by the survivors also suffered from this deficiency. Of the slightly more than 300 names on these lists, approximately half were incomplete. The same problem applied to the material published in volume IV of the *Yahadut Lita* series, which recounted the fate of practically every Lithuanian Jewish community during the Holocaust. Numerous criminals were mentioned in the entries on the various cities, towns and villages, but 241 of the 346 criminals named in the book were identified only by their last names. The volume was, nonetheless, a very important tool in our research effort. Besides listing the full names of 105 criminals (89 of whom were as yet unknown to us), among them several for whom we possessed a last name but not a first name, it directed us to numerous survivors and other sources of information that we hoped might help us find the missing first names.[2] I then compiled a master-list of Lithuanian criminals whose first names were missing and began a systematic effort to uncover them. At this point the list had 440 entries, and was larger than the list of Lithuanian criminals whose full names we possessed.

The search for the first names of the Lithuanian murderers affords us an insight into the documentation available in Israel on the crimes committed against the Jewish communities in that country. My first step was to examine the *sifrei yizkor* or memorial books published by the individual communities. Surprisingly, very few of the Lithuanian communities published books of their own. Given the high educational and intellectual level of Lithuanian Jewry, one would have anticipated that practically every community would have published a memorial volume. Apparently the small size of most of the communities and the relatively low percentage of survivors convinced the Lithuanian Jews that it would be best to publish a joint memorial book. The result was the four-volume series entitled *Yahadut Lita*, the last volume of which is devoted to the fate of the Jewish communities during the Holocaust. This book includes numerous names of criminals and sources of information, but as noted above suffers unfortunately from the classic problem of the lack of first names. In all, I found very few memorial books on Lithuanian Jewish communities, and the number of first names obtained from these volumes was quite limited. The book on Skuodas[3] had the first name I was looking for, the volume on Krekenava[4] did not have any first names and the book on Kedainiai[5] had several. I also found a few more last names to add to my list, but these books could obviously not solve the entire problem.

The next step was to examine the various publications on the subject that had been published in the Soviet Union. Considerable attention has been focused in Lithuania on Nazi war crimes and more than 20 books have been published on this subject over the course of the past three decades. These works cover a wide range of topics and deal with the issue on a national as well as regional or local level.[6] Several books contain extensive documentation and the number of criminals named in these works is quite large.[7] Using these sources, I was able to find the first names of almost 10 per cent of the criminals whose names I was missing.

These works are also of interest because they very much reflect Soviet ideology and politics. The material is presented in accordance with the Communist Weltanschauung using the special terminology which has evolved behind the Iron Curtain to describe the events of the Second World War. The Nazis are usually referred to as "Hitlerite fascists" and the Communists as "progressive" or "democratic" forces. The role of the Communists in the resistance and their suffering under Nazi occupa-

tion were usually considerably exaggerated and the unique fate of the
Jews as victims was in most cases downplayed. Regardless of their ideo-
logically-slanted presentation,[8] these books contained valuable information for the purposes of our investigation.

In this context I want to note the assistance I received from Chaya
Lifshitz who worked as a researcher for many years at Yad Vashem. Lifshitz was born in Lithuania and lived there until she came to Israel in
1969. Prior to her *aliya*, she worked on several publications related to
this subject and brought with her to Israel a complete set of all the
books on Nazi war criminals which had been published in Lithuania.
She had even more books on this topic than the Yad Vashem Library.
Lifshitz directed my attention to works which I would never have found
using the existing research tools available at Yad Vashem, and made
available considerable material from her own personal library. She also
informed me about two very important private collections of documentation on the destruction of Lithuanian Jewry. One belonged to Leib
Kunichowsky, whose story is related in Chapter 4. The second, which
included extensive lists of Lithuanian Nazi war criminals, had been
brought to Israel by a Lithuanian Jew in the 1970s and would ultimately play a significant role in our efforts to prosecute Nazis in various countries in the Western world.

After examining the Soviet publications regarding Nazi war criminals, I began contacting survivors and other Jews from the various
Lithuanian communities in an effort to find the missing first names. In
this respect, the material in volume IV of *Yahadut Lita* was a veritable
gold mine. Each entry included a list of all the available sources, published as well as oral, on each town, village or city.[9] With the help of
Igud Yotzei Lita (Association of Lithuanian Immigrants in Israel) I was
able to obtain the addresses and phone numbers of the individuals who
had been interviewed as well as of additional survivors. Thus began a
final effort to find the information which would enable us to determine
whether these criminals were residing in the United States.

From the outset I was not particularly optimistic about our chances
of finding the missing information in this manner. The number of survivors from the provincial communities in Lithuania was extremely
small and in many cases the information in *Yahadut Lita* came from
Jews who had escaped to the Soviet interior before or during the initial
stages of the Nazi occupation and returned to their native towns after
the war. In theory this did not pose a problem because what we were

seeking was not eyewitness testimony but rather the criminals' first names. The individuals in question had in most cases grown up in these towns and might possess such information even if they had not been there during the war. Indeed, many of those who returned from the Soviet interior made special efforts to determine the identity of the murderers who had killed members of their family and quite a few played an active role in attempts to bring collaborators to trial. The problem, however, was that in some cases there were no survivors from a specific town; whatever information was available came from Jews from the same area who were not acquainted with the local Lithuanians.

In other cases those who submitted the testimony had indeed been born in a specific place, but had left that town or village long before the war. Despite these obstacles I believed that such an effort would be worthwhile. Even if only a few names were found, and only a few of those were actually living in the United States, we still owed it to the victims to make this minimal effort. I also hoped we might obtain the names of additional criminals hitherto unknown to us, who might also have escaped to the United States. Each enquiry regarding the first name of a criminal was therefore accompanied by a request for names (even if only a last name) of additional Lithuanian criminals, as well as for names of other Lithuanian Jews—survivors as well as those who escaped to the Soviet interior or even emigrated prior to the outbreak of the war—who might have known the suspects and could provide the missing information.

This investigation encompassed 99 Lithuanian Jewish communities and the first problem was how to proceed. The most logical thing to do was either to establish a priority list based on chances of success (number, age and memory of survivors, size of town, etc.) or simply do it alphabetically. I allowed a personal consideration to influence this decision and began my search with the criminals who had participated in the murder of the Jews in my maternal grandmother's place of birth, a town named Seduva, located in central Lithuania about 25 miles west of Panevezys. We knew how the Jews of Seduva had been killed and we possessed the names of two of the Lithuanians who had played a leading role in the murders. In both cases, however, we lacked the criminals' first names. One was a teacher named Grinius, who had been head of the local "Activists," the other was a man named Blazys who had also actively participated in the atrocities.

The results of their activities were typical of the fate of the Jewish communities in the provincial towns of Lithuania. The local "Activists" led by Grinius began attacking the Jews even before the Germans arrived and within a short time they had concentrated them in a ghetto in the village of Pavertitch, three miles from Seduva. On August 3, 1941 ten Jews who were ostensibly taken to work were shot on the road to Radviliskis. In mid-August 27 additional Jews, including the rabbi of the town Mordechai David Henkin, were shot behind the village of Kauleliskiai and 35 Jews employed as agricultural laborers on "the Red Estate" were murdered about the same time. The final *Aktion* took place on August 25, 1941 in the Liaudiskiai forest, five miles from Seduva. A total 664 men, women and children were shot to death and buried in a pit by the Lithuanians who marked the event by extensive drinking and a festive meal which lasted the entire night following the murders.

Three Jewish families were initially spared the fate of their brethren; those of Dr. Patovksy, the local doctor, who was the only physician in the area and of two men—Cooper and Noll—who had served in the Lithuanian Army. They were murdered with their families a few weeks later. The only survivor of the massacre of the Jews of Seduva was Shulamit Noll, who was among the Jews taken to be murdered but miraculously survived. She was not shot and was able to crawl out of the pit which the Lithuanians, in their haste to celebrate the murders, neglected to cover. With the assistance of a priest's valet and a local farmer she hid in the area throughout the war and was able to survive.[10] The fact that there was an eyewitness who was a native of the town was very good but there was no guarantee that she knew the first names of the murderers, nor was there any indication in the available sources whether she was alive, and if so where she was presently living.

My first step was to call Baruch Gofer of Tzur Shalom near Haifa who was originally from Seduva. Over the years he had collected material on the town in the hope of publishing a memorial book. I learned of his activities from Professor Dov Levin of Yad Vashem and the Hebrew University, a Lithuanian survivor and an expert on the Holocaust in that country.[11] For many years Professor Levin had taken a keen interest in the work of OSI and on numerous occasions went out of his way to be of assistance. He told me that if there was anyone who knew the pertinent information about the Jewish community of Seduva it was Baruch Gofer. Gofer, indeed, gave me several leads, the most important of which was that Shulamit Noll, the sole survivor of the massacre, was alive and living in the Tel Aviv area. He did not know her exact address but directed me to those who did. In the course of our conversation I mentioned that my grandmother was originally from Seduva and he informed me that I had relatives in Tel Aviv whom I had never heard about. This proved to be more than an interesting anecdote because they were the ones who gave me Shulamit Noll's married name and address. In addition, they also supplied the name and address of Gershon Kirpitchnik, another survivor, who was originally from Seduva and had spent most of the war in hiding in the Seduva area but had not been present at the massacre. Kirpitchnik, unlike Noll, had lived for many years after the war in the Soviet Union and had only recently arrived in Israel. He had not been interviewed before and there was no indication in the available documentation that he had survived and/or was residing in Israel.

I called Shulamit Lipkis nee Noll, who was living in Holon, and explained my problem to her. She initially seemed hesitant over the phone, perhaps I had called at a bad moment. In order to put her at ease, I told her that I had obtained her name from my relatives from Seduva and that my grandmother had been born there, but I have the impression that those facts did not really make any impression. Mrs. Lipkis told me that she remembered both criminals and was even able to relate some identifying facts. Grinius, according to Lipkis, had served as the principal of the Lithuanian high school in Seduva and Blazys had been a teacher in the same school. She did not, however, know the first name of either criminal.

Mrs. Lipkis asked me to write to her, in case she might remember some more information and also told me about another person whom it might be worthwhile to contact since he had attended the school where both suspects had worked. When I called her shortly afterwards to confirm that she had received the letter, she told me that she did not have any further information but that she planned to visit Gershon Kirpitchnik and would ask him regarding Blazys and Grinius. A few days later I called Kirpitchnik myself but had trouble communicating with him as the only language we had in common was Yiddish, which I have difficulty speaking. I therefore wrote to him and he subsequently replied that neither he nor any of the other Jews from Seduva who had attended the local high school (and with whom he had discussed the matter) remembered either man's first name. Kirpitchnik did, however,

provide some important information. He related that he had seen Grinius in 1954 in the Lithuanian resort of Druskininkiai. This meant it
was almost impossible that he was living in the West and thus I was
able to remove at least one name from my list of question marks. (All
the Lithuanian criminals living in the West had escaped to Central
Europe, primarily to Germany, during the final stages of the Second
World War. Those who remained in Lithuania after the arrival of the
Soviets were unable to leave, and therefore if Grinius had been living in
Soviet Lithuania in 1954 it was more than reasonably certain that he
was either still there or had died in the meantime.

Kirpitchnik's reply ended our active search for the first names of the
criminals from Seduva, but we subsequently received some additional
information from an unexpected source. Professor Levin was able to
obtain a Lithuanian phonebook, published in 1939, which listed the
names and professions of all those with telephones throughout Lithuania. Among the lucky few with telephones in Seduva was a teacher
named Anupras Blazys. While this could under no circumstances be
considered conclusive proof as to the identity of the criminal, it was definitely a lead worthy of further investigation. The phonebook led us to
possible answers to many of the question marks on our list of Lithuanian criminals. In view of the fact that quite a few of the criminals were
serving in the Lithuanian police or armed forces in 1939 and were
therefore likely to be among the relatively few Lithuanians who had
phones at that time, this information had considerable potential. I have
no doubt that the Lithuanian phone company (if such a thing existed)
never imagined in its wildest dreams what ingenious use could be made
of its product.

While each investigation of this sort yielded different results for differ-
ing reasons, the research on Seduva was fairly typical. In many cases
we were unable to find the information we sought, usually because of
the lack of survivors, although there were other reasons as well. Many
of the individuals listed in volume IV of *Yahadut Lita* as sources of information could not be found via the population registry or had already
passed away. Given the fact that *Yahadut Lita* was published more than
ten years after the information was originally obtained from these individuals, that is hardly surprising. In other cases it turned out that the
person listed as a source had obtained the information from other individuals whose names, for some reason or other, had not been listed. In
addition, there were many cases in which I successfully contacted the

survivor, only to discover that while he or she knew the criminal, they simply could not recall his first name.

I remember one particularly frustrating example regarding a criminal from the town of Semeliskis, a small community in the Trakai district in south-east Lithuania, where about 300 Jews resided prior to the Nazi invasion. Even before the arrival of the Germans, local "Activists" murdered several Jews and confiscated Jewish property. A few weeks later all the Jews were concentrated in a local church which had been converted into a club during the year of Soviet rule. One day all the young, strong men were taken to dig a large pit in a nearby forest. They were murdered and buried there, and the rest of the community shared their fate on October 6, 1941, the first day of the holiday of Sukkot. In addition, the Jews of nearby Vievis and Zasliai were murdered together with the Jews of Semeliskis, a total of approximately 1,000 victims.

The leader of the Lithuanian murderers was the local priest Petraitis.[12] We did not know his first name but the fact that he was a priest and the leader of the killers gave me hope that we might be able to find that information. There were, in addition, several relatively young survivors of Semeliskis living in Israel and thus our chances of success appeared fairly good. The first person I contacted was Yozhik Alpert of Netanya who, according to my sources, was the person most likely to be able to supply the missing information. His reply, in essence, summed up the numerous investigations of this sort, in which our efforts were ultimately unsuccessful. Of course he had heard of Petraitis. He knew him personally. In fact, he had even purchased a cow from him in 1938 or 1939. His first name? He did not know offhand, but would try to remember. Alpert probably tried but to no avail, and thus we were unable to continue our investigation.

Despite numerous setbacks in these cases, our project to determine the first names of the Lithuanian murderers did, on occasion, yield results. These findings took several forms. In some cases survivors were able to provide the first names that we sought. Shulamit Shefek of Kibbutz Amir remembered the names of two of the three Czepunas brothers who had participated in the murder of the Jews of Uzpalis,[13] and Wolf Gudrov of Haifa supplied us with the name of one of the Bielevicius brothers who had played an active role in the murder of the Jews of his hometown of Vievis. In other instances, survivors supplied us with names, albeit in many cases last names only, of additional criminals who were unknown to us up to that point. Chana Brava of Ramat

Gan, for example, did not remember the first name of the Lithuanian criminal Ziliunas,[14] but was able to provide me with the names of six additional Lithuanians who had actively participated in the persecution and murder of the Jews of her hometown of Salakas, three of whose full names she supplied. P. Toker of Petach Tikva sent me the names of five Lithuanians who had played an active role in the murders in Radviliskis and Miriam Krakinowski of Poughkeepsie, New York supplied the names of three Lithuanians who committed crimes in Troskunai.

There were other cases in which survivors confirmed that a specific criminal had escaped from Lithuania and was living in the West, including at least one instance in which the murderer was known to be living in the United States. Additional information was also forthcoming as a result of these inquiries, whether it be leads regarding survivors and/or documentation or specific details concerning the individuals under investigation. Although the project did not yield as much information in practical terms as we might have hoped for, it did produce data regarding quite a few criminals, several of whom were later revealed to be living in the West.

In the spring of 1985 I was informed by OSI that one of the Ukrainian criminals whose name I had sent them was alive and living in the United States. P.S.,* the commandant of the Ukrainian police in a town near the city of Podhajce (Tarnopol district), Poland had played an active role in the murder of the Jews of his town and numerous other communities in the area. His name was listed in the Yad Vashem war criminals index and had been transmitted to OSI in September 1984 on the first list of Ukrainians sent to Washington. David Marwell called to tell me the good news and requested that I began looking for documentation regarding S. and/or survivors who might be able to identify him. This case was particularly important for both of us as it was the first which resulted from "R & D" (research and development) efforts in Israel to uncover additional Nazi war criminals living in the United States which Marwell had been so instrumental in launching. Convinced as both of us were of its enormous potential, we were especially hopeful that this investigation would prove successful in order to ensure the completion of the project. The best way of convincing OSI to continue to allocate the necessary funds to carry out the research was to

---

* Name changed.

prove our thesis convincingly by uncovering Nazi war criminals living in the United States against whom solid evidence could be presented.

As luck would have it, there was indeed abundant material regarding the crimes committed by S. in the Yad Vashem Archives. In fact, this case was one of the relatively rare investigations which I conducted in Israel in which the criminal was specifically named as a murderer in the available documentation. In S.'s case, the testimony was so detailed that even one of his victims was specifically named by several of the survivors. The testimonies also helped confirm that the individual living in the United States was indeed the criminal. S.'s wife's maiden name matched the name of the police commandant's spouse as noted by one of the survivors in his testimony.

In this case we were the beneficiaries of considerable material collected by the Legal Department of the Central Committee of Liberated Jews in Germany, which was established after the war to assist in the prosecution of Nazi war criminals. The Ukrainian police commandant was one of the suspects against whom this department collected evidence, all of which was now in the Yad Vashem Archives.[15] The department had even published an advertisement in the Jewish press calling upon survivors of the Tarnopol district, who knew P. S. as the former Ukrainian police chief who had served in various locations in the district and had organized and carried out pogroms against Jews starting in July 1941, to submit testimony. This call was published in several publications[16] and apparently was helpful in the collection of evidence.

I was able to find statements by nine different survivors regarding S.'s crimes. These witnesses had submitted their testimony in 1947 at which time their ages ranged from 69 to 22, so it seemed that there was a good chance that at least some of them were still alive. The person whose evidence seemed to be particularly important was a woman named Mira Tuchfeld* whose brother-in-law had been murdered by S. She was the youngest of the survivors who had testified against him and specifically noted his active participation in murder and the fact that he had personally told all the Jews in their town that they would be murdered. Her testimony had been submitted to the Legal Department in Munich in April 1947,[17] but there was no indication as to her present whereabouts, nor could we even be certain about her name.

---

* Name changed.

She probably had subsequently married and changed her name and thus finding her was not going to be simple.

In January 1986 David Marwell told me that I should make a special effort to find Mira Tuchfeld. Given the scant information in our possession, the prospects did not appear particularly promising. During the initial months of 1986 I found the testimonies of numerous survivors from the Podhajce area,[18] but had no luck in discovering Mira Tuchfeld's whereabouts. This became even more critical in the wake of OSI's unsuccessful efforts to locate any survivors who could testify against S. While OSI had been able to find several individuals from the Podhajce area, none remembered the Ukrainian police commander, and all their efforts to locate Mira Tuchfeld had also proven fruitless.

It was precisely at this point that a mere coincidence led to the information we were seeking. In late May 1986, I was reading the Israeli daily *Ma'ariv* and happened to notice an advertisement for a memorial assembly for the Jews of Podhajce and its environs which was to take place three days later. According to a custom which has become popular in Israel, Jews from European communities destroyed during the Second World War erect special monuments to commemorate the victims of the Holocaust from their area. These monuments are erected in Israeli cemeteries, usually in the Tel Aviv area, where most of the survivors currently reside. It just so happened that the monument for Podhajce had recently been completed and was to be dedicated in a special ceremony at the Nachlat Yitzhak cemetery in Tel Aviv. I very much doubt whether under normal circumstances the memorial assembly would have been publicized in the press. Thus inadvertently we were the main beneficiaries of this occasion, which turned out to be far more significant than the organizers had ever anticipated.

On June 1, 1986 I attended the memorial assembly hoping to find survivors who knew S. and/or individuals who might be able to direct me to Mira Tuchfeld. I found both in the person of Aron Amitai* of Ramle who provided me with all the information I required. According to Amitai, there were only three Jews from P.S.'s town who had lived there for any length of time during the Nazi occupation. All three—two sisters and one brother—were members of the Tuchfeld family. The brother had passed away after the war but the sisters Mira and Chasia were still alive. The former—the Mira Tuchfeld we were searching for—

---

* Name changed.

was living in Queens, New York while the latter was presently in Vienna. Amitai was also from the town, but he had been drafted into the Red Army immediately before the war and consequently had not been in the town during the Nazi occupation. At the end of the war, however, he returned home to determine the fate of his family and friends and learned of the activities of the Ukrainian police and the role that they had played in the murder of the Jews. When I told him that we were looking for potential witnesses against officers of the local Ukrainian police, he immediately volunteered S.'s name. Amitai related that he knew the family very well since they had been his neighbors and he had grown up together with S. This fact apparently had not had any effect on the Ukrainian police commander since according to Amitai it was P.S. who had murdered his parents.

Besides supplying me with the addresses of the two Tuchfeld sisters, Aron Amitai also gave me the name of a Jewish survivor from the nearby village of Hevaronka who was presently living in Wroclaw, Poland and might be able to provide valuable testimony. I was also able, with his assistance, to obtain the names of quite a few additional survivors of the Podhajce area who until then were unknown to me. One of these individuals even gave me the name of another Ukrainian who had actively participated in the murder of the Jews in that region and had subsequently escaped to the United States. Thus attending the memorial assembly had proven extremely worthwhile and we now had a far better chance of bringing S. to justice. This was further corroborated about a week and a half later when David Marwell called to inform me that thanks to the information obtained from Amitai, Mira Tuchfeld had been located and had indeed identified the suspect.

At this time the P.S. case is still under investigation by OSI and I am hopeful that an indictment will be submitted in the near future. To a certain extent, the S. investigation was a test case which conclusively proved that the research and development project launched in Washington had serious potential. Yet as convincing as this investigation was, it was only one case and thus its implications—as important as they were—were not as significant as those of another discovery made at about the same time. Whereas the P.S. investigation proved that one of the individuals listed in the Yad Vashem index of Nazi war criminals had immigrated to the United States, a fact which indicated that others probably did so as well, the discovery in question led to unequivocal proof that hundreds, if not thousands, of Nazi war criminals had escaped to the West. The documentation in question, moreover, provided precise information on the date of immigration, the means of transport and in the case of those who immigrated to the United States, even included an address of destination. The project, which could at best be considered potentially valuable based on the P.S. investigation, suddenly became extremely significant in the wake of a new discovery which afforded us access to information on hundreds of Nazis living in the United States. "R & D" which had been launched based on an educated conjecture ultimately proved itself conclusively beyond our wildest dreams.

Oddly enough the discovery in question was revealed in the course of one of OSI's most exciting and most famous, yet least practical investigations. In spring 1985 I began research to determine whether Dr. Josef Mengele had been arrested and released by the American authorities after the war. While that question was undoubtedly of importance, and was of interest from a historical point of view, in my mind it was of no practical value whatsoever. The American government had already committed itself to the search for the "Angel of Death;" even if we did prove that the Americans had indeed arrested and released him, what more could they do to atone for this misdeed? If we proved that the arrest and release had never taken place, whatever motivation had originally existed for the Americans to allocate resources toward finding him would no longer exist.

By late spring 1986 more than a year had elapsed since I began working on the Mengele case. Much of our research had focused on the sources of the information regarding Mengele's arrest by the American authorities. Over the course of the investigation, we had eliminated various leads so that by the winter of 1986 we were left with one last possible source, a Polish survivor named David Freimann who had been in Auschwitz during the war and had apparently worked for the Americans afterwards in occupied Germany. My problem was to find him. In this context the most important aspect of the search was the use made of the files of the International Tracing Service (ITS) of Arolson, Germany. Established by the Allied High Commission as a means of providing information regarding the fate of Europeans who had been uprooted during the war, its files were a veritable gold mine of information regarding Displaced Persons.

The ITS files—or to be more precise microfilm copies—have been in the Yad Vashem Archives since approximately November 1957.[19] I had always had the impression that this material related exclusively to Jewish victims of the Holocaust and/or Jewish Displaced Persons because the only cases in which it was used at Yad Vashem was to respond to requests concerning the whereabouts of Jews who had lived in Europe during the war. Imagine my surprise when in studying the files in search of Freimann's name, I discovered that the ITS had entries not only on Jewish victims and Displaced Persons, but on millions of non-Jews as well.

This discovery was extremely important because many of the files included immigration data such as destination, date of emigration, and means of transport. For those who immigrated to the United States, an exact address was usually also supplied. It did not take long to realize what incredible potential the ITS material had in terms of finding Nazi war criminals. Six years of research for OSI had taught me that the overwhelming majority of the Nazis living in the United States had emigrated from occupied Germany as Displaced Persons who, in most cases, had not changed their names or identities. If that were indeed true, we now had a relatively easy and foolproof way of finding them. If I were right, they would be listed in the ITS files which included exact information regarding their immigration. There would no longer be any need to submit long lists of criminals to the Immigration and Naturalization Service in the hope of perhaps finding someone who might have come to the United States; we could now check each case directly.

Rather than leave this theory to the realm of hypothesis, I decided immediately to put it to the test. I took the names of approximately 50 Lithuanians and Latvians accused of committing crimes against civilians during the Second World War and began searching for their names in the ITS files. The results were amazing. I found entries for 16 out of 49 names, and in ten cases there was detailed information concerning their immigration. This meant that at least 16 of the 49 criminals had escaped from Eastern Europe and were living as Displaced Persons in occupied Germany after the war. Of the ten cases in which emigration data was available, five had gone to the United States, two to Canada and one to Australia. In two cases we were not absolutely sure of the final destination as there was more than one entry for the name in question.

These results confirmed my suspicion that the ITS files could lead us to numerous Nazi war criminals who had emigrated to the West. It was true that in some cases we faced problems because we lacked pertinent biographical information, which would have made our research both easier and more accurate, but there was no doubt that this material would significantly advance our research. For the first time we would be able to determine within a matter of minutes whether a Nazi war criminal had left Eastern Europe and emigrated to the West, and if so, to what country. The system was not entirely foolproof because there probably were some criminals who had changed their names and thereby succeeded in eluding capture by this method. The overwhelming majority, however, had not done so and in theory could be discovered in the ITS files.

Although I was aware of the enormous potential of this documentation from the beginning, I wanted to have definite proof of the validity of the system I had devised before I began to think in apocalyptic terms. As case after case was found in the files, however, it became increasingly clear that I had stumbled across a tool which could revolutionize the search for Nazi war criminals. Now that this material had been found and utilized in the proper manner, I sensed that all the work and energy which had been invested over the past six years had laid the foundation for a truly significant breakthrough and that Israel had indeed made a worthy contribution to the research effort.

At this point what remained to be done was the practical application of this system in order to discover Nazi war criminals residing in the United States and elsewhere in the western world. The task consisted of the compilation of master-lists of Nazi war criminals which were then checked against the ITS documentation. These files were available at Yad Vashem on microfilm (3,915 microfilms with 16,268,921 frames to be exact)[20] arranged according to the phonetic alphabetic used by ITS. Using the alphabet was initially difficult because no explanation of its rules was readily available, but after the first few dozen names were completed I was able to proceed with relatively few problems.

Once I began concentrating almost exclusively on this task, my assignment seemed to enter a different dimension. Whereas my research had until then encompassed a wide variety of sources in numerous languages covering various aspects of the persecution and murder of Jews during the Holocaust, I was now focusing exclusively on postwar immigration. The work by then was becoming purely mechanical, almost automatic. I had to crosscheck a list of criminals with a list of Displaced Persons to determine whether the individual in question had been a refugee in Germany, whether he had emigrated, and if so, when and to where. Yet despite the seemingly routine nature of the task, it did have a certain element of excitement to it.

Each reel of microfilm had a tension all its own, each name checked was a mini-adventure. Each search was accompanied by the hope of a "hit," that the name would appear, that the biographical data would fit, that there would be clearcut emigration information and, most of all, in cases in which we did not possess a date of birth, that the criminal would be young. Each of these factors was a separate issue which ultimately affected our chances of identifying and prosecuting the suspects.

Under ideal circumstances we would have possessed complete biographical data—date and place of birth, name of parents and other pertinent information—on every suspect, but that was not the case. Consequently we occasionally encountered various question marks which also added an element of tension and anticipation to each investigation. The best cases were those in which all the information matched and there was unambiguous data on the destination, means of transport and date of emigration. In many cases we were not certain of the age of the criminal. This was always a critical point and the intense hope that the suspect was young accompanied every search in which the criminal's date of birth was unknown. In this respect we were often disappointed as we frequently discovered that the individual in question had indeed emigrated to the United States. Since he had been born in the previous century, we realized that our chances of ever bringing him to justice were practically nil.

There were other disappointments of a similar nature. Sometimes there would be an entry for the criminal in question but no evidence of emigration. In such cases it was possible to surmise that the individual had been living in Germany after the war and had registered as a refugee, but we had no indication as to his present whereabouts. These criminals had either continued to live in Germany or had subsequently emigrated elsewhere. If the latter were true, finding them was even more complicated as there were no leads regarding the country of destination. Such cases were a bit frustrating, but certainly nowhere near as disappointing as those in which no trace of the suspect was found. These criminals had either remained in Eastern Europe, in which case there was a reasonable chance that they had been tried and punished for their crimes, or had escaped to the West but had changed their names. It was the latter type of case which was particularly upsetting: it was obvious that there was scant hope that such criminals would ever be apprehended. Luckily, the overwhelming majority of the Eastern European collaborators did not adopt new identities and therefore we are presently able, at least in theory, to trace them and bring them to justice. The fact that many others fled and will never even be identified as escaped Nazi criminals so that their names, for the sake of the historical record, could be added to the "lists of shame" of those admitted to the Western democracies, remains a source of frustration.

Working on the ITS files was a research effort with its own rules and regulations and some interesting ironies as well. I mentioned the fact that the ITS arranged its files according to a phonetic alphabet. Besides getting used to reading y as i, v as w, d as t, double letters as single ones, and various other phonetic constructs too complex to relate in this context, mistakes were sometimes made either in the files or the master-lists in my possession which considerably complicated our efforts. I was once looking for a man who, according to my records, was named Petras Bitler and had played an active role in the murder of the Jews of Skuodas, Lithuania.[21] By accident I came across an entry for Petras Bitlierius who fitted the description perfectly. He was the right age and had been in Skuodas during the war. Under Bitler, however, there was no entry for a Petras and if not for the lucky accident of having come across the card for Bitlierius, I would never have found the person we were looking for who was indeed the criminal in question and who had emigrated to the United States (51 West Warren Avenue, Detroit, Michigan) in November 1950.

Another similar case involved a high-ranking criminal named Argods Fricsons who had served as the head of the Latvian Security Police in Liepaja and was in charge of the special murder squad which had killed the Jews of that city. Fricsons' name was quite well-known. It had appeared on practically every list of Latvian war criminals compiled after the war.[22]

For some reason, however, when I drew up my list of Latvians I mistakenly recorded it as Frickops not Fricsons. Thus it was hardly surprising that I did not find his name listed as a refugee in the ITS files. Luckily, however, there was another Latvian criminal named Fricsons on my list who had committed crimes in Valmiera and whose first name was unknown to me. As a result, I had to peruse all the various Fricsons listed, and in the course of this search I found the data on Argods Fricsons. I then checked the pertinent information regarding this suspect and realized that he was indeed the criminal in question.

According to the documentation in the ITS files, Fricsons had emigrated to Australia after the war, a fact confirmed by various Soviet publications.[23] These were not the only cases in which suspects were accidently found whose files in ITS were spelled slightly differently than the version on my master-list. Instances such as these demonstrate how careful we had to be in dealing with this documentation and how seemingly harmless errors could often have significant consequences.

Although the research on the ITS files was a very serious matter, I was not oblivious to some of the interesting ironies discovered. One of the things which I found quite amusing and actually gave me a great deal of satisfaction concerned the microfilms. Most had been produced by the Agfa film company, which on the face of it was hardly a likely candidate to supply materials that would ultimately lead to the prosecution of Nazi war criminals. Agfa was part of the I.G. Farben industrial empire which had several factories at Auschwitz which made extensive use of inmate labor.[24] I doubt whether the directors of the company had any idea to what good use their materials were put after the war. Who knows, perhaps those same microfilms were produced by concentration camp inmates?

Another interesting irony concerned the names of the criminals. There were several cases in which perpetrators and potential victims shared a common family name. In view of the pride with which most people relate to their names, such a discovery could be irritating to say the least. Not that I found any Jews named Hitler, Himmler, Goering or Goebbels, but I did discover some named Brasch,[25] Bruns[26] and Sidabras,[27] for example, which were the names of a Baltic German, a German and a Lithuanian who were accused of committing serious crimes against Jews during the Holocaust. Another discovery in a similar vein related to first names. In the course of my research I came across quite a few female first names which I had always thought were uniquely Hebrew, but were in fact borne by Lithuanians and Latvians as well. Dalia, for example, is the name of a flower in Hebrew and a fairly popular girl's name. To my surprise I found a few Lithuanian females with that exact name. The same applied to other strikingly Hebrew names which are common in Israel such as Maya and Tamara. It is hardly a comforting thought to think that the mother, wife, daughter or sister of the person who murdered one's relatives bears the same name as the person who represents the continuity of the people victimized.

These ironies were merely distractions or diversions that added some humor to what was essentially a mechanical task. As time went by and the statistics began to take shape several things became increasingly clear. One was the scope of the problem. It is one thing to read about thousands of Nazi war criminals who escaped justice; it is another to discover them one by one and see for oneself how they emigrated unhindered to the Western democracies. A second problem related to the countries other than the United States which had admitted Nazi war criminals. My research clearly indicated that although the United States had allowed the entry of more Nazi collaborators than any other Western democracy, the number of criminals who emigrated to other countries was also quite substantial. The leading culprits in this respect were Canada and Australia, but other countries were guilty as well. The scope of the problem in these countries could not be ignored. Every day that went by I discovered additional criminals who had escaped to Australia and to Canada, as well as many whose present whereabouts were unknown, which meant that they were either in Germany or had emigrated elsewhere in the West.

These findings forced me to confront the following dilemma. At that time there were only two Western governments which had special mechanisms to deal with this problem—the United States and West Germany. In my capacity as researcher in Israel for the Office of Special Investigations, the most I could do was to find the names of those suspects who had emigrated to the United States, transmit them to Washington and assist in the relevant investigations. What would happen to the information regarding those criminals who were living elsewhere? What was being done to see that they too would be prosecuted as was the case in the United States? As I uncovered case after case of criminals who had emigrated to Canada or Australia it became obvious that this information had to be used to induce those governments to take the necessary steps. I could hardly do so in my capacity as researcher for OSI, so I had to find a means to utilize this information, a way to arouse and mobilize public opinion and create effective political pressure in the various countries which were harboring Nazi war criminals.

The first institution that I thought of in this context was the Simon Wiesenthal Center of Los Angeles. Not only because of my tenure as its first director but because I thought that their expertise in arousing public opinion was precisely what was needed in this particular case. In addition, I knew that the Center had traditionally pursued an activist stance vis-à-vis Nazi war criminals and would not be afraid to confront the governments in question. Being personally acquainted with Rabbis Hier and Cooper I knew that they would understand the necessity for such a campaign, and would be able to implement it with the maximum resources and minimum bureaucracy.

Several months previously I had approached them regarding the possibility of establishing a computerized data bank on Nazi war criminals in order to facilitate prosecution. My original concept had been based, however, more on theory and hope than on the anticipation of attainable results. I had envisioned its establishment as being just as much for the sake of historical record as for practical purposes. Now that I had the data which could provide a solid basis for a campaign to convince governments to initiate prosecution, the circumstances had obviously changed. Ironically enough, shortly after I discovered the potential of the material in the ITS files, the Center informed me that they had accepted my original proposal regarding the establishment of the data bank. I told them, however, that in view of the documentation recently discovered, we had best concentrate on initiating prosecution in countries outside the United States since we now had the conclusive proof necessary to launch such an effort. The Center's positive response led to the establishment of its branch in Jerusalem and the initiation of a campaign designed to induce additional Western governments to bring the Holocaust criminals to justice.

Leaving the Office of Special Investigations was a difficult step to take. On a certain level, it was a dangerous gamble, because working for OSI put me at the pinnacle of practical work in this field. To my mind the most effective contribution which a historian can make towards the prosecution of Nazi war criminals is to engage in historical research on behalf of a governmental body which has the power to punish the criminals. I now planned to leave such a post to work for a private agency which could not prosecute a single Nazi war criminal. Nonetheless, I decided to make that move because my gut feeling was that only a major international public opinion campaign orchestrated by an organization like the Wiesenthal Center, using the information I had uncovered, could finally succeed in forcing reluctant Western governments to take action. What I was doing for OSI was undoubtedly important but could be done by someone else. As far as Canada, Australia and the other governments were concerned, they had to be convinced as soon as possible to initiate prosecution, or the criminals would die with their crimes unpunished.

During the course of the many weeks that I worked on the ITS files I was particularly perturbed by a single thought—the material at Yad Vashem had been there for 30 years before anyone realized its enormous potential and utilized it to search for Nazi war criminals. Now time was obviously running out and whatever could be achieved had to be done immediately and effectively. If the only way to do so was via a private agency, so be it. If it meant leaving OSI, then I really had no choice. History only rarely knocks at the same door twice.

Notes

1. The lists were compiled by the Association of Lithuanian Jews under the auspices of the Central Committee of Liberated Jews in the American zone of Germany. YVA, M-9/15(6,6a).

2. See the entries for all the "provincial" Jewish communities in Lithuania, *Yahadut Lita*, Vol. IV, pp. 234-373.

3. *Kehillat Shkod; Kovetz Zikaron*, Tel Aviv, 1958, p. 47.

4. *Krakenovo: Our Town in Lithuania*, Johannesburg, 1961.

5. *Sefer Keydan*, pp. 229-33, 235-36.

6. See, for example, B. Baranauskas, *Hitleriniai Parasiutininkai*, Vilnius, 1966; B. Baranauskas, *Hitlerininku Penktoji Kolona Lietuvoje*, Vilnius, 1961; S. Bistrickas, *Ir Susaudytieji Prabyla*, Vilnius, 1960; M. Elinas and D. Gelpernas, *Kauno getas ir jo Kovotojai*, Vilnius, 1960.

7. *Documents Accuse*, Vilnius, 1970; *Masines Zudynes Lietuvoje (1941-1944)*, Vilnius, 1965.

8. The opening sentence in the chapter on "Directives to Mass Killings and Persecutions" is a typical example. "Directives to kill and persecute Communists, supporters of a socialist order and other patriots as well as Jews in Lithuania had been worked out in Nazi Germany." In the chapter on "Mass Execution, Its Executors and Consequences" the murder of the Jews is noted, but the emphasis is on the execution of "Soviet activists, anti-fascists and new settlers who had received land from the Soviet state." *Documents Accuse*, pp. 119, 181-86.

9. *Yahadut Lita*, Vol. IV, pp. 234-373.

10. "Seduva," ibid., pp. 363-64.

11. Levin is probably the most prolific scholar involved in research on Lithuanian Jewry during the interwar period and the Second World War. See, for example, *Lochamim ve-Omdim al Nafsham*, Jerusalem, 1975; together with A.T. Baron, *Toldoteha shel Machteret*, as well as numerous articles.

12. "Semeliskes," *Yahadut Lita*, Vol. IV, pp. 323-24.

13. "Uzpalis," ibid., p. 242.

14. "Salakas," ibid., pp. 321-22.

15. The material is in YVA, M-21. I am not naming the specific file since the case is still under investigation.

16. The advertisement appeared in various papers published by Dsiplaced Persons, among them *Undzer Weg*.

17. See above, note 15.

18. See, for example, the testimonies of Leah Feldberg (0-3/2946), Nachum Pushtig (0-3/2983), and Yitzhak Lev (0-3/3063), YVA.

19. Dr. Josef-Kurt Sella, "The 'ITS' Microfilm Project of Yad Vashem" (internal), YVA, pp. 1-2.

20. Ibid., p. 10.

21. YVA, M-9/15(6).

22. See, for example, YVA, M-21/III/8, 37; WLA, 539/24; Ezergailis, p. 34.

23. J. Silabriedis and B. Arklans, *"Political Refugees" Unmasked!*, Riga, 1965, p. 62.

24. Hilberg, p. 591; Joseph Borkin, *The Crime and Punishment of I.G. Farben*, New York, 1978.

25. WLA, 539/22, 24, 27; YVA, M-21/476.

26. *The Black Book*, edited by Ilya Ehrenburg and Vassili Grossman, New York, 1981, p. 305.

27. Mendel Sidarsky, Uriya Katzenellenbogen and Y. Kissin (eds), *Lite*, Vol. 1, New York, 1951, p. 1819.

7

As a Lobby for Increased
Israeli Involvement

For the thousands of Israelis who thronged to attend the trial of Ivan Demjanjuk,[1] the fact that the man accused of being "Ivan the Terrible" from Treblinka was being tried in Jerusalem appeared to be the most natural thing in the world. What could be more fitting, after all, than that the Jewish state prosecute the perpetrators of the worst crime in the annals of Jewish history. What could be more natural than that the sovereign entity which had been created in the wake of the Holocaust and had served as a haven for tens of thousands of survivors bring to justice the criminals who had participated in the annihilation of thousands of Jewish communities. From its establishment, Israel had been cognizant of its special role in prosecuting those responsible for the crimes of the Final Solution. Shortly after it attained independence, the Jewish state passed a special law to enable its courts to try Nazi war criminals.[2] This policy was also clearly reflected in the capture and trial of Adolf Eichmann, head of the Jewish department of the Gestapo (IV-B-4), who had escaped to Argentina after the war and was kidnapped by Israeli agents in 1960.[3] Given the fact that Demjanjuk could not be punished for his crimes in the United States, Israel's extradition of the man accused of the murder of hundreds of thousands of Jews appeared, at least on the surface, to be the logical outcome of traditional Israeli policy.

The truth, however, was quite different. Rather than being the natural result of Israel's attempts to fulfil its historic obligations vis-à-vis the victims of the Holocaust, the Demjanjuk trial could best be described as a step taken by the Israeli government with great reluctance. Rather than being the fulfillment of a long-sought goal, the extradition of the man accused of being "Ivan the Terrible" was considered by various government of officials as an unpleasant and unnecessary task forced upon Israel. The stark contrast between the motivation which prompted the passage of the Nazi War Criminals and Collaborators Punishment Law by the Knesset in 1950 and the apathy of the Israeli government vis-à-vis its practical application throughout most of the past four decades is a reflection of the serious changes which have taken place in Israeli society and the ambivalence and confusion of present-day Israeli leadership regarding some of the contemporary implications and obligations of the Holocaust.

Over the course of the past 45 years, the attitude of Israeli officials regarding the prosecution of Nazi war criminals has undergone significant changes and can be divided into several periods. During the Second World War and its immediate aftermath, the leaders of the *Yishuv* (Jewish community of Palestine) viewed the prosecution and punishment of the perpetrators of the Holocaust as an important goal. Although at this point, prior to the establishment of the state, the ability of the Palestinian Jewish community to bring the perpetrators to justice was obviously severely limited, various measures were taken to facilitate the achievement of that goal. This assistance usually took the form of attempts to apprehend the most wanted criminals and ensure their prosecution by the occupation authorities, although in several instances steps were taken by individuals to execute Nazis who had participated in the implementation of the Final Solution.

As early as 1942 the Jewish Agency, which constituted the official leadership of the Jews in Palestine, began collecting evidence regarding the crimes committed by the Nazis and their collaborators. Jews who managed to escape from occupied Europe during the course of the war were interviewed for this purpose and lists of Nazi war criminals were compiled.[4] These lists were sent to Europe with Jewish Agency emissaries after the war and attempts were made to locate the most prominent criminals in order to bring them to justice. Although the primary objective of the delegation from Palestine was to facilitate the exodus of Holocaust survivors from Eastern Europe and to arrange for their (illegal) immigration to Palestine, efforts were also made to see to it that those responsible for the murders paid for their crimes. One of the functions of the Vienna office of the Jewish Agency headed by Arthur Ben-Natan was to collect evidence and witnesses against Nazi war criminals and turn them over to the judicial authorities. Most of the criminals were tried by the Soviet, Polish or Czech authorities who adopted a far more stringent policy than their American or British counterparts. Tuvia Friedman, a survivor of Radom, Poland, who subsequently was to devote many years to the hunt for Nazi criminals, played a leading role in this operation which was headed by Alex Gatmon.[5]

Besides the efforts to bring Nazis to justice before the courts, Palestinian soldiers from the Jewish Brigade were involved in attempts to avenge the mass murder of Jews during the Holocaust. These soldiers, who were under the command of the Hagana (the military arm of the Jewish Agency) sought out and executed Nazis who had played an active role in the implementation of the Final Solution. These measures were usually taken without the official approval of the political leadership, however, which wanted to concentrate on the organization of illegal immigration to Palestine. Only in a few cases were the leaders of the Hagana willing to approve revenge activities and even then with extreme reluctance. While several groups of survivors were carrying out the execution of tens of prominent Nazis and were actively pursuing plans for mass revenge, the Palestinian Jewish leaders for the most part adhered to a legalistic approach.[6]

The establishment of the State of Israel in May 1948 in no way altered or diminished the desire of the Jewish leadership to bring the Nazi murderers to trial, although the difficult circumstances in which the nascent state found itself undoubtedly dictated a different set of priorities. The major objectives became winning the War of Independence and absorbing the masses of new immigrants who flocked to the Jewish state. Nonetheless, in 1950, shortly after the conclusion of the war, the Knesset passed the Nazi War Criminals and Collaborators Punishment Law which authorized the Israeli judicial system to prosecute and punish the perpetrators of the Holocaust. This law, which was passed shortly after the Law of Return, which granted automatic Israeli citizenship to any Jew seeking to live in Israel, is considered one of the classic pieces of Jewish legislation passed by the Israeli parliament. In the words of Justice Minister Pinchas Rosen, the law was a declaration vis-à-vis the past. "We will neither forget nor forgive. This is an accounting with the past . . . In passing these laws we are fulfilling an obligation, an elementary and natural obligation."[7] Beyond the declaratory value of such statements, the law constituted a manifestation of the application of Jewish memory in sovereign terms. Not only could the Jewish state commemorate the martyrs, she now for the first time had the political and judicial authority to extradite, prosecute and punish the perpetrators of the Holocaust.

It is not clear whether those who drafted the law had any particular criminals in mind when they formulated this piece of legislation. No concrete plan of action accompanied the law, nor were any trials of

Nazi criminals held in the immediate wake of its passage by the Knesset. Israel recognized the need to create the legal framework that would enable the Jewish state to play an active role in bringing those responsible for the murder of European Jewry to the bar of justice. Once the legal groundwork had been established, however, the law remained a purely theoretical matter until 1960 when Adolf Eichmann was captured and put on trial in Jerusalem. During the decade between the passage of the law and its initial application, no attempt was made to extradite Nazi war criminals to Israel and none were put on trial. There are indications that during this period Israel was involved in clandestine activities to liquidate leading Nazis who had not been prosecuted, but the existence and scope of these activities remain unconfirmed and unclear to this day. The only practical results of the law, in fact, were the trials of several Jews who had served as kapos or had assisted the Nazis, who were discovered living in Israel.[8]

The Eichmann trial marked an important watershed in the Israeli attitude toward the Holocaust. The testimonies of the witnesses riveted the attention of the Israeli public and exposed the entire population to the story of the persecution and destruction of European Jewry. Rather than confining the proceedings to the crimes committed by Eichmann, the prosecution utilized the opportunity of a trial held in Jerusalem to present a comprehensive survey of the scope of the Final Solution.[9] For the first time in its brief history, Israel squarely faced the horrors of the fate of European Jewry during the Second World War. The public exposure of those events, which had been experienced by so many Israelis but remained taboo in numerous homes, had a profound effect on countless Israeli Jews, especially the younger generation. For many Israelis, the trial was their first meaningful exposure to the subject.[10] Besides the psychological impact which the proceedings had on the Israeli public, the trial had practical results as well. The most important in terms of the prosecution of Nazi war criminals was the establishment by the Israeli police of a special office for the investigation of Nazi war crimes. This office, which was an outgrowth of the police unit which investigated Adolf Eichmann, was to handle all cases related to the crimes committed during the Second World War.

Over the course of the more than 25 years since its establishment, the unit has conducted numerous investigations and has assisted the judicial authorities in many countries. The members of the unit have interviewed thousands of survivors and have provided documents and witnesses for the prosecution of countless criminals throughout the world. During the initial period of its operation most of the cases investigated were of Nazis tried in West Germany, but in recent years the majority of the cases have been those initiated by the Office of Special Investigations in the United States.[11] Until Ivan Demjanjuk was extradited, however, not a single one of the investigations conducted by the unit resulted in a trial held in Israel. While Israeli assistance to prosecute Nazis was always forthcoming, there was no active involvement in prosecution by the Israeli government during the 25 years which elapsed between the Eichmann trial and that of Ivan Demjanjuk.

Throughout the entire period between those two trials, only three times did Israel attempt to bring a Nazi to justice in Jerusalem, all of which were unsuccessful. The most recent attempt was the search for Dr. Josef Mengele which has been described elsewhere in this book. In that case, Israel operated in conjunction with the West German and American authorities. In view of the West Germans' determination to bring Mengele—if found alive—to trial in Germany, Israeli involvement seemed more symbolic than practical.[12] The other two efforts were extradition requests submitted by Israel during the late 1970s. One was for the extradition of Gustav Franz Wagner the deputy commandant of the Sobibor death camp, who was living in Brazil,[13] and the second was for the extradition of the Dutch war criminal Peter Menten, who had played an active role in the murder of the Jews in Galicia.[14] Both requests, which were rejected on legal grounds, were initiated during the tenure of Shmuel Tamir as Minister of Justice (1977-1980). Tamir considered the prosecution of Nazi war criminals a basic moral obligation of the Jewish state, and sought to apply Israel's commitment on a practical level. His activities constituted an exception to previous and subsequent Israeli policy vis-à-vis the trial in Israel of Nazi war criminals. None of the other Israeli ministers of justice during the past two and a half decades took an active interest in this subject and as survivors passed away and memories receded, official Israeli activity and interest dissipated.[15]

Ironically, this process was taking place at a time when other countries were beginning to attempt to deal with this problem. The most important example in this respect was the United States where revelations concerning the presence of numerous Nazi war criminals prompted the establishment in 1979 of the Office of Special Investigations.[16] The initial trials of suspected Nazi war criminals in the United

States sparked additional interest and paved the way for the passage of special legislation to facilitate the prosecution of the perpetrators of the Holocaust. OSI's success, moreover, focused public attention on the critical role played by the collaborators of Eastern European origin in the implementation of the Final Solution. The action taken in the United States also aroused interest in countries such as Canada and Australia which, like America, had admitted large numbers of Displaced Persons of Eastern European origin as immigrants after the war. For years there had been allegations that numerous Nazi war criminals had found haven in these countries[17] and the prosecution efforts in the United States served as a catalyst for the official commissions of inquiry which were subsequently established in both Canada and Australia.[18]

The Nazi war criminals residing in the United States could not be tried for their wartime crimes because they were not committed in US territory nor were they carried out against American citizens. They therefore were tried for lying on their immigration and/or naturalization forms, the maximum penalty for which was deportation from the United States.[19] The fact that these individuals could not be punished for their actual crimes paved the way, at least in theory, for active Israeli involvement. Israel could demand their extradition under the Nazi War Criminals and Collaborators Punishment Law and thereby ensure that they received their just due. In these cases extradition requests were particularly important because of the legal constraints under which the trials were conducted in the United States. Under normal circumstances, the alleged Nazi war criminals tried by OSI were not incarcerated prior to and/or during the trial and consequently several were able to escape. Both Juozas Kisilaitis of the Lithuanian Auxiliary Police battalions[20] and Stefan Leili, a guard at Mauthausen,[21] left the United States prior to their trial and thereby escaped prosecution. In cases in which an extradition request was submitted, however, the suspect was immediately put in jail pending the outcome of legal proceedings.

Despite the opportunities for increased Israeli involvement created as a result of OSI's activities, that agency's initial successes did not lead to any change in Israeli policy. Although discussions regarding the possibility of extradition to Israel of a Nazi war criminal living in the United States were conducted as early as 1981,[22] initially no steps were taken to achieve that goal. Furthermore, Israel never actively pursued Nazi war criminals living in Canada, Australia or any of the other Western democracies, despite the fact that substantial information regarding their whereabouts existed in Israel and was readily available to the Israeli authorities. Evidence of Israeli disinterest was manifested, for example, in the extradition treaty signed with Canada in 1967, which extended only to crimes committed after that date in the territory of either state.[23] Instead of attempting to prepare a legal framework which would enable prosecution, the Israeli government chose to ignore the issue. Instead of actively seeking out the perpetrators and attempting to ensure that they paid for their crimes, Israel exhibited an incomprehensible apathy. Instead of speaking out on behalf of the victims, as they were wont to do on so many occasions in the past, the silence from Jerusalem was deafening.

It was under those circumstances that I began working for OSI in Jerusalem in the autumn of 1980. At that time I was hardly cognizant of the problematic stance of the Israeli government vis-à-vis the prosecution of Nazi war criminals. I was more concerned about finding documents and witnesses for the investigations conducted in Washington, since my primary objective at this point was to convince my superiors of the necessity of an OSI presence in Israel. The thought never crossed my mind that Israel might be doing less than it could to prosecute the perpetrators of the Holocaust. I more or less accepted as given that the Nazis living in the United States could not be punished since the maximum penalty for lying during the immigration and/or naturalization process was deportation, and even that modest goal had not yet been achieved in a single case tried by OSI. I was not aware of Israel's potential in terms of extradition and at this point no one was yet thinking along those lines.

My initial months were spent doing research on our top-priority cases. In discussions with Allan Ryan and Deputy Director Art Sinai prior to returning to Israel I had raised the possibility of adopting a high-profile presence in Jerusalem, which I believed would assist us in finding witnesses, but the heads of OSI insisted that I confine my activities to research at Yad Vashem. My first step, therefore, was to convince OSI that there were additional archives in Israel which contained valuable documentation related to the cases we were investigating. OSI had no knowledge of these other archives so step one was to obtain approval to expand our research to Beit Lohamei ha-Gettaot (Ghetto Fighters' Kibbutz),[24] Tel Aviv University (Weiner Library); and Givat Chaviva (Moreshet); as well as the collection of testimony at the Hebrew University (Oral History Division, Institute of Contemporary

Jewry) and Bar-Ilan University (Institute for Holocaust Research). Once the principle was established that my mandate was to uncover whatever pertinent material existed in Israel, I was also able to expand the search to private collections, some of which proved quite helpful.

Given the fact that OSI was run by lawyers, not historians, and that the individuals in question had little or no idea at this point as to the scope of the documentation on the Holocaust in Israeli archives, it is hardly surprising that at times I found myself in mild disagreement with my superiors. In most cases I was able to convince them to alter the original assignment, although at times it was not that easy to persuade them to adopt my point of view. Another example of the problems faced in this context were the instructions which OSI director Allan Ryan issued to his staff regarding the use of material at Yad Vashem. During his visit to Israel in June 1981, I had discussed this issue with him at length and had attempted to impress upon him the potential value of the documentation. The instructions he issued were, however, that Yad Vashem should only be consulted if the case in question appeared to have merit and all domestic sources had been exhausted. But what about those cases which did not appear to have any merit because there was no material in the United States? Perhaps there was documentation in Israel which would enable OSI to prosecute? If Ryan's instructions were implemented, OSI would never even know about such documents. I therefore appealed to Ryan to change this procedure and ensure that at least a preliminary investigation would be made in Israel regarding every bona fide case. Ryan agreed and on September 17, 1981 cabled that instructions had been issued to the OSI staff to consult with Israel even in cases in which US sources were negative, if it was believed that the effort would prove worthwhile.[25]

This was a classic example of the type of differences of opinion which I had with the leaders of OSI during the initial years of my assignment. As far as historical research was concerned, we were usually able to reach an agreement. However, there were other areas of investigation in which we did not see eye to eye—for example the search for witnesses. OSI insisted that I restrict my efforts to historical research and not launch any public campaigns to seek out survivors. I thought that we would be severely negligent in fulfilling our task if we did not utilize the media and whatever other means existed of finding potential witnesses. This was the reason that I had suggested the possibility of opening up an OSI office in Israel, which would have significantly raised our profile and aroused public consciousness on the issue. As long as my activities in Israel were confined to documentation, however, it was obvious that we would not be able fully to utilize Israel's potential in this critical area.

In discussions with the directors of OSI, I often had the impression that in principle they were amenable to such suggestions. The problem was that they were afraid of angering the Nazi war crimes unit of the Israeli police, who were officially responsible for finding and interviewing survivors. The fear in Washington was that the Israelis would consider the opening of an OSI office in Israel as an "invasion" of their territory and an insult to their professional capabilities. Since OSI was dependent on the Israeli police for assistance in various official aspects of the investigation process, they naturally wanted to maintain good relations with the unit's commander, Lieutenant Colonel Russek and members of his staff. This meant in effect that any public search for witnesses had to be conducted solely by the Israeli police. If the Nazi war crimes unit had been a dynamic, ingenious and imaginative group of tireless investigators with unlimited resources at their disposal, that would not have constituted a serious problem. Unfortunately that was not the case.

My contact with the Israeli police and the opportunities I had to view their methods at first hand convinced me of the necessity to conduct a public search for witnesses. The best way to do so would have been to open an office or at least actively publicize our activities and the results of the trials in the United States, but OSI remained adamant throughout that no such steps be taken. Even my work in Israel as a researcher was a source of friction with the Israeli police and OSI did not want to exacerbate an already-delicate situation.

Almost from the beginning of my assignment, Menachem Russek adopted a skeptical view of my activities in Israel, which he apparently considered an encroachment on his "turf." I could relate quite a few amusing incidents about the different means he found to indicate his displeasure, all at my expense, but that is not the point. Nor was this solely a question of power, jurisdiction or the questionable efficiency of government bureaucracy, all of which were undoubtedly elements of this problematic relationship. The most interesting aspect, to my mind, was the tension between Russek, who was a survivor, and myself, a university-trained scholar of the Holocaust born after the war. I think that he found it difficult to accept that a person who had not lived through the horrors could be as, or even more, knowledgeable than someone like himself who had survived those events. This gap between survivors and non-survivors is a fact of life in the post-Holocaust Jewish world. At times it constitutes an obstacle in dialogue between survivors and their offspring as well as in the work of organizations and institutions which seek to commemorate the Holocaust. When confronted by OSI's decision to hire a university-trained expert to carry out research which ostensibly was part of his job, he may well have felt uncomfortable.

As long as Lt. Col. Russek's displeasure was confined to the interpersonal level, it did not pose a problem. As time went on it began affecting our work, however, since he usually opposed any initiatives which he knew I had originated. Both Allan Ryan and Neal Sher tried to induce the colonel to accept me as a regular member of the OSI staff,[26] but their efforts were only partially successful.

My contact with the Israeli police strengthened my conviction that our activities could very much benefit from more extensive exposure. The problem was how to do so with OSI's approval and without incurring the wrath of the Israeli police. This was no easy task since my mandate precluded activities of this sort. I could not reveal any of the confidential information which journalists were so eager to obtain but which would result in headlines which might jeopardize the investigations. Thus I found myself attempting to provide the media with information about the trials which had taken place in the United States as well as some innocuous details regarding the research carried out in Israel on behalf of OSI. It would be very hard to determine what impact, if any, the few news items and articles which appeared had; it was obvious, however, that as long as I did not receive permission from Washington to proceed, no real progress would be made. I discussed the issue several times with Allan Ryan during his tenure as director. Although he agreed that more extensive publicity in Israel could prove beneficial, neither he nor his successor ever approved any such initiatives. On the contrary, whenever an opportunity arose for a public response they insisted that it be handled by Washington. It should be noted, however, that even if permission had been forthcoming, it is not clear to what extent we would have been successful. At this point, in the early 1980s, there was relatively little interest in Israel in the trials of collaborators of Eastern European origin who were indicted for lying to the US immigration authorities and were not liable for punishment for their wartime crimes.

Besides making me aware of the need for more extensive publicity about OSI's activities, my contacts with the Israeli police also raised serious question marks in my mind regarding government policy vis-à-vis the prosecution of Nazi war criminals. If the Nazi war crimes unit represented the primary effort of the State of Israel to bring the murderers of European Jewry to justice, then it seemed obvious that this was not a priority as far as the government was concerned. The unit consisted of several elderly men all either on the verge of, or in some cases even past, retirement age.[27] Although a few were quite intelligent and most very experienced, years upon years of this work, combined with their advanced age had taken their toll. While they were anxious for our activities to succeed, the exhaustive efforts necessary to conduct such investigations were not always in abundant supply. In addition, there was not a single trained historian on their staff. In short, it did not take many trips to the offices of the Nazi war crimes unit in Jaffa to begin to realize that the State of Israel was hardly obsessed with the fact that time was rapidly running out on efforts to prosecute Nazi war criminals. The continued existence of the unit ostensibly constituted proof that Israel was continuing to fulfil its historic obligation, but in reality this amounted to little more than the proverbial fig-leaf.

The doubts I had regarding the seriousness of the Israeli commitment to bring Nazi war criminals to justice crystallized in late April 1983. At that point the issue, which until then had been primarily theoretical, assumed a more definite form. Acting Director Neal Sher was scheduled to come to Israel to discuss the possibility that the United States would extradite the Rumanian Orthodox archbishop Valerian Trifa to Israel to stand trial for his crimes. This was a surprising development in view of the fact that OSI had hitherto refrained from pursuing extradition to Israel. The Trifa case presented special problems, however, which induced the Americans to seek new solutions to deal with the prelate who had been ordered deported by the courts. In cases such as this, if the court does not order the accused deported to a specific country, he can choose his destination. If that country refuses to admit him, the government can send him to any country of its choice. In most cases they try to send him either to his country of embarkation or the country where he resided prior to his emigration.

Trifa, who had headed the student division of the Iron Guard, the Rumanian fascist movement, and had played an active role in anti-Jewish activities, chose Switzerland as his country of destination. The Swiss, however, refused to allow his entry, as did the Germans (country of prior residence) and Italians (port of embarkation). The Rumanians, who had tried Trifa in absentia after the war and had sentenced him to life imprisonment, indicated to the Americans that they were not interested in the Orthodox prelate. Thus OSI found itself in a serious predicament, which threatened to complicate its future operations. If no country was willing to accept Trifa, he could continue to live in the United States, albeit without the privileges of citizenship. Such a result, after years of protracted legal proceedings, would undoubtedly weaken support for OSI's activities. Under those circumstances, the possibility arose of extradition to Israel which solved the destination problem and at the same time ensured trial and punishment.[28]

My spontaneous reaction to the possibility of Trifa's extradition to Israel was extremely positive. Although I had not worked on the case, I was elated that an OSI subject would finally be punished for his crimes. At this point the thought never even crossed my mind that Israel might not agree to take him. After all, the problem had always been that the non-Jewish world was shirking its responsibility on this issue. The Jews were all in favor of prosecution, or so I thought. In reality, however, the situation was quite different. All my contacts with the Israeli police should have warned me that on a practical level one had to distinguish between Israeli rhetoric and action. Indeed, according to a well-placed source in the Israeli police, representatives of the Israeli Foreign Ministry, Justice Ministry and the police's Nazi war crimes unit had discussed the issue and agreed unanimously that Israel should refuse to extradite Trifa. My contact was unable to relate the specific arguments marshalled by the representatives of the various ministries, but he was certain of the conclusion.

Even though all indicators pointed in this direction, I could not believe that Israel could respond in such a manner. It was as if she was negating one of the basic foundations of her own existence. Under those circumstances, the only hope of averting what appeared at that point to be a mistake of historic proportions would be to reveal the truth to the general public. If government officials had doubted the wisdom of extraditing Nazi war criminals, perhaps public opinion could remind them of some of the reasons for doing so. Although such activities were definitely not part of my official assignment, I felt I had a responsibility to alert the public to what was about to happen. Regardless of the lack of interest exhibited earlier by the local media in the trials conducted in the United States, this information was bound to arouse considerable attention since it was a classic "man bites dog" story. Israel, the Jewish state, was rejecting an opportunity to prosecute a Nazi war criminal.

The person I chose to reveal the information to was Avraham Ben-Melech, Israel Radio's correspondent for Jewish affairs. Over the years he had evinced an active interest in this issue and had broadcast numerous programs on the subject of the Holocaust. Within approximately an hour and a half after our conversation, Kol Yisrael broadcast the story about Trifa as the leading item on its 10 a.m. and 11 a.m. news broadcasts.[29] Ben-Melech's scoop, moreover, paved the way for extensive news stories in all of Israel's major newspapers. Over the course of the next few days, *Ha-Aretz*,[30] *Ma'ariv*,[31] *Yediot Achronot*[32] and the *Jerusalem Post*[33] all carried major stories regarding Sher's visit and the possibility of Trifa's extradition to Israel. There was also extensive coverage regarding these events in the United States, including a page one story in the *New York Times*.[34]

The most important development was that the news stirred a serious public debate on the issue of Israeli involvement in the prosecution of Nazi war criminals 38 years after the end of the Second World War. Given the natural assumption that Israel wanted to and should be involved in such activities, views to the contrary were initially featured prominently. MK Shevach Weiss, for example, a survivor of the Holocaust, and presently one of the most vocal advocates of increased Israeli participation in prosecution, was quoted in *Ha-Aretz* to the effect that "Israel does not have to become the world dumping ground for countries who because of irrelevant internal considerations refrain from trying Nazi or fascist war criminals."[35] The lead editorial in the same newspaper on that day was entitled "Will We Become Contractors for Nazi Trials?" and opposed Israeli involvement. According to *Ha-Aretz*, although the prosecution of Nazi war criminals is important both morally and from an educational point of view, Israel has more pressing tasks. Trifa and his like were not criminals on Eichmann's level and therefore it would hardly be worthwhile for the Israeli government to stage any mini-Eichmann trials that would arouse anti-Semitism throughout the world. Most important, according to *Ha-Aretz*, was the apprehension that a "festival of Nazi trials" would distract the government and the public from dealing with Israel's contemporary economic, social and foreign policy problems all of which required urgent attention.[36] Columnist Annette Dulzin (wife of the chairman of the Jewish Agency executive Aryeh Leon Dulzin) also added her voice to those urging Israel to refuse the American request. In an opinion piece published in *Yediot Achronot*, which was subsequently reprinted in the *New York Times*, as well as in an interview on the prestigious Israeli TV show *Zeh ha-Ze'man*, she called for practical considerations to determine Israeli policy. Neither she nor any of the others who publicly opposed Trifa's extradition to Israel were against the prosecution of Nazi war criminals per se; they believed instead that Israel did not necessarily have a role to play in cases such as these.[37] The fact that Trifa and others like him might escape punishment as a result of an Israeli decision to refrain from action did not perturb these advocates of pragmatism at all costs.

The voices of those who opposed Israeli involvement were not the only ones raised on this issue. Advocates of active Israeli participation spoke out in the media and pressed for Israel to fulfil its historic obligations vis-à-vis the victims of the Holocaust. Three prominent public figures who publicly supported Trifa's extradition to Israel were former Justice Minister Shmuel Tamir, and former Attorney-Generals Gideon Hausner and Moshe Ben-Zeev. In an interview with *Galei Tzahal* (IDF radio), Tamir, who was the only Israeli Justice Minister ever to initiate an extradition request for a Nazi war criminal, called upon Israel to do its utmost to bring the murderers to trial.[38] Hausner and Ben-Zeev published opinion pieces in the press advocating a positive Israeli response to the American offer. Ben-Zeev's article "The Crimes of the Nazis are Still Burning" which was published in *Ha-Aretz* on May 13, 1983, focused on the legal aspects of the proposal and stressed the importance of the Americans' recognition of Israel's right to try Nazi war criminals under the law passed by the Knesset in 1950. His essay concisely summarized most of the legal, historical and philosophical arguments presented by proponents of increased Israeli involvement in the prosecution of Nazi war criminals. For years, Ben-Zeev pointed out, no country had ever recognized Israel's right to implement the law and even the Eichmann trial in no way changed this situation. In fact, the only application to date of the law, besides the Eichmann trial, had been against Jewish collaborators found living in Israel.

And now surprisingly Israel is being offered the international recognition that the Nazi Punishment Law lacked for so many years. The United States—for its own reasons—has offered to transfer the Nazi criminal archbishop ValerianTrifa and apparently other Nazi criminals as well in order that they be tried here in accordance with the Nazi Punishment Law. The United States seeks to deport these criminals and cancel their American citizenship which was obtained fraudulently but has been unable to find a country willing to accept them. Thus this rare set of circumstances motivated the United States to recognize a right which Israel has been claiming for years: that she is the Jewish state even for the Jews who are not living within her boundaries and that she can try anyone who harms Jews in accordance with her laws, as long as no other country has a superior legal claim.

Ben-Zeev noted that if a similar proposal had been made years ago, when the law was originally passed, the Israeli government and people would have been overjoyed. Now instead of gladly accepting the opportunity to fulfil Israel's historic obligation, all sorts of practical arguments were being advanced which ignored the basic *raison d'être* of the Jewish state. He appealed to overcome the hesitation on this issue and not be blinded by exaggerated pragmatism.

For the sake of our mental health and our national honor, we must stop the hesitation of the various pragmatists. Just as by passing the law we only fulfilled—in the words of the then Minister of Justice—"a natural and elementary obligation" so too today as long as it is possible we will once again fulfil a "natural and elementary obligation" if we apply the law and try every Nazi criminal still on the face of the earth who can be brought to trial. We have neither the right nor the need to categorize the Nazi criminals beforehand into large and small categories. All activated the mighty destruction machine against our people. The banalization of the Holocaust is manifested not only in our overusing those events in superfluous and irrelevant contexts but also in refraining from performing deeds that must be done at a certain point in time and our responding with equanimity to this lack of action.

The educational, moral and national value of every trial of a Nazi war criminal, even if he is not on Eichmann's level, which will be held in Israel is a value which will last for generations. The significance of

such a value must take precedence over any practical argument based
on contemporary needs.[39]

Former Attorney General Gideon Hausner, the prosecuting attorney
at the Eichmann trial, also expressed strong support for increased Israel
involvement. In an interview conducted in late May he was resolute in
his stance on this issue. "There can be no other response to the U.S. but
to accept all Nazi criminals, at all risks."[40] In an opinion piece which
appeared in *Ma'ariv* in early July and subsequently in the *Jerusalem
Post*, Hausner further elaborated on the importance of the issue. He,
like Ben-Zeev, noted the legal significance of the American request that
Israel try Trifa, stressing that it constituted recognition of Israel's right
to protect Jews the world over.

> Whatever pragmatic considerations exist in this matter it is unthink-
> able that the State of Israel be apathetic as an ugly wave of the hatred
> of Jews rises and engulfs many countries. It is important to ensure
> that there be as widespread agreement as possible that Israel has spe-
> cial status regarding the defense and security of the Jews in the
> Diaspora and "the Trifa precedent" will help in achieving that goal.
> We should therefore accept the American proposal. Let the nations of
> the world see that the State of Israel is ready to try and punish those
> who harm Jews anywhere. It is incumbent upon the government to
> overcome its doubts and to decide that Trifa will indeed be brought to
> the bar of justice in the State of Israel.[41]

The public debate in Israel regarding this issue undoubtedly had its
effect on the government. On May 31, 1983 Minister of Justice Moshe
Nissim declared in the Knesset that the State of Israel had a historical
obligation to bring every Nazi war criminal to justice and preferably in
Israel.[42] This declaration, which hardly reflected the realities of Israeli
policy, preceded the high-level meetings held in early June between
Israeli Attorney-General Dr. Yitzhak Zamir and US Deputy Assistant
Attorney-General Mark Richard who came to Jerusalem to discuss the
extradition of Trifa.[43]

At this point, the problematics of the case had become more clear.
There appeared to be two major reasons for Israel's hesitancy to accept
the American proposal. The first related to the evidence against Trifa.
Although there were suspicions that Trifa might have personally participated in murder, the only firm evidence against the Rumanian arch-

bishop indicated that he had actively engaged in incitement against Jews. This crime was among those listed as chargeable under the provisions of the Nazi War Criminals and Collaborators Punishment Law. The fear was, however, that Trifa might receive a light sentence of only several years' imprisonment. What would happen after he completed his jail term? Israel would either have to find a country willing to accept him or perhaps might be forced to allow the elderly prelate to remain in Israel.

The second argument related to a legal problem. According to the formulation of the law, the crimes liable to punishment had to have been committed in a "hostile country," which was defined as Germany, one of the Axis countries, or any territory which was under the de facto jurisdiction of Germany or one of its allies. One of the main charges against Trifa was that he had incited a large-scale pogrom in Bucharest in January 1941. At that time Rumania had still not severed diplomatic relations with the Allies and doubts therefore existed whether Trifa could be tried for his crimes in Israel unless the law were changed.

Those who favored his extradition noted that there was no doubt as to Trifa's participation in incitement, which was one of the crimes specifically listed as chargeable under Israeli law. The results of his activities were extremely serious, moreover, since quite a few Jews were murdered in the course of the Bucharest pogrom. Even if the sentence he received was relatively light, that was preferable to the current situation in which he stood an excellent chance of escaping punishment. As far as the second problem was concerned, an expert on the history of Rumanian Jewry during the Holocaust pointed out that at the time Trifa committed his crimes, there were approximately 600,000 German troops stationed in Rumania. Thus a claim could be made that the country was under de facto German jurisdiction, which would enable prosecution and punishment. Another argument was that since the law was passed ex post facto, if need be various amendments could be made to cover cases such as Trifa's.[44]

These arguments did not convince the Israeli government to accede to the American request to extradite Trifa, but the public debate conducted on this issue ultimately did have an effect. In early October 1983, approximately two and a half months after the latest in the series of consultations between high-level officials of the American and Israeli Justice ministries, Attorney-General Dr. Yitzhak Zamir announced that Israel was about to submit an extradition request to the United States for a Nazi war criminal residing in that country. Zamir did not identify the criminal or his crimes and said that the extradition process would take months if not years. He reiterated, moreover, that the Israeli government would continue to do everything possible to bring Nazis to justice despite whatever difficulties existed and whatever damage such activities would cause in the international arena.[45]

The criminal in question was not Trifa, but rather Ivan Demjanjuk, a Ukrainian living in Cleveland who was accused of having operated the gas chambers at the Treblinka death camp. Although Israel never officially rejected the American proposal to extradite Trifa, its response in effect was negative. Despite the fact that there were solid answers to the various questions regarding this case, the government failed to exhibit the motivation and zeal necessary to overcome the existing obstacles. Perhaps if the Rumanian Jews in Israel had pursued the issue more actively or if their leaders had been more influential, the outcome might have been different. The practical result of Israel's refusal was that Trifa was able to obtain entry to Portugal, where he lived in relative peace and tranquillity, unpunished for his crimes, until his demise at the age of 72 in early 1987.[46]

As noted above, the Trifa case had a positive effect because it focused public attention on Israeli policy vis-à-vis the prosecution and punishment of Nazi war criminals. Given Israel's previous record on the prosecution of Nazi war criminals and the reluctance of the Israeli Justice Ministry to deal with this issue, I very much doubt whether Israel would have submitted an extradition request for Demjanjuk if not for the public uproar created in the wake of the refusal to take Trifa. In view of the manner in which the Demjanjuk trial has influenced Israeli public opinion on the issue of Nazi war criminals, the importance of the Trifa case should not be underestimated. On a personal level, the Trifa case convinced me once and for all that Israel had no serious intention of actively pursuing Nazi war criminals and was even reluctant to take action against those who were almost literally being thrown into her lap. It became clear that despite the existence in Israel of a legal framework for prosecution and the unequivocal declarations of contemporary Israeli leaders regarding their determination to bring all the murderers to justice, no such plans existed on an operative level. For someone like myself, who chose to live in Israel because it was a state whose policies and priorities were ostensibly guided by Jewish interests, this was a very painful conclusion. It was accompanied by the realization, however, that the issue was far from over. On the contrary, if anything, the Trifa case proved that numerous prominent Israelis strongly advocated more active Israeli involvement in prosecution and that the government could be influenced on this issue. The next step was obvious; the means had to be found to influence the government to intensify its efforts to bring Nazis to justice. The problem was that it was extremely difficult to do so while working as a researcher for OSI.

Under the existent circumstances, there appeared to be two possible alternatives. I could either attempt to become part of the Israeli decision-making process or establish an independent lobby to mobilize public opinion on this issue. Neither option initially appeared particularly promising.

Several months later an unexpected opportunity suddenly presented itself to meet with a high-ranking official of the Ministry of the Interior and present my case for an appointment to the Nazi war crimes unit. The meeting took place in the wake of a lecture I gave in my hometown of Efrat on the prosecution of Nazi war criminals. Although most of my remarks related to the research done in Israel for OSI, I devoted the last few minutes to a discussion of past and present Israeli policy. Among the audience was a neighbor who had worked for several years as a close aide to Minister of the Interior Yoseph Burg. He was shocked to learn of Israel's refusal to extradite Trifa and the apathy of successive Israeli governments. When we discussed the issue afterwards, we agreed that one way of attempting to change government policy was to be appointed head of the Nazi war crimes unit of the Israeli police force. He volunteered to set up a meeting with the Ministry of the Interior officials responsible for the Israeli police and to recommend my candidacy for the post. The meeting took place in early 1984 at the offices of the Ministry of the Interior in Jerusalem. The official I met with was Rafael Markowitz, director of the police division of the Ministry of the Interior who was Minister Burg's right-hand man on police affairs. His position was extremely important because Burg was simultaneously serving as Minister of the Interior, Minister of Police and Minister of Religious Affairs as well as heading the autonomy talks with the Egyptians, so his personal involvement in each ministry was relatively limited. I briefly outlined my activities on behalf of OSI and explained the background to my request. I pointed out that despite the passage of so

many years, there was still considerable work to be done and that the
unit—if it could be revitalized—was the framework best-suited to carry
out these activities. Markowitz was noncommittal. He indicated that he
was relatively unacquainted with the issue and wanted an opportunity
to investigate on his own before making any decision. We agreed that I
would summarize my proposals and submit them to his office.

The memorandum which I prepared for the Ministry of the Interior
outlined the research carried out in Israel for OSI and presented proposals designed to maximize Israel's potential for finding the witnesses and
documents necessary to prosecute Nazi war criminals. The main suggestions concerned the use of the media and investigative work among
recent immigrants, primarily those from the Soviet Union. The major
point was that unless steps were taken to rejuvenate the ranks of the
unit, no real progress would be made and our last chance to prosecute
at least some of these murderers would be lost. Although the memorandum dealt with the professional aspects of the issue and not with the
reasons why it was so important that Israel take the appropriate measures, I could not resist adding an ideological element. My conclusion
called for a rejuvenation of the ranks of the unit and noted that the
issue was "not a matter of perhaps. This is our obligation vis-à-vis the
victims, ourselves, and future generations."[47]

Markowitz never officially replied in writing, but it was obvious that
the response was negative. I am not certain exactly why, but I think the
major reason was that the authorities did not want to change the basic
Israeli policy on this issue. It was clear that any revitalization of the
unit would ultimately lead to increased pressure for more active government involvement. Since there was no readiness to change existing
policy it would have been counterproductive to institute major personnel changes. The low-level activity of the Israeli police remained
unchallenged and the apathetic approach of the various government
ministries remained unchanged.

During the following months there were no particular developments
of note. Annette Dulzin's article against holding trials in Israel appeared
in the *New York Times* in May[48] but did not have any particular impact
in Jerusalem or Tel Aviv. She made clear her stance that the murderers
should be tried and punished; she simply thought that it should be
done in West Germany, not in Israel. The fact that the West Germans
refused to try non-Germans, who were the overwhelming majority of
the criminals in question, did not in any way faze Mrs. Dulzin.

In August, US Attorney-General William French Smith announced that Valerian Trifa had left the United States for Portugal,[49] a development which once again focused public attention on the question of Israeli policy vis-à-vis the prosecution of Nazi war criminals. As could be expected, various government ministers and officials utilized the occasion to reiterate Israel's commitment to the trial and punishment of perpetrators of the Holocaust, but no practical measures were taken to initiate additional extradition requests. According to the *Jerusalem Post*, Yitzhak Feinberg, spokesman for the Justice Ministry, stated that Israel might seek Trifa's extradition from Portugal if enough evidence could be obtained to convict him. He noted that "if Trifa has been thrown out to wander like a nomad that's part of what we want. . .But we are not completely satisfied yet and don't see this as the end of the road."[50] Justice Minister Nissim went even further in an interview with *Ma'ariv* on August 16, 1984. According to Nissim, Israel had never refused to extradite the Rumanian archbishop. The view was that "it was preferable from a legal point of view if Trifa would be one of several Nazi war criminals extradited to our hands." Since the United States did not want to wait until the legal proceedings against the others could be completed, it agreed to deport Trifa to Portugal.[51] While it is apparently true that Israel never officially responded in the negative to the American request with regard to Trifa, Nissim's explanations do not accurately reflect Israeli policy, which in effect remained unchanged. Besides Demjanjuk, no efforts were being made to extradite any of the other Nazi war criminals residing in the United States.

Further corroboration of Israel's reluctance to widen the scope of the extraditions was forthcoming several months later when Israel turned down a second American request that it extradite a Nazi war criminal living in the United States. The individual in question was Karl Linnas who had served in the security forces at a concentration camp in Tartu, Estonia and had participated in the execution and physical abuse of civilian prisoners. Linnas had been stripped of his citizenship in 1981 and was subsequently ordered deported to the Soviet Union. The American authorities feared that such a step might be interpreted as US recognition of the Soviet annexation of Estonia. Another issue was the general reluctance of the Americans to deport anyone to the Soviet Union, whose human rights record was hardly exemplary and whose judicial system was so politicized.[52] The Americans turned to Israel in the hope that she might be willing to extradite Linnas and thereby ensure his trial and punishment by a Western court of law.[53] Once again, however, Israel chose not to accede to the American request.

Israel never officially rejected the Americans' proposal, nor ever formally explained why she chose not to prosecute the Estonian war criminal. The major problem was apparently the fact that there were no witnesses living outside the Soviet Union who could testify regarding Linnas' crimes. While there was solid evidence that Linnas had committed far more serious crimes than Trifa, the legal situation as far as Israel was concerned was similar. As long as no witnesses could be found in Israel, or at least in the West, Israel preferred not to assume responsibility.[54] It is possible that the fact that the majority of the victims at the Tartu camp were non-Jews also mitigated against Israeli involvement.

The Linnas case hardly attracted any public attention. After the refusal to take Trifa, Israel's reluctance to prosecute Nazi war criminals was no longer such a sensational scoop. The fact that Israel's request for Demjanjuk's extradition had still not been decided by the American courts also helped alleviate whatever pressure might have been mobilized to induce Israel to take Linnas.

These three cases (Trifa, Demjanjuk and Linnas) which Israel was forced to consider during the years 1983-85 ultimately led the Justice Ministry to establish criteria for the extradition of Nazi war criminals by Israel. In a meeting with Justice Ministry officials, a lawyer, representing an American group anxious to encourage active Israeli involvement in prosecution(Holocaust Survivors and Friends in Pursuit of Justice), was told that Israel would only attempt to extradite suspects who fulfilled three criteria. The first was that the individual had actively participated in murder, the second was that he was relatively young, and the third was the existence in the West, preferably in Israel, of survivors who could provide eyewitness testimony.[55] Although these criteria significantly reduced the number of alleged war criminals who could be extradited to Israel, there were still more than enough candidates to ensure active Israeli involvement for years. During this period, however, that was hardly the case. While preparations were under way for the Demjanjuk trial, no efforts were being made to extradite additional Nazi war criminals to Israel.

On April 15, 1985 Ivan Demjanjuk was ordered extradited to Israel by a US Federal Court in Cleveland, Ohio. The landmark decision rendered by the judges, which recognized Israel's right to demand the extradition of Nazi war criminals,[56] should have sparked renewed interest and pressure for more active involvement by the Israeli government. That was not initially the case, since Demjanjuk had the right to appeal against the decision at several different judicial levels and there were still serious doubts as to whether he would actually be extradited to Israel. Before his arrival in the country, there was relatively little public interest in his case and in the larger issue under consideration. Years of disappointments concerning the apprehension and punishment of Nazi war criminals and the rejection of the few Israeli extradition requests submitted in the past had apparently conditioned the Israeli public toward a pessimistic view of Israel's ability to play an active role. Some of those doubts undoubtedly dissipated approximately ten months later, on February 28, 1986, when an El-AI plane brought Ivan Demjanjuk to Israel to stand trial in Jerusalem, the first war criminal since Adolf Eichmann to be tried under Israel's Nazi War Criminals and Collaborators Punishment Law.[57]

Demjanjuk's arrival aroused enormous public attention in Israel, especially regarding Israeli policy and the fate of various other cases being tried in the United States. Several reports appeared in the press regarding Israel's refusal to extradite Linnas,[58] and *Ma'ariv* reported in late March that the Israeli police were collecting evidence against the Latvian collaborator Elmars Sprogis, whose extradition to Israel was planned. The source of the information was Brooklyn District Attorney Elizabeth Holtzman who was one of the leaders of the campaign for the prosecution of Nazi war criminals in the United States and had played an instrumental role in the establishment of the Office of Special Investigations.[59] It is not clear on what basis Holtzman made her statement nor is there any indication that Israel ever took any practical measures to extradite Sprogis. His case is particularly important, however, because it demonstrates the critical role Israel *could* have played in the prosecution of certain Nazi war criminals in the United States whose cases were somewhat problematic.

Sprogis had served as Assistant Chief of Police in Gulbene, Latvia in 1941 and was subsequently appointed Chief of Police in Madona, Latvia. According to the evidence in OSI's possession, he personally ordered and assisted in the murder and arrest of the Jews in Gulbene and supervised and participated in the murder of Soviet prisoners of war in Madona. The court ruled, however, that the evidence presented by OSI against Sprogis was neither clear nor unequivocal.[60] Under normal circumstances OSI would have appealed the decision, but in this case there were several complications. Sprogis, unlike most of the other defendants in OSI cases, had admitted on his immigration forms that he had served in the Latvian police and was nonetheless admitted to the United States. OSI feared that if his case reached the Supreme Court, a precedent decision might be rendered in which membership in the Latvian police and sending Jews to a place where it was known that they would be murdered might be classified as "passive activity" and insufficient grounds for denaturalization and deportation.[61] Under such circumstances, an extradition request by Israel could have served as a possible solution. OSI was convinced that the evidence in its possession was sufficient to convict Sprogis. His extradition to Israel would create not only an opportunity to overturn his acquittal but a chance to ensure he was punished for his crimes, which could never happen if he remained in the United States. The same would have applied in the case of Karlis Detlavs, a Latvian who served in the local auxiliary security police and participated in the persecution and murder of Jews in Riga.[62] The Detlavs case was lost prior to OSI's establishment and there was reason to believe that if tried again he would be convicted. Since OSI had lost its appeal before the Board of Immigration Appeals, extradition by Israel could have facilitated the prosecution and punishment of a Nazi war criminal who otherwise would remain free in the United States. (In this case the issue became academic when Detlavs died in Baltimore in 1983.)

A call for Israeli utilization of extradition on a wider scale was very forcefully expressed in a series of op-ed pieces in the *Jerusalem Post* by Paul Korda, a young American-born attorney who worked for approximately two years in the International Department of the Israeli Justice Ministry. A child of survivors, Korda was appalled at what he considered to be the indifference of the Israeli authorities on the issue of Nazi war criminals and called for the extradition of all those who would otherwise not be punished for their crimes. He pointed to the various cases of criminals who had escaped justice (Trifa, Koziy, Arthur Rudolph, Vanya Awdziej, Juozas Kisielaitis) either because they had been deported to countries where they were not put on trial or because they had escaped from the United States prior to their trials, and called upon Israel to fulfil its historic obligation. In his words,

The Jewish state must bear a major responsibility for punishing the perpetrators of the Holocaust because they waged a genocidal war against the Jewish people, slaughtering one-third of its members, at a time when there was no Jewish state to defend Jews. . . We must not shrink from our historic responsibility because future generations will judge us not only by what we did but also what we failed to do.[63]

While Korda's articles effectively focused on Israel's reluctance to play an active role in the prosecution of Nazi war criminals, they had little practical impact and in no way altered Israeli policy. This was made clear in a meeting I had on March 12, 1986 with Dr. Nimrod Novick, who at that time was a political adviser to Prime Minister Shimon Peres. The meeting was initiated by Gideon Greif on behalf of the Israeli organization of children of survivors (*Dor ha-Hemshech le-Moreshet ha-Shoa ve-ha-G'vura*) in order to attempt to apply increased pressure on the government to take action against Nazi war criminals and especially against Dr. Josef Mengele. Greif presented the case for more active Israeli participation in the hunt for Nazi war criminals and in their prosecution and I explained the current situation regarding the presence of Nazis in Western democracies. Novick was basically in agreement with our demand vis-à-vis the top echelon of German Nazis, but rejected our position that Israel extradite the others who were primarily collaborators of Eastern European origin. In view of the fact that there were almost no top Nazis left to be prosecuted, that those few still alive were either in hiding and/or living under the protection of their host governments, and that the overwhelming majority of those who could be prosecuted were the Lithuanians, Latvians, Ukrainians, etc. whom Novick believed should not be brought to Israel, his stance was hardly encouraging. What was even worse in my opinion was the reason why he opposed holding additional trials of Nazi war criminals—aside from those of high-ranking Germans—in Israel. According to Novick, such trials would strengthen extremism in Israel because they would reinforce "the entire world is against us" mentality of certain sectors of the population. Although he did not specify exactly whom he was referring to, it was clear that he meant those with a right-wing orientation. In the context of Israeli politics the reference was to the supporters of right-wing political parties such as Likud and Ha-Techiya, as well as religious parties who ostensibly might benefit from the "patriotic" atmosphere generated by such trials. His opposition appeared to be electoral rather than ideological, a response which struck me as quite cynical given the nature and scope of the crimes committed by the suspects in question.

Although Novick clearly stated that his views were his own and did not represent those of the Labor Party or of Prime Minister Peres, I think that on a practical level they accurately reflected the negative attitude of Israeli leaders on both sides of the political spectrum. Despite the bombastic declarations issued periodically by ministers and government officials regarding Israel's determination to bring the murderers to trial, operative policy had for years been determined by pragmatic *realpolitik*, which ignored or minimized Israel's historic obligations. Novick, for example, was willing to admit that Israel had a moral obligation on this issue, but in his opinion it applied only within the narrow constraints of contemporary Israeli priorities.[64] He was, in effect, merely euphemistically describing the reality of years of Israeli inactivity. If Gideon Greif or I had any illusions about mobilizing support in government circles for increased Israeli participation in the prosecution of Nazi war criminals, this meeting clearly indicated that we faced a difficult uphill battle.

The attitude toward this issue began to change in Israel in spring 1986. The Demjanjuk investigation was taking longer than anticipated and each time his custody was extended the media reported on various aspects of his case. By this time I was seriously negotiating with the Simon Wiesenthal Center regarding the possibility of establishing a computerized data bank on Nazi war criminals. Apparently the prospect of leaving OSI combined with my frustration with Israeli reluctance to play a more active role in prosecution prompted me to adopt a more public stance. I began getting actively involved in the preparation of several major stories which appeared in the media. Of particular note was a special broadcast by Kol Yisrael (Israeli Radio) entitled *Ha-Mirdaf She-lo Radaf* (The Unchased Chase) which was written and produced by Avraham Ben-Melech and broadcast on, and immediately after, Martyrs and Heroes Remembrance Day. Ben-Melech's program noted Israel's relative inactivity on the issue and included interviews with former head of the Mossad, Isser Harel, and former Justice Minister Shmuel Tamir, both advocates of Israeli involvement. In addition, it featured an attempt to locate survivors from various areas under investigation by OSI, an effort which yielded several potential witnesses,[65] and once again confirmed the necessity of utilizing the media in these types of investigations.

Shortly thereafter, the *Jerusalem Post* ran a page one story in its Friday edition (the Israeli equivalent of the Sunday newspapers) exposing Israel's reluctance to extradite additional Nazi war criminals from the United States, noting that at least four Nazis had already escaped from America before they could be deported (Trifa, Koziy, Hrusitzky and Kisielaitis). This article represented a breakthrough because for the first time Justice Ministry officials admitted that something was amiss in the Israeli effort. Dennis Goldman, director of the International Department, explained that Israel unlike the US did not have a special office to prosecute Nazis and declared that Israel was "making the most of the minimal resources we have." My response, which was the first time that I publicly attacked Israeli policy, was that money could not be an issue in matters such as this: "Israel is the country that's supposed to look out for the interest of the victims and see that these guys don't slip away . . . That's the moral obligation of this country—to see that the murderers of the Jewish people come to justice."[66] This story was followed by a report in a similar vein which appeared the following Sunday in the Israeli daily *Ma'ariv*. The only difference was that in the interim, Justice Ministry officials issued another one of the standard statements regarding Israel's determination to extradite Nazi war criminals. It was accompanied, however, by the admission by government officials that no such plans existed at the moment. *Ma'ariv* noted that this policy was attacked by Israeli Nazi-hunters who expressed reservations in view of the fact that four criminals had already escaped from the United States.[67] These articles, which I initiated, set the stage for the escalation of the campaign once I left the Justice Department and joined the Wiesenthal Center. One of the issues which I discussed with Rabbis Hier and Cooper before assuming my new position was the possibility of influencing Israel to play a more active role in prosecution. As an Israeli-by-choice, I considered this goal an important priority and was hopeful that in my new capacity I would finally be able to launch a campaign to mobilize public opinion and influence government policy. The leadership of the Center agreed, although they did initially have certain reservations. As committed supporters of the State of Israel they were a bit hesitant about launching a campaign which might tarnish Israel's image and at the same time diminish the responsibility of other countries, primarily those which had sheltered Nazis for years, to bring the perpetrators of the Holocaust to justice.

From the very beginning, I thought that the only possible means of convincing the government to play a more active role in the prosecution of Nazi war criminals was to mobilize public opinion. Experience had shown elsewhere that governments could be moved on this issue, but only if the public was aroused to express its outrage. If such efforts had succeeded in the United States, Canada and Australia, there was good reason to believe that we could achieve our goal in Israel as well. The key was the local media which has an inordinate influence on Israeli politicians and government officials, but whose response on this issue had hereto been lukewarm. There were several journalists who were usually willing to cooperate and felt a sense of responsibility to cover such stories. The problem was that they rarely determined what was broadcast and/or printed in the media. The decision was ultimately in the hands of the editors whose response had usually left something to be desired. For many of them, the Holocaust was a subject best confined to *Yom ha-Shoa* (Martyrs and Heroes Remembrance Day) and Nazi war criminals were best prosecuted elsewhere. Nonetheless we invested considerable efforts in obtaining media coverage in the hope that such exposure would ultimately not only inform the public but also influence the decision-makers. In this respect we were perhaps the major beneficiaries of the Demjanjuk trial. Besides sensitizing the public on the issue of the prosecution of Nazi war criminals living in Western democracies, his extradition afforded us a plethora of opportunities to focus attention on Israeli policy.

During the initial months following the establishment of the Jerusalem office, our public opinion campaign focused on the existence of hundreds, if not thousands, of Nazi war criminals in the West, Israeli inactivity on the issue and the philosophical or ideological basis for increased Israeli involvement in prosecution. All three were interconnected because whatever hope existed of persuading the public to apply pressure on the government to change its policy was based on our ability to convince them of the existence of a serious problem and the fact that Israel had a very important role to play. In order to do so, we utilized the discovery of the ITS files and the submission of the lists of suspected Nazi war criminals to Western governments to prove our contention that there were still numerous murderers alive in democratic countries who could be brought to trial. Within the first few months major stories appeared in the weekend editions of the *Jerusalem Post*,[68] *Ma'ariv*[69] and *Davar*.[70] These articles focused on Israeli policy and the recent findings which enabled us to compile the various lists of suspected Nazi war criminals. They stressed the inactivity of the Israeli government and contrasted it with the renewed interest in the issue in the West, noting that official government commissions of inquiry had been established in Canada and Australia.

These points were further developed in several op-ed pieces which I wrote for *Ma'ariv* in late 1986 and early 1987. They dealt with practical as well as theoretical problems and called for a change in government policy, noting that Demjanjuk was only the tip of an enormous iceberg of thousands of Nazis living in the West.

> How can one explain the fact that Israel, the country established in the wake of the destruction of European Jewry and which declares time and again in every possible forum that she is the inheritor of the six million Jews murdered during the Holocaust does not take political and legal steps to advance this issue?

Part of the answer stemmed from a certain ambivalence which existed in Israel vis-à-vis the Holocaust, an ambivalence which was rooted in the painful historical memories of that period as well as in the ongoing debate in Israel regarding the Jewish content of the State and our attitude towards the past. One school of thought sought to see Israel as a liberal Western democracy whose Jewishness was expressed primarily in the fact that the majority of its citizens were Jews, the language Hebrew, and the holidays Jewish. On the other hand there were those who sought to strengthen the Jewish component of Israeli life and expected the state to develop and implement policy based on Jewish priorities. While the former, for the most part, were not particularly perturbed by the fact that thousands of Nazis were living unpunished in the West, the latter obviously expected Israel to do its best to see that these criminals were prosecuted. The Demjanjuk trial—the symbolic trial in Israel of one Nazi war criminal—appeared to be a compromise between these two approaches.

> But one show trial in Jerusalem will not solve the problem which is enormous in scope. It is unthinkable that we will ignore our moral obligation to serve as a mouthpiece for the victims of the Holocaust. That was, after all, one of the reasons for the establishment of the

State, to grant sovereign expression to the Jewish people. It is unthinkable that on the one hand we seek to grant posthumous Israeli citizenship to the victims of the Holocaust (a provision to that effect is included in the Yad Vashem law which is currently being implemented) and on the other we refrain from fulfilling our concomitant obligations. And it should be noted that when material advantages were in the offing Israel presented itself as the inheritor of the six million to receive reparations from Germany. Every privilege is accompanied by certain responsibilities and we must not attempt to evade them. It is very likely that in the wake of the Demjanjuk trial, the government and the public will be convinced that determined action by Israel must be undertaken to prosecute as many Nazi criminals as possible, but by then who knows if we still will be able to do anything?[71]

In these articles as well as in numerous interviews for the local and foreign press, I tried to counter the various arguments presented against increased Israeli involvement. Besides the points enumerated above, there were practical arguments such as the complex legal problems involved in trying criminals for crimes committed over 40 years ago, the financial burden of such proceedings and the fact that Israel had more pressing problems to deal with. On a more philosophical level, various claims were made that a series of Nazi trials would create an image of a vengeful Israel, would strengthen extremism and paranoia internally and at the same time diminish the significance and uniqueness of the Eichmann trial. There was also the fear—especially in the case of Demjanjuk—that the media might turn the trial into a circus.

These arguments paled in my opinion, in comparison to the realities of contemporary Jewish life in which the State of Israel is the only sovereign entity which could act on behalf of the Jewish people—dead or alive. In this case there is an analogy between the Jews murdered by the Nazis and the victims of terrorism. If terrorists are prosecuted by the states whose citizens were among the latter, who, if not Israel, will seek to bring those who victimized the former to trial? As far as the passage of time was concerned, the issue was sharpened by a rhetorical question. "If someone murdered your parents or your children and was able to elude justice for 40 years, would that in any way diminish your desire to see that person punished for the crime?" The issue, I stressed, was justice not vengeance and justice operated on two levels, symbolic and practical. While the Demjanjuk trial undoubtedly had symbolic significance as the trial of the implementer-collaborator—and in that respect complemented (rather than diminished) the Eichmann trial—it did little to solve the far more serious problem of the thousands of Nazi murderers living unpunished throughout the world. In that respect the Demjanjuk trial could best be compared to the release of Prisoner of Zion Anatoly Shcharansky which, while undoubtedly of symbolic significance, did little to solve the far greater problem of the hundreds of thousands of Soviet Jews who sought to leave Russia. Justice had to be achieved not only on a symbolic level but on a practical level as well, and Israel had a role to play. The fact that this responsibility entailed a painful confrontation with the past was true, but ultimately the bottom line was that "Israel has to be Israel . . . It is the inheritor of the six million and it has the responsibility to see that justice is done."[72]

Besides attempting to mobilize public opinion via the media, efforts were made behind the scenes to influence various government officials. We appealed, for example, to President Herzog, prior to his state visit to Australia, to raise the issue of Nazis residing in that country with his hosts.[73] We also met with Aryeh Mekel, political advisor to Prime Minister Shamir and with MK Dan Meridor, one of the prime minister's closest colleagues. In these meetings we called upon the government to play a more active role by attempting to extradite additional criminals to Israel and by trying to influence those governments to whom lists of suspects had been submitted, to ensure that these individuals were investigated. We pointed out that Israel's readiness to prosecute would encourage other governments to do so and would considerably strengthen Israel's moral case to demand action from others.[74]

At this point, in late 1986, our appeals to government officials had relatively little effect. One of President Herzog's aides told me upon his return that the president had raised the issue during his visit to Australia, but there was no evidence in the media reports that the topic had even been discussed. As far as the prime minister was concerned, we were told that the issue was being handled by the Justice Ministry,[75] which under the circumstances was a euphemistic rebuff.

During this period we also attempted to utilize various news events to focus public attention on the topic. The best example was the visit to Israel in late January 1987 of Australian Prime Minister Bob Hawke. Several days prior to his arrival we sent cables to Prime Minister

Shamir, Foreign Minister Peres and Justice Minister Sharir urging them
to raise the issue of Nazi war criminals in Australia, pointing out that
an Australian commission of inquiry had already recommended government action.[76] On the day of Hawke's arrival, I submitted a list of
15 suspected Nazis who emigrated to Australia to Dr. Merrilees, the
Australian ambassador to Tel Aviv. At a press conference held the same
day, the Center called upon the Australian government to adopt the
findings of the Menzies Commission which recommended that legal
action be taken against those found guilty and urged the Israeli government to press the issue with the visiting Prime Minster.[77] In addition, I
published an op-ed piece in *Ma'ariv* on the next day entitled "An Open
Letter to a True Friend" in which I explained the gravity and scope of
the problem and noted that it was unthinkable that Australia, which
had fought in the Second World War to keep the world safe for democracy, would continue to offer shelter to Nazi war criminals.

> I do not know if this subject will be raised in the official talks you will
> conduct here but I am certain that my appeal expresses the feelings of
> many people in Israel, the country which absorbed the majority of the
> survivors of the Holocaust and which views itself as the inheritor of
> the six million. You who know us well and identify with us, certainly
> understand this well. Please translate this feeling into practical action
> so that justice will finally be implemented not only heard. We wish
> you a pleasant visit and hope that by your next visit this painful prob-
> lem will no longer exist. Not because the criminals had died a natural
> death in Australia but because they were put on trial and received
> their just due.[78]

The impact of these steps was evident by the numerous questions on
this issue posed by journalists to the Australian Prime Minister in the
course of his visit.

Two other events which were utilized in a similar manner were
former Supreme Court Judge Chaim Cohen's opposition to the Demjanjuk trial and the death in Portugal of Valerian Trifa, whom Israel had
refused to extradite from the United States. In an interview to *Zomet ha-
Sharon*, a local newspaper, Cohen, one of Israel's most prestigious
jurists, said that he feared that Demjanjuk might be convicted for emotional reasons and that if he were attorney-general (a post he filled in
the past) he would not have assumed the responsibility for submitting
an indictment against Demjanjuk because of the problems involved in
trying criminals 40 years after the crimes had been committed.[79]

Cohen's statements provided us with an excellent opportunity to remind the public that such trials were being held all over the United States and that, if anything, there was growing awareness the world over of the necessity of prosecuting these criminals. After all, no one was advocating the fabrication of evidence to convict Nazi criminals. In fact, many Nazis ultimately escaped punishment because of the specific problems noted by Cohen. Nonetheless there were more than enough cases where sufficient evidence existed for a conviction and to ignore such evidence simply because of the passage of time would be a perversion of justice.[80] Trifa's death in Portugal, unpunished for his crimes, less than four years after Israel refused to request his extradition provided another opportunity to point to Israel's lack of energy in pursuing the Nazis living in the West. In an op-ed piece entitled "Trifa: A Sad Reminder" which appeared in *Ma'ariv* on February 19, 1987 a few days after the opening of the Demjanjuk trial, I pointed to the Rumanian archbishop's historic role as the first Nazi war criminal offered to—and rejected by—the State of Israel. His case was symptomatic of Israeli policy vis-à-vis the middle and lower echelon Nazis living in the West who could still be prosecuted. Most would probably die unpunished for their crimes unless Israel began to play a more active role in prosecution.

> This fact, which is of course unfortunate, would not have been so tragic had we tried with all our might to prosecute the maximum number of criminals. But it is scandalous if such a thing happens because in Jerusalem they did not deem it necessary to give this subject the serious treatment that it deserves. Perhaps in a different country it would be possible to comprehend the adoption of such a policy, but woe is us if such a thing happens in the state of the Jews. Trifa's death is indeed a concrete reminder that we are already well on our way towards the fulfillment of this sad assessment.[81]

There were also other events which helped arouse public awareness on the issue during this period. The debate in the United States regarding the deportation of Karl Linnas to the Soviet Union attracted considerable attention[82] and the ongoing developments in the Waldheim case were reported extensively in the media.[83] Other events which helped keep public attention at a relatively high level were: the Barbie trial,[84] the Wiesenthal Center's efforts to induce the British government to investigate and prosecute Nazis living in England,[85] and the findings of government commissions of inquiry established in Canada[86] and Australia[87] to determine whether Nazi war criminals were residing in these countries. All these developments were reported in the Israeli media, and contributed to public awareness on the issue, but the event which undoubtedly had the most profound influence on public opinion was the trial of Ivan Demjanjuk.

Prior to the trial, there were serious doubts as to whether there would be sufficient public interest in the proceedings. The fact that Demjanjuk had been a small cog in the machinery of the Final Solution, a man who was neither an initiator nor a planner or even an officer, the fact that he was a Ukrainian collaborator rather than a German, and the doubts regarding his identity all contributed towards the feeling among many observers that the trial would not capture the public's imagination. The latter issue in particular interested the Israeli press which took particular delight in exposing all sorts of "evidence" which seemed to indicate that this was a case of mistaken identity. The lengthy delay (almost six months) in submitting the indictment against Demjanjuk and the fact that he sat in a comfortable Israeli jail cell for practically an entire year before the trial actually began also reinforced the doubts regarding the sagacity of the Israeli extradition of the individual accused of being "Ivan the Terrible" at Treblinka.[88]

On a personal level I had no reservations about the extradition, but was extremely frustrated by the lengthy delays which I feared might deter Israel from extraditing additional Nazi war criminals. I was fairly certain that Demjanjuk would be convicted, but to my mind the most important issue was not his guilt or innocence but the world-wide attention which would focus on the Treblinka death camp and how the trial would affect local public opinion and influence Israeli policy vis-à-vis the prosecution of Nazi war criminals. In that respect, I considered his trial the most potent means available of influencing the public but prior to its opening it appeared that, if anything, the prosecution of Demjanjuk might actually have a negative effect.

In media interviews I pointed out that the delays stemmed from the extensive preparations necessary to present the history of the camp and that the trial was, in effect, the trial of Treblinka and the collaborators rather than merely of the individual criminal.[89] I also explained why the various evidence presented as proof of mistaken identity was not conclusive, but nonetheless the doubts persisted and there did not appear to be intense public interest in the trial. This was an important reason for the choice of the small hall in the Binyanei ha-Uma convention center as the venue for the proceedings. It had approximately 300 seats and the fear was that even those would not be filled unless an attempt was made to bring in organized groups of schoolchildren, students and soldiers.

The opening day of the trial seemed to confirm our worst fears. There were numerous journalists in attendance, but quite a few empty seats in the hall. The proceedings, moreover, dealt with tedious legal points that were hardly the kind of exciting testimony that would arouse the public's imagination. As it turned out the opening day did not in any way reflect what subsequently happened. From the second day on, the Israeli public came in droves to attend the trial. Starting with the testimony of Dr. Yitzhak Arad, chairman of Yad Vashem and the author of a scholarly work on Treblinka, the appearance of the prosecution witnesses aroused considerable interest. Kol Yisrael transmitted the trial live and wherever one went—in offices, on public transportation, in the street—people could be seen listening to the broadcast, glued to their radios. The lines stretched longer and longer and people waited for hours for an opportunity to attend the trial.[90] People began showing up at 6 a.m. to be able to ensure their entry to the morning session which commenced at 8:30 a.m. The interest was so great that the seating capacity of the hall was expanded and a special hall with several hundred places was built where viewers could watch the proceedings on closed circuit TV. The initial decision not to film the trial was reversed, and Educational TV began broadcasting the morning sessions in their entirety.[91] Needless to say, throughout this period the media also provided extensive coverage.

Interest in the trial reached new heights as the survivors of Treblinka took the stand. Tens of thousands of Israelis listened intently as they told their story of mass murder and atrocities in the human hell created by the SS and run by the Germans and their Ukrainian henchmen. The country literally almost held its breath as Pinchas Epstein and Eliyahu Rosenberg identified the suspect as "Ivan the Terrible" from Treblinka.[92] Even after the survivors had completed their testimony and gave way to other prosecution witnesses—handwriting experts, police investigators from the Israeli Nazi war crimes unit, German prosecutors and historical experts—interest in Israel remained extremely high. What was particularly gratifying was that the interest in the trial encompassed all of Israeli society. Contrary to initial expectations, those in attendance came from every sector of the population—young and old, Ashkenazi and Sephardi, observant and secular, in short Israelis from every walk of life and ideological belief. The Binyanei ha-Uma convention center became the only place in Israel where ultra-Orthodox and secular voluntarily sat together at a time when intracommunal strife was rife.[93]

What impact—if any—would the interest in the trial have on Israeli public opinion? Would this interest have a practical effect vis-à-vis the extradition to Israel of additional Nazi war criminals? These were questions which I continuously asked myself as I closely followed the trial which captured public attention in Israel almost by storm. On May 18,1987 *Ma'ariv* published the results of a public opinion poll conducted on its behalf by Modi'in Ezrachi under the direction of Dr. Micha Hoppe. The question posed to 1,236 persons representing the urban and rural adult population in Israel (excluding Arab villages, kibbutzim and Jewish settlements in Judea and Samaria) was: "Should the State of Israel request the extradition of additional war criminals of the same rank as Demjanjuk?" The response was clear cut. 64.9 per cent answered that Israel should request the extradition of every criminal regarding whom information existed. 21.8 per cent responded that extradition requests should only be submitted in cases in which there was no doubt regarding the suspect's identity. 8.1 per cent said that Israel should not request the extradition of criminals of Demjanjuk's rank and 5.2 per cent did not respond. The results were overwhelmingly in favor of additional Israeli extradition requests.[94] The question now became whether this groundswell of public support would effect Israeli policy on this issue.

Slightly more than two months after the Modi'in Ezrachi poll was published in *Ma'ariv*, we had an opportunity to check whether the government had changed its stance. In mid-July a delegation from the Wiesenthal Center met in London with Home Office officials and submitted extensive documentation regarding the wartime crimes of Antanas Gecas, an officer in the 12th Lithuanian Security Police battalion, and two other suspected Nazi war criminals living in England.[95] The Home Secretary, Douglas Hurd, had previously made clear to Center representatives that Britain would under no circumstances agree to deport British residents to the Soviet Union, nor could such individuals be tried in England unless British law were changed. When I raised the possibility of extradition to Israel, Hurd did not reject that option out of hand, and inferred that such a step, albeit difficult, might provide a solution.[96] Under those circumstances the response of the Israeli government became extremely important. Following our meetings in London, our entire delegation came to Israel, to meet initially with Foreign Minister Shimon Peres and Justice Minister Avraham Sharir, and later with Prime Minister Yitzhak Shamir to enlist their assistance in the Gecas case.

If I had any doubt as to the effect of the Demjanjuk trial and the Center's efforts to encourage a more active Israeli stance regarding the prosecution of Nazi war criminals, these meetings clearly indicated that progress had been made. Foreign Minister Peres, who had never evinced any particular interest in this issue, was extremely forthright. In response to our appeal for Israel to play an active role in the Gecas case, he replied that although he considered the primary responsibility to be Britain's, Israel would fulfil its obligations. "We will not let him go free. If the British will not do it, then we will have to do it. We cannot allow a criminal of this sort run around free."[97] Justice Minister Sharir was equally as determined that Israel fulfil its role in this case. After hearing about the documentary evidence submitted by the Center to the Home Office and the various possible alternatives currently being considered by the British authorities, Sharir addressed the question of Israeli involvement. "My response is 100 per cent positive. It is our duty. I cannot imagine how the government of Israel could let such a man get away with it . . . This is my obligation as a Jew and as Justice Minister of the State of Israel."[98] Prime Minister Shamir also indicated his concern in his meeting with a delegation from the Center, although he was perhaps not as resolute as his Cabinet colleagues.[99] I cannot imagine such statements being made before the Demjanjuk trial opened and certainly not before we began our efforts to focus public attention on the lack of Israeli initiative in bringing Nazi war criminals to justice.

* * *

On April 18, 1988 Ivan Demjanjuk was convicted by the Jerusalem District Court of participation in the mass murder of Jews at Treblinka. In the words of Chief Justice Dov Levin, "We determine unequivocally, without hesitation or doubt, that the accused John Demjanjuk who stands before us is Ivan known as "Ivan the Terrible," gas chamber operator at the Treblinka death camp."[100] A week later, Demjanjuk was sentenced to death,[101] and these events naturally led to renewed discussion of Israel's role in the prosecution of Nazi war criminals.[102] In this respect, the official government rhetoric sounded wonderful, but in terms of concrete action the situation remained unchanged.

Thus, for example, on April 26, 1988 the Justice Ministry declared its intention to bring additional suspected Nazi war criminals to justice. According to a statement issued by the ministry on the day after Demjanjuk was sentenced to death, "In any case where there is a chance to extradite a Nazi criminal to Israel and put him on trial here, we will act with utmost energy to do so."[103] Even before this statement was issued, I had cabled Justice Minister Sharir urging him "to initiate efforts to prosecute additional Nazi war criminals in the State of Israel" and to extradite Nazi labor camp commandant Josef Schwammberger from Argentina,[104] but as usual the government did not take any concrete action, nor were our other attempts to induce the Justice Ministry to make good on its pledges regarding the prosecution of additional Nazi war criminals successful. In case after case, our appeals to Israeli officials to extradite Nazi war criminals fell on deaf ears.

When Dan Meridor replaced Avraham Sharir as Israeli Justice Minister in late 1988 we hoped that the situation might improve. At that point our efforts in Isrsael focused on attempts to convince the Justice Ministry to establish a special Nazi war crimes unit which would specialize in such cases and press for extradition and prosecution. On July 16, 1989, Rabbi Hier, Rabbi Cooper and I met in Jerusalem with Dan Meridor to press the case for the establishment of such a unit. To our surprise, the Israeli Justice Minister indicated that he was seriously considering a plan to set up a Nazi-hunting unit at the Justice Ministry[105] and in fact had a candidate in mind to head the unit which he hoped would be established in the near future.[106]

If such a unit had been established, perhaps Israel's record vis-à-vis the prosecution of Nazi war criminals would have been considerably better, but that was not the case. Despite various attempts by the Center to remind, encourage or urge Justice Minister Meridor to carry out his plan to set up a Nazi war crimes unit,[107] no such agency was ever established and the results speak for themselves. With the exception of Demjanjuk, not a single Nazi war criminal has been extradited to the State of Israel. In fact every request submitted by the Center to the Justice Ministry to extradite a Nazi war criminal to stand trial in Israel was rejected.[108] And while it is true that certain legal problems made extradition difficult, if not impossible, in most of the cases in question, neither the Justice Ministry, nor the the government showed any desire to attempt to overcome the existent obstacles. If a Nazi war crimes unit had been established it would have served as a lobby and could perhaps have influenced the decision-making process and achieved practical results. Without such a unit, our chances of achieving any degree of success were obviously severely reduced.

According to Dan Meridor, the reason that the unit was not set up was primarily financial,[109] but I believe that the Demjanjuk case also had a certain impact. The fact that it dragged on for so long and that certain doubts existed regarding his identification as "Ivan the Terrible" also played a role in dampening whatever little enthusiasm existed in government circles for Israel to adopt a more activist stance vis-à-vis the prosecution of Nazi war criminals. In that respect, Demjanjuk's acquittal by the Israeli Supreme Court despite the unequivocal evidence regarding his service in the Sobibor death camp in essence marked the ignominious end of Israeli efforts to bring the perpetrators of the Holocaust to the bar of justice. Given the fact that he was allowed to return to the United States despite the Supreme Court's findings that he participated in the implementation of the Final Solution, I find it highly unlikely, if not impossible, that Israel will ever again attempt to prosecute a Nazi war criminal. If anything, the Demjanjuk verdict constitutes unequivocal proof that the Jewish state is simply not intrerested in *stam wachmannim* (ordinary camp guards) or low-level murderers, and given the fact that almost all the criminals being uncovered and prosecuted these days are in that category, it appears quite clear that the Israeli Nazi War Criminals and Collaborators Law has become, on a practical level, entirely redundant.

I never thought that every Nazi war criminal should be tried in Israel. Such a plan is neither realistic nor feasible—nor is it fair to place exclusive responsibility for prosecution and punishment upon the erstwhile victims. At the same time, I always believed that Israel should have played a far more active role in the efforts to bring the perpetrators of the Holocaust to the bar of justice. To do so would have required significant resources and the creation of a special mechanism to deal with the problem in an effective manner. The ranks of the Nazi war crimes unit of the Israeli police would have to have been expanded and revitalized, and a special litigation unit should have been established in the framework of the Israeli Ministry of Justice. Whatever the cost, such an

effort should have been undertaken, not only out of a sense of obligation to our ancestors (victims and survivors) and our past, but also
because this issue constitutes one of the important foundations of
Israel's sovereign existence, making it a cornerstone of present and
future as well.

Notes

1. Glenn Frankel, "Demjanjuk Proceeding Unites Israel; Curiosity, History
Draw Cross Section to Nazi Trial," *Washington Post*, February 20, 1987.

2. "Chok le-Asiat Din ba-Nazim u-be-Ozreihem 5710-1950" (The Nazi War
Criminals and Collaborators Punishment Law), *Sefer Chukim*, 5710 (1950),
No. 57, August 9, 1950, p. 281. On this date the legislation officially became
law in the State of Israel.

3. Isser Harel, *Ha-Bayit be-Rechov Garibaldi*, Tel Aviv, 1975.

4. Central Zionist Archives, S-25/9290, 7821, 7886, 7888.

5. Interview with Asher Ben-Natan, July 18, 1985; interview with Manus
Diament, July 19, 1985. Michael Bar-Zohar, *Ha-Nokmim*, Tel Aviv, n.d., pp. 72-
79.

6. Ibid., pp. 24-58.

7. Moshe Ben-Ze'ev, "Pish'ei ha-Nazim Adayin Boarim," *Ha-Aretz*, May 13,
1983, p. 14.

8. Tom Segev, *The Seventh Million*, New York, 1993.

9. "Ha-Aretz Kula Atzra Neshimata," *Ma'ariv*, April 11, 1961, p. 1. See also
testimony of the witnesses regarding the crimes committed against Jews all
over Europe, *Mishpat Eichman; Aiduyot*, Vol. I-II, pp. 42-1249.

10. Nili Keren, "Nosei ha-Shoa ba-Chevra ha-Yisraelit u-be-Ma'arechet·ha-
Chinuch ba-Shanim 1948-1981," *Yalkut Moreshet*, No. 42, December 1981,
p.196.

11. On the activities of the unit see, for example, Refael Bashan, "Ha-Matzod
ha-Mishpati Achar ha-Natzim," *Yediot Achronot*, November 26, 1982, pp. 14-
15, 61; Inge Deutschkron, "Sgan-Nitzav Russek Mechake le-'Ivan ha-Ayom,'"
Ma'ariv, April 29, 1984, p. 15. According to Lt. Col. Russek, the Israeli unit
handled 4,200 cases during its initial 24 years of operation (1960-84) and
recorded the testimony of 35,000 survivors. Of the cases investigated by the
unit, 292 criminals were put on trial, of whom 102 received life imprisonment. Gidon Alon, "Eichmann Lo Haya ha-Acharon," *Ha-Aretz*, November 25,
1983, p. 17.

12. *Mengele: The Complete Story*, pp. 307-8, 313- 14.

13. Gustav Wagner participated in the euthanasia killings at Hartheim and
later served at Sobibor. He was known for his cruel treatment of the inmates.
Miriam Novitch, *obibor: Martyrdom and Revolt*, New York, 1980, pp. 55-58,

131, 144, 149-50; Gitta Sereny, *Into That Darkness*, pp. 130, 357.

14. For details on Menten's crimes see Hans Knoop, *The Menten Affair*, New York, 1978, pp. 6-7, 58-73.

15. Chagai Segal, "Medinat Yisrael Lo Rotza La'asot Din ba-Natzim u-be-Ozreihem," *Nekuda*, No. 117, January 15, 1988, p. 43.

16. Rochelle Saidel, *The Outraged Conscience*, pp. 103-21.

17. The Deschenes Commission Report lists the various allegations made regarding the presence in Canada of Nazi war criminals, "War Criminals in Canada?," pp. 245-49. Various Soviet publications pointed to the presence of Nazi war criminals in Australia as well as in other countries. See, for example, *Documents Accuse*, pp. 285-98; *"Political Refugees" Unmasked!* p. 62.

18. The reports published by the commissions of inquiry appointed in Canada and Australia refer extensively to the activities of OSI; see, for example, Deschenes Commission Report, pp. 168-99 and the Menzies Report, pp. 141-45.

19. *Quiet Neighbors*, pp. 246-72.

20. Kisilaitis escaped to Canada, see Neil Macdonald, "Comment on Jews Spoils Lithuanian's Humble Image," *Edmonton Journal*, May 7,1985.

21. Leili escaped to West Germany, see Alfonso A. Narvaez, "A Court Strips Ex-Nazi Guard of Citizenship," *New York Times*, December 31, 1986.

22. Memorandum by Bruce Einhorn regarding "Jurisdictional Problems Affecting Extradition of OSI Subjects to Israel," July 10, 1981.

23. Deschenes Commission Report, p. 92. In discussing the various countries and agencies which submitted information regarding Nazi war criminals in Australia, the Menzies Report does not mention the State of Israel, pp. 25-30.

24. For details on the documentation at Beit Lohamei ha-Gettaot, a kibbutz in northern srael founded by Holocaust survivors who had played an active role in Jewish resistance in Eastern Europe, see Jacob Robinson and Yehuda Bauer (eds), *Guide to Unpublished Materials of the Holocaust Period*, Vol. I, Jerusalem, 1970, pp. 10-13.

25. Cable of Allan A. Ryan Jr. to American Embassy Tel Aviv (State 247231), September 17, 1981.

26. See, for example, letter of Allan A. Ryan Jr. to Lieutenant-Colonel Menachem Russek and Efraim Zuroff, July 13, 1982, in possession of the author.

27. According to Lt. Col. Russek, five of the eight members of his staff had already reached retirement age in 1984, but were continuing their work on a part-time basis. Inge Deutschkron, "Sgan-Nitzav Russek Mechake le-"Ivan ha-Ayom,'" *Ma'ariv*, April 29, 1984, p. 15.

28. David K. Shipler, "U.S. Asks Israel to Take Pro-Nazi Tied to Anti-Jewish Riots in 1941," *New York Times*, April 28, 1983, pp. 1, 3; Stuart Taylor Jr., "Steps to Deport Nazi Backers Cause Legal Concern" *New York Times*, May 9, 1983.

29. Kol Yisrael news broadcast, April 27, 1983, 10 a.m.

30. "Artzot ha-Brit Rotza le-Hasgeer le-Yisrael Poshi'm Nazim Nosafim," *Ha-Aretz*, April 29, 1983.

31. Baruch Me'iri and Razi Guterman, "Bodkim Efsharut shel Hasgaret Nazim le-she-Avar me-Artzot ha-Brit le-Yisrael," *Ma'ariv*, April 28, 1983, p. 15.

32. Yossi Bar, "Artzot ha-Brit Rotza le-Hasgeer le-Yisrael Romani she-Shiteif Pe'ula im ha-Nazim," *Yediot Achronot*, April 28, 1983, p. 2.

33. Robert Rosenberg, "Israel Wary about Trying Ex-Nazis from U.S.," *Jerusalem Post*, May 3, 1983, p. 2.

34. See note 27.

35. See note 29.

36. *Ha-Aretz*, 29 April 1983, p. 9.

37. Annette Dulzin, "Israel, Don't Try Nazis," *New York Times*, May 6, 1984.

38. Tamir was very outspoken in his criticism of Israeli policy and accused Israel of agreeing not to pursue Nazi war criminals energetically in return for financial aid and lucrative trade agreements with Germany. This assertion appeared in two different sources. See the article by Chagai Segal (note 14) and David Bedein, "Wiesenthal Center Hires OSI's Man in Israel," *Baltimore Jewish Times*, September 26, 1986.

39. Moshe Ben Ze'ev, "Pish'ei ha-Natzim Adayin Boarim," *Ha-Aretz*, May 13, 1983, p. 14.

40. Roberta Fahn Reisman, "Israel's Moral Obligation: Bring Nazis to Justice," position paper by Anti-Defamation League of Bnai Brith, p. 3.

41. Gideon Hausner, "Lishpoat Oto," *Ma'ariv*, July 4, 1983, p. 5; and "The Case for Trying Trifa in Israel," *Jerusalem Post*, July 8, 1983, p. 7.

42. See note 39, p. 1.

43. Robert Rosenberg, "Trifa May Not be Subject to Prosecution in Israel," *Jerusalem Post*, June 7, 1983, p. 3.

44. See note 14, pp. 23-4; note 39, pp. 1-4; Ernie Meyer, "Trifa Stayed a Step Ahead of Justice," *Jerusalem Post*, February 11, 1987, p. 6.

45. Tzadok Yechezkeli, "Prof. Zamir Nevakesh be-Karov me-Artzot ha-Brit le-Hasgeer le Yisrael Poshei'a Nazi," *Yediot Achronot*, October 3, 1983, p. 6.

46. Ari L. Goldman, "Valerian Trifa, an Archbishop with a Fascist Past, Dies at 72," *New York Times*, January 29, 1987, p. B6.

47. Memorandum of the author to Rafael Markowitz, March, 1984.

48. See note 36.

49. Statement by US Department of Justice, August 14, 1984.

50. "Israel May Ask Portugal to Hand Over Killer Trifa," *Jerusalem Post*, August 16, 1984, p. 2.

51. Baruch Me'iri, "Safek im Trifa Yuchal le-Heshafet ba-Aretz," *Ma'ariv*, August 16, 1984, p. 2.

52. Richard Cohen, "More Mindless Anticommunism," *Washington Post*, April 23, 1987, p. A23; Opinion editorial in same issue, p. A22.

53. Baruch Me'iri, "Yisrael Adayin Lo Hichlita Levakesh Hasgaret ha-Poshei'a ha-Nazi Linnas," *Ma'ariv*, December 31, 1984, p. 12.

54. Ron Dagoni, "Be-Yisrael Lo Nimtza Mi she-Ya'eed Neged ha-Poshei'a ha-Nazi Karl Linnas," *Ma'ariv*, March 19, 1986, p. 5.

55. Interview with David Martin, August 1, 1985, Tel Aviv.

56. Robert Rosenberg, "Treblinka Gas Chamber Operator Faces Trial Here," *Jerusalem Post*, April 17, 1985, p. 1.

57. Peter Kerr, "Ukrainian Facing a Trial in Israel," *New York Times*, February 28, 1986, p. A10.

58. See, for example, Ron Dagoni, "Yisrael Serva Lekabel Nazi he-Atzur be-Artzot ha-Brit," *Ma'ariv*, March 18, 1986, p. 5.

59. Ilan Becher, "Tzifuya Hasgarato shel Poshei'a Nazi Nosaf, *Ma'ariv*, March 30, 1986, p. 1.

60. Elmars Fridrichs Ernests Sprogis file, SWCA; Henry Friedlander and Earlean M. McCarrick, "Nazi Criminals in the United States: Denaturalization after Federenko," *Simon Wiesenthal Center Annual*, Vol. 3, New York, 1986 pp. 68-72.

61. This explanation was provided by a leading OSI attorney at a meeting in Jerusalem on April 3, 1986.

62. *Quiet Neighbors*, pp. 60, 354.

63. Paul Korda, "Never Too Late to Try Nazis," *Jerusalem Post*, March 2, 1986. See also by the same author, "Negligent about Nazis," *Jerusalem Post*, February 13, 1986, p. 8.

64. Meeting with Dr. Nimrod Novick, March 12, 1986, Jerusalem.

65. "Ha-Mirdaf she-Lo Radaf," Kol Yisrael, May 6, 1986, channels alef and bet, 3-5 p.m.

66. Andy Court, "U.S. Legal Loophole Allows War Criminals to Escape," *Jerusalem Post*, May 30, 1986, p. 1.

67. Baruch Me'iri, "Yisrael Lo Tevakesh me-Artzot ha-Brit le-Hasgeer le-Yadeha Nazim Nosafim," *Ma'ariv*, June 1, 1986, p. 2.

68. Andy Court, "Searching Questions," *Jerusalem Post Magazine*, September 12, 1986, p. 11.

69. Alex Doron, "Nechsefu Ye'adei ha-Bricha Shel Posh'im Nazim," *Ma'ariv*, October 12, 1986, p. 22.

70. Yisrael Landres, "Lama Rak Demjanjuk," *Davar*, December 12, 1986, pp. 16-17.

71. Efraim Zuroff, "Demjanjuk u-Ma Hal'a?," *Ma'ariv*, October 8, 1986, p. 11; see also by the same author, "Lo ba-Rosh," *Emda*, January 1987, pp. 14-15; "Michtav Galui le-Yedid Emet," *Ma'ariv*, January 27, 1987, p. 11; Trifa: Tizkoret Aguma," *Ma'ariv*, February 19, 1987, p. 11. In the debate in the

Knesset on the reparations from Germany, Foreign Minister Moshe Sharett presented the Israeli position as follows: "The government of the State of Israel is demanding the sum of the reparations for itself because it views the State of Israel as the bearer of the rights of the slaughtered millions and as privileged and commanded to demand their just due as the sole sovereign expression of the people, affiliation to whom doomed them to extinction." *Divrei ha-Knesset*, Vol. VII, p. 1320. Quoted in Zerach Warhaftig, *Palit ve-Sarid be-Yemei ha-Shoa*, Jerusalem, 1984, p. 487.

72. See, for example, Glenn Frankel, "War Crimes Trial Poses Questions for Israelis," *Washington Post*, October 2, 1986; David Bedein, "Wiesenthal Center Hires OSI's Man in Israel," *Baltimore Jewish Times*, September 26, 1986; Yedidya Atlas, "Israel Extradition Policy Change Noted," *Jewish Week*, June 26, 1986, p. 15; Yedidya Atlas, "Governments Pushed to Pursue Nazis," *Jewish Standard*, November 21, 1986.

73. Letter of Efraim Zuroff to President Herzog, October 26, 1986, SWCA.

74. Meetings with Aryeh Mekel and MK Dan Meridor, November 25, 1986, Jerusalem.

75. Letter of Aryeh Mekel to Efraim Zuroff, December 19, 1986, SWCA.

76. Cables of Efraim Zuroff to Yitzhak Shamir, Shimon Peres and Avraham Sharir, January 22, 1987, SWCA.

77. Rafael Mann and Aryeh Bender, "Hawk Hitchil Bikuro ha-Mamlachti be-Yerushalayim be-Mezeg Avir So'er," *Ma'ariv*, January 27, 1986, p. 2.

78. Efraim Zuroff, "Michtav Galui le-Yedid Emet," *Ma'ariv*, January 1986, p. 11.

79. Amira Lam, "Ha-Dvarim she-Oriru et ha-Sa'ara," *Tzomet ha-Sharon*, No. 187, November 21, 1986, pp. 12-13.

80. Ernie Meyer, "Haim Cohen Blasted for Remarks on Demjanjuk—'Tampering with Justice,'" *Jerusalem Post*, November 20, 1986, p. 4.

81. Efraim Zuroff, "Trifa: Tizkoret Aguma," *Ma'ariv*, February 19, 1987, p. 11.

82. See, for example, "U.S. Court Orders 'Nazis' Aide' Deported to USSR," *Jerusalem Post*, May 11, 1986, p. 4; Andy Court, "Estonian Camp Head Next in Line for Deportation," *Jerusalem Post*, May 21, 1986, p. 3.

83. See, for example, Wolf Blitzer, "Washington Has New Doubts about Waldheim," *Jerusalem Post*, October 31, 1986, p. 1; "Revealed Plan to Dump Waldheim," *Jerusalem Post*, February 10, 1987, p. 1.

84. See, for example, Michel Zlotowski "'Butcher of Lyon' Goes on Trial Today," *Jerusalem Post*, May 11, 1987; "Barbie Trial Uproar Over Accusations Against Israel," *Jerusalem Post*, July 2, 1987.

85. Y. Finkelstone, "Britanya Misarevet Lachkor u-le-Garesh Ne'eshamim be-Pishei Milchama Nazi'im," *Ma'ariv*, March 3, 1987; Yochanan Lahav, "Britanya Asuya le-Shanot ha-Chok le-Hasgarat Nazim," *Yediot Achronot*, March 5,

1987.

86. Alex Doron, "Ha-Shachen ha-Tov Hoo Nazi," *Ma'ariv,* March 20, 1987, p. 6; Nomi Morris, "Canada to Allow Trials of Alleged Nazi Criminals," *Jerusalem Post,* March 15, 1987, p. 2.

87. Ernie Meyer, "Australian Commission Urges Steps against Ex-Nazis," *Jerusalem Post,* December 29, 1986, p. 3; Gidon Alon, "Doch Rasmi: 70 Poshe'i Milchama Nazim Mitgor'rim be-Australia," *Ha-Aretz,* December 26, 1986.

88. Tova Tzimuki, "Ha-Chulya ha-Chalasha," Davar, October 1, 1986; Boaz Evron, "Histabachnu," *Yediot Achronot,* October 17, 1986; Nadav Shra'gai, "John o Ivan," *Ha-Aretz,* April 11, 1986, p. 17.

89. See, for example, Gidon Alon, "Zeh Yiyeh Mishpat Treblinka ve-Lo Rak Mishpato shel Demyanyuk," *Ha-Aretz,* September 20, 1986, p. 2.

90. Glenn Frankel, "Demjanjuk Proceeding Unites Israel; Curiosity, History Draw Cross Section to Nazi Trial," *Washington Post,* February 20, 1987, p. A13.

91. Tzadok Yechezkeli, "Otam Zeh Me'anyein," *Kol Yerushalayim,* March 6, 1987, pp. 8-9.

92. Ernie Meyer, "Survivor Confronts Ivan Demjanjuk," *Jerusalem Post,* February 25, 1987, p. 1; Ernie Meyer, "High Drama in Court as Survivor Confronts "Ivan,'" *Jerusalem Post,* February 26, 1987, p. 1.

93. Ernie Meyer, "State of Defense," *Jerusalem Post,* September 4, 1987, p. 8.

94. "Shnayim mi-Kol Shlosha Yisraelim Rotzim she-Posh'im Nazim Yusgeru le-Yadeinu," *Ma'ariv,* May 18, 1987, p. 2.

95. Seumas Milne, "UK Risks Regarded as Soft on 'Ex-Nazis,'" *Guardian,* July 21, 1987.

96. Meeting with Home Secretary Douglas Hurd, March 2, 1987. Seumas Milne, "Nazi War Suspects may be Handed to Israel," *Guardian,* March 3, 1987.

97. Meeting with Foreign Minister Shimon Press, July 27, 1987, Jerusalem. Gabi Brun, "Mechonat ha-Yiri'ya Hayta Lo Kemo Ekdach," *Yediot Achronot,* July 28, 1987.

98. Meeting with Justice Minister Avraham Sharir, July 27, 1987,Jerusalem. Bernard Josephs, "Israel Will Try Alleged War Criminal if UK Won't," *Jerusalem Post,* July 28, 1987, p. 2.

99. Meeting with Prime Minister Yitzhak Shamir, August 3, 1987, Jerusalem; Aryeh Bender, "Shamir Yivdok Im Sar ha-Mishpatim Sharir et Chomer ha-Ra'ayot Neged Gekas," *Ma'ariv,* August 4, 1987.

100. Howard Goller, "Israeli Court Says Demjanjuk Guilty of Nazi War Crimes," Reuters, April 18, 1988.

101. "G'zar Din Mavet," *Ma'ariv,* April 26, 1988, p. 1

102. See for example Tzadok Yechezkeli, "Yisrael Lo Tevakesh Od Poshim Nazim mei-Artzot ha-Brit," *Yediot Achronot,* April 20, 1988.

103. Susan Sappir, "Israel Vows to Bring More Nazis to Trial," Reuters, April 26, 1988.

104. Cable from Efraim Zuroff to Avraham Sharir, April 26, 1988, SWCA.

105. David Horovitz, "Justice Ministry May Set Up Nazi-hunting Unit," *Jerusalem Post*, July 31, 1989.

106. Meeting with Dan Meridor, July 16, 1989.

107. See for example letter of Rabbi Marvin Hier to Dan Meridor, October 13, 1989, SWCA.

108. Among the cases in which we requested that Israel press for extradition were those of Ferdinand Aus Der Funten and Franz Fisher who played a leading role in the deportation of Dutch Jewry. See cable from Efraim Zuroff to Dan Meridor, January 27, 1989, SWCA.

109. In a conversation with the author Meridor claimed that Finance Minister Yitzhak Mod'ai had refused to allocate the extra funds necessary to establish the unit.

8

The Motivation for Prosecution

During the course of the more than thirteen years that I have been actively involved in efforts to bring Nazi criminals to justice, I have often been asked two annoying but—given the subject—inevitable questions. The first is: Why? The question takes several different forms depending on the attitude of the questioner. For those opposed to the efforts to prosecute Nazi war criminals, the why in this case usually means: Why bother? Why is this important or necessary, and/or why now after so many years have passed? The implication of this question is that there is no particular significance to the crimes committed which would warrant a special effort to prosecute these criminals at this late date. This attitude may stem from a variety of factors. There are those who claim that these crimes were not committed, a view commonly referred to as "Holocaust denial" which at present is relatively peripheral but whose existence cannot be viewed with equanimity.[1] Other opponents are often motivated by the ethnic or national prejudices of those whose countrymen are accused of committing some of the most horrifying atrocities of the Second World War. Organizations of Lithuanian, Latvian, Ukrainian, Estonian, Croatian, Rumanian and Byelorussian émigrés have consistently opposed attempts to bring their guilty compatriots to trial. The accusations levelled by these groups are usually dangerously close to those of the deniers. Besides claiming that these investigations are motivated by animosity directed against their particular nationalities, they assert that the allegations have been fabricated by the Soviet Union. In order to strengthen their case, moreover, they often deliberately attempt to distort history by casting exclusive responsibility for the murder of the Jews upon the Germans and Austrians. They frequently attempt to highlight the efforts of those few noble members of their nationality who rescued Jews during the Holocaust, presenting them as the norm when in fact they were usually the exception which proved the opposite.[2]

Those who ask why are not confined, however, to those ideologically opposed to these efforts. The same question is often posed by those ignorant of the events, their scope and significance. There are individuals who cannot understand, for example, why a particular effort should be made to investigate crimes committed more than 50 years ago in a remote village in some small East European country which until recently no longer existed. Others often ask why the perpetrators of the Holocaust should be investigated, while the prosecution of countless criminals who committed other serious atrocities has never even been an issue in the Western democracies currently involved in trying Nazi war criminals. Sometimes the question is motivated not so much by ignorance or ideological opposition but rather by prosaic factors related to the suspects under investigation. The time which has elapsed since the crime was committed and the fact that the individuals in question have in most cases been exemplary citizens in their adopted countries are adduced to discourage prosecution. The advanced age of the defendants and the complicated legal issues involved are also factors which prompt a measure of skepticism in the minds of many individuals as to the wisdom of the efforts to bring the perpetrators of the Holocaust to justice. An additional argument often used in this context relates to the nature of the crimes committed. There are those who point to the fact that the crimes were carried out in the course of war as an exculpating factor. Another issue which is often raised ascribes the efforts to punish the perpetrators to personal motives such as the desire for revenge, which cannot be equated with the quest for justice. Many, or all, of these arguments are marshalled by those ideologically opposed to the prosecution of Nazi criminals, but these factors undoubtedly affect many other people who might consider current efforts to prosecute Nazis as questionable at best, ill-advised and ill-timed at worst.

The second question which invariably comes up time and again relates primarily to the emotional or psychological strain borne by those involved in the campaign to bring Nazis to justice. This question is far more personal and is posed by supporters as well as by opponents. The former usually ask in admiration, sometimes as a compliment, while the latter at times pose this query as an insult. In some form or other, this question is often presented by those ostensibly neutral as well. In their case it generally stems from the human interest angle, from a desire to understand what appears to be an interesting phenomenon. The question is how, how can someone devote years of one's life to dealing with such horrible events? How can someone spend the better part of his waking hours day in and day out reading about, studying and investigating the gory details of man's inhumanity to his fellow man, or on a more particularistic level, the details of the brutal annihilation of one-third of one's people. The questions imply the emotional difficulties inherent in such a task and hint at the traumatic effect which those asking the questions assume work of this sort must inevitably engender.

These questions, put to me so frequently over the past thirteen years, did not begin with my transition from Holocaust scholar to Nazi-hunter. I had been asked similar questions during the years I worked at Yad Vashem[3] and at the Wiesenthal Center in Los Angeles. In those days, however, the question of how was far easier to respond to given the nature of my activities. Researching rescue activities, editing a scholarly publication, preparing educational materials as well as an occasional lecture or VIP tour were not that difficult to cope with for a young person whose immediate family had been relatively untouched by the events. I used to respond jokingly, but truthfully, by saying that questions of that sort were the only part of the work which I found difficult. The transition to full time research on Nazi war criminals not only increased the frequency and intensity of the questions but also made them more difficult to answer. Not because of any reduction in ideological motivation (if anything the opposite occurred) but because the task at hand was indeed considerably more difficult. At the end of my first six months at OSI, during which I did research on the mass murder of Jews in Byelorussia, I felt as if that effort had been emotionally equivalent to more than six years of less psychologically-trying tasks at Yad Vashem and the Wiesenthal Center. Not that the material was so different, the events, after all, were exactly the same. The requirements of this work, however, forced me to focus on the atrocities. Gory details had to be thoroughly researched and could no longer be avoided; the ultimate horror of individual participation in mass murder on a scale unknown in human history had to be squarely faced. These were, after all, deeds committed by human beings, people ostensibly like you and me.

The answers to these questions are rooted in the events themselves. The best explanation for the why and how of the efforts to bring the murderers to the bar of justice is a clarification of the nature of the crimes, their historical significance and contemporary implications. In this case, the elementary quest for justice is reinforced and magnified by the manner in which the crimes were committed, their enormous scope and their importance as a watershed event in the annals of mankind, as well as in the history of the Jewish people.

The Holocaust was undoubtedly a unique historical event. Although it is similar in various respects to other large-scale tragedies in Jewish as well as general history, it has assumed a preeminent position in our historical consciousness. If we examine the three most important criteria in this respect—the intent of the perpetrators, the implementation of the mass murder and the implications of the tragedy for the victims—we see that the Holocaust stands out as a singular disaster. No other large-scale catastrophe in Jewish history or in the annals of mankind was as devastating as the annihilation of European Jewry. Several factors combine, moreover, to make the Holocaust an event of universal moral and historical significance which transcends the confines of its chronological framework. The Nazis' determination to murder every single Jew in Europe, the racial criteria applied in defining Jews, which in effect eliminated any avenue of escape for the individual of Jewish origin, the lack of assistance extended to the victims both inside occupied Europe and from the Free World, the studied attempt by the perpetrators to dehumanize the victims while obliterating their religion, the utilization of the advances of modern technology for mass murder and the participation of significant segments of the spiritual and intellectual elite in the annihilation process make the Holocaust an event which casts its pall on Western civilization. If we add the scope of the mass murder, the demographic losses which to this day have still not been recouped, the destruction of the vibrant center of Jewish communal life, learning, culture, education and politics which had developed over the course of a millennium in Europe, the radical changes wrought in the Jewish world in the wake of the events and the psychological scars borne by the erstwhile victims of Nazi genocide, we realize that in Jewish terms in particular, the Holocaust is a sui generis event which will undoubtedly continue to influence Jews the world over for generations.[4]

The Nazis' choice of the Jew as primary victim is also of particular import. For the Jew, in Nazi ideology, was the symbol of the liberal and democratic forces which the Nazis thought were destroying the fabric of German national life and undermining the German state. The Nazis, who sought to build an empire based on race, coercion, repression and power, believed that the only way they could possibly succeed was to destroy all opposition, and eradicate those who espoused moral standards which negated the distorted norms of the Third Reich. The Jews, who in ancient times had given the world the Ten Commandments and more recently had been in the forefront of the struggle for equality, liberalism and democracy, were viewed as the embodiment of the Devil, the archetype of the enemies of Nazism.[5] The fact that a regime could devote such enormous resources to the brutal annihilation of millions of innocent men, women and children whose only crime was their very existence, is a clearcut indication of the perversion of Nazi ideology and the serious threat it posed to humanity as a whole.

The efforts to prosecute the perpetrators of the Holocaust must be viewed in this context. If basic elementary justice—the principle that if an individual harms another person he or she must be held accountable—represents one of the foundations of contemporary society, the significance of the Holocaust can be equated to a lighthouse built on that foundation which shines as a beacon of warning. The evil unleashed by Nazism was not completely eliminated with the defeat of Germany and the fall of the Third Reich. Society must be ever-vigilant and ready to combat the evils of obsessive anti-Semitism, totalitarianism, fascism and other forms of government based on the repression of human freedom and the suppression of human rights. The attempts to bring Nazi war criminals to trial are part of this effort. Not because I believe that these elderly criminals will initiate a renaissance of Nazi ideology or foment a totalitarian uprising, but because their prosecution constitutes an unequivocal statement by the powers that be that those who committed the crimes of the Holocaust will be held accountable. This determination to achieve justice constitutes a powerful weapon in efforts to ensure that such catastrophes will not recur since it reinforces the foundations upon which society is based. No society which condones murder can survive because ultimately it will be destroyed by violence. By bringing the murderers of European Jewry to trial, the various governments are acknowledging the seriousness of the crimes and their historical significance, and making it known that justice, even if delayed, will always be pursued. This is the cornerstone of Western civilization and a concept which must be zealously guarded if democracy is to survive.

In that context it would be worthwhile to deal with a related issue which often arises in discussions regarding the attempts to bring Nazi war criminals to justice. Given the considerable difficulties involved in the prosecution of Nazis, I am often asked why I, or Israel, or some other private body did not attempt to achieve justice by organizing teams of vigilantes to liquidate Nazi war criminals the world over. While such a solution does have a certain appeal in view of the fact that so many of the murderers have already died in peace and tranquillity, unpunished for their crimes, the adoption of this policy is basically counterproductive. The proverbial "bottom line" is that it is ultimately governments which bear the responsibility not only for meting out justice to this or that individual criminal but for the preservation of society as well. This is the reason that it is so important that governments be convinced of the need to assume this responsibility. There is no comparison in terms of public impact and influence on the population of punishment implemented by the state at the conclusion of a judicial process and measures taken against a person suspected of crimes by unknown individuals. As we have already seen in numerous cases, the public trials of these criminals have played an important role in educating the public regarding the Holocaust and undermining the propaganda of Holocaust deniers. Another argument against independent revenge attempts is that violence has its own dynamics and while one may know where it starts one can never tell where it will end. No one issues licences to those seeking to engage in such activities and while one group might be extremely careful and ensure that the intended victim is indeed guilty of his crimes, there is no guarantee that others will do so as well. While governments may be at times reluctant to deal with the issue, slow in their handling of cases and frequently lenient in the punishments meted out, they are still indispensable in the attempts to bring the perpetrators of the Holocaust to justice. In this respect, in the short run, we pay the price of their inactivity, inefficiency and misplaced mercy, but in the long run contribute towards strengthening the frameworks which are the primary defence against a recurrence of similar catastrophes.

International terrorism is a contemporary problem which relates to the issue under consideration. In reality, it may legitimately be considered one of Nazism's offspring. The indiscriminate murder of innocent men, women and children simply because of their religious affiliation or national origin smacks of the type of perverted morality espoused by the Nazis. Just as the Nazis sent German patriots of Jewish origin who had been awarded the Iron Cross first class for bravery in the ranks of the German Army in the First World War to the gas chambers, Arab terrorists indiscriminately murder Jews, among them individuals sympathetic to Palestinian aspirations, simply because of the fact that they are Jews. The scope of these latter crimes cannot be compared to those which took place during the Second World War, but there is a chilling similarity. The fact that people attending a synagogue service in Vienna or Paris or Istanbul or those eating in a Jewish restaurant in Paris were ipso facto identified as potential victims is cause for serious concern. This is precisely the point regarding the vital necessity of government responsibility. Terrorist groups do not pose much of a danger as long as they are unable to use the power and resources of governments, and as long as governments refuse to countenance their activities. If international terrorism is indeed a serious problem today, it is because on the one hand various governments continue actively to assist the terrorists and on the other those governments victimized were initially slow to respond and often adopted a lenient policy which only inspired further terrorist activity. Here too the efforts invested in bringing those responsible to justice play a crucial role in ensuring the ultimate failure of terrorist philosophy and aims.

In summation, the issue of the prosecution of Nazi war criminals exists on two levels which are basically interdependent. As a committed Jew, who identifies with the pain of the past and is concerned about the future, I cannot remain apathetic in response to the fact that hundreds, even thousands of murderers and accomplices who brutally butchered European Jews are living freely, unpunished for their crimes. As someone who has the appropriate training and expertise, I feel I have an obligation to contribute to the prosecution effort. In that respect I often think of the victims. Their fate has been the subject of countless books, plays and films. Their story has been told and retold, used as a lesson by some, denied by others, bandied about in so many different contexts that its perimeters have become frayed. If only Jewish organizations had invested half as much effort in bringing the murderers to justice as has been invested in using the horrors of those crimes to elicit support for a variety of causes—some more worthy, some less worthy—the problem would not exist in its presently unmanageable proportions. I often ponder what the victims might say if they were to learn that 40 years later their fate has become one of the major pillars of Jewish life yet so little has been done by the Jewish Establishment to induce the governments in question to bring their murderers to the bar of justice. Obviously six million people—least of all six million Jews—would not respond unanimously to this question, but the feeling that they deserve more in this respect is definitely a source of motivation.

This principle also applies as far as future generations are concerned. One of the questions I often asked my parents once I had become aware of the events of the Holocaust, was what they had known about the murders in Europe and what they had done to alleviate the plight of European Jewry. They replied that they had known in general that Jews were suffering very badly under the Nazis and that they had attended demonstrations on their behalf. The feeling that they conveyed very strongly was that they had not done enough. They had tried to do something (and I subsequently learned that they had even been more active than they told me about) but their response had been totally inadequate and out of all proportion to the crimes. This question of the response of American Jewry to the Holocaust intrigued me. The first seminar paper I wrote at the Hebrew University dealt with news of the Final Solution in the Jewish and general press during the period from June 1941 (when the mass murders began) until September 1942 (when Western governments began receiving reports on the scope of the annihilation). The findings were quite surprising. The information, initially unconfirmed, at times from unreliable sources, was published report after report after report. In those days, of course, it was difficult to believe that such things could take place, and the manner in which the news was presented often encouraged its dismissal as atrocity propaganda. The fact remains, however, that even at that relatively early date considerable data was available. The fact that so much information was available in the United States regarding the murders in Europe,[6] as well as my parents' response, also served as a motivation to become involved in attempts to bring Nazis to justice.

I believe that as time goes by the knowledge and awareness of the events of the Holocaust in the Jewish community will continue to grow and perhaps wield even a greater influence than they do today. It would not be surprising, therefore, if future generations of Jews will ask why more was not done to bring the murderers of European Jewry to justice. That will undoubtedly be a legitimate and appropriate question, for which I hope to have an adequate answer.

Besides my motivation as a Jew, there were other—more universal—considerations which induced me to become involved in the efforts to prosecute Nazi war criminals. Regardless of its public image, this is not an exclusively Jewish issue. First of all there were many non-Jews among the victims of the murderers whom we seek to bring to justice. While it is true that the Jews were the Nazis' primary target, they certainly were not the only victims. These criminals were responsible for the persecution and murder of countless innocent non-Jews. Beyond the issue of the national origin or religious affiliation of the victims, however, lies a more serious issue—the moral significance of the crime. The Holocaust was a watershed for Western civilization, a series of events which tested each and every level of modern society. It affected not only occupied Europe but neutral states and the Free World as well. Those events constituted a test of the response to evil, a test which every government, organization and individual living during that time had to undergo. This question was posed throughout the world because there was almost no civilized place which was not affected by those events.

In Germany the question was how to respond to Nazism. Does one join the party, remain indifferent or actively fight against the Nazis' anti-Semitic policy and help their potential victims? How did people in Germany respond to the persecution and expulsion of their Jewish compatriots? In the satellite states, governments had to decide to what extent to cooperate with the Nazis in the war effort in general, and vis-à-vis the persecution of the Jews in particular. The high percentage of Slovak Jews murdered was undoubtedly a function of the enthusiasm of Josef Tiso's government to assist the Nazis in their diabolical plans. The Slovaks' zeal in deporting the Jews was manifest in the sum of 500 marks per Jew they deposited in the Nazis' coffers. The response of the Bulgarian government, which refused to deport the Jews from Bulgaria proper and thereby saved their lives, is concrete proof that the attitude of local governments had an important impact on the success or failure of Nazi policy.[7]

This same question existed on an individual level as well. The personal responses of local residents in the areas occupied by the Nazis and/or satellite states ranged from participation in mass murder squads to the noble acts performed by Righteous Gentiles. No one was forced to join the *Ypatingas burys*, Lithuanian auxiliary police battalions or the Arajs Commando on the one hand or Zegota (a Polish group established to rescue Jews),[8] the Danish resistance[9] or the Dutch underground[10] on the other. There was an element of choice. People made different choices and the results speak for themselves. The fact that at least several hundred Jews survived in hiding in Berlin, the heart of the

Nazi regime,[11] is clear proof that individuals did have freedom of response. Indeed if far more people had acted differently, those horrible events we refer to as the Holocaust would not have taken place or would have been considerably reduced in scope. The noble deeds of the Righteous Gentiles,[12] moreover, make the opposite choice made by the criminals that much more reprehensible. Contrary to the image often projected by those who actively participated in the crimes, there was another choice of action available.

The test posed by the Holocaust existed not only in occupied Europe but also in the Free World where governments were forced to respond to Nazism and to the persecution of innocent civilians. Unfortunately, insufficient attention and resources were devoted to the latter problem. Even after the Allies had committed themselves to the armed struggle against the Third Reich, relatively little was done to alleviate the plight of its victims. The Bermuda Conference, the failure to bomb Auschwitz, the refusal to open the gates of Palestine or to alter US immigration quotas and/or requirements are all testimony to a lack of sensitivity to the plight of those singled out for death by the Nazis. The failure of the various governments to assist refugees and/or to adopt measures to help erstwhile victims in occupied Europe was undoubtedly to no small extent a result of a lack of public support for such measures.[13] The test faced by the populations in the Free World was quite different from the one which confronted the peoples of occupied Europe and the satellite states, but it too had profound moral implications. The information regarding the mass murders was available in the West and the people there were certainly free to act. The question was of collective and individual response to the evil perpetrated in Europe.

Given the above historical context and the significance of the Holocaust as a watershed event, the need for positive action on this issue becomes clearer. Society must broadcast an unequivocal message that those who participated in the crimes of the Holocaust will be brought before the bar of justice. Until recently the message was, unfortunately, the very opposite. Despite extensive knowledge regarding the existence of numerous Nazi war criminals in various countries, including Western democracies, governments chose to ignore the problem.[14] The implication appeared to be clear. If you committed a serious offence, but were able to elude the law for 30 or 40 years, society will allow you to live out your "golden years" in tranquillity, regardless of whether you murdered ten people or a hundred or even a thousand. The fact that those crimes took place elsewhere long ago was sufficient reason to ignore them, especially if the criminal had been on his best behavior ever since arriving in his adopted home. The cold war created new realities and new rivalries and the criminals were also able to benefit from that terrible combination of governmental ignorance and apathy.

Now, however, the information has been researched and publicized and the whereabouts of the criminals are rapidly being discovered. All the excuses which once existed are being eliminated and discredited one after the other and what remains are the bare facts, the existence of thousands of Nazi war criminals the world over, including a significant number in the bastions of Western democracy. What is being done to solve the problem? We have the beginnings of answers in various countries, most notably the United States, which initiated its effort to prosecute Nazi war criminals in 1977.[15] A decade ago, the United States was the only Western country, besides West Germany, that had taken any purposeful steps to solve this problem. Nowhere else had even the initial step of investigation been initiated by the governments in question. During the past nine years, however, commissions of inquiry, or variations thereof, were finally established in Canada,[16] Australia,[17] Great Britain,[18] New Zealand,[19] and Iceland,[20] and in most cases legal measures were actually adopted by those countries. The manner in which these governments were finally convinced to undertake the necessary steps to enable the prosecution of the Nazi war criminals in their countries, the practical results achieved thereby, and the role of the Wiesenthal Center in these efforts are the final subjects of this volume.

Before presenting an analysis of the efforts in each country, it would be worthwhile to recount the background to this campaign. In early 1986, while working as a researcher for the Office of Special Investigations, I was toying with the idea of establishing a computerized data bank on Nazi war criminals in order to advance research and prosecution. I broached the idea with my former colleagues at the Wiesenthal Center, Rabbis Hier and Cooper, who I assumed would support such an initiative if it were combined with a practical campaign to step up prosecution. In essence, the two issues were irrevocably intertwined since any effort to persuade a government to adopt the necessary legal measures would be dependent on our ability to collect the maximum documentation.

It took several months for the Wiesenthal Center to respond to the proposal, and in the meantime I discovered the emigration data in the ITS files. On a practical level I now had the names and postwar emigration destinations of numerous suspects, information which could serve as a solid basis for the political campaigns necessary to convince various Western governments to initiate prosecution. Thus when the Wiesenthal Center replied in the affirmative to my original proposal, I told them that we now had an opportunity to achieve our ultimate goal. Instead of concentrating on the collection of names in the hope of perhaps being able to find information regarding their present whereabouts, we now had a proven method of finding at least hundreds, if not thousands, of Nazis who had definitely emigrated to the West. In short, the time had come to press the host governments on the basis of the information in our possession. The Center agreed to the revised proposal and immediately set out to launch the project.

Before presenting the results of those efforts in the various countries, it is important to explain briefly our sources of information. Contrary to the claims made by émigré groups that all the information against the suspects was based on Soviet sources, a considerable portion of the material came from Jewish sources, primarily from the testimonies of survivors. If we take our lists of Lithuanian suspects, for example, at least three of the major sources were compiled primarily or exclusively on the basis of survivor testimony. The first was a list of 1,284 perpetrators culled from the testimonies in the Kunichowsky collection.[21] The second was a list of several hundred Lithuanian war criminals compiled by Jewish survivors in the DP camps in Germany immediately after the war.[22] The third was volume IV of the *Yahadut Lita* series, which presents the fate of all the Lithuanian Jewish communities during the Holocaust in encyclopaedic form. This volume, which contained the names of hundreds of Lithuanian collaborators and provided valuable information regarding the crimes committed, was also based primarily on Jewish sources.[23] In the case of Latvia, the same applies. We were able to draw upon extensive lists of criminals compiled by survivors after the war,[24] as well as on names collected by Yad Vashem in the course of research on a volume which relates the fate of Latvia's Jewish communities during the Holocaust.[25] We also used information from Soviet publications as well as Soviet-held documentation,[26] but none of the lists were based exclusively on such data.

In this context, the issue of documentation and research emanating from the Soviet Union should be clarified. A distinction must be made between historical documentation which was held in Soviet archives and Soviet research based on such documentation. Given the fact that a high percentage of the crimes committed by the criminals presently residing in the West were carried out in areas that were once part of the Soviet Union, it is hardly surprising that much of the pertinent documentation was held for decades in Soviet archives. The Red Army occupied these areas and in many cases captured important historical material which the Germans and their local collaborators left behind. The term "Soviet documentation" is in fact a misnomer, because the material in question is not Soviet but rather German or Lithuanian, Latvian or Ukrainian, etc. It was Soviet-held documentation because it was in archives in the Soviet Union. As far as Soviet research is concerned, the situation is to some extent different, because ostensibly there is a greater possibility of manipulation or falsification. In that respect, it must be pointed out that all the numerous books and articles published in the various Soviet republics regarding the role of local collaborators merely confirm and corroborate what we already know from numerous other sources.

The fact that the Soviet Union had a politicized judiciary which often perverted justice, as was proven time and again in the case of Soviet Jews,[27] cannot change the fact that numerous Lithuanians, Latvians, Ukrainians and Estonians collaborated with the Nazis. The fact remains that there has to date never been a case of a trial of a Nazi war criminal in which a document produced from a Soviet archive was discovered to be forged. Dr. Hans Engelhardt, West German Justice Minister and a member of the Christian-Democratic Party, confirmed in a letter to the Wiesenthal Center that the German judicial authorities had never encountered a case of forged Nazi documentation being sent from the Soviet Union in the investigation of a Nazi war criminal.[28] In view of the fact that West Germany has tried more Nazi war criminals than any other Western democracy,[29] Engelhardt's statement is particularly important. It should also be added that the Soviet-held documents have been carefully tested in the course of numerous trials conducted in the United States and have invariably been authenticated by the courts.[30]

It is only natural to pose questions regarding a regime which has on numerous occasions exhibited its cruelty and duplicity, yet for various reasons the Soviet Union consistently provided reliable documentation on this issue. The Soviet Union suffered tremendous losses during the Second World War and was therefore genuinely anxious to ensure that those who collaborated with the Nazis were punished. Any attempt to level false charges against émigrés would, if discovered, ipso facto jeopardize the efforts to convict or extradite others and would ultimately be counterproductive given the important role of Soviet-held documentation in the prosecution of Nazis who committed crimes in areas that were once part of the Soviet Union. In addition, the Soviet Union viewed itself as the premier anti-fascist force in the world. It is unlikely that they would risk endangering that image by fabricating evidence or testimony against Nazi war criminals. Given all of the above, there was certainly no reason to reject materials from the Soviet Union automatically, let alone Soviet-held documentation. Such material proved reliable in the past and has been extremely helpful in the process of investigation and prosecution. As with material from other sources, it is likewise best corroborated by additional documentation and rarely provides by itself a sufficient basis for conviction. The best proof of the validity of this approach is that many of the individuals who have been named as Nazi war criminals in Soviet publications have been convicted by American courts.[31]

Following the dismemberment of the Soviet Union, the questions regarding the authenticity of Soviet documentation became irrelevant, since almost all the areas where the crimes were committed ceased being part of the Soviet Union. Once the former Soviet republics gained or regained independence and the pertinent docuements continued to be found by war crimes researchers in the same archives, the claim could no longer be made that the material in question had been fabricated by the Communists.

Let us now turn to the campaigns waged by the Wiesenthal Center in various Western countries to convince governments to prosecute Nazi war criminals.

Notes

1. For an overview of the phenomenon of "Holocaust denial" see Deborah E. Lipstadt, *Denying the Holocaust; The Growing Assault on Truth and Memory,* New York, 1993; Yehuda Bauer, "Tofa'at ha-Revizyonism—Hakchashat ha-Shoa u-Mashma'uta ha-historit," *Ha-Shoa ba-Historiographiya,* Jerusalem, 1987, pp. 571-81.

2. See the study of the efforts of émigré groups in the United States to

undermine the activities of OSI. Eli Rosenbaum, "The Campaign Against the U.S. Justice Department's Prosecution of Suspected Nazi War Criminals," New York, 1985, pp. 37-40. In early 1977 Juozas Prunskis, Director of Information for the Lithuanian-American Council wrote to the Association of Lithuanian Jews in Israel and asked them to issue a statement indicating that many Lithuanians had rescued Jews during the Holocaust. Yaakov Oleisky, the president of the Israeli association, replied by noting the extensive role played by the Lithuanians in the murder of Jews in Lithuania. Yaakov Oleisky, "Chelkam shel ha-Lita'im be-Hashmadat ha-Yehudim," *Yalkut Moreshet*, No. 32, December 1981, pp. 177-82. Prunskis later wrote a pamphlet regarding the rescue of Jews by Lithuanians as part of the effort by the émigrés in the US to combat the facts which came to light regarding the active participation of Lithuanians in the murder of Jews. *Lithuania's Jews and the Holocaust*, Chicago, 1979. This issue came to the fore again in the wake of revelations by the Wiesenthal Center that the Lithuanian goverment had rehabilitated numerous Nazi war criminals. See, for example, Dov Levin, "Lithuanian Attitudes toward the Jewish Minority in the Holocaust; The Lithuanian Press, 1991-1992," *Holocaust and Genocide Studies*, Vol. 7, No. 2, Fall 1993, pp. 247-262.

3. Efraim Zuroff, "Working at Yad Vashem; Travails of a Holocaust Professional," *Hadassah Magazine*, November 1978, pp. 16-17, 38-39.

4. Efraim Zuroff, "The Uniqueness of the Holocaust," Holocaust Curriculum for Jewish Schools, a project of the American Association for Jewish Education, reprinted in Ivan Tillem (ed.), *The 1987-1988 Jewish Almanac*, New York, 1987, pp. 105-10.

5. George L. Mosse, *The Crisis of German Ideology: Intellectual Origins of the Third Reich*, New York, 1964, pp. 294-311.

6. Several studies of the American press during the Holocaust have subsequently been published. Deborah E. Lipstadt, *Beyond Belief: The American Press and the Coming of the Holocaust 1933-1945*, New York, 1986; Haskel Lookstein, *Were We Our Brothers' Keepers? The Public Response of American Jews to the Holocaust 1938-1944*, New York, 1985.

7. Helen Fein, *Accounting for Genocide: Victims and Survivors of the Holocaust*, New York, 1979, pp. 99-102, 159-64. On the events in Slovakia see Livia Rotkirchen, *Churban Yahadut Slovakia*, Jerusalem, 1961. On the events in Bulgaria see Nissan Oren, "The Bulgarian Exception—A Reassessment of the Salvation of the Jewish Community," *Yad Vashem Studies*, Vol VII, January 1968, pp. 83-106.

8. Joseph Kermish, "The Activities of the Council for Aid to Jews ('Zegota') in Occupied Poland," Yisrael Gutman and Efraim Zuroff (eds), *Rescue Attempts During the Holocaust*, Jerusalem, 1977, pp. 367-98.

9. Leni Yahil, "The Uniqueness of the Rescue of Danish Jewry," ibid., pp. 617-25.

10. B.A. Sijes, "Several Observations Concerning the Position of the Jews in Occupied Holland During World War II," ibid., pp. 527-57; *Ha-Machteret ha-Chalutzit be-Holland ha-Kvusha*, Beit Lohamei ha-Gettaot, 1969.

11. There is no exact figure for the number of Jews who survived in hiding in Berlin. In June 1945 the Jewish community listed the number as 1,123, but other estimates indicate lower totals. Leonard Gross, *The Last Jews in Berlin*, New York, 1982, p. 345.

12. See, for example, Mordechai Paldiel, *The Path of the Righteous; Gentile Rescuers of Jews During the Holocaust*, Hoboken, 1993; Moshe Bejski, "The "Righteous Among the Nations" and Their Part in the Rescue of Jews," *Rescue Attempts During the Holocaust*, pp. 627-47.

13. On the response of the American government see Henry L. Feingold, *Politics of Rescue: The Roosevelt Administration and the Holocaust 1938-1945*, New Brunswick, 1970; Saul S. Friedman, *No Haven for the Oppressed: United States Policy Towards Jewish Refugees 1938-1945*, Detroit, 1973; David S. Wyman, *Paper Walls: America and the Refugee Crisis 1938-1941*, Amherst, 1968; and idem, *The Abandonment of the Jews; America and the Holocaust 1941-1945*, New York, 1984. On the response of the British government see Bernard Wasserstein, *Britain and the Jews of Europe 1939-1945*, London, 1979.

14. There was considerable information regarding the presence in the United States of numerous Nazi war criminals as early as the beginning of the 1960s. *The Outraged Conscience*, pp. 19-29, 47-67; Howard Blum, *Wanted! The Search for Nazis in America*, New York, 1977.

15. *Quiet Neighbors*, pp. 29-64; *The Outraged Conscience*, pp. 123-38.

16. The Deschenes Commission was officially established on February 7, 1985 by Order-in Council PC-1985-348.

17. The Menzies Review was established on June 25, 1986.

18. The British comm1sion of inquiry headed by Sir Thomas Hetherington was established on February 8, 1988.

19. The New Zealand government instructed the Solicitor-General to investigate the matter in May 1990.

20. A panel of lawyers was appointed to investigate the question on March 22, 1992.

21. YVA, O-71.

22. YVA, M-9/15(6,6a); WLA, 539/25.

23. *Yahadut Lita*, Vol. IV, pp. 234-373.

24. YVA, M-21/III/8; M-21/476; WLA, 539/22, 23.

25. Dov Levin (ed.), *Pinkas Ha-Kehillot; Latvia ve-Estonia*, Jerusalem, 1988.

26. See, for example, *Documents Accuse*, Vilnius, 1970; E. Avotins, J. Dzirkalis and V. Petersons, *Daugavas Vanagi: Who Are They?*, Riga, 1963; J. Silabriedis and B. Arklans, *"Political Refugees" Unmasked!*, Riga, 1965.

27. William Korey, *The Soviet Cage: Anti-Semitism in Russia*, New York, 1973,

pp. 201-75.

28. Letter of Dr. Hans Engelhardt to Rabbi Marvin Hier, June 24, 1987, SWCA.

29. Deschenes Commission Report, pp. 31-32. For details on the prosecution of Nazi war criminals in West Germany see Adalbert Rückerl, *The Investigation of Nazi Crimes 1945-1978: A Documentation*, Heidelberg and Karlsruhe, 1979.

30. *Quiet Neighbors*, p. 84.

31. Among those named in Soviet publications and convicted by American courts were: Liudas Kairys, Sergei Kowalczuk, Karl Linnas, Boleslavs Maikovskis, Kazys Palciauskas.

9

Australia—Nazis Down Under

The first list of suspected Nazi war criminals which I compiled was submitted to the Australian authorities. On October 1, 1986 Rabbis Hier and Cooper met in New York with Australian Foreign Minister Bill Hayden and handed him a list of 40 alleged Nazi war criminals who had emigrated to Australia after the Second World War.[1] The list consisted of 25 Latvians, 13 Lithuanians, one Pole, and one Ukrainian who had been accused of committing crimes during the Second World War. These ranged from service in a mass murder squad to writing and disseminating pro-Nazi propaganda. The majority were suspected of active participation in mass murder, most in the course of service in either the Latvian or Lithuanian police. As for the age of the suspects, two were over 80 and three were under 65. Ten were in their late sixties (65-70), while nine were aged 70-75 and ten were in their late seventies (75-80). In several cases there was an element of doubt as to the age of the suspects. As could be expected, most of the crimes had been committed in Latvia (Riga, Valka, Smiltene, Valmiera, Karsava, Liepaja, Bauska, etc.) and Lithuania (Kaunas, Panevezys, Anyksciai, Vievis, Simnas, Zagare, Alsedziai, Raseiniai, Rokiskis and Telsiai), although some of the Latvians were accused of committing crimes in Byelorussia (Minsk) as well. A significant majority (60 per cent) were accused on the basis of documentation found in Israeli archives—primarily Yad Vashem[2] and the Wiener Library at Tel Aviv University[3]—while a minority were named in Soviet publications.[4]

Prior to their immigration to Australia, the suspects had been living in Displaced Persons' camps in occupied Germany. They were able to register as DPs and obtain assistance from various international aid organizations. A few (4) left Europe as early as 1948, but the majority did so in 1949 (22) and 1950 (8). Almost all arrived in Australia by boat, most having gone via Bagnoli transit camp and Naples. Several ships, such as the *Svalbard* in 1948, the *Nelly*, *Wooster Victory* and *Stewart* in 1949, had several suspects on board.

The list which the Wiesenthal Center submitted to Foreign Minister Hayden was accompanied by a letter to Prime Minister Bob Hawke, in which Rabbi Hier asked the Australian government to investigate the charges and if necessary create a legal apparatus to deal with the problem. He noted that this list was only preliminary and that based on the material which I had recently found, we were likely to discover the names of "at least several hundred suspected Nazi war criminals. . . believed to be living in Australia." He noted, moreover, that the biological clock was "running out" on these criminals and that the danger existed that justice would not be achieved. "Future generations must learn that the crime of genocide has no time limit and that even forty-five years after the event, governments will overcome any impediment in exercising their responsibility to bring those who committed such crimes before the bar of justice." The letter also included basic statistics on the fate of Lithuanian and Latvian Jewry during the Holocaust and was accompanied by a particularly graphic description of the brutality of the Lithuanians who participated in the murder of the Jews of Kaunas from the memoirs of Rabbi Efraim Oshry, a survivor of that city.[5] Despite intense interest and pressure from the media, the Center did not make public the names of the initial 40 suspects. At a press conference held after the meeting, Rabbi Hier explained that the Center had refrained from publicizing the names in order to give the Australian government an opportunity to investigate and, if necessary, take legal steps against the accused. He warned, however, that if the government failed to act, the Center would release all the pertinent information to the media.[6] This policy, which the Center pursued in its dealing with each government to which a list of Nazi war criminals was submitted, was designed to ensure that those under investigation would not be given advance warning and that innocent people would not be harmed if by some chance there was a case of mistaken identity.

The initial list of 40 suspects was not the first such list submitted to the Australian government. A few months previously, the issue of Nazi war criminals had received extensive coverage in the Australian media. On April 13, 1986 the Australian Broadcasting Corporation began a series of radio programs entitled "Nazis in Australia" produced by Mark Aarons and on April 22, 1986 Australian TV focused on the issue in a documentary entitled "Don't Mention the War." Both programs charged that substantial numbers of Nazi war criminals had entered Australia and that to some extent this had happened because American and English intelligence agencies had deceived and withheld information from the Australian authorities. These programs also alleged that several Australian officers had played an active role in this deception.

In late June 1986, in response to these charges, the Australian government established an official commission of inquiry headed by retired civil servant Andrew C. Menzies which was to examine the allegations and report its findings to the government. In the wake of the establishment of the Menzies Commission, lists of Nazi war criminals were submitted to the government by various sources, among them government agencies such as OSI, private organizations and individuals.[7] By the time it completed its investigations several months later, the Menzies Commission had received allegations regarding close to 200 persons, including the Wiesenthal Center's initial list of 40 suspects.[8] The most important contribution made by the Center, however, was the revelation that key documentation had been found which would enable the discovery of hundreds of Nazi war criminals who had emigrated to Australia. We stressed this point in order to emphasize the necessity of a thorough investigation by the Australian government and the adoption of legal measures to ensure that those guilty be brought to justice. Given the fact that the government had already launched an official inquiry, the key in our opinion to the problem in Australia was to ensure that the investigation be done thoroughly, efficiently and quickly. The hope was, of course, that the commission would recommend prosecution or extradition and that the government would promptly adopt and implement legislation to that effect. At this point, our particular role was to provide the names of the maximum number of suspects to the Menzies Commission, a task for which we were eminently qualified, following the discovery of the ITS files.

Our next step, therefore, was to continue our research and compile additional lists of Nazi war criminals who immigrated to Australia. The initial list we submitted received very extensive coverage in the Australian press and sparked considerable public debate regarding the steps which should be taken by the government. Many newspapers, among them the prominent Melbourne daily *The Age*, came out in favor of thorough investigation and prosecution.[9] We did not play any role in the public discussion, preferring to concentrate vis-à-vis Australia on our research efforts. Shortly after our list was handed over to the Australians, moreover, the Center was contacted by the Menzies Commission which requested our assistance in obtaining the pertinent source material. On October 21 and 29, 1986, I met with David Richey, the First Secretary of the Australian Embassy in Tel Aviv, and directed him to the documentation sought by the commission. The fact that the commission was not acquainted with most of the documentation I had used in compiling the list emphasized the importance of the participation of professional Holocaust historians in the investigation effort. It also underlined the necessity of our active involvement.

Our next step was to submit an additional list of ten suspects to the Australian authorities via the Australian Embassy in Washington. The list, which was submitted on November 25, 1986,[10] consisted of the names of six Lithuanians, three Latvians and one Estonian. Among the suspects were several individuals who had served in the *Ypatingas burys* (Vilnius Sonderkommando) and the Arajs Commando, two of the most notorious murder squads which operated in Eastern Europe. Several of the suspects had served with the local police in Lithuania or Estonia or with the Latvian SS, and had participated in persecution in various capacities. Most had arrived in Australia in 1948 and 1949. We had found their names in various sources, among them lists of war criminals compiled by survivors immediately after the war,[11] rosters of the *Ypatingas burys*,[12] material from Simon Wiesenthal's Documentation Center in Vienna,[13] as well as Soviet publications.[14]

Shortly after this list was handed over to the Australian government, the Menzies Commission completed its inquiry and submitted its findings to Special Minister of State Michael J. Young. The report confirmed the existence of a serious problem and called upon the government to take action. This constituted a serious breakthrough because until then the government had consistently refused to deal with the issue, and had rejected all requests for the extradition of Nazi war criminals to the Soviet Union. Menzies noted that at least 70 individuals who had entered Australia had been accused of committing serious war crimes, "indeed crimes involving the murder of many persons, in some cases hundreds of persons, in circumstances of the utmost cruelty and depravity." While Menzies was unable to investigate these charges fully, and thus was unable to determine the question of guilt, he made clear that the seriousness of the allegations was such that the government had to address the issue.

The argument that the culprits, by coming to this country, have turned their back on such events has, in my view, no validity. . . In the

Australian system of justice, lapse of time has never been regarded as justification for withholding prosecution action for the most serious crimes such as murder. Neither has a blameless life after the crime, although this is certainly a matter to be considered in mitigation of sentence. Some of the offences the subject of allegations recorded by the Review are of such seriousness that, if the allegations are confirmed by a full investigation, justice, however long delayed, should be and be seen to be, administered.

Menzies recommended therefore that the government take forthright action in dealing with the issue.

> In my view the Chapter should not be closed in regard to serious war crimes and I recommend that the Government make a clear and positive statement to that effect and that it will take appropriate action under the law to bring to justice persons who have committed serious war crimes found in Australia.[15]

On a practical level, the Menzies report recommended three possible courses of action once the charges against the suspects had been proven: extradition, revocation of citizenship followed by deportation in cases in which citizenship had been acquired less than ten years ago, deportation of non-citizens, or the revision of the Australian War Crimes Act to enable prosecution in Australia. In order to carry out the necessary investigations, Menzies called for the establishment of a special "clearly identified organization dedicated to the task of dealing with war criminals," and suggested that it be located in the office of the Director of Public Prosecutions. This unit would deal with extradition requests, investigate the charges against those accused of war crimes and, if the War Crimes Act were amended, prepare the prosecution of those criminals against whom sufficient evidence was found.[16] At the same time, Menzies recommended that the government clearly state that it was not contemplating any reduction in the standards of justice applied in these cases nor in the safeguards available under Australian law to individuals accused of such serious offences.[17]

Menzies also addressed himself to the question of how the suspects had entered Australia. According to his report, there was no evidence of collusion by the Australian authorities with Nazi war criminals to facilitate their entry, nor was it Australian policy to allow or assist the entry of known or suspected Nazis.[18] Nonetheless, many criminals were able to immigrate to Australia because of the inefficiency of the screening process employed by the Australians. The questions posed by Australian screening officers were "limited and not of a very searching nature" and there was unjustified reliance on the inadequate screening process of the International Refugee Organization. This was particularly true regarding the cases of the East European collaborators who constituted a significant percentage of the suspected Nazis who emigrated to Australia.[19] In short, the Australian experience in this respect was very similar to that of the Americans.

We considered the recommendations of the Menzies Commission a very positive step. Although on the philosophical and emotional level I was perturbed by the fact that Menzies had excluded those criminals who had not committed murder from consideration,[20] I realized that on a practical level there was hardly any chance of prosecuting anyone in Australia besides those who had committed the most serious atrocities. Given OSI's success in convicting even propagandists this was unfortunate, but nonetheless one could not fail to be impressed by the findings and recommendations of the Australian commission of inquiry. In the relatively brief period of approximately five months, the commission had succeeded in achieving a feat which had taken other government commissions considerably longer. Most importantly, its recommendations called for specific legal steps which we hoped the government would introduce. The problem was that we had absolutely no guarantee that the Australian government would adopt any of the recommendations made by the Menzies Commission.

Our policy during this period was, therefore, to continue our research efforts to discover the names of as many Nazi war criminals as possible who had entered Australia in the hope that this information would help convince the government to take the necessary action. We received important assistance for our research effort from an unexpected source shortly before the Menzies Commission published its findings. Chaya Lifshitz, a former colleague at Yad Vashem, had previously introduced me to Y.S., a Lithuanian Jew living in Israel who for years had collected information regarding Lithuanian war criminals. Y.S., many members of whose family had been murdered in Lithuania during the Holocaust, had decided to collect data regarding the murderers when he returned to his native Lithuania after service in the Red Army during the war. As an official of the Soviet agency which investigated the wartime activities of Lithuanian applicants for government service, he was in a unique position to obtain the names of hundreds of collaborators who had played an active role in the murder of the Jews.

Y.S. had smuggled the pertinent data out of Soviet Lithuania when he made *aliya* in the mid-seventies, but by the time we met some ten years later, he was initially loath to turn over the material due to his hereto unsuccessful efforts to interest government agencies in pressing for the prosecution of these criminals. (Shortly after his arrival in Israel he had contacted the Nazi war crimes unit of the Israeli police and had offered them his data on the condition that they launch a prosecution effort, but no concrete results were achieved.) In this respect the most convincing arguments for giving the material to the Wiesenthal Center were our ability to determine the postwar emigration destinations of the criminals and our efforts to bring them to justice. Y. S.'s material significantly helped our research effort and thereby assisted our campaigns to convince various governments to prosecute Nazi war criminals.

In late January 1987 we had an extraordinary opportunity to intensify our efforts vis-à-vis Australia when Prime Minister Bob Hawke visited Israel. The first-ever visit to Israel by an Australian head of state, the occasion was covered extensively by both local and foreign, especially Australian, media. Where, if not in Israel, could public opinion and pressure be marshalled to draw attention to the issue of Nazi war criminals in Australia. Given the findings of the Menzies report, our focus was very specific. We pressed for the adoption by the Australian government of the recommendations submitted by its own commission of inquiry.

Rabbi Cooper came up with the idea of presenting another list of suspects to Prime Minister Hawke during his visit to Israel, in order to draw public attention to the issue of Nazi war criminals in Australia. I compiled a list of 15 Lithuanian suspects who had emigrated to Australia after the war and asked Dr. Robert Merrillees, the Australian ambassador to Israel, for permission to present the list to Prime Minister Hawke personally in the course of his visit. Dr. Merrillees replied that "programming constraints" precluded such a meeting and proposed that we meet in Tel Aviv after the Prime Minister's visit.[21] I related the story to Aryeh Bender, a journalist sympathetic to the issue, who turned the incident into a page-two news item, which appeared in *Ma'ariv* on the day before Bob Hawke arrived in Israel. "They Are Preventing Us from Presenting a List of Nazis Living in Australia to Bob

Hawke," read the headline which helped focus public attention on probably the only unpleasant aspect of the Australian prime minister's visit.[22] It is possible that the headline also slightly softened Dr. Merrillees, because when I notified him that I intended to submit the list on the day of Bob Hawke's arrival, rather than after the trip, he did not object.[23]

At the same time, we attempted to persuade the Israeli leaders who were going to meet with Hawke to express Israeli concern that the Nazi criminals living in Australia be prosecuted. We therefore cabled Prime Minister Shamir, Foreign Minister Peres and Justice Minister Sharir urging them to discuss the issue with the Australian Prime Minister.[24] I had my doubts whether they would do so, but was certain that if no one even reminded them that the issue existed they would certainly not do anything. None of the three ministers responded to our request, which is a good indication of the importance with which they regarded this question. I pointed out in the interview with *Ma'ariv* that the Prime Minister's Office was apparently trying to evade the issue for fear of embarrassing the Australian leader. I noted, however, that since Bob Hawke was a good friend of Israel, there was no fear of his being embarrassed. The fact that the issue was raised did not necessarily mean that it had to be presented in a deprecatory or threatening manner.[25]

On the morning of Bob Hawke's arrival in Israel, I went to Tel Aviv to submit our third list of suspects to Dr. Merrillees at the Australian Embassy. If the circumstances of the meeting were unpleasant for the Australian ambassador, the timing, from his point of view, could hardly have been worse. At this point, all he wanted to know was whether this list was our final submission. When I replied that, on the contrary, we would be submitting many additional names in the future, I had the distinct impression that he was genuinely disappointed. I submitted the list along with a letter to Prime Minister Hawke in which we called upon him to take the necessary steps to adopt the recommendations of the Menzies Commission. "I can think," I concluded the letter, "of no more appropriate venue than Jerusalem to indicate your determination to do so."[26] Following the submission of the list at the Australian Embassy, the Center convened a press conference in Jerusalem to report on my meeting with Dr. Merrillees and the contents of our latest list. All the suspects were Lithuanians, most of whose names we had obtained from the lists prepared by Y.S. Almost all had served in the Lithuanian police, and had participated in the mass murder of Jews in communities such as Kaunas, Seduva, Rietavas, Ariogala, Salakas and Linkuva. Among them was a member of the infamous *Ypatingas burys* (Vilnius Sonderkommando), as well as the head of the Kaunas battalions of the Lithuanian police. Most were in their seventies and almost all had arrived in Australia during the years 1948-49. At the press conference I stressed the importance of the adoption of the recommendations of the Menzies Commission by the Australian government and called upon Israel to raise the issue in a friendly way with Bob Hawke.[27]

These points were further clarified and emphasized in an op-ed piece which appeared in *Ma'ariv* the next day, along with an extensive report of the press conference.[28] Entitled "An Open Letter to a True Friend," it welcomed Prime Minister Hawke to Israel, but noted that the presence of tens, if not hundreds of Nazis in Australia cast a shadow over his visit. After describing the crimes committed by two of the more notorious criminals who had emigrated to Australia, I pointed out that the government had already taken a positive step by establishing the Menzies Commission, which had recommended that legal action be taken against those convicted of war crimes. The problem was, however, that these recommendations were meaningless as long as they were not adopted by the government.

Time is against us. Every day that passes without practical measures being taken to punish the criminals increases the Nazis' chances of dying in their beds in peace and tranquillity. It is unthinkable that Australia, whose soldiers fought bravely against the Axis forces and which sacrificed so many young men to preserve democracy in the world, will grant a haven to lowly murderers who collaborated with the Nazis . . . I do not know if this subject will be raised during the formal talks you will conduct here, but I am certain that my appeal expresses the wishes of many people in Israel, the country which absorbed most of the survivors and which views itself as the inheritor of the six million victims. You who are closely acquainted with us and identify with us, certainly understand this feeling well. Please translate this feeling into practical measures so that justice will not only be heard but will finally be carried out as well. We wish you a pleasant visit and hope that by the next time you come this painful problem will no longer exist. Not because the criminals died a natural death in

Australia, but because they were put on trial and received what they deserve.[29]

The steps we took to focus public attention on the issue of Nazi war criminals in Australia and the extensive coverage of our efforts in the Israeli media had an effect. This was evident, for example, in the questions posed by journalists to Prime Minister Hawke in the course of his visit. I was present when Hawke came to Yad Vashem the day after our press conference, and was extremely gratified to hear that the first question posed to the Australian leader at the conclusion of his visit was "What's with the Nazis?" This question, moreover, was repeated at the summary press conference Hawke held at the King David Hotel upon the conclusion of his trip. While Hawke was noncommittal in response to these questions, the pressure they represented was nonetheless extremely important since it constituted a reminder that while the victims may be dead and buried, there are others who will demand that justice be carried out. That demand had a unique urgency and significance when presented in Jerusalem at the conclusion of a visit to Yad Vashem, where the Australian Prime Minister was exposed to the horror of the crimes and was obviously very moved by what he saw.[30] I have no doubt that if not for the Center's efforts, the issue would never have been raised during Bob Hawke's visit and a golden opportunity to press for determined action would have been squandered. From a Jewish point of view, the fact that the issue was raised in Israel was also very important. It would have been unthinkable for the Prime Minister of Australia to have visited Israel at a time when his government was debating whether to prosecute Nazi war criminals or not and none of his hosts in the Jewish state would have urged that perpetrators of the crimes of the Holocaust be brought to justice.

It is obviously difficult to determine what effect Hawke's visit to Israel had on his attitude towards the issue of Nazi war criminals and on the decisions ultimately taken by the government. The events in this case seem to indicate, however, that the trip had a positive impact. In late February 1987 Australian Attorney-General Lionel Bowen announced in Canberra that the government planned to establish a special unit to investigate the allegations against Australian residents suspected of committing war crimes.[31] The unit, headed by Robert F. Greenwood QC, a well-known and highly respected attorney, began investigating the various cases shortly thereafter.[32] Even more important, a bill was submitted to the Australian parliament whereby the Australian War Crimes Act of 1945 would be amended to enable the trial and punishment of Nazi war criminals by Australian civil courts. According to the proposed new law, the jurisdiction for the trial of war crimes would be transferred from military to civilian criminal courts where defendants would face a maximum penalty of life imprisonment for wilful killing and up to 25 years' imprisonment for other offences.

The proposed legislation makes deportation and internment in death camps or concentration camps serious crimes and excludes the possibility of acquittal on the grounds that the individual was following orders. According to the formulation of the new law, a serious crime became a war crime when it was committed in the course of persecution on political, racial or religious grounds with the intent of wholly or partially destroying a particular ethnic, racial, or religious group. The bill covers those crimes committed in Germany, the territory it annexed or occupied as well as the satellite states, and includes the entire range of acts of persecution committed during the Holocaust, with the exception of propaganda activities.[33]

In the meantime our research continued and additional names of suspected Nazi war criminals who emigrated to Australia were uncovered. In September 1987 Robert Greenwood and Robert Gray, chief investigator of the Australian Special Investigations Unit, came to Israel to discuss our research and meet with local officials at Yad Vashem, the Israeli police and the Justice Ministry. I utilized the opportunity of their visit to present an additional list of suspects to the Australian authorities and thereby focus public attention on the issue of the passage of the proposed legislation which would enable the prosecution of Nazi war criminals in Australia. The list submitted to Greenwood had twelve suspects, bringing the number of names uncovered in Jerusalem and transmitted by the Wiesenthal Center to the Australian government to 77.[34] Like the previous list, it consisted exclusively of Lithuanians, most of whose names were obtained from the material prepared by Y.S. They were accused of active participation in the murder of Jews in various towns throughout Lithuania and had arrived in Australia during the years 1948-49. Most of the suspects were aged between 65 and 75, although there were three over the age of 80.

In the course of the meetings I explained the sources of our documentation and the scope of the material available in Israel which might be of assistance to the Australian authorities. I also made clear our inten-

tion of continuing the research I had initiated to determine the whereabouts of as many Nazi war criminals as possible, a process which I
predicted would yield many more suspects for the Australian authorities.[35]

This was indeed the case as our research, primarily on the Baltics,
proceeded apace. By October 1987 Robert Greenwood announced that
his unit already possessed the names of more than 250 suspected Nazi
war criminals (compared to the 70 names initially examined by the
Menzies Commission which began its work in June 1986), of which 77
had been supplied by the Wiesenthal Center, including four individuals
named on our list of top twenty suspects.[36] This number rose again on
February 22, 1988 and November 7 of the same year when the Center
submitted additional lists of 15 and 28 suspects respectively to the Australian authorities, bringing the number of suspects whom we had
identified who had emigrated to Australia to 120. The first list was
made up exclusively of Lithuanians and was based on the data provided
by Y.S.[37] The second list included 22 Lithuanians and 6 Latvians, most
of whom had served in indigenous police units. In this case, the sources
of the information were varied. Some of the suspects were named in
Yahadut Lita, while others were listed in the Yad Vashem Archives,
Wiener Library, the Y.S. lists or Soviet publications.[38]

By this time we had also received confirmation from the Australian
authorities that the overwhelming majority of the suspects whose
names we had submitted had indeed emigrated to Australia, although,
as could be expected, not all were still alive. This information confirmed
the working premise of our research effort and the validity of the data
in the ITS files. The fact that quite a few of the most notorious criminals on our lists were discovered residing in various Australian cities[39]
increased our motivation and quite possibly influenced the outcome of
the campaign to pass war crimes legislation in Australia.

The Australian War Crimes Amendment Act was finally passed after
a lengthy, and at times acerbic, debate in Parliament on December 21,
1988. It had been passed relatively quickly in the lower house (House
of Representatives) shortly after its submission in 1987, but was
delayed for more than a year in the Senate. During that period a Senate
all-parliamentary committee investigated the legislation and supported
it after suggesting several amendments. In mid-1988 the opposition
(Liberal and National parties) launched a campaign against the bill
which led to an amendment which restricted its application to crimes

committed in Europe (thereby excluding from prosecution Australian servicemen who committed crimes in the Pacific). Another amendment stipulated that a judge could halt the proceedings if he believed that a defendant was unable to obtain sufficient evidence to defend himself.[40] And while it appeared that this latter amendment might prove problematic, the passage of the bill was a highly significant victory for those seeking to being the perpetrators of the Holocaust to the bar of justice.

In the wake of the passage of the war crimes bill, the Center continued its efforts to uncover the Nazi war criminals who had emigrated to Australia, sending additional lists of suspects to the Special Investigations Unit which had been established in Sydney. On June 21, 1989 Greenwood informed me that two of the three "investigations nearing the stage where they may be referred to the Attorney-General with a recommendation for prosecution" had been submitted by the Wiesenthal Center and that in all, 28 of our cases (20 Lithuanians and 8 Latvians) had "current potential." At the same time, at least 33 of our suspects had already passed away in Australia by the time they were tracked down by the local authorities.[41]

While this news was ostensibly cause for guarded optimism, reality proved otherwise. Our research yielded numerous suspects who had emigrated to Australia, but little progress was made in terms of prosecution. On October 23, 1989 I met Greenwood in London and submitted a list of 32 persons who had emigrated to Australia after allegedly serving in the infamous 12th Lithuanian Auxiliary Police Battalion which had actively participated in the mass murder of Jews in Lithuania and Byelorussia.[42] Six months later, on April 22, 1990, an additional list of 55 suspects was sent to the Special Investigations Unit, which was based on the testimonies in the Kunichowsky Collection, which had been donated to Yad Vashem several months previously. Those named were primarily Lithuanian policemen or members of local vigilante squads who had participated in the murder of Jews in various Lithuanian towns and villages such as Alytus, Kelme, Semeliskis, Ceikiniai, Vidukle, etc.[43]

The relatively large number of cases of suspected Nazi war criminals who had emigrated to Australia whom we were able to identify, did not necessarily yield a plethora of prosecutions. As noted above, many of the criminals had already died in Australia by the time we discovered their postwar escape. In other cases, there was a lack of incriminating documentation and/or witness testimony. Not that such material did

not exist or had never existed. On the contrary, in numerous cases witnesses had once been available, but had subsequently passed away. In
other cases, documents regarding crimes committed in areas which
were once part of the Soviet Union were not readily available, since
researchers were never granted full access to local archives.

It was only in late July 1990, therefore, that the first Nazi war crimes
trial to be held in Australia was scheduled to begin. Ivan Polyukhovich,
a 74 year old Ukrainian living in Adelaide, was charged with the murder of 24 persons and with involvement in the murder of an additional
850 Jews from the Serniki Ghetto in the Volhynia region of the
Ukraine.[44] The night before the trial was to open, however, Polyukhovich who was free on $20,000 bail, was found shot in the chest about a
block from his suburban Adelaide home.[45]

A police investigation subsequently established that Polyukhovich's
wound was self-inflicted, but considerable damage was done. The trial
was postponed and costly delays resulted.[46] Even though his botched
suicide attempt might have been interpreted as an admission of guilt, it
did not create any additional public support for the prosecution of Nazi
war criminals. In fact, about a month later, Australian Attorney General Michael Duffy announced that the government would cease funding the Special Investigations Unit at the end of June 1992. In his
statement, Duffy said that more than 650 allegations had been received
since the unit was established in May 1987, but that its work "could
not last indefinitely." According to the Attorney-General, SIU director
Greenwood had identified 12 cases as likely to result in prosecution and
the unit was concentrating its resources on those cases. In addition,
there will be "some limited resources for the Unit to investigate up to
five other cases."[47]

The financial argument, i.e. the high cost of funding the SIU and the
trials, was a major factor in the government's lukewarm attitude
toward the continuation of the Nazi war crimes investigations. As time
passed by, with mounting costs but meager results in the courtroom,
pressure mounted to abandon prosecution efforts which had never
been overly popular to begin with.[48] Despite solid support from the
organized Jewish community,[49] the war crimes bill and the trials
encountered staunch and vocal opposition from local ethnic groups,[50]
right-wing extremists[51] and numerous politicians[52] and public figures.[53] The arguments they marshalled ranged from the anti-Semitic[54]
to the legal, but invariably it was the financial considerations which

found the widest support[55] both in public opinion and in government circles. With Australia in the throes of a deep economic recession not many people understood why millions of dollars (3.9 million dollars each for 1990/91 and 1991/92)[56] were being spent to prosecute ostensibly law-abiding senior citizens.

Despite waning government support for the investigation of Nazi war criminals, we continued our research in Jerusalem. During the summer and fall of 1990 we submitted the names of 50 additional suspects who had committed crimes in Lithuania to the Australian authorities. One name, that of Augustinas Medrausys, head of the Lithuanian police and "partisans" in Bazilionai, was obtained as a result of our efforts in New Zealand. Medrausys, who is alleged to have played a leading role in the persecution and deportation of the Jews of his hometown, emigrated to New Zealand on May 6, 1949 and apparently resided in Auckland until 1981, when he moved to Australia.[57] The other names were culled from the testimonies in the Kunichowsky collection and consisted primarily of members of local Lithuanian police units or vigilante squads.[58] The submission of the list was followed by intensive efforts to locate the survivors and/or other potential witnesses during the winter and spring of 1991.[59]

In April 1991 Robert Greenwood, who had headed the SIU since its inception, resigned to return to his law practice three months before the end of his contract. His resignation did not augur well for the continuation of the prosecution effort, which was also hampered by a constitutional challenge launched by Ivan Polyukhovich's lawyers.[60] We did not realize it at the time, but the SIU's days were numbered, and the loss of Greenwood, who possessed considerable expertise and charisma, was indeed a very serious blow.

While our work continued as usual, the results were hardly encouraging. Deputy director Graham Blewitt replaced Greenwood as the head of the SIU, the standard government line regarding the 12 best cases most likely to result in prosecution was repeated time and again, and those opposed to the trials continued to point to the huge expenses and the lack of results. The sentiments of the latter were expressed by shadow federal Attorney-General Andrew Peacock who in May 1991 described the SIU's record as "somewhat akin to an episode of 'Yes, Minister' where Sir Humphrey Appelby boasted of the efficiency of a hospital that had no patients."[61]

In the summer of 1991 it appeared as if things might be moving in a positive direction when Heinrich Wagner (born 1922) and Mikolay Berezowsky (born 1913) were charged with murder under the War Crimes Act. Both were living in Adelaide and were accused of participating in the murder of Jews in the Ukraine.[62] At the same time, however, it became increasingly clear that the SIU's days were numbered. Thus, for example, on September 5, 1991 Graham Blewitt told the Senate Estimates Committee that he was confident that "June 1992 is a reasonable deadline and that the investigations will be finished by then."[63] Given the fact that by this time the Soviet Union had been dismembered, and numerous exciting new research possibilities in the Baltics, the Ukraine and Belarus were opening up, it seemed unlikely that the unit would be able to conclude its investigations by that date. I therefore wrote to Jeremy Jones of the Executive Council of Australian Jewry to determine how the Jewish community had responded to this development.[64] The answer, supplied by local Jewish leader Isi Leibler, was that the SIU would indeed not be opening any new files (for which there was no budget) but that they were continuing with the current prosecutions, which, if successful, would result in quite a few good cases. "In the unlikely event that in the near future any major war criminal is unearthed in our midst, I would campaign for a revival of the unit. However they have done a good job based on all the information placed at their disposal."[65] In other words, the Jewish community was not going to contest the government's decision regardless of its problematic practical implications. In the meantime, the Polyukhovich trial opened in March amidst gruesome testimony regarding the murder of the Jews of Serniki and attacks by Nazi trials opponents due to the high cost of the proceedings.[66]

In April there was more bad news, this time from Lithuania. Graham Blewitt admitted in a newspaper interview that the SIU was recently forced to drop 12 cases against Lithuanian Nazi war criminals because of the refusal of Lithuanian witnesses to testify. According to the SIU director, in the wake of independence, numerous witnesses had reversed their decision to testify against suspects living in Australia. As a result of this development, the SIU which had hoped to prosecute at least a dozen war criminals (among them many Lithuanians and Latvians named by the Wiesenthal Center) would continue to investigate only one additional case besides the three suspects already charged.[67] In practical terms, this meant that years of our work and mutual cooperation would be rendered, in practical and judicial terms, worthless. This assessment was confirmed by Graham Blewitt who informed me on May 4 that as far as the SIU is concerned "all possible avenues of inquiry to locate witnesses who can implicate SIU suspects in war crimes have been completed." Blewitt, moreover, had suspended further investigation of SIU's Lithuanian cases and, in fact, "None of the Lithuanian suspects in Australia would be charged." Blewitt admitted that had the investigations been carried out "many years ago," he was "sure that the result would have been different,"[68] but it was clear that he accepted the imminent closure of the SIU as a fait accompli.

With little to lose under such circumstances, all we could do was to register our protest in the most vocal manner possible. An excellent opportunity to do so presented itself when Australian Foreign Minister Gareth Evans visited Israel in mid-May. I prepared a list of 19 new suspects to submit to Evans[69] and wrote op-ed pieces in *Yediot Achronot*, Israel's largest daily, and the *Jerusalem Post*. The article in the former, entitled "Their Situation was Never This Good," focused on the case of Leonas Pazusis who had served in the *Ypatingas burys* murder squad and was living in Brisbane:

> At the end of the day his gamble on Australia as a country of refuge was successful. It is true that he never imagined that a special investigations office would be opened and that a law would be passed which would endanger him, but the entire matter was in reality no more than an unconvincing rhetorical exercise, the proof being that after five years of work and millions of dollars in expenses, indictments were submitted against only three Nazi war criminals - all Ukrainians. Not a single Lithuanian, Latvian or Estonian has been put on trial despite the fact that quite a few of those living in Australia served in special murder squads. And now it is clear that they will never be brought to trial.

> June 30 will go down in Australian history therefore as the day the Nazis celebrated their final victory in that country and the Australian government, at least on this issue, completely lost its sense of shame.[70]

The second article entitled "Nazi liberation day 'Down Under'" explained why the closure of the SIU was a terrible mistake:

It appears that the high cost of attaining justice, the meager results to date, and the ostensibly unpleasant task of prosecuting elderly immigrants have grounded the hunt for the Nazis in Australia. But these reasons can hardly justify such a step, given the severity of the crimes and the fact that at least in theory there is currently far greater potential to investigate and prosecute Nazi war criminals than ever before.

With the dismemberment of the Soviet Union, the areas in which the overwhelming majority of the crimes committed by the criminals residing in Australia are now independent. For the first time, countries such as Lithuania, Latvia, Estonia and the Ukraine can freely and fully cooperate with judicial authorities in the West.

If that has not been the case until now, closing the unit is the worst possible response. Under such circumstances, the message being conveyed by the Australian government is that the declared intention of western democracies to bring Nazi war criminals to justice is mere rhetoric.

Instead of closing down the SIU, the Australian government should apply whatever pressure necessary to make clear to the newly independent former Soviet republics that their fullest cooperation is a prerequisite for joining the democratic family of nations, let alone receiving Western financial aid.

The closure, moreover, will have a negative effect not only in Eastern Europe, but elsewhere in the Western world. Imagine how it will affect the governments of New Zealand and Iceland, where Nazi war criminals have been discovered, but which have not yet decided whether to take any legal action. Consider the impact in England and Scotland where a law enabling the prosecution of Nazi war criminals was recently passed but no indictments have yet been submitted.

On a practical level, it is time to think not about the high cost of justice, but rather about the fact that by closing its Special Investigations Unit, Australia is in essence granting a pardon to practically every Nazi war criminal currently living in that country.

Among them are quite a few suspects whose identities and whereabouts are known, but against whom the authorities have until now not been able to find sufficient evidence for conviction according to the perhaps too stringent demands of the Australian War Crimes Act.

But there are also many others whose wartime activities and postwar escape to Australia will only be revealed during the coming years as additional documents and witnesses from the former Soviet Union became available for the first time.

Ever since the War Crimes Bill was passed in early 1989, none of these criminals could live in tranquility in Australia, as they were never sure if they would be caught and tried.

While that was hardly a punishment commensurate with the crimes committed, it was at least a small measure of justice. Now, however, even that miniscule element of accountability will vanish, eliminated by the Australian government itself.

Instead of closing the SIU on June 30, 1992, Australia should announce its intention to renew the effort to prosecute the perpetrators of the Holocaust and not relent until full justice is achieved.[71]

Besides the list of suspects and the articles, we also succeeded in getting Prime Minister Yitzhak Shamir to raise the issue with Evans, which apparently was not that difficult since the Australian minister harshly criticized Israeli policy in Judea, Samaria and Gaza and had recently decided to renew Australia's dialogue with the PLO.[72]

While these articles did not have any practical effect, they did elicit a highly critical response from Michael Sullivan, the First Secretary of the Australian Embassy in Tel Aviv[73] and Australian Jewish leader Isi Leibler, both of whom claimed that the Australian government had honorably fulfilled its responsibilities on the war crimes issue. While Sullivan's response was, in a certain sense, understandable, it was Leibler's missive which was particularly offensive. Instead of criticizing his government's lack of political will to continue the investigations, Leibler preferred to blame the Wiesenthal Center for submitting "often poorly researched" lists which, in his words, led to "sending investigators on exorbitantly expensive wild-goose chases that contributed to growing public resentment at funds perceived to be ill spent."[74] Why such expensive wild-goose chases were undertaken if the SIU did such a good job is a question Leibler prefers to ignore, just as he failed to acknowledge the very important fact that by closing the Nazi war crimes unit when it did, the Australian government basically rewarded recalcitrant Baltic witnesses and missed a golden opportunity to prosecute numerous Lithuanian and Latvian murderers. Another pertinent factor which Leibler neglected to mention was that despite his own efforts there was, by this point, little support even in his own community for the continued prosecution of Nazis, a fact which made the government's decision to close the SIU much easier and hardly surprising.[75]

In late June, Mikolay Berezowsky was formally charged with participation in the mass murder of Jews, mostly women and children, in the Ukrainian village of Gnivan in 1942. Prosecutors charged that, as the head of the local police, Berezowsky had participated in the arrest of 102 Jews in Gnivan who were forcibly marched to a pit in a forest outside the village where they were murdered.[76] Less than a week later, the SIU was officially closed, with only a skeleton staff, headed by Graham Blewitt, remaining to complete the prosecution of the three men already charged.

Shortly thereafter there was more bad news from Canberra as the government decided, contrary to the recommendation of the SIU, that it would not complete the investigation of a fourth suspect whose case was considered to be the most promising Nazi prosecution in Australia. The individual in question was Karlis Ozols, who had served as an officer in the notorious Latvian Arajs Kommando and was living in Melbourne. Ozols's name was on the first list submitted by the Wiesenthal Center to the Australian authorities in October 1986.[77] The decision was a particularly serious blow since both the SIU and the Department of Public Prosecutions had succeeded in establishing a prima facie case against Ozols and the case appeared to be particularly convincing.[78] The decision by the Attorney-General was therefore a clearcut indication that governmental Nazi-hunting in Australia had officially been halted. In theory, Nazi war criminals could still be prosecuted under the War Crimes Act, but such cases would never actually be brought to trial because the Australian Federal Police, whose responsibility such cases became, lacked the expertise and budget necessary to deal with the problem.

To further complicate matters, the Berezowsky case was dismissed by Magistrate David Gurry who found that the 78 year old Ukrainian had no case to answer on the charge of being involved in the murders in Gnivan. According to Gurry, the prosecution had indeed proved that Berezowsky was a member of the local police and had collaborated with the Nazis, but they had failed to prove that he had been involved in the round-ups and murder of the Jews.[79] If we had hoped that the actual trials would help us enlist public support to reopen the SIU, the Berezowsky decision, if anything, had the opposite effect.

In the meantime, it became increasingly clear that the government had stopped the Ozols investigation primarily for political reasons. Thus when the cabinet endorsed Attorney-General Duffy's decision on the case both Leslie Caplan, president of the Executive Council of Australian Jewry and World Jewish Congress co-chairman Isi Leibler responded with dismay. The latter was particularly incensed in view of his public support of the Australian government's efforts on this issue. In Leibler's words:

> This is deeply distressing to all people concerned with the pursuit of justice. The Government has evidently lost its nerve in the face of vociferous public opposition to the war crimes trials already under way.
>
> While I understand the Government's political vulnerability with a federal election less than a year away, the moral issues involved in bringing Nazi war criminals to book should far outweigh any perceived electoral gain.
>
> I am particularly incensed in view of the fact that I have gone out on a limb, both here and internationally, to defend Australia's record in this regard, which I believe, until this latest move, has been exemplary. It is even more riling to learn that the Government has decided to capitulate and pull the plug on further investigation into a major alleged war criminal despite the recommendation of the Director of Public Prosecutions that a prosecution be brought.
>
> This would have been by far the most important of all the cases to have come to trial in Australia, and I am told that the cost involved in completing the investigation would be negligible in the context of the large sums that have already been spent.
>
> Even at this late stage, I strongly urge the Government to reconsider its decision, which not only reeks of political expediency and moral bankruptcy, but is deeply offensive to the many Holocaust survivors who have attempted to rebuild their lives in this country and to all people of good will.[80])

The protests by Australian Jewish leaders did not succeed in changing the government's decision regarding Ozols. By this time, public sentiment was solidly opposed to the trials[81] and the government, with an election approaching, was determined to halt the investigations. Discussions with local Jewish leaders Caplan and Leibler regarding the possibility of jointly submitting an additional list of suspects did not yield concrete results. In fact there were even individuals like *Australian Jewish News* editor Sam Lipski who indicated that he would oppose such an initiative "at every point."[82] Without the support of the local Jewish community, our chances of reversing the government's decisions on the SIU and the Ozols case were practically nil, and thus we found ourselves conducting a virtually hopeless battle against the Australian authorities.[83]

Whatever little hope existed for additional prosecutions was dashed when Ivan Polyukhovich, the first person tried for Nazi war crimes in Australia was acquitted on May 18, 1993. The jury of nine men and three women reached its verdict after being told by Judge Brian Cox that it would be dangerous to convict Polyukhovich on the evidence presented to the court and that they were duty-bound to consider that the defendant could have more strongly defended himself if the charges had been brought closer to the time of the alleged offenses.[84] Thus less than three years after shooting himself on the eve of his trial, Polyukhovich walked out of the Adelaide courtroom a free man, and dozens if not hundreds, of Nazi war criminals living in Australia breathed a sigh of relief.

At this point, after consulting with individuals who had played an active role in the prosecution effort, we decided to make one last attempt to induce the government to at least put Ozols on trial. On May 27, 1993, I wrote to Prime Minister Paul Keating and Attorney-General Michael Lavarche offering the services of the staff of the new office we planned to open in Vilnius, Lithuania to help complete the Ozols investigation.[85] If accepted, our offer would have saved the Australian government as much as tens of thousands of dollars, an argument which we hoped would convince them to proceed with the case. Our proposal was rejected, however, on the grounds that "it would not be possible to appoint a private organization as, in effect, the agent of the Australian Government, to carry out investigations outside Australia."[86] In short, Ozols remains to this day, if still alive, a free man in Australia.

At this point, in late 1993, more than seven years of work to prosecute the Nazi war criminals living in Australia have yielded an important war crimes law, several years during which local Nazis feared prosecution, but little justice in practical terms. Three individuals who collaborated with the Nazis in the Ukraine have to date been charged with war crimes. One (Polyukhovich) was acquitted, in one case (Berezowsky) the charges were dismissed in the committal stage, and the trial of the third (Wagner) was dropped when the defendant suffered a heart attack and doctors advised that the continuation of the trial could result in his death,[87] hardly impressive results given the fact that hundreds, if not thousands of Nazi collaborators emigrated to Australia after World War II. In that context, Graham Blewitt's assessment of the Wiesenthal Center's efforts to uncover Nazi war criminals in Australia and assist in their prosecution together with the Special Investigations Unit accurately describe the difficult conditions under which we sought to achieve justice Down Under:

There can be no doubt that many dozens of war crimes cases would have been prosecuted in Australia if there had been the political will to do so in the early decades after the Second World War. It is certainly not your fault, not ours, that most of the war crimes suspects who came to this country, and the witnesses to their crimes are now dead. For my part, I would like to thank you for your untiring efforts in trying to make our task in Australia as successful as possible.[88]

Notes

1. "Australia Given Names of 40 Linked to Nazis," *New York Times,* October 2, 1986.

2. See, for example, YVA, M-21/III/8, 37, 41; M-21/272; M-9/15(6,6a); 0-53/22;0-33/672.

3. See, for example, WLA, 539/22, 24, 25, 27.

4. Among the publications consulted were *Daugavas Vanagi* and *"Political Refugees" Unmasked!*

5. Letter of Rabbi Hier to Prime Minister Hawke, September 30, 1986, SWCA.

6. Bruce Baskett, "40 Nazis Here—Hayden Gets List," *Herald,* October 2, 1986, p. 1.

7. "Review of Material Relating to the Entry of Suspected War Criminals into Australia," submitted to Special Minister of State Michael J. Young by A.C.C. Menzies, November 28, 1986, p. 7.

8. Ibid., pp. 27, 118.

9. See, for example, "Track Down the War Criminals," *The Age,* October 6, 1986, p. 13; "Holocaust Criminals," *Canberra Times,* October 9, 1986.

10. Letter of Geoffrey Dabb, Counsellor Australian Embassy in Washington to Martin Mendelsohn, December 2, 1986, SWCA.

11. YVA, M-9/15(6, 6a).

12. Roster of *Ypatingas burys*, SWCA.

13. Letter of Simon Wiesenthal to Rabbi Marvin Hier, October 9, 1986, SWCA.

14. Raul Kruus, *People Be Watchful!*, Tallinn, 1962, pp. 7, 17-18, 32, 46-47, 85, 100, 102, 106, 111, 134, 138; *Daugavas Vanagi*, pp. 38, 61; *Tiesa*, July 26, 1979.

15. Menzies Report, pp. 12-13.

16. Ibid., pp. 167-71.

17. Ibid., p. 180.

18. Ibid., p. 179.

19. Ibid., pp. 64-67.

20. Ibid., p. 12.

21. Cable of Dr. R.S. Merrillees to Efraim Zuroff, January 22, 1987, SWCA.

22. Arye Bender, "Mon'im me-Etanu Hagashat Reshimat Nazim ha-Garim be-Australya le-Bob Hawk," *Ma'ariv*, January 25, 1987, p. 2.

23. Cable of Efraim Zuroff to Dr. R.S. Merrillees, January 23, 1987, SWCA.

24. Cables of Efraim Zuroff to Prime Minister Shamir, Foreign Minister Peres and Justice Minister Sharir, January 22, 1987, SWCA.

25. See note 22.

26. Letter of Efraim Zuroff to Prime Minister Hawke, January 25, 1987, SWCA.

27. "15 Posh'ei Milchama Nazim Chayim be-Australia," *Yated Ne'eman*, January 28, 1987.

28. Rafael Mann and Arye Bender, "Hawke Heichel Bikuro ha-Mamlachti be-Yerushalayim be-Mezeg Avir So'er," *Ma'ariv*, January 27, 1987, p. 2.

29. Efraim Zuroff, "Michtav Galui le-Yedid Emet," *Ma'ariv*, January 27, 1987, p. 11.

30. Upon leaving the Israeli Holocaust memorial, Hawke said that, "Anyone who wants to understand the commitment of the Jewish people to the creation of the State of srael, their commitment to ensure srael will have the right to exist behind secure and recognized boundaries into the future, only has to come here to Yad Vashem to understand the depth of that commitment." Michelle Grattan, "PM is Given List of 15 More Alleged Nazis in Australia," *The Age*, January 28,1987.

31. Andrew Gleeson, "Bill on War Criminals Ready Soon: Bowen," *The Age*, February 25, 1987.

32. Alex Doron, "Australia be-Ikvot ha-Nazim: Yotzrim Reshet Beinle'umit le-Isuf Meida al 250 Posh'im," *Ma'ariv*, September 22, 1987, p. 4.

33. Bernard Freedman, "Civilian Trials for Nazi War Criminals?," *Australian Jewish Times*, November 5, 1987, pp. 1, 8.

34. Douglas Davis, "The Nazi Spectre in Australia," *The Australian*, September 17, 1987.

35. Meeting with Robert Greenwood QC, September 13, 1987, Jerusalem.

36. Rod Frail, "Nazi Suspect Lists Grows to 250," *The Age*, October 15, 1987.

37. List of suspects sent by Efraim Zuroff to Robert Greenwood, February 22, 1988, SWCA.

38. List of suspects sent by Efraim Zuroff to Robert Greenwood, November 7, 1988, SWCA.

39. "Alphabetical List and Status of Wiesenthal Allegations," February 1, 1988, SWCA.

40. Brian Timms, "Australia to Prosecute Alleged World War Two Criminals," Reuters, December 21, 1988; "Background: Nazi War Crimes Trials in Australia," prepared by the Executive Council of Australian Jewry.

41. Letter of Robert Greenwood to Efraim Zuroff, June 21, 1989, SWCA.

42. Letter of Efraim Zuroff to Robert Greenwood, October 23, 1989, SWCA.

43. Letter of Efraim Zuroff to Robert Greenwood, April 22, 1990, SWCA.

44. Bernard Freedman, "Kaddish Said over Rovno Mass Grave," *Australian Jewish Times*, July 27, 1990, p. 1.

45. "First Defendant Charged with War Crimes Shot on Eve of Trial," Associated Press, July 29, 1990; "Trial Could Last for Two Years," *Sun-Herald*, July 29, 1990.

46. Bernard Freedman, "Adelaide War Crimes Suspect May Never Stand Trial," *Australian Jewish News*, August 17, 1990, p. 3.

47. "War Crimes," release by Attorney-General Duffy, August 31,1990, SWCA.

48. "War Crimes Poll," *Australia/Israel Review*, December 8-22, 1988, p. 7.

49. Among the organizations and individuals who lobbied for the passage of the war crimes bill and supported the prosecution effort were: the Executive Council of Australian Jewry (Leslie Caplan - president; Jeremy Jones - executive director), Jewish leader Isi Leibler, the Zionist Federation of Australia (Mark Leibler - president); journalist Mark Aarons and former OSI lawyer John Loftus.

50. See for example "War Crimes," *Australia/Israel Review*, January 26 - February 9, 1988, p. 5 and November 19-27, 1989, p. 7.

51. See for example "Justice to be Done," *Australia/Israel Review*, March 31 - April 19, 1988, p. 8.

52. See for example "War Crimes - Complications Set In," *Australia/Israel Review*, May 9-20, 1988, p. 6; "War Crimes" and "Ethnic Stereotyping," ibid., October 13-26, 1988, pp. 6-7.

53. See for example Bob Santamaria, "The Crimes of War and of Dangerous Legislation," *Australian*, November 24, 1987; Chris O'Conner, "Leave Nazis to Die in Peace Plea," *News*, December 8, 1987; Michael Barnard, "Truth, Justice and Vengeance," *The Age*, June 7, 1988; idem., "Latest Fascinating Chapter in the War Crimes Farce," *The Age*, October 3, 1989.

54. On claims for example that the war crimes legislation was being supported by the Jewish community to divert attention from Israeli actions in Lebanon and the territories see "War Crimes Opinion," *Australia/Israel Review*, December 8-22, 1988, p. 7.

55. See for example Bill Mandle, "A High Price to Pay for Hate Hype," *Canberra Times*, September 12, 1990.

56. "War Crimes," release by Attorney-General Michael Duffy, August 31, 1990.

57. Letter of Efraim Zuroff to Robert Greenwood, August 22, 1990, SWCA.

58. Letter of Efraim Zuroff to Robert Greenwood, October 8, 1990, SWCA.

59. See letters of Efraim Zuroff to Senior Investigator Bill Beale December 12, 1990; February 6, 1991; March 10 and 14, 1991, SWCA.

60. Wilson da Silva, "War Crimes Investigations Hit by Court Fight, Resignation," Reuters, April 3, 1991.

61. Bernard Freedman, "Peacock Slams War Crimes Unit," *Australian Jewish News*, May 19, 1991.

62. Fax of Bill Beale to Efraim Zuroff, September 5, 1991, SWCA.

63. Memorandum of Jeremy Jones to Peter Adler, October 8, 1991, SWCA.

64. Letter of Efraim Zuroff to Jeremy Jones, October 8, 1991, SWCA.

65. Letter of Isi Leibler to Efraim Zuroff, March 10, 1992, SWCA.

66. "Trials and Errors," *Australia/Israel Review*, March 24 - April 6, 1932, p. 6

67. Bernard Freedman, Lack of Co-operation May Force End to Trials," *Australia/Israel Review*, April 3, 1992; Sigrid Kirk, "12 War Crimes Cases Dropped," *Sydney Morning Herald*, April 7, 1992.

68. Letter of Graham Blewitt to Efraim Zuroff, May 4, 1992, SWCA.

69. Letter of Efraim Zuroff to Gareth Evans, May 11, 1992, SWCA.

70. Efraim Zuroff, Mei-Olam lo haya Matzavam Tov Yoter, *Yediot Achronot*, May 12, 1992.

71. Efraim Zuroff, "Nazi Liberation Day 'Down Under,'" *Jerusalem Post*, May 13, 1992.

72. David Makovsky, "Australian FM Attacks Policies in Territories," *Jerusalem Post*, May 15, 1992, page 2A.

73. Michael Sullivan, "Prosecuting Nazi War Criminals," (letter to the editor), *Jerusalem Post*, May 20, 1992.

74. Isi Leibler, "Australia's Special Investigations Unit" (letter to the editor), *Jerusalem Post*, May 21, 1992.

75. Efraim Zuroff, "Curious Defense" (letter to the editor), *Jerusalem Post*, July 3, 1992. The exchange of letters on this issue continued throughout the summer of 1992.

76. Jeremy Jones, "Second Australian Charged under New War Crimes Act," *JTA Daily News Bulletin*, June 24, 1992, p. 3.

77. "Suspected War Criminals List - Australia," suspect no. 35, SWCA.

78. Bernard Freedman, "Investigations Dropped into Alleged War Criminal," *Australian Jewish News*, August 7, 1992, p. 3; idem., "Government Drops Fourth War Crimes Investigation," *Australian Jewish News*, September 4, 1992.

79. "Australian Cleared of Killing Jews in Ukraine," *Jerusalem Post*, July 30, 1992.

80. "Leibler Slams 'Political' War Crimes Decision," media release by the World Jewish Congress, September 9, 1992, SWCA.

81. See for example "No More War Crimes Trials" (editorial), *Sydney Morning Herald*, September 8, 1992.

82. Letter of Sam Lipski to Rabbi Laibl Wolf, April 9, 1993, SWCA.

83. Among the projects which we supported was an international letters of protest campaign initiated by New York businessman Aryeh Rubin entitled DLANG (Don't Let Australian Nazis Go). See fax of Efraim Zuroff to Aryeh Rubin, October 20, 1992 and responses by J.P. Gallagher (February 26, 1993) and Owen Walsh (March 4, 1993) on behalf of the Australian government, SWCA.

84. "Australian Acquitted in First Nazi War Crimes Case," Reuters, May 18, 1993.

85. Letter of Efraim Zuroff to Prime Minister Paul Keating, May 27, 1993, SWCA.

86. Letter of Deputy Secretary Norman S. Reaburn to Efraim Zuroff, July 5, 1993, SWCA.

87. Jeremy Jones, "Australia Ends Prosecution of Nazi War Criminals There," *JTA Daily News Bulletin*, December 14, 1993, p. 4.

88. Letter of Graham Blewitt to Efraim Zuroff, July 23, 1992, SWCA.

10

England and Scotland—The Second Battle of Britain

Unlike Australia where the government had already established a commission of inquiry before we submitted our first list of suspects, in Great Britain it was the Wiesenthal Center which first exposed the presence of Nazi war criminals and demanded that legal action be taken against them. On October 22, 1986 Rabbis Hier and Cooper met with Donald Ballantine, the British consul in Los Angeles, and handed him a list of 17 suspected Nazi war criminals who had emigrated to Britain after World War II.[1] The list which was compiled in Jerusalem named eleven Latvians and six Lithuanians living in Great Britain who were alleged to have taken part in the persecution or murder of innocent civilians. Their crimes covered the entire gamut of assistance provided by local collaborators for the Nazis—from service in mass murder squads to writing anti-Semitic propaganda. Among the suspects were two individuals who had served in the *Ypatingas burys* (Vilnius Sonderkommando) and one who had been an officer in the 12th battalion of the Lithuanian Auxiliary Police. Other suspects alleged to have committed serious crimes were the police chief of Telsiai, Lithuania; the deputy chief of the Latvian police in Riga; and the chief of the Latvian police in Tukums and Kuldiga, all of whom were accused of participation in murder. Among the other suspects were two high-ranking officials of the collaborationist Latvian administration, one who served as Minister of Finance, and another who headed the Labor Office and supervised the drafting of men for the Latvian Legion as well as the recruitment of Latvians for forced labor in Germany. Unlike the Australian list, the source of most of the allegations were Soviet publications,[2] although additional material on some of the suspects was found in archives in the United States,[3] and Israel (Yad Vashem,[4] and the Wiener Library[5]). The list was accompanied by a letter from Rabbi Hier to Prime Minister Thatcher in which the Center asked that the British government carefully investigate the charges and "if necessary create the required legal apparatus to deal with them."

Although we did not publicize the names of the suspects, the news regarding the submission of the list made quite an impact in Great Britain. The local media made enormous efforts to discover the identities of the suspects as well as their current whereabouts, but with one exception we refused to confirm or deny the names. The individual in question was Antanas Gecas, formerly Gecevicius, a Lithuanian who had served as a junior lieutenant in the 12th battalion of the Lithuanian Auxiliary Police, which had actively participated in the murder of Jews in Kaunas, Lithuania; Slutzk, Minsk, Dukara and Koidanov, Byelorussia. Gecas, who at that time was 71-years old and living in Edinburgh, Scotland, was identified by the press and admitted that he had served with the unit in question. He also confessed to the media that he had been present at an execution of Jews but claimed that he had never personally participated in such atrocities. In an interview with the *Sunday Times*, for example, he claimed, "I took no part in the shootings; that's abhorrent and I'm a Catholic."[7] Given the confession by Gecas which followed a "leak" from the Soviet Embassy in London and a request from the British Board of Deputies, Rabbi Hier believed that there was no longer any reason to deny that Gecas was one of the suspects. The publication of his name turned Gecas into both the major target and a symbol of the efforts to prosecute Nazis in Britain. The fact that we were able to obtain extremely incriminating evidence about his crimes also reinforced his role in this respect.

Ironically, Gecas initially showed no fear of prosecution and even indicated his willingness to stand trial in Israel or anywhere else except the Soviet Union.[8] Those of us who were aware of Israel's ambivalent attitude regarding the extradition of Nazi war criminals chuckled sadly upon learning of the Lithuanian's readiness to face charges in Jerusalem. If only Israel were as anxious to extradite him as he ostensibly appeared to be to stand trial there. The Israeli response to Gecas' offer was, after all, not the key issue, but rather whether Her Majesty's government would take the necessary measures to investigate the allegations and prosecute the guilty.

The 17 suspects on our list were living in various parts of England, with quite a few residing in London. The specific whereabouts of the criminals did not initially appear to be of any particular significance, but the fact that our number one suspect was from Scotland ultimately had a very important effect on our campaign. On October 23, 1986, the day after our list was submitted, I received a phone call from Bob

Tomlinson of Scottish Television who was trying to confirm whether Antanas Gecas of Edinburgh was among the names we had submitted. At this point Gecas' name had still not been publicized, so I did not divulge the information. I did suggest, however, that if he were looking for evidence regarding the Scottish suspect it might be worthwhile to speak to the Office of Special Investigations regarding the activities of the Lithuanian Auxiliary Police battalions. This was in fact one of the luckiest circumstances of our efforts in Britain. An officer named Jurgis Juodis who had served in the same unit as Gecas was living in St. Petersburg, Florida and had already been investigated and indicted by OSI in 1981 for his wartime activities.[9] In fact among the individuals questioned in this investigation was none other than Antanas Gecas, who willingly admitted his service in the notorious Lithuanian police unit.[10] The fact that the Americans had indicted someone who had served in a more or less equivalent capacity was a powerful argument in favor of prosecuting Gecas. Although we had decided not to publicize the names of the suspects, I directed Tomlinson to Eli Rosenbaum of OSI, who had played an active role in that investigation, because I had the feeling that he was more intent on ensuring that Gecas be prosecuted than on obtaining a scoop.

The fact that a Nazi war criminal was living in Scotland so angered Bob Tomlinson that he was determined to do whatever he could to force the British government to take action. During the coming months, we were in close contact as he set out to produce two documentaries on the subject of Nazi war criminals in Britain.[11] Tomlinson is not a Jew but he took the issue extremely personally. His empathy with the victims and his desire to see justice done were reinforced by his indignation that a criminal like Gecas could be living in Scotland. Over the course of the next year and a quarter, he and his colleagues at Scottish Television were to play a key role in exposing the crimes committed by the suspects living in Britain and the adamant refusal of successive British governments to deal with the issue. As it turned out, they proved to be excellent partners in the campaign to convince the British government to initiate investigation and prosecution. Another non-sectarian group which was to participate actively in these efforts was the All-Party Parliamentary War Crimes Group headed by former Home Secretary Labor MP Merlyn Rees. Founded and organized by MP Greville Janner in late November 1986, this group maintained close contact with the Center from the beginning of its campaign and played a highly significant role in the efforts to convince the government to take action.[12]

During the initial weeks following the submission of our list, public attention naturally focused on Gecas and considerable information appeared in the press on the crimes committed by the Lithuanian battalions in Byelorussia. The fact that Gecas had been interviewed by OSI was also revealed, as well as his admissions regarding his service in the unit.[13] Various newspapers named other individuals as suspects, some of whom were indeed on our list, but those names were never confirmed by the Center. Other names publicized were of suspects whose identities were leaked to the press by the Soviet Embassy in London.[14] Additional attention was focused on British policy in a half-hour documentary by Scottish Television entitled "Britain: A Nazi Safe House?" Broadcast in late January 1987, the film revealed that successive governments had refused to take action against Nazi war criminals in Great Britain and that it was the British who urged an end to the war crimes trials in Germany several years after the conclusion of the Second World War. The film highlighted the fact that three suspected Nazi war criminals had emigrated to Great Britain after the war and had lived there undisturbed, one of whom (Dering) had even received an OBE. The three individuals named in the film were Antanas Gecas, Kiril Zvarich, a Ukrainian policeman, and Dr. Wladyslaw Dering, a Pole who participated in medical experiments carried out by the Nazis in Auschwitz.[15]

Several months elapsed before the Center received a response from the British government. In early February 1987 we were informed that Home Secretary Douglas Hurd had agreed to meet with a delegation to discuss the allegations against the suspects living in Britain.[16] Shortly afterwards, public attention was once again focused on the issue with the publication of The Paperclip Conspiracy by correspondent Tom Bower. The book revealed that Britain, as well as the United States and other countries, had actively recruited and granted asylum to Nazi scientists who later worked on various top-level projects.[17] At the same time MP Greville Janner threatened to use his parliamentary immunity to disclose the names of the 17 suspects on the Wiesenthal Center list in Parliament.[18] These events helped keep public interest at a high level during the period prior to our meeting with the Home Secretary which was scheduled to take place in London in early March.

Prior to our arrival in England, however, several interesting developments took place. Rabbi Hier received a letter from Charles Powell, Mrs. Thatcher's private secretary, in which he outlined the legal situation in Britain vis-à-vis the prosecution of Nazi war criminals. The letter, which was sent as a preliminary statement regarding British policy, did not forebode well for our meeting. According to Powell,

> The jurisdiction of the United Kingdom courts is generally confined to crimes committed within the national territory, and there is little scope to bring proceedings for offences committed abroad, particularly where the accused were not British citizens at the time the offences took place. An extraterritorial prosecution is seldom a practical proposition, given the nature of our legal system and our laws of evidence.

British policy, Powell explained, has traditionally been to deal with crimes committed overseas by extradition. He noted that the United Kingdom had ratified the UN Convention on the Prevention and Punishment of Genocide and therefore could in theory extradite persons accused of war crimes. The problem was, however, that extradition could only take place in cases were there was "an extradition treaty with the requesting state and subject to the terms and conditions of that treaty." Contrary to recent allegations, it had never been a government policy to refuse requests for the extradition of Nazi war criminals. Despite the fact that the Prime Minister had asked Powell to "make clear her deep revulsion at the atrocities committed during the Nazi era," and had therefore "considered most carefully" the issue raised in the letter by Rabbi Hier, the Prime Minister's private secretary wanted to make clear that the possibility of taking action is "likely to be severely limited by the legal considerations . . . outlined above." The evidence so far presented, according to Powell, did not provide the basis for legal action. The government would nonetheless continue to study the issue and examine how other countries had dealt with the problem.[19]

Powell's letter was a clear indication that the government was not about to take any action against Nazi war criminals. This was further reinforced by a detailed legal note sent by Home Secretary Hurd to the All-Party War Crimes Group several days before our arrival in London. Hurd reiterated the legal principles outlined in Powell's letter to Rabbi Hier, but added specific details which the Prime Minister's private secretary had merely alluded to. The Home Secretary noted, for example, that according to existent British law, war criminals could not be extradited to either the Soviet Union or Israel because Britain had no extradition treaty with the former and the treaty with the latter covered only offences committed within either country. In a meeting with MPs from the All-Party War Crimes Group, Hurd also revealed that not all of the 17 suspects whose names had been submitted by the Wiesenthal Center were presently living in Britain. According to the Home Secretary, six had been discovered in England, while three had already died there. Two others were probably living in Britain and the remaining six had still not been found.[20] These pronouncements, made immediately prior to our meeting with Hurd, were apparently designed to set the stage for the government to turn down the Center's request for legal action.

Prior to our arrival, two additional factors entered the equation. Scottish Television revealed the existence of a new list of 34 suspected Nazi war criminals living in Britain which it submitted to the Director of Public Prosecutions.[21] This new information put added onus on the British government to take action, but at the same time those opposed to our efforts received assistance from an unexpected quarter. A serious debate erupted among the leaders of British Jewry regarding this issue. Eric Moonman, executive vice-chairman of the Board of Deputies, said that the Center lacked "quality evidence" and cautioned against "an indiscriminate campaign of allegations."[22] Statements of this sort by a Jewish leader were music to the ears of the reluctant British officials and we feared that they would seriously jeopardize our attempts to mobilize public opinion. We arrived in London fully cognizant that we faced a difficult uphill battle.

On Monday March 2, 1987 a delegation of the Center headed by Rabbi Marvin Hier met at the Home Office with Douglas Hurd and senior members of his staff. Rabbi Hier began by outlining the Center's recent activities, emphasizing its success in discovering the postwar whereabouts of numerous Nazi war criminals. He reiterated the Center's plea that the perpetrators of the Holocaust be brought to justice and noted that, according to officials of the West German Justice Ministry, Nazi documents submitted by the Soviet Union in war crimes cases had never been found to be fabricated. I then presented a survey of the evidence which had served as the basis for the allegations and explained why evidence from Soviet archives was not necessarily suspect. I also pointed out that similar allegations based on the same sources had proven sufficient to induce the governments of Canada and Australia to establish official commissions of inquiry.

In reply, Mr. Hurd officially informed us of the results of the investigation by the Home Office of the names we had submitted and basically reiterated the points made in the legal note he submitted to the All-Party War Crimes Group. The Home Secretary made it clear that the government would need more substantial documentation before it would take any measures and at this point had no intention of initiating its own investigation of the charges. The only question that the government was ready to examine was whether the suspects had violated British immigration law. The Home Secretary, in short, was throwing the issue back at us. If we wanted the government to prosecute these criminals, we would have to uncover the evidence ourselves.

Rabbi Hier pointed out in response that the ability of a government to investigate charges of this sort was far superior to that of a private organization and therefore the British government should create an independent agency similar to those established elsewhere. Hurd, however, was not convinced and we found ourselves in the strange position of being asked by Her Majesty's government to do its work for her. The Home Secretary also made it clear that the legal options were limited and totally ruled out—on political grounds—extradition to the Soviet Union. He noted that one of the options under consideration by the Home Office was deprivation of citizenship . When I asked Mr. Hurd whether he would be willing to consider extradition to Israel, he responded that that would require a change in British law and in the treaty with Israel, but he did not totally reject that possibility. We asked the Home Secretary for the names of those suspects who had been found in Britain in order to obtain the necessary documentation. In that respect, Rabbi Cooper suggested that perhaps Mrs. Thatcher could, during her upcoming visit to Moscow, induce her hosts to be more cooperative in providing documentation on Nazi war criminals from Soviet archives. Hurd promised to brief the Prime Minister regarding this issue and to send us the names of the suspects found living in Britain.[23]

The Home Secretary held a press conference immediately after our meeting at which he outlined the government's position and explained the available options. He made clear that more documentation would have to be produced before action would be taken and that ultimately the evidence presented would determine the government's policy, although the alternatives for practical action were limited. While he did not rule out steps such as deprivation of citizenship, the general impression conveyed by the media was that the government had basically turned down our request.[24] This created enormous interest in the press conference we held shortly thereafter. Since the government had declined to investigate the allegations, the media hoped that we would publicly name the suspects.

We did not do so, however, because despite the government's refusal to establish a commission of inquiry, we believed that the issue was not yet lost. The government's willingness to accept additional evidence and provide us with the names of the suspects living in Britain, and the fact that they did not totally reject prosecution or other measures such as deprivation of citizenship meant that we still had hope of achieving our goal. At this point, however, our chances of success were still dependent on cooperation with the government, to whom we had given our assurances that we would not reveal any of the names on our list. The media were extremely disappointed by our stance, but it would have been counterproductive to violate our agreement with the British government simply to obtain a few headlines whose only practical result would probably have been a few libel suits.

We now began to focus on two major objectives—obtaining additional evidence and mobilizing public opinion to put pressure on the government. As far as the first task was concerned, it was obvious that we were to a large extent dependent on the cooperation of the Soviet authorities and their willingness to provide documentation and witnesses. The second task appeared quite difficult in view of the opposition of a significant portion of the British press to our campaign. Unlike the situation in Australia, where most of the media initially supported the demand to investigate and if necessary take legal action against Nazi war criminals, many of the newspapers in Britain were far from enthusiastic about such a prospect. Some, in fact, were adamantly opposed to our efforts. The most blatant was the*Times* which, in an editorial published the day after our meeting with the Home Secretary, presented our efforts as a vengeance campaign which was incompatible with the principles of Christian mercy upon which British law was based. According to the*Times*, the efforts to bring Nazis to trial might cause suffering to innocent people, and since Britain had no special historical accounts to settle with the Nazis, the matter was best ignored.[25]

Other newspapers were hardly more sympathetic. The *Daily Telegraph*, for example, compared the issue of Nazi war criminals to the question of granting refugee status to Tamil immigrants and praised Douglas Hurd's decision not to launch an investigation.

Nazi-hunting has become a new and frankly distasteful blood sport. It is no reflection of anti-Semitism or of indifference to past atrocities, to feel an overwhelming revulsion against the notion of further war crimes trials, almost half a century after the alleged horrors took place. There is a futility, a sterility, about continuing a search for vengeance beyond certain limits of time and space.

The fact that a respected newspaper like the *Daily Telegraph* chose to refer to crimes committed during the Holocaust as "alleged horrors" and portrayed our efforts to prosecute the perpetrators as a "search for vengeance"[26] are clearcut indications of the staunch opposition, which bordered on outright hostility, of certain segments of the local media.

This negative attitude was also expressed by various columnists. Peter Simple of the *Daily Telegraph* was probably the most vitriolic. He concluded a sarcastic description of our meeting with the Home Secretary with the following recommendations:

The more I hear about this meeting between the zealots of the Simon Wiesenthal Center and Mr. Hurd, the more sorry I feel for Mr. Hurd whose duty it evidently is to placate them even in their most outrageous suggestions, such as changing the fundamental laws of this country. In their enthusiasm for more and more show trials they seem almost to have forgotten what country they are in. So much so that British Jews themselves are showing signs of uneasiness and fears, by no means unjustified, of a "backlash.". Many of them may well be wishing that the zealots of the Simon Wiesenthal Center had never come here at all, and that they would go back to Los Angeles and stay there.[27]

This attitude was also expressed in very strong terms in Parliament. Ivor Stanbrook, Conservative MP for Orpington, for example, said that there was "something distasteful and abhorrent about the activities of Nazi hunters."[28]

These were not the only opinions expressed regarding this issue. On February 27, 1987, even before we met with the Home Secretary, the *Independent* called for a government inquiry. In an editorial entitled

"The past that we should never forget," the paper noted that "There is a deeply felt and valid impulse to hold individuals responsible for their deeds. . ." and called upon the government to investigate fully the charges and how the suspects acquired British citizenship.[29] The *Guardian* also called for concrete steps in this matter. On 4 March it editorialized that

> if there is no statute of limitation on murder, there cannot surely be one on genocide. This holds good morally even for a country where there can be no such charge. If the 17 used deceit to obtain British nationality in order to evade punishment, they thereby laid themselves open to being stripped of it if detected. Even four decades after the event, such lies should not be passed over as no longer relevant, and it is right and proper that the Home Office react to an allegation from a respected source by investigating the validity of the naturalization of the 17.

The *Guardian* suggested therefore that if a solid case existed against the suspects, West Germany should be asked to apply for their extradition, because "That is as much as we can do." Neither paper supported a change in the existent law to enable prosecution in Britain or a revision of extradition policy and/or treaties which could result in extradition to the Soviet Union or to Israel. The *Guardian*, in fact, expressed gratitude that no war crimes trials could be held in Britain and came out against retroactive legislation to deal with this issue.[30] Thus the battle over public opinion in Britain looked as if it was going to be extremely difficult.[31] Although we had the support of the All-Party War Crimes Group, Scottish Television, several of the more popular newspapers,[32] and most of the Jewish community (despite the attempt by Moonman to thwart our effort), the chances of being able to apply serious pressure on the government did not seem particularly promising.

Another problem we faced was even more serious. It was obvious that if we could not obtain additional documentation, our chances of convincing the government to take legal steps against the criminals were not good. The problem was that the crimes committed by the individuals in question had taken place in Lithuania, Latvia and Byelorussia, all of which were part of the Soviet Union. As noted above, the sources of most of the allegations were publications printed in the Soviet Union which were based on documentation in Soviet archives.

(In several cases we had additional material from Israeli and American sources, but most of the key documents could not be obtained in the West.) We now had to obtain the original records in order to convince the British government to take action. The problem was that we had no guarantee that we would be able to carry out the necessary research. For several months our legal counsel in Washington, Martin Mendelsohn, had been negotiating with officials at the Soviet Embassy to obtain visas for a team of researchers from the Center, but the Russians had still not responded in the affirmative. Following our meeting at the Home Office, I once again raised the issue with Rabbi Hier and we agreed that I should apply for permission in person. Given the enormous publicity in the British media regarding the issue, the involvement of Soviet officials who had leaked an additional list of 34 suspects, and the existence of a local Soviet embassy (a "luxury" I did not enjoy in Israel), we decided that I would attempt to meet with Soviet officials in London and ask for a visa to do research in Soviet archives.

I decided to approach Guennadi Shabanikov, the first secretary of the Soviet Embassy, who had been interviewed by the media several times regarding the issue of Nazi war criminals in Britain. He had also been helpful to Bob Tomlinson of Scottish Television, so we assumed that he was the best person to turn to. Our chances of success were very doubtful, however, because of several factors. While it was true that the Wiesenthal Center and the Soviets shared a common goal vis-à-vis the prosecution of Nazi war criminals, our activities on behalf of Soviet Jewry were well known. In addition, the fact that I was an Israeli further complicated matters, even if there was already talk of *glasnost* in Moscow. I was not particularly optimistic therefore when I phonedShabanikov on Wednesday March 4, 1987 after delivering a lecture at London Hillel House. Contrary to my expectations, the Soviet official was quite friendly and accommodating, and we agreed to meet the same day at the embassy.

So many thoughts went through my mind as I travelled to that meeting. Most were of the refuseniks I had met in Moscow, Riga, Vilnius and Leningrad and of the fact that I was about to meet face to face with a representative of the regime which was oppressing them. I also thought of my friend Dr. Ari (Leonid) Volvovsky who was serving a three-year sentence in a labor camp in Siberia. He had been arrested for spreading anti-Soviet propaganda, but in reality was being punished for his desire to make *aliya* to Israel and his determination to live as an observant

Jew. I toyed with the possibility of raising his particular case and fantasized that the discussions witt Shabanikov would be so successful that it would be possible to do so. I also thought about the various stories I had read and heard about the KGB, bugging devices, kidnappings and the like, all the usual sinister images usually associated with the Soviets. I also wondered how my Russian hosts would respond to my skullcap and whether it would affect the results of the meeting. I jokingly thought to myself that it would probably trigger some sort of alarm system.

The meeting, as it turned out, was surprisingly cordial. I began by summarizing our discussions with the Home Secretary and by analyzing our chances of persuading the British government to take legal action. I then outlined the situation in Canada and Australia and explained the extent to which we had used Soviet publications in our research. Given our recently-acquired ability to determine the postwar emigration destinations of Nazi criminals, the chances of prosecution were considerably increased and made the co-operation of the Soviet authorities absolutely critical. Shabanikov took copious notes throughout our discussion, but was noncommittal vis-à-vis my chances of obtaining a visa. The only thing he was willing to say was that he would pass on my request to the pertinent authorities in Moscow.

While we were able to agree on the need to prosecute the "scoundrels" (his term) still alive in the West, we had serious differences of opinion on several other subjects we discussed in the course of our 90 minute meeting. Shabanikov was extremely interested in discussing Israel's attitude towards the Soviet Union and especially the question of Israeli participation in an international conference. I explained that I certainly could not speak on behalf of the Israeli government, but as a resident of Israel it appeared that there were four issues on which Soviet policy would have to change before Israel would agree to an international conference with Soviet participation. The first was Prisoners of Zion, Jews who had been imprisoned for Zionist activity in the Soviet Union. The second was freedom of emigration for Soviet Jews. The third was Soviet support for terrorist organizations, particularly those dedicated to the destruction of Israel, and the last was the Soviets' consistent support for the Arabs over the course of the past four decades. Shabanikov did not even attempt to reply to the specific points I raised. His response was the typical Soviet reply. Israel should first participate in an international conference and then, if things went well, progress could undoubtedly also be made on the other issues. I told him that I doubted whether most people in Israel would be amenable to such a proposal and ended the meeting by giving him the address of the Center's offices in Los Angeles and Jerusalem.[33] While I was pleased that I finally had an opportunity to present my case personally before the Soviets, I was not particularly optimistic about my chances to obtain a visa to the Soviet Union. Given the extremely important issues at stake, I could only hope that Shabanikov would be able to convey the message. It was now all up to the Soviets. Douglas Hurd had indeed entrusted the task to us, but we were almost entirely dependent on the Russians. Time and again they had expressed their intense desire that Nazi war criminals be punished. Now they would have a clearcut opportunity to prove the seriousness of their intentions. The question was whether they would be willing to cooperate with an activist Jewish organization which had accorded high priority to the struggle for Soviet Jewry.

On March 10, 1987 Douglas Hurd sent us the names of the six suspects from our list who had been discovered living in England. In his letter to Rabbi Hier the Home Secretary noted that despite the difficulties in prosecution and/or extradition under the existent British law, there were other possible options such as deprivation of citizenship and/ or deportation. He also noted that the law could be amended, but emphasized that before the government could contemplate making such a recommendation, it would require "much more evidence." Hurd reiterated his willingness to investigate the immigration records of the six suspects and the historical evidence already submitted by the Center. The Home Office would continue its attempts to determine the whereabouts of the others, but there was no indication of government readiness to establish a special agency to investigate the allegations.[34]

In effect, what our visit had achieved was the crystallization of the issue. We now knew exactly what the position of the British government was and what we had to do to achieve our goal. The problem was, however, that the issue was not exclusively dependent on us. In lectures in London and Manchester,[35] I stressed the need for public opinion to put pressure on the government to take action, but I knew that that was only half the solution. The other half was unfortunately in Moscow, not in Jerusalem.

This fact was impressed upon us in a very convincing manner several weeks after my return to Israel. In early April 1987 Bob Tomlinson informed me that he had received permission to do research in the Soviet Union on the Nazis living in Britain. I immediately called Shabanikov to enquire about my visa request and told him that if the Soviets were really serious about their desire to see the Nazi criminals living in Britain prosecuted they would allow us access to the Soviet archives, since the Center was the agency authorized by the Home Office to deal with this issue. In this respect, the Home Secretary's letter to Rabbi Hier could not have come at a more opportune time. The problem was, however, that the Soviets apparently preferred to cooperate with Scottish Television which had never displayed any interest in Ida Nudel, Yoseph Begun or Ari Volvovsky rather than with an activist Jewish organization, even one with official authorization from the Home Office. Shabanikov told me quite curtly that although what I was saying was logical, he did not yet have an answer. I would simply have to wait to hear either directly or via Los Angeles.[36]

The discovery about this time that three additional Nazis from our original list of 17 were alive and living in England provided us with another opportunity to press our case with the Soviets.[37] The news that the number of Nazis alive in Britain had officially risen to nine prompted many enquiries from the media regarding our progress in finding the documentation demanded by the Home Office. All such questions were immediately referred to Mr. Shabanikov, who admitted that we had agreed on the need to prosecute the Nazis but could not explain why the Soviet Union was not willing to admit researchers from the Wiesenthal Center.[38] Our attempts to publicize the problem were a bit risky, but our frustration with the Soviets was growing rapidly, as was our fear that their intransigence would ultimately ruin whatever chance existed of convincing the British to prosecute.

In late April 1987 General Vassili Patrenko, the liberator of Auschwitz, visited the Wiesenthal Center in Los Angeles, and this event presented an opportunity to discuss the issue with the Soviets. The general, who was the keynote speaker at the Center's *Yom ha-Shoa* assembly was accompanied by numerous Soviet Embassy officials and Rabbis Hier and Cooper made special efforts to attempt to clarify the matter. Patrenko personally promised to try to help,[39] and on this basis Rabbi Hier also appealed to Soviet ambassador Dubinin.[40] Month after month went by, however, with no real progress made. At one point Martin Mendelsohn was told that in principle he could travel to the Soviet Union alone, but months passed without his trip being approved.

Efforts were even made to approach the Soviets via American oil magnate Armand Hammer, all to no avail.[41] Thus, as spring turned into summer, the prospects for Britain looked extremely bleak.

During this period we continued our research regarding the cases in other countries, hoping against hope that the Soviets would allow us to obtain the necessary material. What was particularly frustrating was that in the meantime a crew from Scottish Television had been admitted to do research on the British cases. That was beneficial for the cause perhaps, but with all due respect to their good intentions, they were hardly experts on the subject. Whatever problems existed vis-à-vis material from Soviet archives might now be magnified. All we could do, however, was wait and hope that they would succeed or that the Soviets would change their minds.

Bob Tomlinson and his crew returned from the Soviet Union in June 1987 with superb documentation. The most important material was witness testimony against Antanas Gecas and Kiril Zvarich. Tomlinson sent us copies of the documents and we immediately renewed our search for additional material. We focused on Gecas for two reasons. Zvarich's name did not appear on our list and, based on our knowledge of the Juodis case, we knew that there was a good chance of obtaining documentation in Israel on the Lithuanian Auxiliary Police battalions. At the same time, we asked to meet again with Home Office officials to present the material and discuss the cases. In this respect we were the beneficiaries of British policy, which viewed us as the exclusive agency for research on the war crimes committed by British residents during the Second World War. When BobTomlinson sought to present the material he had obtained in the Soviet Union to the Home Office, he was politely told that the Center was the agency authorized to do so. What the Soviets had hoped to achieve via Scottish Television was therefore ultimately carried out by the Wiesenthal Center, which never obtained permission to research those cases in the Soviet archives.

We scheduled our meeting at the Home Office to coincide with the screening on national television of a special documentary film on Nazi war criminals prepared by Scottish Television. Prior to our trip to England, we were able to find additional documentation not only on Gecas but also on two other suspects from our original list, both of whom had served in high posts in the Latvian collaborationist administration. The documentation regarding Gecas perfectly complemented the material obtained by Scottish Television in the Soviet Union.

Whereas the latter consisted of eyewitness statements regarding Gecas' personal involvement in ordering the murder of innocent men, women and children and his own participation in these atrocities,[42] the former presented a documentary framework regarding the crimes committed by his battalion in Lithuania and Byelorussia. Among the documents presented were rosters of Gecas' battalion, the order of October 6, 1941 instructing his unit to travel to the Minsk-Borisov-Slutzk areas of Byelorussia,[43] a segment from the memorial volume on Slutzk in which the role of the Lithuanians in the murder of the Jews is described,[44] documents from the trial of Major Franz Lechthaler, the German commander in charge of Gecas' battalion in which the role of the Lithuanian police in the murder is described,[45] as well as statements made by Gecas to OSI officials in conjunction with the Juodis investigation. Gecas, as noted above, admitted his service in the Lithuanian Auxiliary Police, as well as his presence at various executions. He even confessed that in one case his own unit carried out the murders, although he maintained that in most cases the Lithuanians merely protected the areas in which the Germans carried out the executions.[46]

While the documentation we collected in the West was quite substantial, the case against Gecas became even more convincing when this material was combined with witness testimonies obtained in the Soviet Union. Tomlinson returned with statements signed by three Lithuanians who had served under Gecas and who described his personal participation in the atrocities in graphic terms which left little room for doubt. Moteyusa Migonis, for example, testified that he had heard Gecas order the murder of (and saw him personally shoot) civilians in Slutzk and in a village not far from Minsk.[47] Juozas Aleksynas related how Gecas had carried out mass executions of Jews from the Minsk Ghetto on at least two occasions and in each case had personally gone into the pits to finish off those victims who were still alive.[48] Leonas Mickevicius testified that Gecas had done the same thing to Jews murdered in Kletzk.[49] All three had served under Gecas' command in Byelorussia and thus had a superb vantage point from which to view his activities. All three identified Gecas' photograph and described him accurately. Despite Tomlinson's studied efforts to confuse them in order to ensure the veracity of their statements, they submitted extremely convincing testimony.

On Friday July 17, 1987 a delegation of the Wiesenthal Center headed by Rabbi Hier met with Deputy Under-Secretary of State David

Faulkner and officials of the Home Office. We described the extensive documentation regarding Gecas which the Center had collected and presented a letter from West German Justice Minister Hans Engelhardt confirming that there had as yet never been a case of a Nazi war crimes trial held in West Germany in which a German document from a Soviet archive had proven to be false.[50] Rabbi Hier pointed out that Jurgis Juodis, who was accused of participating in the same crimes as Gecas, had been indicted by OSI which had authenticated the documentation in question. He also noted that the brutality of the Lithuanian Auxiliary Police battalions in Byelorussia was legend and had even shocked the Germans. One of the documents previously presented to the Home Office contained the plea of Carl, the German Gebietskommissar of Slutzk. Following the Lithuanians' slaughter of the Jews, he had appealed to his superiors that they refrain from sending that unit to the area under his jurisdiction. In his words, "I beg you to grant me one request: in the future, keep this police battalion away from me by all means."[51]

In the course of his presentation Rabbi Hier also noted the Center's efforts to obtain permission to conduct research in Soviet archives and called upon the British government to establish an independent agency to investigate the documentation and charges. I then presented the preliminary documentation that Center researcher Robert Rozett had uncovered in Jerusalem regarding the two high-ranking Latvian collaborationists,[52] and explained the historical background to their activities. I noted their role in the recruitment of local men for the Latvian SS Legion and their involvement in sending tens of thousands of their countrymen to work in Germany for the Nazi war effort. Given the serious nature of the crimes and the extensive documentation submitted to the Home Office, especially in the Gecas case, any British decision short of a full-scale investigation must, Rabbi Hier concluded, be considered an attempt to side-step the issue.

David Faulkner replied by thanking the Center for its efforts, but was extremely cautious and noncommittal regarding any steps which the government might take. Although he admitted that the documents submitted were precisely the sort of material which the Home Office sought, he refused to undertake to conduct the type of investigation demanded by the Center. While Faulkner and Home Office officials agreed that the charges against Gecas appeared to be very serious and that the fact that he was free was a bad message for the younger generation, our hosts continued to stress the existent legal obstacles which prevented prosecution. They indicated that deprivation of citizenship was the most likely, if not the only, possible alternative available to the British government.[53] In short, the government was still reluctant to take any action, so now the documents had to speak for themselves. In March, the Home Secretary had cast the onus of the investigation upon us, and we had now returned with extensive proof in one case and important preliminary documentation regarding two additional suspects. Once those facts were known we hoped that the public would apply pressure of its own.

In this respect our timing could not have been better. Our meeting with Faulkner had been scheduled to coincide with the screening of "Crimes of War," the new Scottish Television documentary on Nazi war criminals in Britain, and the two events succeeded in attracting considerable coverage.[54] For an entire week we managed, with the able assistance of Lydia Triantopoulis and Brian MacLaurin, the directors of public relations for the Wiesenthal Center and Scottish Television respectively, to keep the issue in the forefront of the news. These efforts were aided by two revelations publicized during the week following our meeting with Faulkner. The first related to the list of 34 suspected Nazi war criminals living in Britain which had previously been leaked by the Soviet embassy in London to Scottish Television. On July 21, 1987 the Home Office confirmed that at least seven of the suspects were indeed living in Britain, bringing the number of confirmed Nazi war criminals residing in England to 16.[55] In addition, the All-Party Parliamentary group revealed documentation which indicated that in April 1948 Britain had attempted to recruit Klaus Barbie as an intelligence agent.[56] Both revelations added to the pressure upon the government to launch a full-scale investigation of the Nazis living in Britain.

On Wednesday July 22, 1987, Channel 4 broadcast the Scottish Television documentary "Crimes of War" nation-wide and on Thursday it was shown again in Scotland. The Scottish broadcast was followed by a symposium entitled "Crimes of War: Time for Justice?" in which the moral, legal, religious and historical aspects of the problem were discussed by a forum which included professors, MPs and the Bishop of Edinburgh. Prior to participating in the program, Brian MacLaurin suggested that I utilize the opportunity of my visit to Scotland to confront Gecas. What better way of focusing attention on the fact that a man accused of mass murder was living in peace and tranquillity in an Edinburgh suburb? Although I had some reservations about the theatrical aspects of our "confrontation," I realized that the current situation required extraordinary measures. So even though this was hardly the type of activity historians usually engaged in, I agreed to Brian's suggestion.

I have to admit that the idea of a face-to-face confrontation with a man accused of participation in the murder of thousands of Jews made me more than a little uneasy. What if he were armed? What if he tried to assault me physically? What would I say to him? What kind of response could I expect? These were some of the questions which went through my mind during the flight from London to Edinburgh and the drive to the suburb of Newington. Brian and I had no idea whether Gecas would let me in or even come to the door, but we realized that this would be an excellent opportunity to reiterate clearly the demand that Nazi murderers be brought to justice. Brian reassured me that nothing would happen since in Britain the possession of guns was illegal, and he also prepared the setting by inviting the media. By the time I arrived at the corner of Moston Terrace, the scene had been set. Television crews, journalists and photographers were all there to immortalize what appeared to be a classic confrontation between the hunter and the hunted.

I arrived at the door to find it open on a chain. I knocked twice but no one answered, so I rang the bell. After the second ring, a woman (who did not come to the door) asked what I wanted. I identified myself as Mr. Zuroff from the Wiesenthal Center and asked to speak to Mr. Gecas. She instructed me to speak to his lawyer Nigel Duncan in Wilson Street. When I enquired whether she was certain that Gecas would not see me, she again referred me to his solicitor, so I told her to tell him that I had been there to speak to him. At that point I turned to leave, but was held back by several of the photographers who, apparently, had missed the shot that they wanted. I was sent back to Gecas' door, ostensibly to ring the bell. This added a touch of comic relief to the events which were of course quite serious.

After leaving Gecas' house, I held an impromptu press conference in front of his garden. I explained that I had come to hear his response to the charges levelled against him. Unlike Gecas, who never gave his victims a chance, we were willing to give him an opportunity to prove his innocence. Moreover, in view of the recent confirmation by the Home Office that at least seven and probably more of the suspects on the Scot-

tish Television list were indeed living in Britain, the government could
no longer ignore the problem of Nazi war criminals. On a personal
level, I concluded, there also was a reason for this trip. One of the sites
of mass murder shown in the Scottish Television documentary was
Ponary, a forest outside Vilna (Vilnius) where tens of thousands of Jews
had been murdered. Among the victims was my great uncle whose
name I bore. I had come, therefore, to show Gecas that the children
and nieces and nephews of the victims would never forget the crimes
committed. The fact that I had come from Israel to submit the documentation regarding his crimes was the ultimate proof that Gecas had
not been victorious. While he was hiding inside, the full truth would be
told and hopefully justice, although delayed, would be achieved.[57]

The problems we faced in our efforts to realize that goal were clearly
enunciated in the course of the discussion which followed the broadcast
of the Scottish Television documentary. Entitled "Crimes of War: Time
for Justice?," it pitted advocates of prosecution against opponents in a
civilized, though at times bitter, debate, chaired by Scottish TV personality Sheena McDonald. The participants, besides myself, were: Richard
Holloway, the bishop of Edinburgh; MP Peter Archer (Labor) of the All-
Party Parliamentary Group; MP Ivor Stanbrook (Conservative), a
staunch opponent of our campaign; Professor Neil MacCormack of
Edinburgh University; and Professor Bernard Crick of London University. Although the majority of the participants supported the Center's
demand that the government investigate the issue, the vociferous opposition of the minority revealed the depth of the hostility with which our
efforts were regarded in certain circles. I found myself accused by MP
Stanbrook of seeking vengeance and by Professor Crick of initiating a
campaign designed to induce younger Israelis to identify with the Holocaust but which in reality was trivializing those events. According to
Stanbrook, my evidence was no more than allegations; in Crick's view, I
was merely an agent of the Likud, a right-wing Israeli political party. It
was not particularly difficult to refute those arguments but the fact that
prominent public figures could publicly make such accusations was
somewhat disconcerting. I believe that the eloquent and convincing
arguments presented by Bishop Holloway, RichardHolloway, Professor
MacCormack and MP Archer on behalf of a thorough investigation by
the British government were an effective antidote to the charges levelled against the Center's campaign and helped present the issue in its
proper moral, philosophical and historical perspective.[58]

The television debate in Scotland was the culmination of a hectic week of meetings, press conferences, and interviews. Prior to returning to Israel, however, I had to attend to one last important matter in London. Shortly after our meeting with David Faulkner, the Home Office had confirmed that at least seven suspects on the list submitted by Scottish Television were living in Britain. Upon hearing this news, I had called N. Nagler of the Home Office to indicate our willingness to be of assistance in investigating these cases. He did not respond immediately but promised me an answer prior to my return to Israel. I received the positive response just before boarding the flight back to Tel Aviv. The names were then sent to Los Angeles,[59] expanding the scope of our research and increasing our chances of being able to convince the British government to take the necessary steps against Nazis living in England.

Following the meeting with Home Office officials in London, Rabbis Hier and Cooper came to Israel to discuss the Gecas case with Israeli cabinet ministers. We believed that Israeli interest would add to the pressure on the British government; who, if not Israel, should be involved in such a case? Although the existent extradition treaty between Israel and England did not cover cases of this sort, Home Secretary Hurd had not totally rejected such a possibility. This was another reason why the Israeli position was significant and in this respect we were not disappointed. Both Foreign Minister Peres and Justice Minister Sharir indicated their willingness to bring Gecas to justice in Israel, if Britain, whom they viewed as the bearer of primary responsibility, would not take action.[60] Regardless of whether the declarations by these ministers will ever be translated into action, their forthright response was a welcome development. The Home Office formally announced the next day that it was investigating the charges against Gecas,[61] a step which it had hitherto refrained from taking. Until this point all they had been willing to do was to investigate the suspects' immigration records. This new development constituted a clearcut indication that the Home Office realized that the documentation we had submitted merited serious consideration.

Given Justice Minister Sharir's willingness to take action if necessary against Gecas, I was surprised and perturbed when Israeli television announced on its main news broadcast on August 17, 1987 that Israel had decided not to ask for Gecas' extradition. What was even more alarming was the basis for the decision. According to journalist Zvi

Goren, the Israeli Justice Ministry had reached the conclusion that the documentation on Gecas was insufficient to indict him.[62] This was particularly dangerous because it gave the British an excuse to close the Gecas case and thereby drop the entire issue. The question was whether the news was accurate and on what basis the decision had been made. A quick investigation revealed that the information was not accurate and that the Justice Ministry had still not made a decision.

We never did discover who leaked the inaccurate news, but it obviously was a ministry official who was against trying Gecas in Israel. Some damage was initially done because Reuters carried a story based on the report by Israeli television.[63] I was able, however, to convince the Justice Ministry to issue a formal statement the next day in which they announced that Israel had not yet made any decision regarding Gecas. This news was broadcast on Israeli television the next night and Reuters carried a story which rectified the mistaken impression created by its initial report. I also used the opportunity to point out that whatever difficulty existed in this case related to the nature of the evidence and not its content. The testimonies, for example, were excellent, but the witnesses were Soviet citizens and this created a problem for Israel which had no diplomatic relations with the Soviet Union. I therefore called upon the Soviet Union to allow the witnesses to testify in the West.[64] The damage was thereby more or less undone, but the episode is a classic example of how months and even years of work can be nullified by one small well-placed lie by a top or even middle-echelon bureaucrat.

At the same time that we were attempting to convince the Israeli Justice Ministry to ask for Gecas' extradition, Bob Tomlinson was trying to persuade the Soviets to be more cooperative. Those efforts were apparently successful. On August 24, 1987 the Soviet Foreign Ministry called in Noel Marshall, the British charge d'affaires in Moscow, and submitted a formal extradition request for Antanas Gecas,[65] and in an interview with Scottish Television, Mrs. Kolesnikova, the Soviet prosecutor, indicated that if necessary, efforts would be made to enable witnesses living in the Soviet Union to testify in the West. The Home Office in response made clear that they would welcome any person who could assist in the investigation of the case and indicated unofficially that they were examining various ways of amending the criminal code to enable the prosecution of Nazi war criminals in England.[66]

During the autumn of 1987 the All-Party Parliamentary Group and various interested groups such as the Union of Jewish Students, and *Searchlight* magazine continued to pressure the British government. A postcard campaign which had been suggested by the Center during our first trip to England was finally launched, rallies were held and other means were utilized to mobilize public opinion on the issue.[67] In mid-November 1987 at a meeting with the All Party Group, Home Secretary Hurd formally announced that he was "seriously considering" amending British law to enable the prosecution of Nazi war criminals living in the United Kingdom. At this point the Home Office was deliberating regarding several other options such as deprivation of citizenship on the basis of false declarations made in the course of the immigration and/or naturalization process, deportation or extradition. The feeling among most members of the All-Party Group was, however, that an amendment of the British criminal code was the best solution.[68] Despite the initial tendency of the Home Office to reject totally the Center's demand for investigation and prosecution, Douglas Hurd now seemed to realize that certain steps had to be taken. The question was what might those steps be?

We finally received our answer on February 8, 1988 when Douglas Hurd announced the establishment of an independent inquiry to examine the evidence against alleged Nazi criminals living in Britain. The inquiry was to be carried out by Sir Thomas Hetherington, former Director of Public Prosecutions, and William Chalmers, former Crown Agent in Scotland, who were commissioned to advise the government regarding the steps to be taken in this matter after examining the available evidence.

In the Home Secretary's words:

> The allegations are very serious and must be pursued, but I do not believe that the material now before us would justify me in proposing to Parliament a change in the law.
> The inquiry which I have announced will enable us to form a clearer view of the weight to be given to the allegations and will enable us to determine whether it would be right to propose a change in the law to extend the jurisdiction of the courts.[69]

The proposed inquiry, Hurd explained, would probably last a year and would focus on seventeen individuals living in the U.K. against whom there are allegations of participation in war crimes. While some MP's like Stanbrook were critical of the step taken by the government, Hurd's decision to establish a commission of inquiry did have widespread support which included opposition MP's as well.[70]

The establishment of the British commission of inquiry did not end our role. Ten days after the announcement by House Secretary Hurd, I met in London with Undersecretary of State for Home Affairs David Faulkner and submitted the names of two additional Lithuanian suspects who had emigrated to Great Britain after World War II, along with additional documentation on several of our Latvian suspects. At the meeting we also discussed the work of the commission and I offered the Center's fullest cooperation and assistance to the British investigators.[71] Another important meeting held during the same trip was with Sergei Chashnikov, Second Secretary of the Soviet Embassy in London, with whom I participated on a television show on Scottish Television. In response to my request for permission to bring a delegation of researchers to the Soviet Union, Chashnikov suggested that it be done in the framework of a governmental delegation such as one sent by OSI. I explained to the Soviet diplomat why such a delegation was impossible and outlined our role in the war crimes issue. Chashnikov asked me to submit a formal request to the Embassy outlining our activities and expressed the hope that permission would be granted. At the same time, I also urged that Soviet witnesses be allowed to travel to the West to testify against Nazi war criminals.[72]

In the meantime, our research effort continued and on June 8, 1988 Rabbi Hier sent the name of an additional Lithuanian suspect who emigrated to Great Britain to Home Secretary Hurd. The individual in question was alleged to have participated in the murder of the Jews of Skapiskis and we obtained his name from the lists provided by Y.S.[73] A month later, an additional list of 13 suspects, most of whom were in camps for East European military personnel in Britain after the war, was submitted to the British authorities by Rabbis Hier and Cooper. The individuals in question, 12 Byelorussians and a Ukrainian, had mostly served in the Byelorussian police and were identified as war criminals in 1948 by the Soviet Embassy in London.[74] This submission brought the number of British suspects identified by the Wiesenthal Center to 33 (11 Latvians, 9 Lithuanians, 12 Byelorussians, 1 Ukrainian).

By mid-summer, the British authorities already had the names of 250 alleged Nazi war criminals living in the country[75] and the commission of inquiry had begun its work in earnest.[76] Although many of the names possessed by the commission were in fact no more than hunches or suspicions, the figure proved a basic premise of our campaign. We realized that the information in our possession was in reality only the tip of the iceberg in terms of the Nazi war criminals who had emigrated to Great Britain. At the same time, we believed that once the government began its own official inquiry a great deal of important information and many suspects would be uncovered. Thus the number of suspects under investigation by the commission was hardly surprising.

While we continued our efforts to locate additional suspects, we also began working together with the commission on specific cases. On July 14, 1988 I met in London with commission secretary David Ackland and gave him the names of 60 potential witnesses living in the West[77] who might be able to testify in various cases particularly that of Andrei Pestrak, a Ukrainian who had served in the local police in the towns of Maniewicze, Trojanowka and Poworsk. In addition, we discussed the possibility that measures would be taken to insure that the suspects would not escape from Great Britain before they could be prosecuted. While no such legal restrictions existed, Ackland said that a possibility being considered was the application of a law designed to prevent football hooligans from going abroad. In the meantime, however, in theory the Nazis could, in theory, leave, although the names of all the suspects had been brought to the knowledge of all overseas agencies investigating Nazi war criminals.[78]

In the fall of 1988 a book I wrote about my experiences at OSI and the efforts to prosecute Nazi war criminals in Western democracies was scheduled to appear. Entitled *Occupation: Nazi-Hunter*, the book was an attempt to explain to public opinion in Great Britain and elsewhere why in my opinion it was still important to bring the perpetrators of the Holocaust to the bar of justice even at the end of the eighties. Published by Ashford Press of Southampton, it was to appear on October 17 at which time I was scheduled to launch a publicity tour in various cities in Great Britain. None of that happened, however, as in late September, Antanas Gecas obtained an interim injunction barring the distribution of the book in Scotland on the ground that it would prejudice a libel suit he had initiated against the*Times* of London, as well as a possible trial if Nazi war criminals would indeed be brought to justice in Great Britain.[79]

Ashford contested the injunction and Jane Tatum, Ashford's managing director, and I travelled to Edinburgh to appear at the hearing which began on October 12, 1988. To further complicate matters, Gecas decided to sue me for £75,000 claiming slander and damages. During a break in the proceedings, taken because the judge's nose suddenly begin to bleed, two messengers at arms attempted to serve me with a summons. I refused to take it, the messenger threw it at me, and the court clerk claimed that it had been properly served.[80]

Gecas' major claim was that if the book would appear, a former member of his unit living in Scotland might be afraid to testify on his behalf in his libel suit against the *Times*. According to Gecas' lawyer Donald Robertson, the individual in question feared that he could be extradited to the Soviet Union.

Besides this argument, Robertson attacked me personally as well as the book, claiming that it had not been written in the spirit of cool reasonable discussion. Thus while he admitted that he did not have the slightest doubt that "I was a totally sincere and dedicated man," that was precisely the problem:

> This book is an indictment. He is certainly not a judge. He is more of a prosecutor, a hunter—and a hunter out for a kill.
>
> This book is not designed to stimulate reasonable, calm discussion about a matter of public interest. It is concerned to accuse and to represent that there is no possibility of these persons, and in particular Mr. Gecas, not being guilty.
>
> There is no suggestion anywhere that there could be the least likelihood that they are not guilty of the terrible crimes of which they are accused.
>
> This book does not contain comment, certainly not fair comment on a matter of public interest.
>
> What it contains is false statements of the gravest imputation that Mr. Gecas and everybody else in that 12th Battalion were guilty of war crimes of the most horrific kind, that they took part in executions and mass murders and that he was a supporter of the Nazi cause.

In addition, Gecas, according to Robertson, had been subjected to a campaign of vilification, the members of his family had been threatened and their home attacked.[81] Our lawyers claimed that the material in the book was accurate and that they posed no serious risk of prejudicing Gecas' libel suits. The book was fair comment on a matter of public interest and banning its distribution in Scotland would be futile as it could still be read in any other part of the United Kingdom. Gecas' story, moreover, had already appeared in more than thirty newspaper articles so the information in the book was neither new nor revealing.[82]

Despite these arguments, Lord Cowie ruled on October 14, 1988 that the injunction banning the distribution of *Occupation: Nazi-Hunter* should remain in force. In his opinion, the book's publication could seriously prejudice Gecas' libel action against the*Times* and therefore the ban issued a month previously by Lord Kirkwood should continue. At the same time, he rejected the contentions that the book defamed Gecas or that it might prejudice any future criminal proceedings against him:

It seems to me that if the allegations in the book are calculated, whether intentionally or not, to prejudice his case against Times Newspapers by influencing against him witnesses who may give evidence in that action, that would amount to an improper and unwarranted interference with the conduct of that action and can be restrained by interdict.

Lord Cowie claimed, moreover, that his decision applied worldwide not only in Scotland.[83]

Needless to say I was shocked by what I considered to be "a scandalous ruling."[84] To make matters worse, Ashford, instead of fighting the injunction, decided to accept Lord Cowie's decision and withdraw the book. In response, managing director Jane Tatum, who had been the driving force behind the book's publication, resigned in protest. According to Tatum, Ashford was "commercially and morally wrong" to withdraw the book and she intended to attempt to publish it herself.[85] Although she did not succeed in doing so, Jane Tatum's courage in opposing Ashford's cowardice was a strong source of comfort and consolation at a very trying time.

Three days after his initial victory, Gecas went to court again, this time to obtain an injunction barring me from publishing the book anywhere in the world. Initially Lord Cowie had refused to grant such since in his view the injunction against Ashford was sufficient. In the wake of Jane Tatum's comments in the weekend papers that she intended to publish the book herself, Gecas went to court against me (as the holder of publication rights) again. Once again Gecas' lawyers portrayed me as a villain determined to get around the injunction. Gecas, on the other hand, was depicted as the victim of a smear campaign, an elderly man living in virtual siege, who had received razor blades and a bullet in the mail and had had posters accusing him of crimes against humanity put up in his neighborhood. Since I was not present to contest the action, it was hardly surprising that Judge Lord Dervaird granted Gecas' request, creating an ignominious situation in which in my words, it was "now more likely [that I would] end up in a Scottish jail than Mr. Gecas."[86]

The delay in the publication of the book and Gecas' victory in court were difficult defeats, which in my mind did not augur well for our efforts to convince the British government to prosecute the Nazi war criminals living in the United Kingdom. Nonetheless we continued our efforts as did others, primarily the All-Party War Crimes Group. In mid-November 1988 they published a "Report on the entry of Nazi War Criminals and Collaborators into the UK 1945-1950" which clearly showed how governmental apathy allowed numerous Nazi war criminals to enter Great Britain after World War II. The carefully researched and fully documented report also proved that our assertions regarding the presence of Nazi war criminals in the UK were correct and noted how faulty screening and labor recruitment had facilitated the entry of war criminals into Great Britain.[87]

The report on the emigration of Nazi war criminals to Britain, was followed by a second study entitled "Nazi war criminals in the United Kingdom: the Law," which examined the various legal issues which affected the possible prosecution of Nazi war criminals in Great Britain. After examining such issues as retroactivity, extra-territorial jurisdiction, and the taking of evidence overseas, it concluded that "should sufficient evidence be found that Nazi war criminals may be living in the UK, a change in the law to enable their prosecution would not only be appropriate, but would allow justice to be properly served."[88] Both reports received widespread media coverage[89] and provided a solid basis for the demand that the perpetrators of the Holocaust living in Britain be brought to the bar of justice. In this respect, the existence of a powerful lobby like the All-Party War Crimes Group was a superb asset, which made a tremendous contribution to the efforts to pass the necessary war crimes legislation.

Our efforts received another extremely important boost when the British commission of inquiry completed its investigation. On July 24, 1989 Home Secretary Douglas Hurd announced in Parliament that the commission had unequivocally recommended that the government take action against the Nazis living in Great Britain and had endorsed a change in the law to enable the prosecution in British courts of individuals, presently British citizens or residents of the United Kingdom, who committed murder or manslaughter during World War II.[90] The commission reached its conclusion after carefully examining in depth seven of the 301 allegations submitted to the authorities. In four of the cases, it concluded that there was "a realistic prospect of a conviction for murder on the evidence available were the jurisdiction of the British courts to be widened." (In the meantime one of these four suspects had died and a second suspect supplied medical evidence indicating that it was unlikely that he was healthy enough to stand trial.) In the other three cases where there was as yet insufficient evidence for a conviction, further investigations were recommended. In addition, the commission found 75 additional cases in which it believed that further investigations should be carried out. At the same time, however, the commission found numerous cases in which no action was required either because the subjects were already dead (56 cases); had left the United Kingdom (13); were not found in the United Kingdom and apparently never resided there (25); or had not committed murder or manslaughter and were therefore not considered under the mandate of the commission (49).[91]

The commission also examined four different legal means of dealing with the problem: deprivation of citizenship and deportation; extradition; prosecution in military courts; and legislation to enable prosecution in ordinary criminal courts. In the opinion of the commission, neither deprivation of citizenship and deportation nor prosecutions in a military court could be considered satisfactory. The former was a lengthy process which held no guarantee of success and the latter, if legally permissible, meant that the suspects would be tried without a jury, a proposal which is unsuitable in times of peace more than 40 years after the crimes were committed. Since most of the crimes in question took place in areas that were presently part of the Soviet Union, extradition was also problematic. The commission therefore recommended that legislation be passed to enable prosecution in Great Britain and that it be introduced and put into effect as quickly as possible given the age of the suspects and witnesses.[92]

In its final report the commission also dealt with the possible objections to the passage of such legislation and the arguments marshalled by those opposed to the trials. Yet while they recognized the validity of these claims, the members of the commission believed that the enormity of the crimes committed left Great Britain no choice but to take action. In the words of the report:

> Despite the evidence that we have found arguments can be advanced in favor of taking no action with respect to war crimes. It has been said that there is little point in attempting to punish old men, who have lived peacefully in this country for over 40 years, particularly as it is claimed that this country made a decision at the time not to continue with prosecutions. It is undoubtedly true that the passage of legislation and the investigation and trial of such cases, should it be decided to follow this course, would require additional manpower and resources which would be costly and it could be argued that such money would be better used for other purposes. As we indicate below (Paragraph 9.99), there would be considerable problems in bringing evidence before the courts, the solutions to which would be expensive and possibly only partly effective. Some of the subjects of the allegations whom we have interviewed have protested their innocence and have maintained that the whole issue is a Soviet plot to blacken the emigre community. Superior orders may be cited as a defence.

> 9.18. Although we recognize the substance of some of these arguments, when weighed in the balance against the atrocities of which we have heard, we find them lacking. The crimes committed are so monstrous that they cannot be condoned: their prosecution could act as a deterrent to others in future wars. To take no action would taint the United Kingdom with the slur of being a haven for war criminals.[93]

The response to the report, authored by two of Great Britain's most prominent jurists, was for the most part very favorable both in Parliament as well as in the media. Both government and opposition MP's welcomed the findings and expressed support for the commission's recommendations.[94] The *Independent*, for example, editorialized that it was "Not too late for justice"[95] and the *Guardian* supported this stance as well.[96] And while there were MP's and others who opposed the idea of trying war criminals in Great Britain,[97] it was clear that we were closer than ever to achieving our goal of bringing the perpetrators of the Holocaust living in the UK to the bar of justice.

Given the recommendations made by the commission of inquiry and the government's declared intention of implementing them, our role now focused on the practical implications of that decision. Everything possible had to be done on the one hand to speed up the legislation and on the other to insure that in the meantime the murderers did not escape.[98] Another important issue was the fact that the commission had not recommended the establishment of a special investigations unit,[99] a decision which we believed was a serious mistake.

In the fall, the focus moved to Parliament. The All-Party War Crimes Group sponsored an international conference entitled "Time For Justice," at which the directors of governmental Nazi war crimes units in the United States (Neal Sher) Australia (Robert Greenwood) and Canada (Bill Hobson) met with MP's and explained the practical mechanics of Nazi-hunting. Designed to enlist public opinion and parliamentary support prior to the debate on the war crimes bill which was going to be submitted to parliament, the conference attracted considerable media attention.[100] I utilized the opportunity of attending the conference to meet with Michael Boyle of the Home Office and submit the name of an additional suspect who served in the 12th Lithuanian Auxiliary Police Battalion and emigrated to Great Britain after the war.[101] At this time, Scottish Television was investigating suspicions that Gecas had worked for British intelligence after the war and had therefore been granted immunity,[102] so the discovery of another member of his unit who had come to Great Britain was potentially important. I also submitted lists of members of this unit who had escaped to the West to the heads of the Australian (32 names) and Canadian (22) Nazi war crimes units.[103] (The Americans had already checked the roster of the unit against their immigration records and had denaturalized several Lithuanians who had served in its ranks.)[104] The problem was, however, that the Home Office refused in principle to gather any evidence or conduct any investigations whatsoever until Parliament passed appropriate legislation,[105] so in the meantime our research would have no practical impact.

The situation began to change on December 12, 1989 when the government submitted a proposal to the House of Commons that legislation be passed to enable the prosecution in Great Britain of individuals who were currently British citizens or residents "for acts of murder and manslaughter or culpable homicide committed as war crimes in Germany, or German-occupied territory, during the Second World War." As expected, the proposal aroused considerable emotion pro and con in the British parliament. Home Secretary David Waddington explained that no responsible government could ignore the allegations presented by the Wiesenthal Center in 1986. The proposal before the house was not intended to criminalize actions which were not criminal at the time. On the contrary, "it is a proposal to give our courts power to try here actions which undeniably were criminal and which the perpetrators must have known were wicked and criminal at the time they perpetrated them . . . We are talking about premeditated acts of cold-blooded mass murder perpetrated on defenseless civilians." The government, Waddington explained, had not yet decided whether to submit a bill but would determine its position in the light of the debate and vote in Parliament. Greville Janner described how members of his family had been rounded up and burnt to death in a locked synagogue. Nonetheless, he asserted that "I do not want revenge. I just want justice. I do not understand why if there was sufficient evidence people should not be brought to trial." Among the supporters of the proposed legislation were also leading MP's such as Sir Bernard Braine, Merlyn Rees, Roy Hattersly, Ivan Lawrence and many others.

Needless to say, there were also those who opposed the idea of war crimes trials in Great Britain. Former Prime Minister Edward Heath was adamantly opposed to passing what he categorized as "retrospective legislation" to deal with the crimes of World War II. "Those of us who served six years through the war fought it out and we had the Nuremberg trials and we disposed of it. We are now moving into a better, more peaceful and wider Europe . . . . This is not the moment to start passing legislation of this kind." Sir John Stokes questioned whether the laws of England should be changed in order to right serious wrongs. In his words, "These trials would be more of a lottery than a long, complicated, and involved procedure, involving overturning the whole bases of English law in order to bring to trial a few old men. Mercy should overcome justice particularly when so many years have elapsed."[106]

Despite these arguments, the House of Commons in a free vote, overwhelmingly supported the proposed change in the law by a margin of 348-123. Prime Minister Thatcher voted in favor of the bill as did eight other Cabinet ministers and Opposition leader Neal Kinnock. Liberal Democrat leader Paddy Ashdown and Social Democrat leader David Owen both opposed the measure as did Chancellor of the Exchequer John Major, and two other Cabinet ministers. Attorney-General Sir Patrick Mayhew, did not vote.[107] The overwhelming majority in favor of the bill was a clear sign to the government to proceed with practical steps to pass the necessary legislation to enable war crimes trials. Buoyed by the victory in parliament, the Center called for the necessary investigations to begin immediately.[108]

A significant step in that direction was taken on March 8, 1990 when Home Secretary David Waddington introduced a bill in parliament to enable the prosecution of Nazi war criminals in Great Britain. According to the provisions of the proposed bill, live evidence could be taken by satellite from witnesses abroad and testimony taken in East European courts could be recorded on video and introduced as evidence. In addition, written statements from witnesses already deceased could also be admitted. In addition, in an effort to speed up the process, committal proceedings were being dropped (as they had been in cases of serious fraud).[109] Eleven days later the bill was passed in the House of Commons by a wide margin (273-60) and the government announced that it was establishing a team of 9 police officers to carry out the necessary investigations.[110] Explaining the rationale for the bill, Waddington admitted that most people would prefer to get on with their lives, rather than dealing with the crimes of the past. "But sometimes one is brought face to face with facts that cannot be buried, with deeds so terrible that they cannot be forgotten. As long as one of those responsible survives, the world will cry out for justice."[111] That sentiment was echoed in the popular press in the wake of the passage of the bill,[112] although the *Times*[113] and various columnists[114] doubted the sagacity of the decision. Yet despite the doubts expressed in various quarters against the bill it was passed in the House of Commons for a third time by a significant majority of 135-10 on April 25, 1990.[115]

The passage of the bill three times in the House of Commons did not, however, ensure its becoming law. It still had to be approved by the House of Lords, where opposition to its passage was widespread. The extent of the opposition was reflected by the Lords' rejection by a vote of 137-62 of an amendment which would have allowed Scottish courts to accept evidence recorded on video or by live satellite hookup.[116] (The acceptance of such evidence was permissible in England and Wales.) In addition, some of the most prominent members of the House of Lords publicly expressed unequivocal opposition to the passage of the war crimes bill. Thus for example Lord Donaldson, one of Britain's most senior judges, said in early May that he was filled with "complete horror" regarding the changes in the law that were necessary to enable the prosecution of Nazi war criminals.[117] To make matters worse, according to the *Guardian*, if the bill was rejected by the Lords, the government planned to abandon its war crimes initiative altogether.[118] Although Mrs. Thatcher's personal secretary refused, in a letter to Rabbi Hier, to confirm that that was indeed the case,[119] we remained extremely concerned that the perpetrators in Britain might succeed in eluding justice.

With the future of Nazi-hunting in Britain ostensibly in the balance, the House of Lords convened on June 4, 1990 to discuss and vote on the proposed legislation. Since I had been scheduled to deliver a lecture in Manchester the same week, I travelled to London to attend the debate in the House of Lords. It was not, to put it mildly, a pleasant experience. Speaker after speaker rose to attack the bill, passionately urging their colleagues to reject the proposed legislation. Many objected in principle to the bill since they considered it retroactive legislation. Others considered it a proposal initiated by, and primarily for the benefit of, Jewish interests and as such untenable.

If the arguments marshalled in opposition to the bill had been based on fact it would have been bad enough, but in most cases the reasoning presented for the bill's rejection was inherently faulty. In this respect, three examples will suffice. Many lords used the argument that Great Britain had already decided to stop war crimes trials in 1948, but in reality that decision only applied to the British zone of occupied Germany. (No one even dreamed at that time that Nazi criminals would emigrate to England, Wales or Scotland.) A second claim was that convictions could never be obtained since the crimes had been committed so long ago, an assertion clearly rejected by the war crimes inquiry. The third argument was that the bill was in essence "racist" since it applied only to the perpetrators of the Holocaust, but it was common knowledge that they were the only mass murderers currently living in Great Britain.[120]

Despite their advanced age and the extremely lengthy debate (69 peers requested permission to speak) the lords in most cases presented their positions with considerable feeling and conviction. Among the leading peers who opposed the legislation were Lord Hailsham of St. Marylebone, the former Lord Chancellor; Lord Shawcross, Britain's chief prosecutor at Nuremburg; Lord Donaldson of Lymington, the Master of the Rolls, as well as former Prime Minister Lord Callaghan and former Foreign Minister Lord Carrington. The opponents minced no words in their condemnation of the proposal.[121] In Lord Hailsham's words:

This is not a Jewish question at all. It is a question of justice, and what is being offered is not the justice which this country is expecting . . ."

Only seven cases were carefully investigated [by the War Crimes Inquiry]. Only four would merit a trial. One of these is dead. One is too ill to stand trial. One would almost certainly get off. That leaves one. For that we are being invited to commit an indelible stain to the standards of British justice. We are not to be bullied in this House; not to be blackmailed; not to be intimidated, but to do that which is right in the sight of the Lord, and I know where my conscience will lead me to vote."

According to Lord Shawcross, he had been in favor of increasing the efforts to prosecute the perpetrators of the Holocaust shortly after the war, but events in Palestine, such as the activities of the Stern Gang and the bombing of the King David Hotel had not helped those who favored his position:

In the atmosphere of those days it would have been impossible to continue war crimes trials, wherever the criminals happened to be. Now younger people who had no experience of the war and perhaps have more simplistic ideas of right and wrong, want us to do so.

The average age of the members of the Commons who made very eloquent and sincere speeches in favor of this Bill was five years at the beginning of the war.

Of course we can revive the policy of retribution, but we cannot in my view do it without imposing an indelible blot on every principle of British law and justice.

Those in favor of the bill although fewer in number, also presented their case eloquently and passionately. In his speech Britain's Chief Rabbi Lord Jakobovitz spoke of the significance of justice in the war crimes context:

I would hope that a commitment to bring criminals to justice, and to fight evil wherever and whenever it is to be found, unites all decent men and women irrespective of belief.

Some opponents of the Bill, many speaking here, are among the staunchest friends of the Jewish people, but I am bound to add that so were some of those who were appeasers of the Nazis in the 1930's.

A vote now preventing suspected arch-criminals who had succeeded in our lifetime in turning the foul teachings of racism into rivers and lakes of innocent blood would give a wrong signal to a world seeking reassurance that civilized governments and legislatures would never allow such evil to triumph with impunity . . ."

A vote against the Bill would make it certain that for millions of victims there could and would be no justice, not even in theory or symbolically. It had been said that the Bill was 40 years too late; but 40 years of moral negligence was no excuse for persisting in it after it had been brought to light.

Lord Beloff, another staunch supporter of the bill, could not resist pointing out the prejudice with which the issue was being considered and the current implications of such:

> There are only two lots of people who don't believe in British justice— supporters of this amendment and the IRA.
>
> There seems to me to have crept in a degree of prejudice which is very similar to the prejudice one can read in some official documents of the wartime years when the first rumors of these appalling events reached this country and were largely dismissed. I would not argue that we could have done in this country much to prevent them. It is certainly true some people said, "well the Jews are always complaining, they are probably exaggerating."
>
> If we were to reject this in the present temper of Europe where anti-Semitism is again rife we would be giving encouragement to some of the least attractive elements in the European scene today.[122]

Despite the unequivocal defense mounted by supporters of the bill, including government spokesman the Earl of Ferrers, most of those assembled voted to reject the proposed legislation. Thus the House of Lords voted by a very large margin (207-74) to drop the war crimes bill, the first time in recent British history that the unelected upper house had defeated a bill passed by the House of Commons. The unprecedented vote sent shock waves through the British establishment, and focused attention on the role played by the House of Lords.[123] For those of us involved in war crimes, however, it was a bitter defeat which jeopardized years of efforts. The idea that the lords, many of whom inherited their titles, could prevent the prosecution of the Nazis in Britain after a bill to that effect had passed the House of Commons three times by huge margins was a very bitter pill to swallow.

What made it even worse, however, was the fact that it was obvious that the decision by the House of Lords in no way reflected public opinion in Great Britain. This was clearly evident from four public opinion polls taken shortly after the Lords voted to reject the War Crimes Bill. Thus, for example, on June 6 the *Daily Mail* published a National Opinion Poll in which 60% approved of the bill and 31% opposed it. A day before, BBC Radio 4 asked listeners for their opinion and recorded calls at a rate of 9 to 1 in favor of the bill and against the vote in the House of Lords. Shortly thereafter ITV published the results of its Oracle poll. In response to the question "Should alleged war criminals be tried?", the survey recorded 85% (5,899 calls) in favor and 15% (1,047 calls) opposed.[124] In addition, there was considerable editorial support in the media for the government to press on with the war crimes legislation,[125] so despite this serious setback, all hope was not lost.

Ironically, that was not the only bad news for us in Britain that week. On the day after the war crimes bill was rejected by the House of Lords, the *Times* of London reached an agreement out of court with Antanas Gecas regarding his libel suit against them. Since we had hoped that the *Times* might perhaps fight Gecas in court and thereby expose his wartime crimes, the announcement came as a bitter disappointment. The good news was that the *Times* had not agreed to pay Gecas any damages and that Gecas had not demanded that the *Times* retract its charge that as an officer of a Lithuanian Auxiliary Police Battalion he had participated in atrocities against civilians during World War II. The bad news was that the case would not go to court and that the *Times* had agreed to contribute an undisclosed sum toward his legal costs since his lawyers had taken his case on a no-win no fee basis.[126] With the war crimes bill rejected a day earlier, the Gecas–*Times* settlement was hardly encouraging.

Prior to the vote in the House of Lords, I had prepared an additional list of suspects for submission to the Home Office. The nine individuals in question, all Lithuanians, had (with one exception) been named in the testimonies of the Kunichowsky collection and according to the ITS files had gone after the war to Great Britain, mostly in the framework of the "Westward Ho!" emigration scheme.[127] This plan which was designed to facilitate the emigration to the United Kingdom of foreign workers to overcome manpower shortages, gave preference to refugees from the Baltics[128] (among whom the percentage of Nazi collaborators was extremely high). The idea behind the submission of the list was to emphasize the fact that numerous Nazi war criminals had come to live in Great Britain and that they did not deserve the right to continue to live unprosecuted in the UK. Under normal circumstances, I would have waited until I had completed all the research on the entire Kunichowsky collection prior to submitting the list, but the vote in the House of Lords made the submission of the list at this point particularly important, a fact confirmed by the extensive media coverage of this ostensibly minor event.[129] Unfortunately, despite my efforts to convince them otherwise, Michael Boyle and Paul Regan of the Home Office made clear that no steps would be taken to investigate these suspects until the war crimes bill was passed.[130] Under these circumstances, the key to the issue became whether the government would reintroduce the legislation or abandon the war crimes initiative.

On June 21, 1990 the British government announced that it would indeed introduce the Nazi war crimes legislation during the next session of Parliament which would convene in November. "The government," Sir Geoffrey Howe indicated in response to a question by MP John Marshall, "will be seeking, whether by way of suggested amendments or otherwise, to secure the support of both Houses for the Bill."[131] According to the decision, which was taken by a meeting of ministers chaired by Prime Minister Thatcher and approved by the entire cabinet, the bill would be reintroduced in the exact same form, but with "suggested amendments" to overcome some of the objections raised by the peers. According to the law, a year had to pass from the second vote in the House of Commons before the bill could be returned to the House of Lords and therefore the latter would only receive the bill sometime after March 19, 1991. If the Lords were to once again defeat the bill, the government intended to invoke the Parliament Act (which enables the passage of bills passed by Commons and rejected by the Lords) and send the bill directly to the Queen for royal assent.[132] Given the opposition of several senior ministers to the war crimes bill and the constitutional crisis which could result by involving the Parliament Acts, Mrs. Thatcher's determination to push the bill through was indeed noteworthy. If not for her support, it is likely that the legislation would have been dropped.[133]

In the meantime, our research continued but we found ourselves confronting serious obstacles. The most important related to our inability to obtain the "Westward Ho!" records. Given the high percentage of Baltic immigrants accepted under this scheme, we thought that it would be particularly important to gain access to those documents. All our efforts to do so to date have, unfortunately, been unsuccessful.[134]

Another problem concerned the demise of suspects and witnesses, a natural process which, needless to say, continued totally oblivious of the progress of the war crimes legislation.[135]

The War Crimes Bill was resubmitted to the House of Commons on March 7,[136] and five days later MP's approved by a vote of 177 to 17 a measure allowing the second reading of the bill to be made without amendments and a third reading without debate to insure its speedy return to the House of Lords.[137] On March 18, the bill was debated on the floor of the House of Commons after being introduced by Home Secretary Kenneth Baker. At the conclusion of the debate during which the by-now standard arguments of supporters and detractors were presented, the bill was passed by a vote of 254 to 88.[138]

In the wake of the vote, we announced that we would be submitting the names of 8 additional Nazi war crimes suspects who emigrated to Great Britain after World War II to the British government. These names, like those on the previous list, were for the most part taken from the files of the Kunichowsky collection which named Lithuanians who had played an active role in the murder of Jews. Among those on the list were individuals who had committed crimes in Kelme, Musninkiai, Jonava, Mariampole, Sveksna and Svencionys as well as a member of the 12th Lithuanian Auxiliary Police Battalion.[139]

On April 30, meanwhile, the House of Lords again rejected the War Crimes Bill, this time by the much smaller margin of 131-109, despite offers by the government to consider amendments which would address the points found objectionable by the peers. In response, the government invoked the Parliament Act, sending the bill to the queen for royal assent.[140] Thus within days after its second rejection by the House of Lords, the long-awaited War Crimes Bill was signed by Queen Elizabeth II and officially became the law of the land on May 9, 1991.

Once the War Crimes Bill was passed, the special investigations unit established at Scotland Yard began its activities. We immediately established contact with Director Eddie Bathgate and continued the process of submitting the names of suspects which we uncovered in our research. On July 10, 1991 I sent Bathgate a list of 4 Lithuanian suspects whose names I had uncovered during a visit to Lithuania the previous month.[141] At the same time, I urged him to make every effort to obtain access to the "Westward Ho!" and "Operation Post Report" records and have them cross-checked against our master-list of war criminals from the Baltics.[142] (The latter records contained admissions of collaboration with the Nazis by many Lithuanian, Latvian, and Estonian postwar immigrants to Great Britain and therefore were of enormous potential for the discovery of Nazi war criminals.[143] Unfortunately, to this date, such a research project has never been undertaken.

In January 1992 the importance of the Westward Ho! records was further reinforced when we uncovered an additional suspect who emigrated to Great Britain in that framework. According to a series of articles published in Lithuania in June 1991, one of the local collaborators in the murder of the Jews of Jonava was a men named Stepas Nedzelskis. We discovered that Nedzelskis left for Great Britain with "Westward Ho" on March 16, 1948 from Regensdorf via Munster. We submitted the pertinent documentation to the Nazi war crimes unit on January 27, 1992,[144] but our information arrived too late. Two days later we were informed by Bathgate that Nedzelskis had indeed been living in the United Kingdom but had already passed away.[145]

In early 1992, the war crimes focus temporarily moved to Vilnius as Gecas' libel suit against Scottish Television began with hearings in the Lithuanian capital. The former Lithuanian police officer had sued Scottish Television over its documentary film *Crimes of War*, initially screened in 1987, which claimed that Gecas had participated in the mass murder of civilians in Byelorussia. When Scottish Television produced three elderly witnesses who were unable to travel to Edinburgh to testify, the Court of Sessions, Scotland's supreme civil court, agreed to allow the necessary hearings to take place in Lithuania, with the judge, lawyers for both sides, court officials and shorthand experts in attendance.[146] Although the two witnesses who had served with Gecas in the 12th battalion claimed that they had been forced to embellish their testimony under KGB duress, Juozas Aleksynas graphically described the murders and stated unequivocally that Gecas had issued the orders to carry out the executions.[147] His testimony was to play a key role in the verdict rendered in this case.

Before the Gecas libel case was completed, new revelations regarding his unit created a stir in Great Britain. For years we had assumed that Gecas was one of only a few at most members of the 12th battalion who had emigrated to Great Britain after World War II. We had already uncovered the names of many unit members who had emigrated to Canada and Australia and OSI had discovered quite a few residing in the United States, but as late as February 1992 only three members of the unit including Gecas were known to have been living the United Kingdom.[148] On June 7, 1992, however, Stephen Ward of the *Independent* revealed that an entire company (160 men) of the 12th Battalion had surrendered en masse to the Allies in Italy in 1944 and were subsequently incorporated into the Free Polish Army. Later they became part of the Polish Resettlement Corps and were brought to Britain with few or no questions asked. According to the *Independent,* more than 30 of the men were still in Great Britain.[149] This meant that not only might we be able to find witnesses against Gecas living in Great Britain, but that the scope of the prosecutions would probably be for larger than originally expected.

This revelation was followed by more good news from Scotland. On July 17, 1992, Judge Lord Milligan branded Antanas Gecas a war criminal and rejected the £600,000 libel suit he had launched against Scottish Television which had named him a Nazi war criminal in its documentary *Crimes of War.* In the words of Judge Lord Milligan's verdict:

> I am clearly satisfied on the evidence as a whole upon the standard of proof agreed to apply to this case that the pursuer participated in many operations involving the killing of innocent Soviet citizens, including Jews in particular, in Byelorussia during the last three months of 1941, and in doing so committed war crimes against Soviet citizens who included old men, women and children. I further hold it proved that the pursuer was the Platoon Commander of the platoon in which Antanas [sic] Aleksynas served throughout this period, and that that platoon participated specifically in the first (gravel pit), second (near birch grove) third (water in pit), fourth (Slutsk) and sixth (Minsk) operations as described by Mr. Aleksynas. It inevitably follows that the pursuer committed war crimes against innocent civilians of all ages and both sexes in the course of these specific operations, it not being in dispute that he was in active command of his platoon throughout the period mentioned.[150]

The decision in the Gecas libel suit ostensibly paved the way for his indictment on war crimes charges in Scotland,[151] but that did not take place. For reasons which as yet remain unclear, the Lord Advocate, Lord Roger Earlsferry, announced on February 3, 1994 that the Scottish Nazi war crimes unit was being disbanded and that there was insufficient evidence available for a criminal prosecution in any of the seventeen cases under investigation. While the cases against Gecas and other suspects living in Scotland officially remain open,[152] there appears to be little hope that any will actually be prosecuted. And while it is true that a higher level of proof is required in criminal proceedings than in libel cases, information regarding Gecas has come to light which raises serious question marks about his case.

Gecas, it was recently revealed, worked, following his arrival in Great Britain in 1948 for British intelligence, which perhaps helps explain his admission of wartime service in the 12th Lithuanian Auxiliary Police Battalion and may have had an effect on the decision not to prosecute him. The fact that Gecas himself was apparently never questioned by the Scottish Nazi war crimes unit nor was his house ever searched, also appears quite strange, as does the fact that the witnesses who testified against him in the libel trial were subsequently reluctant to testify against him in a criminal proceeding.[153] The Center protested against the decision not to prosecute Gecas, calling it a travesty of justice,"[154] but it remain to be seen whether anything can be done to induce the Scottish authorities to indict the former Lithuanian murder squad officer.

The developments in the Gecas case once again focused public attention in Great Britain on the war crimes issue and various figures were publicized regarding the scope of the investigations being carried out by the British authorities. According to a report in the *Daily Telegraph*, for example, 97 suspects currently residing in England and Wales were being investigated. An additional 250 individuals had been cleared following investigation because they had already passed away, were not residing in Great Britain, or there was insufficient evidence that they had participated in the murder of civilians.[155]

The number of suspects is likely to rise as research continues based on recently acquired documentation from the newly-independent former Soviet republics. Thus for example the Center sent a list of four additional Lithuanian suspects to the British authorities on May 16, 1993. The individuals on this list had served either in the Lithuanian Auxiliary Police or in the National Labor Defense Battalion which was the predecessor of the police battalions. All emigrated to Great Britain in the framework of the Westward Ho! program.[156]

To date, not a single Nazi war criminal has yet been brought to trial in Great Britain, although one suspect (besides Gecas) has publicly been named as a top-priority case. According to reports in the media, Seimion Serafimowicz, the commander of the Byelorussian police in the town of Mir, and presently living in Daustead, Surrey,[157] is most likely to be among the first people tried in England under the War Crimes Bill. Despite the lack of practical results to date, we are still hopeful that several of the Nazi war criminals presently living in Great Britain will indeed be successfully brought to trial. Like the situation in Australia, one should not underestimate the importance of the passage of the War Crimes Bill, but at the same time the fact that not a single criminal has to date been indicted in the United Kingdom underlines the frustrating gap between war crimes legislation and the implementation of justice, a phenomenon which has plagued our efforts throughout the world.

In retrospect, if I attempt to analyze the modified success we achieved in Great Britain, we see to what extent the success of our efforts was dependent not only on historical documentation and witnesses but on far more prosaic factors. In the Gecas case, for example, we had incredibly good luck. I received his name and address from Zelig Gelinsky, a Lithuanian survivor living in Israel, more than four and a half years before I compiled the British list.[158] Even though I had no apparent use for it at the time, I kept the information, hoping to be able to use it eventually. Even more important was the fact that he was living in Scotland. If he had been residing anywhere else in Great Britain, I am almost certain that Bob Tomlinson and Scottish Television would never have become involved. Without their help there is no question that we could never have possibly succeeded to the extent we did. The two documentaries they produced and the documentation they obtained in the Soviet Union played a critical role in efforts to convince the Home Office to take legal measures against the Nazis in Britain. The fact that the Soviets chose to cooperate with Bob Tomlinson and Ross Wilson was also very important, although had they co-operated with someone else perhaps the results would have been similar. There is no doubt, however, that the Scots proved to be extremely dedicated and energetic in their efforts to expose Gecas and this contributed substantially to the results achieved. Another lucky coincidence was the Juodis case. The fact that Gecas had served in the same unit saved us considerable work. The fact that Juodis had been indicted in the United States helped convince the British that the charges were indeed extremely serious. In this respect we were also lucky that the British made their decision after the Canadians and Australians had decided to initiate legislation enabling them to prosecute the Nazi war criminals in those countries. The success of OSI is also a factor in our favor. Had Britain been the first country to face this issue, they would probably never have even considered acceding to our request.

The role played by Scottish Television highlights the contribution of the media. Without the extensive coverage of the issue, our chances of success would have significantly diminished. The media played a key role in focusing attention on this issue and arousing public opinion. Although several newspapers adopted a very prejudiced view of our activities, the role of the media as a whole was generally positive in terms of acquainting the public with the facts. It is true that some papers lost interest when we refused to publicize the names of the suspects, but it was the media nonetheless that enabled us to keep the issue center stage in the public arena.

The last factor of importance is the assistance provided by local bodies, especially the All-Party Parliamentary Group. One of the reasons why certain Britons objected to the Center's campaign was that we were "outsiders," a non-British organization, which ostensibly had no right to make demands upon Her Majesty's government.[159] In that respect the role of the All-Party group was extremely critical. The campaign conducted so adroitly by Merlyn Rees, Greville Janner and their colleagues added an important dimension to the efforts to convince the Home Office to take action.[160] Without the local support which they did so much to enlist, it would have been impossible to influence the British government to adopt the war crimes legislation. Now it remains to be seen whether any Nazi war criminals will actually be brought to trial in Great Britain.

Notes

1. Tom Tugend and Hyam Corney, "Alleged Nazis in Britain," *Jewish Chronicle*, October 24, 1986.

2. Among the publications in which the allegations appeared were: "Zmonijos Atmintis Kaltina," *Tiesa*, September 25, 1981, p. 2; Vytautas Zeimantas, "Atpildas uz nusikaltimus," *Tiesa*, February 19, 1978. This article included a roster of members of the Vilnius Sonderkommando; *Daugavas Vanagi*, pp. 34-35, 51-54, 80-85, 98, 109, 113, 136-39; *"Political Refugees" Unmasked!*, pp. 21-32, 43, 69, 109-12, 140-41, 163, 174, 182, 192.

3. Ezergailis, "Who Killed the Jews of Latvia?," pp. 10, 35.

4. YVA, M-9/15(6, 6a).

5. WLA, 539/22, 24, 27.

6. Letter of Rabbi Marvin Hier to Prime Minister Margaret Thatcher, Octo-

ber 22, 1986, SWCA.

7. Askold Krushelnycky and Barrie Penrose, "Refugee Accused of War Crimes by Nazi Hunters," *Sunday Times*, October 26, 1986, p. 5.

8. Gordon Airs and Brian McCartney, "I'm No Nazi Butcher," *Daily Record*, October 29, 1986, p. 13.

9. *Quiet Neighbors*, p 355.

10. Signed statement by Antanas Gecas, April 16, 1982; Deposition of Antony Gecas in Jurgis Juodis case, August 12, 1982, C.A. No. 81-1013-CIV-T-H, p. 27, Gecas file, SWCA.

11. The documentaries produced by Scottish Television were: "Britain: A Nazi Safehouse," January 29, 1987, and "Crimes of War," July 22, 1987.

12. Among other MPs active in this group were Peter Archer, Alex Carlile, John Wheeler, Ivan Lawrence, John Gorst, Neil Thorne, Rupert Allason and David Winnick.

13. See, for example, Jenni Frazer. "The Gecas Dossier," *Jewish Chronicle*, November 7, 1986, p. 8.

14. See, for example, Barrie Penrose, "Whitehall Will Plan Next Move on "Nazi" List," *Sunday Times*, November 16, 1986.

15. Maggie Brown, "Secret UK Policy "Created a Safe Haven for Nazis"," *Independent*, January 29, 1987, p. 2.

16. David Horovitz, "Thatcher to Discuss Issue of Nazi Criminals," *Jerusalem Post*, February 2, 1987.

17. Simon Freeman, "Shadow of the Holocaust," *Sunday Times*, February 22, 1987.

18. Michael Wise, "Britain Trails Six Alleged Nazi War Criminals," Reuters, February 24, 1987.

19. Letter of Charles Powell to Rabbi Marvin Hier, February 12, 1987, SWCA.

20. David Horovitz, "Won't Prosecute Nazis, Home Office Declares," *Jerusalem Post*, February 26, 1987, p. 3.

21. Stephen Ward, "Soviets Name 34 Nazi War Criminals Living in Britain," *Independent*, February 27, 1987.

22. David Wastell and Donald MacIntyre, "Jewish Fears over Nazi Criminal Hunt," *Sunday Telegraph*, March 1, 1987.

23. Record of meeting of Wiesenthal Center delegation with Douglas Hurd and Home Office officials, March 2, 1987, London, SWCA.

24. "Press Conference with Douglas Hurd (After a Meeting with Simon Wiesenthal Center Delegation)," March 2, 1987, SWCA.

25. "The Wiesenthal File," *Times*, March 3, 1987.

26. "Case for Inaction," *Daily Telegraph*, March 4, 1987, p. 16.

27. Peter Simple, "Zealots," *Daily Telegraph*, March 4, 1987.

28. Nicholas Comfort, "Hurd in Talks on 'Nazis on Britain' claim," *Daily Tele-*

graph, February 27, 1987.

29. "The Past that We Should Never Forget," *Independent*, February 27, 1987.

30. "Wiesenthal's Seventeen," *Guardian*, March 4, 1987.

31. See, for example, Vivienne Levy, "Time is Running Out for the Nazi Hunters," and Bob Graham, "Two Days that Haunt the Lifetime Memories for a Camp Survivor," *London Daily News*, March 2, 1987, p. 2.

32. See for example, Gordon Airs, "Horrors that shocked even the Nazis," *Daily Record*, November 17, 1986; Peter Bond and James Lewthwaite, "315,000 killed by 17 Nazis in our midst," *Sun*, February 26, 1987.

33. Meeting with Guennadi Shabanikov, March 4, 1987, London.

34. Letter of Douglas Hurd to Rabbi Marvin Hier, March 10, 1987, SWCA.

35. "'Don't Be Quiet on Nazis in Britain,'" *Jewish Telegraph*, March 13, 1987; "Zuroff Spells Out 'Cause for Concern,'" *Jewish Gazette*, March 13, 1987, p. 1.

36. Telephone conversation with Guennadi Shabanikov, April 7, 1987.

37. David Horovitz, "London Finds Three More Alleged Nazis," *Jerusalem Post*, April 15, 1987.

38. Stephen Ward, "Russians Delay Inquiry into 'Nazis,'" *Independent*, April 14, 1987.

39. Stephen Braun, "The Holocaust Remembered: A Reunion and a Promise," *Los Angeles Times*, April 27, 1987.

40. Letter of Rabbi Marvin Hier to Ambassador Yuri Dubinin, May 13, 1987, SWCA.

41. Information provided by Rabbi Hier, June 1987.

42. See the statements of Moteyusa Migonis, March 12, 1987, and Leonas Mickevicius, March 11, 1987, recorded by Assistant Procurator A. Kirijenka in Kaunas, Lithuania; Juozas Aleksynas, March 10, 1987, recorded by Senior Assistant Procurator J. Bakusionis in Alytus, Lithuania, Gecas file, SWCA.

43. Various orders issued to auxiliary service battalions of the Lithuanian auxliary police some of which include rosters of the units: order no. 32 (July 30, 1941); order no. 61 (August 25, 1941); orders to 2nd battalion: order no. 1 (August 26, 1941); order no. 42 (October 6, 1941), Gecas file, SWCA.

44. Statement of Daniel Melodinov, "Yehudei Iutzk ba-Kibush ha-Germani," *Pinkas Slutzk u-Bnoteha*, New York and Tel Aviv, 1962, p. 144.

45. "Strafsache gegen Franz Lechthaler," YVA, TR-10/37, pp. 35-49.

46. See note 10.

47. Migonis statement, p. 3, Gecas file, SWCA.

48. Aleksynas statement, p. 2, Gecas file, SWCA.

49. Mickevicius statement, p. 2, Gecas file, SWCA.

50. Letter of Dr. Hans Engelhardt to Rabbi Marvin Hier, June 24, 1987, SWCA.

51. Letter of Gebietskommissar Carl to the Generalkommissar, Minsk, Octo-

ber 30, 1941, Nuremberg document 1104-PS, *Nazi Conspiracy and Aggression* (Red Series), Vol. III, Washington, 1946, pp. 785-89.

52. See, for example, "The Problem of Latvia's Future" (Memorandum presented by the Latvian General Directors to Himmler on his visit to Riga on October 1943); Cable of Herschel Johnson, American Legation in Sweden to US Secretary of State regarding "Conditions in Latvia as of March 20, 1944," both June 19, 1944, YVA, M-1177/16; letter of director of Labor Office, Riga to all labor offices and branches, February 7, 1944, YVA, JM5754.

53. Meeting of Wiesenthal Center delegation with Under-Secretary of State David Faulkner, July 17, 1987, London.

54. See, for example, Howell Raines, "Britain to Review Citizenship in War-Crimes Case," *New York Times*, July 19, 1987, p. 13; Martin Bailey, "Russian Request for 'War Criminal,'" *Observer*, July 19, 1987, p. 3.

55. "Seven Join List of 'Ex-Nazis,'" *Guardian*, July 22, 1987; "More Ex-Nazis traced in Britain," *Glasgow Herald*, July 22, 1987.

56. Martin Fletcher, "MPs Reveal British Link with Gestapo Chief," *Times*, July 22, 1987.

57. "Nazi-Hunter Fails in Attempt to Confront Gecas," *Scotsman*, July 24, 1987; "Nazi Hunter Fails to Confront 'War Criminal' in Public," *Times*, July 24, 1987, p. 5.

58. "Professor Crick Makes Israel the Target," *Jewish Echo*, July 31, 1987, p. 5.

59. Letter of N.A. Nagler to Rabbi Marvin Hier, July 27, 1987, SWCA.

60. Gabi Brun, "'Michonat ha-Yeri'a Hayta Lo Kemo Ekdach,'" *Yediot Achronot*, July 28, 1987.

61. David Horovitz, "Britain to Study Case of Alleged War Criminal," *Jerusalem Post*, July 29, 1987, p. 3.

62. "Mabat," Kol Yisrael, August 17, 1987, 9 p.m.

63. "Israel Not to Ask for Gecas," *Edinburgh Evening News*, August 18, 1987.

64. See, for example, "Israel Still Reviewing Gecas Case," *Glasgow Herald*, August 19, 1987.

65. Nikolai Pakhomov, "British Authorities Shelter Nazi Criminals," Tass, August 27, 1987.

66. Seumas Milne, "Alleged Nazi Could Face Soviet Witness in UK," *Guardian*, August 27, 1987, p. 5; information provided by Bob Tomlinson, August 26, 1987.

67. "War Crimes Campaign Launched," *Searchlight*, October 1987, p. 10.

68. David Horovitz, "UK May Change Law to Try Alleged War Criminals," *Jerusalem Post*, November 19, 1987, p. 4.

69. "War Crimes Evidence Is to Be Investigated," *Times*, February 9, 1988.

70. Ivor Owen, "Inquiry into Nazi War Crimes Allegations Wins Broad Support," *Financial Times*, February 9, 1988.

71. Letter of Efraim Zuroff to David Faulkner, February 15, 1988, SWCA.

72. Meetings with Sergei Chashnikov, February 16 and 17, 1989, Edinburgh.

73. Letter of Rabbi Hier to Douglas Hurd, June 8, 1988 and accompanying "Suspected Nazi War Criminals - England," both SWCA.

74. Foreign Office Documents 371/110160; 371/66347.

75. "250 Suspected War Criminals in Britain," *Independent*, July 14, 1988, p. 1.

76. "War Crimes Inquiry Team to Visit Moscow for Nazi Suspect Check," Reuters, July 14, 1988.

77. Seumas Milne, "Home Office Handed Names of Western War Crimes Witnesses," *Guardian*, July 15, 1988, p. 3.

78. Report of meeting with David Ackland, July 18, 1988, SWCA.

79. "Judge Blocks Nazi Hunter's Book," *Glasgow Herald*, September 27, 1988. At the same time lawyers for three Latvian emigres living in Great Britain also threatened Ashford with a lawsuit if their clients' names were mentioned in the book. Letter of Shacklocks to Ashford Press, October 6, 1988, in possession of the author.

80. Mark Douglas Home, "Summons for Nazi Hunter," *Independent*, October 13, 1988; John Robertson, "'Bloody Nose' for Judge and Summons-servers in Court," *Scotsman*, October 13, 1988, p. 1.

81. John Robertson, "Author is Branded 'Hunter out for a Kill,'" *Scotsman*, October 14, 1988, p. 11.

82. Kerry Gill, "Writ-serving Attempt During Hearing," *Times*, October 19, 1988.

83. Kerry Gill, "Court Upholds Ban on Publication, *Times*, October 15, 1988, p. 2

84. David Horovitz, "Alleged Nazi Wins Court Battle against Book by Israeli Author," *Jerusalem Post*, October 16, 1988.

85. Arthur Macdonald and John Robertson, "Gecas' Book's Backer May Defy Judge's Worldwide Ban," *Scotsman*, October 15, 1988, p. 1.

86. John Robertson and Brian Pendreigh, "Court Grants Worldwide Ban on Publication of Zuroff Book," *Scotsman*, October 18, 1988, p. 3.

87. "Report on the Entry of Nazi War Criminals and Collaborators into The UK 1945-1950: Summary and Extracts," SWCA.

88. "Summary of Nazi War Criminals in the United Kingdom: The Law," SWCA.

89. See for example Phil Reeves, "MPs Seek Laws to Try War Crimes Suspects," *Independent*, February 7, 1989.

90. Stephen Ward, "Suspected Nazi war criminals to face trial," *Independent*, July 25, 1989.

91. "War Crimes; Report of the War Crimes Inquiry," July 1989, p. 92.

92. Ibid., pp. 95-105.

93. Ibid., p. 94.

94. See for example the comments by MPs Roy Hattersley, Ivan Lawrence, Merlyn Rees, Greville Janner, and John Gorst, *Parliamentary Debates (Hansard)*, July 24, 1989, pp. 732-739.

95. "Not Too Late for Justice," *Independent*, July 25, 1989.

96. "Hunting to the End," *Guardian*, July 25, 1989.

97. See for example the speeches by MP's Ivor Stanbrook and Tony Marlowe in the House of Commons. The latter asserted that the campaign to bring Nazis to trial "has nothing to do with justice and everything to do with smothering the world with a form of moral blackmail as a means of covering the current behavior of the State of Israel." *Parliamentary Debates (Hansard)*, July 24, 1989, p. 735.

98. Julian Robinson and David Winner, "Hurd Acts on War Criminals," *Jewish Chronicle*, July 28, 1989, p. 1.

99. "War Crimes; Report of the War Crimes Inquiry," p. 104.

100. See for example Eileen Macdonald, "124 Nazis in Britain Face Probe into War Crimes," *Observer*, October 22, 1989.

101. Letter of Efraim Zuroff to Michael Boyle, October 23, 1989, SWCA.

102. Undated letter of Paul Murricane to Efraim Zuroff, SWCA.

103. Susan Reid, "Ottawa Given War-crimes List of 21 Believed Living in Canada," *Toronto Star*, October 25, 1989. The list was of 22 names.

104. Among the members of the unit who were denaturalized by OSI were Jonas Klimavicius, Antanas Mineikis, Henrikas Benkunskas, and Matthew Katin.

105. Letter of Michael Boyle to Efraim Zuroff, November 15, 1989, SWCA.

106. "House Gives War Criminals Motion a Big Majority in Free Vote," *Times*, December 13, 1989.

107. Judy Jones and Stephen Ward, "MP's Vote Paves Way for Nazi War Crimes Trials," *Independent*, December 13, 1989.

108. Michael Evans and David Sapsted, "Inquiry Sought into Nazi War Crimes," *Times* , December 14, 1989.

109. Stephen Ward, "Lords May Delay Bill on War Crimes Trials," *Independent*, March 9, 1990.

110. "Former Nazi War Criminals Face Trial in Britain," *Jerusalem Post*, March 21, 1990, p. 3.

111. "Police Team yo Pursue War Crimes Inquiry," *Times*, March 20, 1990.

112. John Beattie, "They Must Be Found", *Daily Star*, March 20, 1990; "Search for Nazis Must Never Stop," *Sun*, March 19, 1990.

113. "A Kind of Wild Justice," *Times*, March 20, 1990.

114. See for example Colin Welch, "Fair Trial or Farce?," *Daily Mail*, March 29, 1990.

115. "War Crimes Bill," *Parliamentary Debates (Hansard)*, April 26, 1990, p. 455.

116. Douglas Davis, "Setback for UK War Crimes Trials," *Jerusalem Post*, May 3, 1990, p. 2.

117. David Utteig, "Top Judge Attacks Nazi Trial Plans," *Sunday Correspondent*, May 6, 1990.

118. Michael White, "War Crimes Bill May Be Abandoned," *Guardian*, May 9, 1990.

119. Letter of Charles Powell to Rabbi Marvin Hier, May 23, 1990, SWCA.

120. "Trip to England June 4-10, 1990, "Report by Efraim Zuroff to Rabbis Marvin Hier and Abraham Cooper, Drs. Gerald Margolis and Shimon Samuels, June 1990, SWCA.

121. Report of Efraim Zuroff to Avra Shapiro, July 10, 1990, SWCA.

122. "Peers Throw Out War Crimes Bill," *Independent*, June 5, 1990; Anthony Looch and William Weekes, "War Crimes Bill Attack Brings Cheers in Lords," *Daily Telegraph*, June 5, 1990; "Lords Majority of 133 against War Crimes Bill," *Times*, June 5, 1990.

123. See for example "Lords in Action," *Times*, June 6, 1990.

124. "The War Crimes Bill—Opinion inside and outside Parliament," prepared by the All-Party Parliamentary War Crimes Group, July 1990, SWCA.

125. "Need for a moral statement," *Independent*, June 6, 1990; "Why the Lords Got it Wrong," *Guardian*, June 6, 1990; "Shocking Decision Shames the Nation," *Mail on Sunday,* June 10, 1990.

126. Kerry Gill, "Settlement in War Crimes Suit" and "Defamation Case against the Times is Settled," *Times*, June 6, 1990, p. 1, 5.

127. "List of Suspected Nazi War Criminals Who Emigrated to England after World War II," June 7, 1990, SWCA.

128. David Cesarani, *Justice Delayed; How Britain became a refuge for Nazi war criminals*, London, 1992, pp. 74-76.

129. See for example "'Nine more UK Nazis' Shock," *Jewish Chronicle*, June 8, 1990, p. 1.

130. Letter of Michael Boyle to Efraim Zuroff, June 18, 1990, SWCA.

131. "Business of the House," *Parliamentary Debates (Hansard)*, June 21, 1990.

132. Nicholas Wood and Sheila Gunn, "Cabinet Will Defy Lords over Nazi Crimes Bill," *Times*, June 22, 1990.

133. John Deans, "Nazis: Maggie Takes on Lords," *Daily Mail*, June 22 1990.

134. Letters of Efraim Zuroff to David Cesarani, September 10, and October 1, 1990, SWCA.

135. See for example Seumas Milne and Stephen Cook, "War Crimes Suspect Dies," *Guardian*, August 24, 1990, p. 8.

136. Sheila Gunn, "Ministers Bring Back War Crimes Bill," *Times*, March 8,

1991.

137. Nikki Knewstub, "MP's Back Move to Speed War Crimes Bill," *Guardian*, March 13, 1991.

138. "War Crimes Bill," *Parliamentary Debates (Hansard)*, March 18, 1991, pp. 23-118.

139. Jenni Frazer and Julian Robinson, "Nazis to Be Named," *Jewish Chronicle*, March 15, 1991.

140. Nikki Knewstub, "Peers Wreck War Crimes Bill," *Guardian*, May 1, 1991.

141. Letter of Efraim Zuroff to Detective Chief Superintendent Eddie Bathgate, July 10, 1991, SWCA.

142. Letters of Efraim Zuroff to Eddie Bathgate, June 19, 1991, and January 27, 1992, SWCA.

143. David Rose, "MI5 List of Nazi Killers Hidden for 40 Years," *Observer*, May 5, 1991.

144. Letter of Efraim Zuroff to Eddie Bathgate, January 27, 1992, SWCA.

145. Fax of Eddie Bathgate to Efraim Zuroff, January 29, 1992, SWCA.

146. Kerry Gill, "UK Court Sits Abroad on War Crimes Denial," *Times*, February 10, 1992.

147. Stephen Ward, "War Crimes Witness Withdraws Claim on Killings," *Independent*, February 12, 1992.

148. Letter of Roderick W. Urquhart to Efraim Zuroff, February 7, 1992, SWCA.

149. Stephen Ward, "War-crimes Platoon Men Living in UK" and David Cesarani "Hidden Legacy of the Fugitives from War," *Independent* July 5, 1992, p. 1, 5.

150. Opinion of Lord Milligan in causa Antony Gecas; Pursuer, against Scottish Television PLC (Defenders), July 17, 1992, pp. 180-181.

151. Stephen Ward, "Gecas May Be Prosecuted as War Criminal," and "War Crimes Trial May Follow Ruling," *Independent* July 18, 1992.

152. "War Crimes," Statement of Lord Advocate, February 3, 1994, SWCA.

153. Ian McKerron and Stephen Grey, "Nazi Mass Killer Was a British Spy," *Daily Express*, February 3, 1994.

154. "Britain Won't Charge Alleged War Criminal," *Jerusalem Post*, February 4, 1994, p. 12.

155. David Millward, "Inquiries into 97 Cases," *Daily Telegraph*, July 18, 1992.

156. "Suspects List - United Kingdom," May 16, 1993, SWCA.

157. Julian Kossof, "Family Says that Suspected Nazi War Criminal Is Innocent," *Jewish Chronicle*, July 2, 1993, p. 6.

158. Letter of Zelig Gelinsky to Lt. Col. Menachem Russek, January 24, 1982, a copy of which was sent to the author at that time.

159. The most strident presentation of this school of thought was made by

Peter Simple, see "Zealots," *Daily Telegraph*, March 4, 1987.
160. See, for example, Robert Harris, "Hurd to Back Nazi Trials at Old Bailey," *Observer*, November 22, 1987, p. 1.

11

Canada—Cases Dropped and Nazis Acquitted

Another country in which the passage of war crimes legislation has not yielded significant results in legal terms is Canada. Following the opening of our Jerusalem office, we submitted our first list of suspected Nazi war criminals to the Canadian authorities on October 30, 1986. Consisting of 26 names, it was submitted in Ottawa to the Deschenes Commission, the official agency established by the Canadian government in February 1985 to investigate the existence in Canada of Nazi war criminals.[1] Unlike the situation in countries like England which at that point had still not established a government mechanism to investigate such allegations, or Australia which had only established a commission of this sort approximately three months before the submission of our list, Canada had initiated an official inquiry long before the Wiesenthal Center submitted the list compiled in Jerusalem.[2] Throughout this period, the Center was represented in Canada by Sol Littman, who had played an active role in lobbying the government to establish a commission of inquiry and had supplied many of the names examined by that body.[3] While still employed by OSI, I had been in contact with the Deschenes commission, and had submitted the names of several suspects supposedly living in Canada as well as of Nazi war criminals who might have emigrated there.[4] Canada was one of the few Western governments which had already extradited a Nazi war criminal, sending Helmut Rauca, who had played an active role in the murder of the Jews of Kaunas, Lithuania, to West Germany for trial in May 1983.[5] All of these factors made our effort in Canada slightly different than the campaigns we conducted elsewhere.

This was clearly reflected in the list submitted by the Wiesenthal Center to the Deschenes Commission. As noted above the list consisted of 26 suspects, but in reality our initial research uncovered 65 names of alleged Nazi war criminals who had immigrated to Canada after the Second World War. The suspects found in Jerusalem were primarily Latvians (25), Lithuanians (20), and Ukrainians (19), whose crimes

317

covered the entire gamut of collaboration from mass murder to propaganda. Some of the suspects were alleged to have committed particularly serious crimes. Among the Latvians, for example, were several individuals who had served in the notorious Arajs Commando which had slaughtered thousands upon thousands of Jews and other innocent civilians throughout Latvia.[6] One of the Lithuanians had been a member of the *Ypatingas burys* murder squad which had carried out the murder of tens of thousands of Jews near the city of Vilnius.[7] Several of the Latvians had served with the local police forces in places such as Riga, Daugavpils, Jelgava, Tukums and Valmiera and had participated in the mass murder of civilians.[8] High-ranking officials of the collaborationist Latvian administration, including several ministers, were among the Latvian suspects who emigrated to Canada.[9] The Lithuanians were mostly either policemen or members of vigilante groups who had carried out the murder of local Jewish communities in towns and villages all over the country. Telsiai, Panevezys, Siauliai and Kedainiai were among the larger Lithuanian towns where these individuals committed their crimes which involved the murder of thousands of Jews.[10] As far as the Ukrainians are concerned, the suspects who immigrated to Canada were either policemen or members of the Galicia Division of the SS.[11]

The documentation regarding the crimes came from various sources. In 40 per cent of the cases the material was found in Israel, whereas in the remainder of the investigations the sources of the charges were various Soviet publications. It is interesting to note, however, that in quite a few instances there was corroboration of the allegations in both Israeli and Soviet material, a fact which reinforced our conviction that the latter documentation deserved thorough scrutiny and could not automatically be rejected. Regardless of the charges by emigre groups that the individuals in question were being framed by the Soviets because of their opposition to Communism,[12] the fact remained that there was considerable documentation in Western sources regarding the crimes committed by many of the individuals named in Soviet publications.

Following consultations with Sol Littman, who was acquainted with many of the names previously submitted to the Deschenes Commission, our original list was pared down to 26 names which were submitted to the Canadian authorities on October 30, 1986. The revised list consisted of the names of eleven Latvians, nine Lithuanians and five Ukrainians, whose ages ranged from under 65 to over 80. The crimes they were accused of reflected the entire range of activities carried out by the collaborationists. Most had arrived in Canada by boat during the years 1948-51, several aboard the SS Samaria. The large majority of the cases (61 per cent) were based on documentation, research and witness testimony uncovered in Israel. The sources of the allegations in the remainder of the cases were Soviet publications. In addition, the Center presented a second list of 37 suspected Nazi war criminals whose names were already known to the authorities. This list was intended to supplement the information in the possession of the Deschenes Commission, especially regarding the suspects' immigration to Canada.

Unlike the success the Center enjoyed elsewhere, the lists submitted in Canada did not achieve the desired effect. There were several reasons for this development. One was that by the time the Commission received the lists in late October 1986, it was already completing its investigation and was unable to research the allegations. Another reason was that quite a few of the names, even on the first list, were already in the Commission's possession. (They claimed that only seven were previously unknown to them.)[13] This mix-up must be attributed to the fact that I had previously submitted a few lists of names to the Deschenes Commission via private individuals. In early July 1985, for example, I gave a list of 20 suspected Nazi war criminals known to be living in Canada to Professor Irwin Cotler, who subsequently submitted it to the Deschenes Commission.[14]

Shortly before that I had assisted Joseph Riwash of Montreal, who had formerly served with the Legal Department of the Central Committee of Liberated Jews in Germany, in his search for suspects who might be living in Canada. Riwash had come to Israel to examine the records compiled by his office which were in the Yad Vashem Archives. Those files did not prove particularly helpful, however, because with the exception of two or three cases,[15] there was no indication in the documents that any of the suspects had emigrated to Canada. Since over the course of the previous few years I had made extensive use of these records in my work for OSI, the archivists at Yad Vashem asked me to assist him. I explained to Riwash that the material in question would not prove helpful to the Deschenes Commission, but that there was other documentation at Yad Vashem which might be important. I directed him to various lists of Nazi war criminals of Eastern European origin,[16] and explained that while these documents did not indicate whether any of these criminals had immigrated to Canada, there was reason to believe that many had done so. If a means could be found to determine whether they had indeed entered Canada, we could thereby possibly achieve a major breakthrough. Riwash seemed to believe that such a check could be undertaken and took the material with him. The irony of this story is that less than a year later I discovered a means of determining the emigration destinations of these criminals, and that the answers we sought were only yards away in the Yad Vashem Archives.

In both cases—the list of criminals submitted via Professor Cotler and the list of potential suspects given to Joseph Riwash—I did not receive any confirmation of the receipt of the material from the Deschenes Commission. In order to be certain that the suspects I found would be investigated, I included their names on the lists sent to Sol Littman, which probably accounts for the misunderstanding regarding the Wiesenthal Center's submission. I subsequently received confirmation of my theory when I read the official report issued by the Deschenes Commission on December 30, 1986. In the chapter on Methodology, the Commission lists my name as one of the "substantial sources" of allegations and notes that I submitted the names of 29 suspects. It also lists Joseph Riwash as the number one supplier of suspects, having submitted 707 names which are described in the report as being "supplied at random by Yad Vashem." It is obvious therefore why most of the names submitted by the Center were already known to the Deschenes Commission. Had the Commission confirmed their receipt when originally submitted via Professor Cotler and Joseph Riwash, the misunderstanding which ensued could have been avoided. It is possible that Riwash did not mention my name as the source of his material, but that was not the case as far as the list submitted via Professor Cotler.[17]

On March 12, 1987, after practically two years of research and several technical delays, the Canadian government finally published the findings of the Deschenes Commission. According to the official commission report, there were 20 cases of suspected Nazi war criminals living in Canada which should be dealt with urgently and more than 200 additional cases in which further investigation was recommended. In more than 600 other cases the charges were either insufficient or the suspects had already died and the Commission recommended that they be closed. Despite the evidence regarding the existence in Canada of Nazi war criminals, the Commission did not recommend the establishment of a special government agency, similar to the US Office of Special Investigations, to deal with the problem. It advocated instead the establishment of a team of full-time lawyers, historians and police officials within existent frameworks and proposed increased funding for the Justice Department and the Royal Canadian Mounted Police, which would be entrusted with the responsibility for these investigations.[18]

On a practical level the Commission made several recommendations to solve the problem of Nazi war criminals in Canada. The most important was an amendment of the federal criminal code which would enable the prosecution and punishment in Canada of all suspected Nazi war criminals.[19] The Commission also called for new procedures to facilitate the revocation of Canadian citizenship,[20] as well as deportation,[21] and recommended that Canada utilize extradition in cases covered by existent treaties. As for extradition to other countries, the report called for the expansion of Canadian extradition policy and the amendment of the Canadian Extradition Act, as well as existent treaties with countries such as Israel, which hereto precluded the extradition of Nazi war criminals.[22] This latter recommendation was rejected by the Canadian government, however. In the words of Justice Minister Ramon Hnatyshyn, the existent extradition policy was considered to be "a carefully developed balance of the considerations which must apply before Canadian residents are sent for trial outside Canada."[23]

The Commission also dealt with several other important questions, the findings on some of which were not made public. Among the issues deliberated in the confidential section of the Deschenes report was a study of the involvement of Canadian politicians and officials in the admission of Nazi war criminals to Canada. According to unconfirmed press reports, research by Alti Rodal of the Commission indicated that war criminals had been given asylum in Canada and recruited as anti-Soviet agents.[24] Another question dealt with by the Commission was whether Dr. Joseph Mengele had ever entered Canada or applied for immigration to Canada. The Commission concluded beyond reasonable doubt that the infamous Auschwitz doctor had neither lived in Canada nor applied for immigration. The Commission was very critical of Sol Littman who had originally raised the possibility that Mengele had applied for a Canadian visa.[25]

Ironically, it was those charges which were apparently a key factor in the government's decision to establish a commission of inquiry on the issue of Nazi war criminals in Canada. In fact, the opening paragraph of the Minute-of-Council establishing the Deschenes Commission stated as follows: "Whereas concern has been expressed about the possibility that Joseph Mengele, an alleged Nazi war criminal, may have entered or attempted to enter Canada . . ." Only afterwards does the minute mention the concern that "other persons responsible for war crimes related to the activities of Nazi Germany during World War II . . . are currently resident in Canada."[26] It is not at all clear therefore whether the Canadian commission would have been established solely on the basis of the second concern. The fact that it took the Canadian government so long to investigate the charges and was apparently prodded into doing so only in the wake of the Mengele rumor is a clearcut indication of the government's reluctance to deal with the issue.

One of the controversial decisions made by the Commission was its exoneration of members of the Galicia Division of the Ukrainian SS. According to the Deschenes report, the charges of war crimes against members of the division had never been substantiated and mere membership was insufficient to justify prosecution "in the absence of evidence of participation in or knowledge of specific war crimes."[27] The problem was, however, that the Commission had not reached its decision on the basis of a thorough investigation of the wartime record of the Galicia Division. Despite demands that such a study be carried out, the Commission refused to launch any such investigation. The reasons for this decision were highly questionable. The Commission explained that it was not created to indict "one or several particular groups of Canadians," or "to revive old hatred that once existed between communities which should now live in peace in Canada."[28]

While the Commission's desire to preserve peace among local ethnic groups is understandable, its refusal to investigate the activities of a particular unit accused of committing war crimes, simply because it was composed of individuals of a specific ethnic origin is a concrete example of an area in which the Commission failed to fulfil its basic function. The best way to put old hatreds to rest is to determine finally the truth regarding the presence in Canada of Nazi war criminals, and not to continue to allow doubts, charges and countercharges to fan inter-ethnic tension. This was not done by the Commission, and even those interested parties who sought to present the pertinent documentation to the Commission were not allowed to do so. Sol Littman was informed in early January 1986 by Commission Counsel L. Yves Fortier QC that "the history of the 14th Volunteer Grenadier Waffen SS Division (Galician) was of no immediate interest to the Commission."[29] The failure to investigate the background and activities of a unit accused of war crimes, 1,200 to 2,000 members of which entered Canada was undoubtedly a major flaw in the investigative process carried out by the Deschenes Commission.

There were other serious problems with the inquiry conducted in Canada, several of which have been publicly exposed by Sol Littman.[30] Most relate to the research methods employed in investigating the various cases of suspected Nazis. The Commission's decision that no names would be forwarded to any East European government is a blatant example. Given the fact that a substantial number of the crimes were committed in Eastern Europe, this decision practically doomed every such investigation to failure. OSI would probably have not been able to file most of its East European cases if not for the material it obtained from the countries in which the crimes were committed. The argument advanced to justify this policy, moreover, does not make any sense. According to the report, a conscious decision was made not to forward names from the master list to East European countries for fear that "for ideological or political reasons, the recipient country might wish to publicize the names of the individuals and attempt to give the impression that the Commission or the Government of Canada had somehow conceded that these individuals were war criminals."[31] The fact of the matter was that none of these countries, some of whom had been dealing with OSI in numerous cases, had ever resorted to such tactics. The serious implications of this faulty approach are clearly delineated in the case by case descriptions which constitute the bulk of the report. In numerous cases the Commission recommends two ostensibly valid and equitable alternatives:

1. Should the Government of Canada not wish, as a matter of policy, to submit the name of the subject to the Yad Vashem archives, to the relevant Eastern bloc government or to the appropriate archival centers, the file ought to be closed.

2. Should, however, the Government of Canada decide to submit the subject's name to the Yad Vashem archive, to the relevant government or to the appropriate archival centers, the matter ought then to be reassessed and a final decision taken, depending upon the result of such inquiry.[32]

One would assume that if the Commission were indeed intent on uncovering the Nazis living in Canada it would have investigated those charges thoroughly by examining whatever documentation existed all over the world. It refrained from obtaining the pertinent material in Eastern Europe, preferring to offer this possibility merely as an alternative rather than as an obvious imperative. The above quote represents the Commission's conclusion regarding over 80 cases.

In that context, one additional criticism can be made concerning the research carried out by the Deschenes Commission. Much of the work described in the case descriptions was superfluous and indicates a lack of professional expertise. Thus in cases concerning suspects who allegedly committed crimes in East Europe, the report notes time and again that "neither the Berlin Document Center, the Central Office of Land Judicial Authorities for the Investigation of National-Socialist Crimes in Ludwigsburg, West Germany, the Central Information Office of the Federal Archives in Aachen-Kornelimunster, the German Military Service Office for notifying the next of kin of members of the former German Wehrmacht in Berlin nor the Berlin Sick Book Depository had any record of the subject."[33]

Anyone acquainted with the documentation regarding the crimes committed during the Holocaust knows very well that none of these archives contain data on most of the Eastern European collaborators. This research is in fact strikingly similar to the screening process employed by immigration officers in the DP camps in Germany after the war. They made sure to check the Berlin Document Center to determine whether a prospective immigrant had been in the SS, little realizing that even the biggest mass murderers from the Baltics and the Ukraine were not listed there.[34] Their efforts, like the research conducted in these archives by the Commission, were practically useless.

It is precisely for that reason that the recommendation by the Deschenes Commission not to establish a special agency like OSI is particularly unfortunate. OSI has proven that war criminals can be successfully prosecuted—even more than 40 years after the crimes were committed—and its success was to a large extent a result of its establishment as a separate unit devoted exclusively to a particular task. The circumstances related to the efforts to prosecute and punish the perpetrators of the Holocaust require a special framework similar to OSI. The recommendation of the Deschenes Commission against the establishment of such a unit was a mistake which ultimately seriously hampered the prosecution effort in Canada.

The reason for this decision, moreover, is the same fear of ethnic tensions which apparently haunted the efforts of the Commission and precluded various steps which could have considerably advanced the efforts to deal effectively with the problem of Nazi war criminals in Canada. To claim that the establishment of an OSI in Canada is "courting dangers which must be avoided at all costs"[35] is an affront to the efforts of the US authorities and an indication that fear of the emigre communities wielded undue influence on the Commission's recommendations. This latter factor may also explain the government's refusal to adopt deportation and extradition, two of the three alternatives proposed by the Commission as a means of solving the problem of Nazi war criminals in Canada. Despite the fact that both have been used successfully by the United States, the Canadian government chose to reject them, preferring prosecution in Canada. The primary reason for choosing the alternative, which ultimately was the most expensive and yielded the least results, was probably their assumption that this solution would prove the least painful to Canada's large ethnic minorities

In mid-September 1987 the Canadian Parliament passed amendments to the criminal code which enable the prosecution of Nazi war criminals in Canada.[36] This legislation became law (Bill 71) shortly thereafter, thereby setting the stage for the trial and punishment of Nazi and other war criminals in Canada. (Unlike the laws subsequently passed in Australia and Great Britain, the Canadian bill covers all war criminals, not only Nazis.)[37]

Shortly after the passage of the law, Sol Littman wrote to Justice Minister Ramon Hnatyshyn urging him to implement the war crimes bill in six specific cases, mostly from the Soviet Union. Littman also sent Hnatyshyn the pertinent evidence which he had collected in these cases noting that: "In the past, Canada has tended to ignore such information".[38] Now that the proposed war crimes legislation had become law, Littman pointed out that there was in effect no reason why the government should not proceed with the prosecution of the Nazi war criminals living in Canada.

While Hnatyshyn did not immediately take action in any of the cases mentioned by the Wiesenthal Center, there were some positive developments prior to and immediately after the passage of the law. These related to the case of Toronto resident Imre Finta who had served as head of the Hungarian gendarmerie in Szeged and had played an active role in the concentration and deportation of the Jews of that city to the

Auschwitz death camp. Finta had been exposed as a Nazi war criminal several years earlier by Sabina Citron, a survivor who headed the Canadian Holocaust Remembrance Association. In response, Finta called her a liar and she sued him for libel. In addition, Canadian television had also broadcast allegations that Finta was a war criminal, and he responded by suing the television station for libel.

Canadian television prepared extensively for the trial, but after it had already obtained evidence in Hungary, Austria, and Israel, Finta withdrew his suit on September 2, 1986. The court ordered the former gendarmerie officer to pay the court costs, and when he failed to do so, Canadian television seized and sold his home at an auction. On November 5, 1987, Finta failed to defend himself against Sabina Citron's libel suit and he was ordered to pay her $30,000 plus court costs. Shortly thereafter, in early December 1987, Finta became the first person charged with war crimes under the new Canadian law.[39]

In the meantime, our research in Jerusalem yielded the names of many suspected Nazi war criminals who emigrated to Canada after World War II. On March 3, 1988, Sol Littman forwarded a list of 21 Lithuanian suspects, whose names had been supplied by Y.S., to Justice Minister Hnatyshyn in Ottawa. Most of the individuals on the list had served in local police units which had carried out the murder of the Jews in various locations in Lithuania.[40] Although the submission of the list received extensive positive coverage in the Canadian media,[41] the government did not appear to be making much progress, in practical terms, on the prosecution of the Nazi war criminals in Canada.

In July 1988 Sol Littman travelled to Lithuania to attempt to do research on some of the suspects the Center had identified in Canada. In Vilnius he met with the deputy procurator of Lithuania and was able to obtain documents and witness statements regarding several of the 21 suspects whose names the Wiesenthal Center had submitted to the Canadian authorities in March 1988.[42] Nonetheless, when the War Crimes Investigations Unit of the Royal Mounted Canadian Police attempted to enlist the assistance of the Jewish community in its search for witnesses in the cases under investigation (including some which had been submitted by the Center), they did not turn to Sol.[43] Apparently his persistent efforts over the years to goad the Canadian authorities into action against Nazi war criminals had left a bitter residue, which did not augur well for future cooperation.

In the meantime, however, we continued our efforts in Jerusalem and Toronto to uncover additional Nazis criminals living in Canada, and before long we were able to submit an additional list of suspects to the Canadian Justice Department. On April 7, 1988 Sol Littman submitted a list of 25 additional Lithuanian and Latvian suspects whose names we had uncovered from a variety of sources. Some appeared on the lists supplied by Y.S., a few were named in Soviet publications, while the majority were taken from documents in Israeli archives and survivor testimony. Given the advanced age of several of the suspects, we realized that it was likely that not all were still alive, but we nonetheless submitted the names of those born before 1900 for the sake of the historical record and on the outside chance that any of them might, against the odds, still be alive.[44] (We also took into account the fact that in many cases Displaced Persons lied to the authorities regarding their dates of birth). At the same time we also gave in additional emigration data on several suspects whose names we had previously submitted to the Canadian authorities. In particular we focused on Ivan Sowhan who had served as chief of the Ukrainian police in Dobromyl and Przemysl, Poland during the war and according to testimony in the Yad Vashem Archives had actively participated in the murder of numerous Jews in both towns.[45]

Six weeks later I met at Yad Vashem with three members of the Canadian war crimes unit who were visiting Israel to find documentation and witnesses. They requested further clarification on nine cases which we had submitted to the Canadian authorities and we also discussed the sensitive issue of the relationship, or lack thereof, between the Wiesenthal Center and the Canadian Nazi war crimes unit. It was obvious that the authorities still viewed us more as adversaries than partners and I tried hard therefore not only to offer assistance but to allay their anxieties.[46] Unfortunately, in this respect, even the best intentions did not always yield concrete results. Less than three weeks later William Hobson, head of the unit, informed Sol Littman that he was confident that the RCMP would "take your offer of assistance [in finding witnesses - E.Z.] into consideration should the need arise."[47] Given the dismal record of the Canadian unit up to that point, it was obvious that the need was already acute, but the readiness for cooperation with the Center was in extremely limited supply in Ottawa.

In October 1989 I met Hobson in London and submitted a list of 22 members of the 12th Lithuanian Auxiliary Police Battalion who had emigrated to Canada after World War II.[48] At the same time, similar lists were submitted to the Australian and British authorities,[49] who had convened (together with the Americans) for a special conference sponsored by the British All-Party Parliamentary War Crimes Group to help convince the British government and British public opinion regarding the need for appropriate legislation which would enable the prosecution of the Nazi war criminals in Great Britain. And while I was impressed by Hobson's dedication and sincerity, I was unable to convince him to allow us to play a more active role in the investigations carried out by his unit. Despite the notable lack of success which had hereto been achieved by the Canadian team, its director still preferred to keep the Wiesenthal Center at arm's length. Perhaps it was because the submission of our lists had created additional pressure on Hobson to achieve concrete results. Thus for example after I submitted the list of the members of the 12th Lithuanian Auxiliary Police Battalion who had emigrated to Canada, the *Toronto Star* harshly criticized the government's record to date:

> In view of the Wiesenthal Center's credentials and the horrible nature of the allegations, Justice Minister Doug Lewis is obliged to order a swift and thorough investigation.
>
> But if experience can serve as a guide, there is considerable doubt that Ottawa will move decisively before the biological clock runs out on these suspects, if indeed they are still in Canada and alive.
>
> Despite its promises of action after the Deschenes Commission reported in 1987 that there were at least 20 solid cases that could be prosecuted in Canada, the federal government has brought only one suspect to trial - and that trial has been proceeding at a snail's pace.
>
> Victims of atrocities deserve better than this.[50]

In that respect, we still had not been convinced that the Canadian government was so good at prosecuting Nazi war criminals, that we could abandon our double function as an independent lobby for government action and a research agency. Thus we continued to be viewed as adversaries by Hobson and his successors despite our best efforts to convince them otherwise.

In early 1990, two additional men were charged with war crimes. In January, Michael Pawlowski was accused of participating in the murder of 400 Jews from the village of Snow on or about September 17, 1942 and about two weeks later, 8 other Jews who had escaped the initial killing, and 80 Poles near the village of Yeskovichi (both Byelorussia) in the summer of 1942. In February, Stephen Reistetter was charged with deporting 3,000 Jews from Bardejev, Slovakia to Poland in April and May of 1942. A few months later most of the deportees were sent to their death in Treblinka. At the time that they were charged, Pawlowski was 72 and living in Renfrew, Ontario. Reistetter, who was 75 years old, was residing in St. Catherines, Ontario. While these indictments represented a significant step forward, it was obvious that the two cases were merely the tip of the iceberg as far as Canada was concerned. In fact, according to Hobson, his unit was actively investigating 45 cases and that additional charges would be laid within six months. (Of the 45 cases then under review 18 were among the 20 identified by the Deschenes Commission as worthy of urgent action.)[51] To our mind, however, this was a conservative estimate, since by this point, we had already begun to review the material in the Kunichowsky collection and were certain that it would yield dozens of new cases for Canada.[52]

Before our new list was submitted, the efforts to prosecute Nazi war criminals in Canada were dealt two extremely harsh blows. The first related to the Pawlowski case. In early May 1990 Justice James Chadwick of the Ontario Supreme Court ruled that a commission established by the prosecution to videotape the testimony of eleven elderly witnesses living in the Soviet Union could not travel there for that purpose. Chadwick explained his decision by noting such factors as the passage of time since the crime was committed; the prepackaging of witnesses and evidence by the Soviet authorities; the limited ability of the defense to investigate and the difficulty of a jury to determine the credibility of videotaped testimony. Although Chadwick left open the possibility of bringing the witnesses to Canada, his decision made the prosecution effort much more difficult than it should have been.[53]

The second blow was even harsher. On May 25, 1991 an Ontario Supreme Court jury acquitted Imre Finta of charges of manslaughter and other atrocities against more than eight thousand Jews. The verdict came as a shock because Finta did not even testify on his own behalf nor did the defence bring a single witness. On the contrary, the only evidence presented to the court regarding the events in Szeged were gruesome stories of how the Jews of that town were rounded up like animals, robbed of their valuables and deported to camps.[54] The problem was, however, that defense attorney Douglas Christie succeeded in stacking the jury with people who were opposed to the war crimes bill and used the courtroom as a forum for anti-Semitic propaganda.[55] If we add the fact that Judge Campbell told the jurors that it would be dangerous to convict Finta of manslaughter because there was no medical evidence as to the cause of death of the deportees, it is perhaps not surprising that the former captain of the Hungarian gendarmerie in Szeged walked out of the Toronto courtroom a free man.[56] Only after the trial, the *Toronto Star* revealed that when he was arrested, Finta admitted that he had signed the order for the deportation of the Jews of Szeged. Since the police failed to inform him of his rights at the time of his arrest, the judge ruled that the information was inadmissible.[57] The prosecution has appealed the case and still await a verdict.

In the summer of 1990 we continued our research on the Kunichowsky collection, seeking additional witnesses for the cases of the suspects who had emigrated to Canada. Thus, for example, on June 14 we published an ad in the *Canadian Jewish News* asking potential witnesses from thirty different Lithuanian towns and villages to contact the Center.[58] To our chagrin, however, the ad did not elicit much information of value (one additional suspect and a few leads on potential witnesses.)[59] Given the extremely high rate of victimology in these locations (over 90%), the meager results were not surprising, but were nonetheless disappointing.

About this time, the Canadian government was suddenly forced to face a new challenge on the war crimes front. Arthur Rudolph, a prominent Nazi rocket scientist who had employed slave labor at the Dora concentration camp during World War II and had voluntarily relinquished his American citizenship and left the country in 1984 rather than face prosecution by OSI, came to Canada in July 1990. Although the trip was ostensibly to visit his daughter, in reality he sought to contest in Canada the agreement he had signed in the United States six years earlier. The Canadian government, however, immediately referred Rudolph to an immigration inquiry on the basis that there were reasonable grounds to believe that he was a Nazi war criminal. Although the hearings in his case were only determined several months later, the German scientist left Canada a month after his arrival. On January 11, 1991, the charges against Rudolph were confirmed and he was ordered deported from the country, a decision subsequently upheld by the Federal Court of Appeal. Rudolph's request to submit the case to the Canadian Supreme Court was rejected on October 8, 1992.[60]

Before this victory was achieved by the Canadian authorities, we made preparations to submit a particularly important additional list of suspects to the Nazi war crimes unit. Comprising 81 suspects, it represented the total number of suspects who had emigrated to Canada from among the 1,284 Nazi collaborators named in the testimonies of the Kunichowsky collection which had finally been deposited in Yad Vashem less than a year previously. Each of the testimonies had been notarized and signed by the witnesses, at least some of whom were still alive. While it is true that in several cases our information was incomplete due to a lack of biographical data, quite a few appeared to have excellent potential. Unfortunately, many appeared to be too old and most likely would have passed away long before we uncovered their emigration to Canada.

Sol Littman and I submitted the list to Peter Kremer, the new director of the Canadian war crimes unit, in Ottawa on October 18, 1990. At the meeting we again tried to present our case for closer cooperation between the Center and the Canadian authorities, hoping that Kremer might view this issue more positively than his predecessor. While we were favorably impressed by the new director, we did not obtain an ironclad commitment from him to work more closely with us. At a press conference we held afterward in the Parliament building, Sol and I stressed the importance of the Kunichowsky collection, its scope and uniqueness, as well as the enormity of the crimes committed by local collaborators in Lithuania, including the intelligentsia and even women. And while we were not certain how many of the suspects were still alive and living in Canada, the documents submitted to the authorities were unequivocal proof of the "extensive scope of the problem and the enormous amount of work still to be done."[61]

In addition to the 81 new suspects whose names were submitted to the Canadian authorities, we also gave them extensive documentation, including witness statements taken immediately after the war, and a lengthy, current list of potential witnesses in Canada, the United States, and Israel, regarding a case which I had previously made known to the Deschenes Commission. The person in question was Antanas Kenstavicius, who at the time was 82 years old and living in Hope, British Columbia. He had served as the commander of the Lithuanian police in the Svencionys district during the war. According to testimony in the

Yad Vashem Archives, Kenstavicius had in the fall of 1941 carried out the expulsion and concentration of all the Jews of the Svencionys district in the former Polish army barracks at Polygon. There the Lithuanian police under his command beat and tortured the Jews, raped Jewish women and stole valuables before the mass murder of the Jews was carried out. Kenstavicius himself was also alleged to have taken part in the persecution of the Jews and to have personally carried out the execution of 33 Polish intellectuals and 3 Jews in the Jewish cemetery at Svencionys. After the war Kenstavicius was in a DP camp in Kempten and emigrated to Canada on April 30, 1948 as a railroad worker. Despite the efforts of the Judicial Department of the Central Committee of Liberated Jews in Germany,[62] no legal steps were taken in this case and Kenstavicius began life anew in Canada, unhindered by his past. Over the coming months we pressed the Canadian authorities regarding this case,[63] but to date Kenstavicius has not yet been indicted.

In early 1991 there was more bad news on the war crimes front. On March 4, 1991, the government decided not to proceed with its case against Stephen Reistetter who had previously been indicted for his role in the deportation of 3,000 Jews from Bardejev, Slovakia to the death camps in Poland.[64] The reason for the government's decision was that two of its witnesses had died, and one had become too ill to testify, but according to David Matas, a noted expert on war crimes cases in Canada, the government could still have proceeded with the case. The government also erred, in his opinion, by acquitting Reistetter, a step which would preclude an extradition request, rather than asking for a stay in the proceedings. According to Matas, the government should have also considered having Reistetter denaturalized and deported.[65]

On June 21, 1991, the government suffered another setback when Justice James Chadwick again ruled that the government could not videotape evidence in the Soviet Union for the Pawlowski case. A month earlier, four of the original eight charges against the former Byelorussian policeman had been dropped due to the death of an elderly witness living in the Soviet Union, and the ruling by Chadwick effectively prevented the prosecution from presenting a credible case. In Chadwick's opinion, the defendant would not have been able to defend himself properly if the testimony were presented to the jury on a television screen and therefore he refused to approve the sending of a rogatory commission to the Soviet Union.[66] When Sol Littman, accompanied by a delegation of concerned lawyers, met some three weeks later with Justice Minister Kim Campbell to discuss the problems plaguing war crimes prosecutions in Canada and to once again offer the Center's assistance, the usual arguments regarding private agencies, privacy, and suspect's rights were marshalled to maintain the status quo.[67] In short, despite the setbacks, the government was sticking to its hereto unsuccessful policies.

In October, however, there finally was some good news. On October 22, 1991 Judge Frank Collier of the Federal Court of Canada ruled that Jacob Luitjens had obtained his Canadian citizenship by concealing his past as a Nazi collaborator in Holland. This decision, which was delivered 29 months after the completion of the presentation of the evidence, paved the way for the deportation from Canada of the retired botany professor who had been convicted in Holland in absentia in 1948 for his crimes.[68] Less than three weeks later, Luitjens was stripped of his citizenship by a cabinet decision, but it was months before the Department of Immigration convened a deportation hearing against him, and even longer before he was finally deported from Canada on November 26, 1992.[69]

On February 27, 1992 Sol Littman met again with Peter Kremer and handed him the names of three additional Lithuanian suspects who had emigrated to Canada after World War II.[70] The meeting, as expected, did not lead to any changes in Canadian policy vis-a-vis cooperation with the Wiesenthal Center. The unit did, however, avail itself shortly thereafter of a guide to the KGB's Nazi war crimes files that our office in Jerusalem prepared based on the testimony of a high-ranking officer in that organization who dealt extensively with the subject while in the Soviet Union. At the same time, we passed on the name of an additional suspect whose whereabouts in Canada were uncovered as a result of our investigations regarding Evald Mikson, an Estonian living in Iceland, who had played an active role in the persecution and murder of the Jews of Estonia. Martin Jensen, one of Mikson's subordinates at the Estonian Political Police, was discovered living at Hillsdale Avenue in Toronto by Thor Jonsson and Karl Birgisson, two Icelandic journalists who were investigating the Mikson case. According to a document signed by Jensen, the Estonian Political Police had, during the period from August 28, 1941 until July 1, 1942, arrested 9,308 Communists of whom 1,159 had been put to death and 693 Jews all of whom were executed.[71] The numerous documents in the archives in

Tallinn which bear Jensen's signature would have helped build a good case against the Estonian emigre, but unfortunately he died on August 8, 1992, several months after we alerted the Canadian authorities to his presence in the country.[72]

In the spring of 1992 the Canadian government announced that it would complete its war crimes investigations by March 1994, a decision which was roundly criticized by the leadership of Canadian Jewry. Although the move was accompanied by a directive to give the Nazi war crimes unit added staff and budget during the final two years of its operations,[73] it was obvious that its closure would primarily benefit the subjects of its investigations, and therefore the highly justified protests.

In July 1992 I met twice in Jerusalem with a lawyer and an investigator from the Canadian war crimes unit. These meetings were the first in which we received specific requests for information regarding suspects whose names the Wiesenthal Center had submitted to the Canadian authorities. Thus we were asked to provide additional information in dozens of cases of suspects who had been discovered living in Canada during the past six years thanks to the lists we had submitted.[74]

Shortly thereafter, Sol Littman used the Access to Information Act to obtain documents regarding the scope of the Nazi war crimes investigations being carried out in Canada. According to Justice Ministry and RCMP documentation, the government had 1,117 ongoing investigations of which about 300 were considered high-priority. In addition, 799 investigations had been concluded either because the suspect had died or there was insufficient evidence to proceed. In response to Littman's question whether the cases had been prioritized, the RCMP replied that it was prepared to do so, but only if he was prepared to pay $12,750 to have the work done. Needless to say, Sol refused.[75]

In December 1992 the Canadian government charged a fifth suspect with Nazi war crimes. Radislav Grujicic, an 81 year old resident of Windsor, Ontario, was charged with ten counts of premeditated murder and one count each of conspiracy to murder and kidnap. As a senior official of the Serbian police in Belgrade, he played an active role in the murder of Communists during the period from June 22, 1941 to October 1, 1944.[76] The filing of the Grujicic case was followed several weeks later by a statement by Kremer indicating that the government hoped to take legal steps against 20 suspected Nazi war criminals within the coming fifteen months, i.e. by the March 1994 date for closing down the Canadian Nazi war crimes unit. He added, however, that

"There are no guarantees there will be any prosecutions,"[77] an assessment which appears to be far more realistic than the hope that legal steps could be taken even against the twenty best cases in Canada.

The practical implication of Kremer's announcement was that the unit would be concentrating its resources and manpower on the cases already under investigation This development posed a serious dilemma for us. I already had in my possession several dozen names of additional suspects whom I had recently uncovered on the basis of documents smuggled out of newly-independent Lithuania. On the one hand, why bother submitting the names which would distract the unit from concentrating on its high priority cases which were (I hoped) close to being brought to trial. On the other hand, I certainly had an obligation to submit whatever relevant information I had in my possession regarding Nazi war crimes suspects residing in Canada, even if only for the historical record. There was, however, one additional factor which ultimately played a role. Perhaps if we submitted the names of additional suspects regarding whose crimes there was solid documentation, the Canadian government might delay the closing down of the Nazi war crimes unit. With that in mind we sent Peter Kremer two lists with a total of 59 individuals who had served in the Lithuanian Auxiliary Police Battalions, and their predecessor the National Labor Defense Battalion, which had played an active role in the persecution and murder of Jews both in Lithuania and elsewhere in Eastern Europe.[78] Among the individuals whose names were on the list were several who were sent on "secret missions" in the summer and fall of 1941, a term commonly used to refer to operations to liquidate Jewish communities. Also of importance was the relatively young age of many of the suspects, quite a few of whom were "only" in their early seventies (born 1921-1923).[79]

As of this writing, March 1994 is only five months away and not a single additional case had been filed by the Canadian war crimes unit. In June 1993 I wrote to Peter Kremer offering the services of an office we planned to open in Vilnius to do historical research and find witnesses for the dozens of cases of Baltic war criminals which the Wiesenthal Center had uncovered all over the world.[80] He declined our assistance, however, noting that the government's "investigations must be conducted independently."[81] Thus another potentially valuable opportunity for meaningful cooperation was rejected and the results speak for themselves. If the Canadian government had been so eminently successful in prosecuting the Nazi war criminals residing in the country our assistance would indeed have been superfluous, but that unfortunately has not been the case. Left to its own resources, the government has failed miserably in its task, with the real winners being some of the worst of Hitler's henchmen. These criminals emigrated to Canada thinking it would be a safe haven. Except for a few years in which a real fear of prosecution existed, it turns out that as far as the overwhelming majority of the Canadian perpetrators of the Holocaust are concerned, they were, unfortunately, absolutely correct.

Notes

1. "Nazi-hunter Gives Official 26 Suspects," *Winnipeg Free Press*, October 31, 1986.

2. The Deschenes Commission was established by Order-in-Council PC-1985-348 on February 7, 1985, Deschenes Commission Report, p. 111.

3. See, for example, "500 Nazis Here," *Calgary Sun*, April 26, 1985.

4. Letter of Efraim Zuroff to the Deschenes Commission, July 6, 1985, SWCA.

5. Sol Littman, *War Criminal On Trial: The Rauca Case*, Toronto, 1983; Deschenes Commission Report, pp. 90-91.

6. YVA, M-9/15(6); M-21/III/37; 0-33/672; WLA, 539/24, testimony of Zelda Hait, Bat Yam, Israel; *Daugavas Vanagi*, pp. 73, 90-91; *"Political Refugees" Unmasked!*, pp. 41, 174-79.

7. Roster of member of Vilnius Sonderkommando, SWCA.

8. YVA, M-9/15(6); M-21/III/8, 37; 0-33/672; WLA, 549/22, 24; *Daugavas Vanagi*, pp. 17, 34, 73, 101, 123; *"Political Refugees" Unmasked!*, pp. 69, 119, 158-67, 183, 188, 192.

9. WLA, 539/22, 24; *Daugavas Vanagi*, pp. 40, 47, 50, 53-56; *"Political Refugees" Unmasked!*, pp. 67-79, 98-108, 132, 137, 158-67, 214.

10. YVA, M-9/15(6); M-21/515; WLA, 539/25; *Yahadut Lita*, Vol. IV, pp. 246-47, 251-52, 306-7, 329-31, 336-38, 360; list of Lithuanian collaborators who emigrated to the West, submitted to Lt. Col. Menachem Russek, Israel police and OSI by Zelig Gelinski, January 24, 1982.

11. YVA, M-21/350; Valery Styrkul, *We Accuse*, Kiev, 1984, p. 131, 139.

12. "The Campaign against the U.S. Justice Department's Prosecution of Suspected Nazi War Criminals," pp. 13-15.

13. Greg Weston, "Nothing New in List of 'War Criminals,'" *Ottawa Citizen*, October 31, 1986, p. A14.

14. Letters of Efraim Zuroff to Professor Irwin Cotler and the Deschenes Commission, both July 6, 1985, SWCA.

15. See, for example, YVA, M-21/III/43; M-21/515; M-9/95.

16. See, for example, the lists of Lithuanian war criminals compiled by survi-

vors after the war, YVA, M-9/15(6, 6a).

17. Deschenes Commission Report, pp. 47-8.

18. Ibid., pp. 827-30.

19. Ibid., pp. 157-63.

20. Ibid., pp. 226-27

21. Ibid., pp. 238-39.

22. Ibid., pp. 87-111.

23. "Report on Ex-Nazis Presented," *Facts on File World News Digest*, March 20, 1987, p. 107.

24. Ibid., p. 107; "Canada Misled on War Criminals, Study Says," *Edmonton Journal*, August 7, 1987.

25. Deschenes Commission Report, pp. 67-82.

26. Ibid., p. 17.

27. Ibid., p. 261.

28. Ibid., p. 254.

29. Letter of L. Yves Fortier, QC to Sol Littman, January 6, 1986, SWCA.

30. See, for example, Neil Macdonald, "Deschenes Report Evaporates in Face of Reality," *Ottawa Citizen*, March 14, 1987.

31. Deschenes Commission Report, p. 59.

32. See, for example, Cases no. 8, 21, 24, 39, 45, 53, 65, 76, ibid., pp. 279, 288, 290, 300, 303, 304, 309, 317, 325. In most of the cases the recommendation regarding research did not include Yad Vashem and was to "the relevant East European country or to the appropriate archival sources."

33. See, for example, Case No. 1, 232, 569, ibid., pp. 275, 417, 628.

34. *Quiet Neighbors*, pp. 21-22.

35. Deschenes Commission Report, p. 829.

36. Nomi Morris, "Canadian Deputies Vote to Allow Trial of War Criminals," *Jerusalem Post*, September 14, 1987, p. 4.

37. David Matas, "Nazi War Criminals in Canada," Report of the Institute for International Affairs of B'nai B'rith Canada, Downsview, 1992, p. 31 (hereafter - Matas Report).

38. "Ottawa gets list in hunt for Nazis," *Globe and Mail*, October 23, 1987.

39. Gary Oakes and Kevin Donovan, "Metro man, 76, Facing Charges in War Crimes Against 8,615 Jews," *Toronto Star*, December 10, 1987, p. 1.

40. Letter of Sol Littman to Ramon Hnatyshyn, March 3, 1988, SWCA.

41. See for example Sherri Aikenhead, "Hunting for Names," *Maclean's*, March 14, 1988, p. 14; Rudy Platiel, "Canada Given New War Criminals List," *Globe and Mail*, March 8, 1988.

42. Sol Littman, "Report; Lithuanian Visit July 9-18, 1988," SWCA.

43. "War Crimes Witnesses," *Canadian Jewish News*, December 15, 1988.

44. "List of Suspected Nazi War Criminals in Canada - List #3," submitted April 7, 1988, SWCA.

45. Yad Vashem Archives M-2/87; letter of Sol Littman to William Hobson, April 4, 1989, SWCA.

46. Memo of Efraim Zuroff to Rabbis Hier and Cooper, "Regarding Meetings at Yad Vashem with Members of the Crimes against Humanity and War Crimes Section of the Canadian Justice Ministry and the Royal Canadian Mounted Police," May 18, 1989, SWCA.

47. Letter of William Hobson to Sol Littman, June 6, 1989, SWCA.

48. Letter of Efraim Zuroff to William Hobson, October 23, 1989, SWCA.

49. David Horovitz, "Nazi Hunter Tracks Down Names of 136 Alleged War Criminals Who Fled to West," *Jerusalem Post*, October 22, 1989.

50. See for example "As the Clock Runs Out," *Toronto Star*, October 31, 1989.

51. Paul Lungen, "Renfrew Man Charged under War Crimes Law," *Canadian Jewish News*, January 4, 1990; Matas Report, p. 24; "Nazi War Crime Suspect Acquitted in Canada," Associated Press, May 25, 1990.

52. Gordon Barthos, "Ottawa Gets War Crime Suspect List," *Toronto Star*, April 25, 1990; Paul Lungen, "Canada Is Expected to Review New War Crimes List," *Canadian Jewish News*, May 3, 1990, p. 4.

53. Paul Lungen, "War Crimes Trial Suffers a Setback," *Canadian Jewish News*, May 10, 1990.

54. "Nazi War Crime Suspect Acquitted in Canada," Associated Press, May 25, 1990.

55. Matas Report, pp. 1-19.

56. See note 17.

57. Ben Kayfetz, "Canadian Acquittal Shocks Community," *Jewish Chronicle*, June 1, 1990, p. 40.

58. "Were You There?," *Canadian Jewish News*, June 14, 1990.

59. See the memo of Sol Littman to Aaron Breitbart, Simon Wiesenthal and Efraim Zuroff, June 18, 1990; memo of Sol Littman to Efraim Zuroff, June 20, 1990, SWCA.

60. Matas Report, p. 42.

61. David Vienneau, "Report Names 81 Alleged Nazis Living in Canada," *Toronto Star*, October 18, 1990, p. 1.

62. See Kenstavicius file, Yad Vashem Archives, M-21/III/515.

63. See for example letter of Efraim Zuroff and Sol Littman to Peter Kremer, December 11, 1990, SWCA.

64. David Vienneau, "Nazi-hunters Cope with Setbacks," *Toronto Star*, March 6, 1991.

65. Matas Report, pp. 29-30.

66. Sean Upton, "War Crimes Case Setback," *Ottawa Citizen*, June 22, 1991 p. 1.

67. Sol Littman, "Meeting With Justice Minister Kim Campbell, Ottawa, July 10, 1991," SWCA.

68. Rudy Platiel, "Court Rules against Luitjens" *Globe and Mail*, October 24, 1991.

69. Matas Report, pp. 31-41.

70. Memo from Sol Littman to Efraim Zuroff along with "Supplementary List of Lithuanian Suspects Who Emigrated to Canada after World War II," March 3, 1992, SWCA.

71. Letter of Efraim Zuroff to Peter Kremer, April 3, 1992, SWCA.

72. Phone conversation with Nazi war crimes unit, October 22, 1992, SWCA.

73. Uri Nir, "Ha-Kehilla ha-Yehudit be-Kanada Mitnagedet Le-Kviyat Mo'ed Acharon La-Chakirot Neged Poshim Nazim," *Ha-Aretz*, May 17, 1992, p. 5a.

74. Letter of Efraim Zuroff to James Mathieson , July 15, 1992, SWCA.

75. David Vienneau, "1,000 Nazi Suspects Probed," *Toronto Star*, August 12, 1992, p. 1.

76. "Canadian Charged with War Crimes Was Once Hired by CIA, Says Group," *Bnai Brith Messenger*, December 25, 1992.

77. Paul Lungen, " Grujucic Pleads Not Guilty to War Crimes," *Canadian Jewish News*, January 28, 1993.

78. Letters of Sol Littman to Peter Kremer, April 2 and 29, 1993, SWCA.

79. "Canada—List of Suspects by Categories," January, 1993 SWCA.

80. Letter of Efraim Zuroff to Peter Kremer June 7, 1993, SWCA.

81. Letter of Peter Kremer to Efraim Zuroff, July 16, 1993, SWCA.

12

Sweden—A Scandinavian Haven for Baltic War Criminals

One of the countries where we encountered stiff government opposition to our efforts to prosecute Nazi war criminals was Sweden. In early October 1986 I compiled a list of fourteen suspects who had escaped to Sweden after the Second World War. While the crimes these individuals were accused of were similar to those committed by the suspects whose names had been submitted to other Western governments, there were several unique features about the Swedish list. First, every one of the suspects was Latvian. Second, with a few exceptions, all had arrived in Sweden directly from Latvia and had not previously been in DP camps in Germany. For this reason, I hardly found any data on their emigration in the ITS records. Unlike most of the names on the other lists we had submitted the sources of the majority of the allegations in these cases were Soviet publications.[1] Our public opinion campaign in Sweden began almost inadvertently. In an interview in the *Jerusalem Post*, Rabbi Cooper indicated that we had found material on Sweden and that the Center was going to submit a list of suspected Nazi war criminals to the Swedish government.[2] Shortly thereafter, Arne Lapidus, the local correspondent of the Swedish daily *Expressen* wrote an extensive story on my research for the Center and our campaign to bring Nazi war criminals to justice. Without identifying the criminals, whose names I refused to divulge, he described some of the crimes they were alleged to have committed, the positions they occupied during the war, and noted where some were living in Sweden.[3] Lapidus' article in *Expressen* made quite an impact. I was literally overwhelmed with phone calls from the Swedish media who were anxious to uncover as many details as possible regarding the suspects, especially their current whereabouts.

Among the most persistent journalists was Ann-Katrin Hagberg of *Folket*, a newspaper in Eskilstuna, where one of the suspects was reportedly residing. Her persistence yielded some interesting results. In her search for the suspect in question, who had served as commander of a local police station in Riga, she uncovered another Latvian living in

Eskilstuna who had served in the Latvian police during the Second World War. Zanis Fonzovs claimed that he had been a member of the local police in the town of Mersags for eight months in 1941 but that all he did was keep the streets clean. He painted a very sanguine picture of the activities of the Latvian police during the war and denied that there were any Nazi war criminals living in Eskilstuna.[4] Fonzovs was not the person on our list, but I thought that since he had served in the Latvian police during the critical period when most of Latvian Jewry was murdered, he too might have played a role in the persecution. As it turned out, however, there were apparently no Jews living in Mersags during the Second World War.[5]

The interview with Fonzovs reinforced my conviction that intelligence activities among the emigre communities could help us uncover numerous suspects, particularly in Sweden, whom we otherwise would have never been able to find. According to Fonzovs, for example, he personally had assisted 1,666 Latvians escape by sea to Sweden.[6] Given the percentage of criminals among those who emigrated to Western democracies, it is most likely that the number of perpetrators living in Sweden was much higher than the number of suspects on our initial list. This was particularly true because the documentation which had enabled us to track down so many of the criminals who had emigrated to the United States, Australia and Canada was for the most part not as effective in uncovering the escapees to Sweden.

Besides creating an uproar in Sweden, the article in *Expressen* put me into an unpleasant situation vis-à-vis Mr. Wiesenthal. The same day that it appeared he phoned me, clearly quite upset, because he was getting calls from all over Europe enquiring whether he had closed down his office. In the course of the interview, Lapidus had asked me two interconnected questions; how I accounted for the renewed campaign to bring Nazis to justice, and why these same Nazis had not yet been discovered. I replied that a new generation of Nazi-hunters had brought renewed energy to the campaign to prosecute the perpetrators of the Holocaust,[7] little thinking that anyone would interpret that comment as an insult or criticism of a veteran like Mr. Wiesenthal who had almost single-handedly kept the issue alive during the many years when most people preferred to forget those events. My intention was merely to describe a new phenomenon that had favorably affected efforts to prosecute Nazis the world over. Perhaps something was lost in the Swedish translation, perhaps there was some sort of misunderstanding regarding my intention. I explained to Mr. Wiesenthal that I certainly had no intention of closing down his office. At the same time he praised the Center's efforts, noting how important it was to ensure that the criminals know that we have not forgotten their crimes.[8]

The extensive coverage of our efforts in the Swedish media aroused considerable opposition among local emigre groups. A spokesman for the Estonians living in Sweden, for example, told the Scandinavian news agency (Tidningarnas Telegrambyra) that the Soviet Union was behind the "attempts to discredit the Baltic people" and accused Simon Wiesenthal of "running errands" for the Russians. According to Ants Kippar, the victims killed by these individuals were Communists who had murdered Estonians. In response to such charges, we were very careful to point out that although our campaign was directed at individuals not at ethnic groups, the evidence of local collaboration and active participation in mass murder in the Baltics was overwhelming. As far as the accusations regarding fabrication of evidence by the Soviets, we maintained that the Soviets' demonstrably poor record on human rights did not ipso facto make authentic documentation regarding Nazi war criminals counterfeit.[9]

Meanwhile, in early November, I uncovered seven additional suspects who were reported to be living in Sweden. This list was composed exclusively of Estonians and was based on Soviet publications.[10] Among the suspects were the director of the Department of Internal Affairs of the Estonian collaborationist government, and officers of the Estonian political and security police. This brought the number of suspects to 21, but the list submitted to the Swedish government had only twelve names, since those born before 1900 and/or those not accused of active participation in persecution and/or murder were deleted. A delegation from the Center handed in the list at the Swedish Embassy in Washington on November 18, 1986 but the ambassador did not accept it personally.[11] Upset by the news reports which preceded its submission, he preferred to entrust that task to one of his subordinates, Ulf Hjertonsson.

On the day that the list was submitted in Washington, as well as the next day, the Swedish press was full of reports on the list, including full details regarding the allegations.[12] *Svenska Dagbladet* carried an interview with Mr. Wiesenthal[13] and Arne Lapidus quickly filed another extensive story from Israel.[14] Government officials were quick to point out in interviews, however, that there appeared to be little chance of

legal action being taken against the suspects. Justice Ministry spokesman Johan Munck noted that there was a statute of limitations in
Swedish law which precluded prosecution of even the most serious
crimes more than 25 years after they had been committed. According
to Munck, even if the suspects were located, they could neither be prosecuted nor deported to any other country. The only legal option available was that they could sue whomever publicly accused them of
committing these crimes. On November 19, 1986 Prime Minister Ingvar Carlsson said that his government would nonetheless examine the
allegations,[15] so at that point we were still hopeful that some measure
of justice might be achieved. At the same time, the emigre groups continued their attack on the Center by accusing us, among other things,
of making a deal with the Soviets to besmirch émigré Balts in return for
the release of Soviet Jews.[16]

I had an opportunity to respond to these charges, as well as to
address the legal issues, in interviews that week on Swedish radio and
television. Ake Wiklund, foreign affairs correspondent for Swedish
radio, focused primarily on the issue of the statute of limitations in an
interview conducted in Jerusalem and Swedish television correspondent Bertil Karlefors pressed me on the question of Soviet evidence in a
news feature filmed in my home in Efrat. As far as the statute of limitations was concerned, I responded by posing a rhetorical question to the
Swedish authorities. What would the government do if it discovered
Olof Palme's murderer one day after the statute of limitations went into
effect? The Swedish law, as far as I knew, had not been handed down
from Heaven and therefore could under certain circumstances be
altered. Given the seriousness of the charges, this appeared to be a case
in which special provision should be made to ensure that justice be
achieved.

Wiklund also asked me about the charges made by the emigres who
accused us of directing our campaign against particular ethnic groups.
I noted in response that the Jewish people had made special efforts to
honor those non-Jews who had saved Jews during the Holocaust.
Among those designated by Yad Vashem as one of the Righteous
Among the Nations was a Latvian named Janis Lipka who had personally rescued tens of Jews from the Riga Ghetto. He too was a Latvian
just like the criminals who had participated in acts of persecution and
murder. Lipka's deeds proved, moreover, that Latvians had a choice:
one did not have to support and abet the forces of evil. On that note, I

added that I found it unthinkable that Sweden, which had produced a hero of the dimensions of Raul Wallenberg, could continue to provide a haven for Nazi war criminals.[17]

The television interview focused mainly on the sources of the material presented to the government. It was known by this time that most of the allegations were based on Soviet publications, a fact which naturally aroused many question marks. In response I pointed out that there were no known cases to date in which evidence provided by the Soviets in Nazi war crimes trials had been proven false. Moreover, all the voluminous historical documentation in our possession from Western sources—both Jewish and non-Jewish—corroborated the massive collaboration of Latvians and Estonians in the implementation of the Final Solution. If the historical evidence indicated that the claims made in these Soviet publications were inaccurate, that would be grounds to question the validity of the allegations. If anything, the historical documentation fully corroborated the charges.[18]

This interview had a very amusing postscript. As part of the interview, Karlefors had me sit at my desk and pull out an index card from a box. To make it more authentic, I pulled out the card of a Latvian war criminal who had indeed been living in Sweden. He had already died but I did not think that the name mattered because I was told that it could not be seen on the screen. Or so we thought. The interview was filmed on Friday morning and shown on Swedish TV on Saturday. On Sunday evening I received a phone call from a journalist in Göteborg who told me that someone from his town had watched the broadcast and thought that his name was on the card that I had pulled from the box. I knew that that was impossible because the person whose card I had pulled had lived in Stockholm and was already deceased, but I was intrigued by the call. Perhaps the emigre in Göteborg had a guilty conscience? Perhaps we would be able to add another name to our list? I asked the journalist what the man's name was and why he was so concerned. Did he have something to hide? The journalist told me the name and related that the man suspected his name was on my list because the Germans had asked him to join the SS in Estonia. (According to the story he related to the journalist, he had been working on the tugboats in Tallinn harbor and had refused to join the SS.)

The journalist then asked me if I would be willing to check whether his name was on the card I had pulled or on any other list I might possess. I agreed to do so and when I responded in the negative, the Estonian got on the line and said "Oh, so now I can come for a vacation in Eilat this winter." I would be the last person to do anything which could adversely affect the Israeli tourist industry, but I explained to the journalist that ours was an ongoing effort and if we did not currently possess material regarding a certain individual, there was no guarantee that we would not find such evidence in the future. I do not know how the Estonian in Göteborg responded. I suppose one would have to check whether he ever made it to Eilat.

Shortly after the Center submitted its list, the Swedish government announced that it had established a panel of lawyers to investigate the charges. The members of the panel were three ministry under-secretaries for legal affairs: Johan Hirschfeldt of the Cabinet Office, Johan Munck of the Justice Ministry and Hans Corell of the Ministry for Foreign Affairs. They completed their investigation in early 1987 and submitted their findings to the government which informed us on February 12, 1987 that it had decided not to take any legal action against the suspects whose names were on the Center's list. In a letter to Rabbis Hier and Cooper, Prime Minister Ingvar Carlsson explained that

> The crimes that the accused persons are said to have committed came under the statute of limitations in Sweden a long time ago. Since 1926 the longest period of limitation in Swedish law has been twenty-five years. The idea of legislation that would retroactively change the legal position for the war criminals of the Second World War was strongly repudiated by Sweden as early as during the period of limitation. The three lawyers have therefore come to the conclusion that a change in this position must be regarded as out of the question. At today's Cabinet Meeting the Government decided not to take further action in response to your request.

Although the Prime Minister expressed his conviction that the crimes committed during the Second World War "must be condemned and must not be repeated" and noted the importance of the knowledge of those events which "must be an important lodestar for existing and coming generations," he opposed making any changes in the existing law. "I am convinced you understand that an amendment of the Swedish law would be contrary to fundamental principles which have been of guidance in legislation in our country for a long time."[19]

The Prime Minister also sent the Center a copy of the commission's findings which were the basis for the government's decision. What emerges from that document is a basic reluctance to squarely face the issue of Nazi war criminals. The commission notes, for example, that since the charges cannot be tried in Swedish courts, "there would be misgivings about trying the charges in some other way, for example by a commission of inquiry of some kind." If governments were to be dissuaded by misgivings, not a single Nazi war criminal would ever have been brought to trial. How can mere misgivings determine policy given the serious nature of the crimes?

The commission revealed either a lack of understanding of the research process in such cases or simply refused to face up to the challenge. Thus the report concluded that "the possibility of procuring basic data that would make a trial of the kind in question meaningful seems improbable." The Swedish government has apparently never heard of OSI, and did not know that tens of Nazi war criminals from the same general areas and who committed crimes of a similar nature to those alleged to have been committed by the suspects in Sweden had been prosecuted in the United States. And even if the possibility of procuring the pertinent documentation "seems improbable," why did the commission recommend dropping the matter? Were the charges not shocking enough? Would not such an answer be more credible after a serious attempt had been made to obtain the necessary documents?

The negative attitude of the commission is clearly reflected in the concluding paragraphs of its report. In response to the Center's request that the government investigate how many Nazi war criminals entered Sweden after the Second World War, the commission recommended in principle that this request be rejected. "To carry out an inquiry into the subject in the present situation would be doubtful from the point of view of principle," the lawyers concluded, "and scarcely meaningful from the point of view of establishing facts."[20] Given the number of suspects whose names we uncovered, one wonders how the results of such an investigation could be "scarcely meaningful," unless it was already obvious to the commission that the Swedish government would not take any action regardless.

We were upset by the response of the Swedish government but were hardly surprised. In the past the Swedish government has been reluctant to take action on similar issues, the Raul Wallenberg case being the most famous.[21] Our own efforts on these cases have, to a large extent, been stymied by the Soviets' refusal to grant access to their archives. The fact that only four of the twelve suspects are currently alive[22] also contributed to the relegation by the Center of our campaign in Sweden to a low priority.

There were no developments of note regarding the issue until late 1988. At that time we learned that a Swedish historian from Göteborg University named Helene Lööw was engaged in research on the entry of Nazi war criminals into Sweden after World War II. According to her findings, the number of criminals who had entered the country was more than one thousand, a figure far larger than we had ever imagined.[23] At a conference of children of survivors held shortly thereafter in December 1988 I attacked the Swedish government for harboring numerous Nazi war criminals and refusing to investigate the issue, noting that in this respect Sweden's image as a "humanitarian" country was not deserved.[24] In response, I received a lengthy letter from Swedish ambassador Mats Bergquist explaining that according to Swedish law, Nazi war criminals could not be punished due to the statute of limitations on all crimes, and that "an amendment of the Swedish law would be contrary to fundamental principles which have been of guidance in legislation in our country for a long time." Despite the ambassador's protestations about how important it was that "these war crimes do not fall into oblivion,"[25] it was obvious, however, that his government was fully intent on seeing to it that the criminals would indeed be allowed to fade unpunished into oblivion.

In the meantime, discussions with Helene Lööw led us to new documentation and interesting revelations. It appears that toward the end of the war, Iver Olsen, the representative of the U.S. War Refugee Board in Stockholm, financed several rescue missions to the Baltic states. The problem was, however, that Olsen's mission was to rescue Jews but instead he facilitated the escape to Sweden of Nazi war criminals. This took place because he entrusted the rescue missions to émigré Lithuanians, Latvians, and Estonians in Sweden. They utilized the opportunity to bring their compatriots, among them Nazi collaborators, to Sweden rather than saving the remnant of Jews still alive in the Baltics. (The terrible irony of the story was that American Jewish organizations, primarily the Joint Distribution Committee, but also the Orthodox Va'ad ha-Hatzala financed the War Refugee Board's activities.)

The pertinent War Refugee Board documents included detailed lists of the persons brought to Sweden.[26] A cross check of these lists with those of Baltic Nazi collaborators immediately yielded an additional list of suspected Nazi war criminals who had entered the country.[27] In addition, Helene Lööw had also uncovered additional cases of Nazi war criminals who had been admitted to Sweden[28] and thus it became clear that the scope of the problem was much larger than we had originally thought when we presented our initial list of suspects to the Swedish authorities. Our problem at this point was, however, that since all the suspects in question were from the Baltics, it was extremely difficult to obtain the necessary documentation and witnesses. Under such circumstances, it was extremely important to convince the government of the country in which the criminals resided to launch an official investigation of the charges since we had had absolutely no success with the Soviets, who were far more accommodating when the requests for documentation and testimony came from governments rather than from private Jewish agencies. The Swedish government refused, however, to launch an investigation and thus we were forced to try to collect all the evidence on our own.

At first we hoped to obtain the evidence from Helene Lööw, but she lacked the primary sources.[29] (Most of her research was based on the findings of the Sandler Commission, a panel established by the Swedish government after World War II to investigate the refugees who had entered the country during the war.)[30] We therefore turned to the Soviets to attempt to obtain the documentation and testimony regarding the suspects in Sweden,[31] but they never replied. Thus our efforts to achieve justice in Sweden were stymied by a combination of negative government policy and a lack of Soviet cooperation.

From time to time the Center has been approached by journalists who want to do stories regarding this issue,[32] but to date we have been unable to change the government's decision, which remains the major obstacle to progress in bringing the perpetrators of the Holocaust presently living in Sweden to the bar of justice.

Notes

1. WLA, 539/22, 24, 26, 27; *Daugavas Vanagi*, pp. 14, 20, 50, 54, 76-82, 101-3, 142-48; *"Political Refugees "Unmasked!*, pp. 17,20,21,25-29,32,62-69, 113-15, 134-37, 148-50, 152, 156, 173, 181-82, 192-97.

2. Tom Tugend, "Wiesenthal Center Listing 2,000 War Criminals," *Jerusalem Post*, October 17, 1986, p. 4.

3. Arne Lapidus, "Nazistika massmordare bor i Sverige," *Expressen*, October 23, 1986, p. 7.

4. Ann-Katrin Hagberg, "Vi ar beredda avsloja namnet pa Eskilstunabon,"

and "Nazist Jagarna Har Fel," *Folket*, October 25, 1986, pp. 1, 4.

5. Material collected for the *Pinkas Ha-Kehillot* volume on the Jewish communities of Latvia and Estonia published in late 1988 by Yad Vashem.

6. Letter of Ann-Katrin Hagberg to Efraim Zuroff, October 27, 1986, SWCA.

7. See note 3.

8. Conversation with Simon Wiesenthal, October 23, 1986.

9. Translation of broadcast by Tidningarnas Telegrambyra provided by Kenneth Ahlborn, October 1986.

10. The two main sources were: Raul Kruus, *People Be Watchful*, Tallinn, 1962 and Vladimir Molchanov, *There Shall Be Retribution*, Moscow, 1984.

11. Don Shannon, "Nazi Hunters Give Sweden 12 Names from Data Bank," *Los Angeles Times*, November 19, 1986.

12. See, for example, Arne Lapidus, "Listan pa de 14 nazi-bodlarna," *Expressen*, November 18, 1986, p. 17; "Listan pa misstankta," *Svenska Dagbladet*, November 19, 1986, p. 6.

13. "Wiesenthals jakt oroar tusentals nazistforbrytare," *Svenska Dagbladet*, November 19, 1986, p. 6.

14. See note 12.

15. "Sweden Says It Can't Act on Suspected Nazis," *Los Angeles Times*, November 20, 1986.

16. Johan Erseus, "Vara Kallor Ar Trovardiga," *Dagen*, November 22, 1986, p. 11.

17. Interview by Ake Wiklund, November 20, 1986, Jerusalem.

18. Interview by Bertil Karlefors, November 21, 1986, Efrat.

19. Letter of Prime Minister Ingvar Carlsson to Rabbis Marvin Hier and Abraham Cooper, February 12, 1987, SWCA.

20. "Summary," which accompanied the response by Prime Minister Carlsson to Rabbis Hier and Cooper, February 12, 1987, SWCA.

21. Abraham Cooper, "If the Swedes Chose, They Could Trade that Soviet Sub for Raoul Wallenberg's Life," *Los Angeles Herald-Examiner*, November 6, 1981. See also Harvey Rosenfeld, *Raoul Wallenberg; Angel of Rescue*, Buffalo, 1982, pp. 126-44.

22. This was confirmed by Prime Minister Carlsson in his letter to Rabbis Hier and Cooper, February 12, 1987, SWCA.

23. "Historian Documents Swedish Aid to Nazis," *Jerusalem Post*, November 20, 1988, p. 2.

24. Charles Hoffman, "Jerusalem Conference Told Sweden Sheltering Nazi War Criminals," *Jerusalem Post*, December 21, 1988.

25. Letter of Mats Bergquist to Efraim Zuroff, January 5, 1989, SWCA.

26. See for example "Report on Evacuation Activities during June-August 1949;" "Evacuation of Latvian Citizens—Report on the Situation by October,

1944;" "Sweden: I. Olsen's Reports," War Refugee Board Records, Box 72, FDR Library.

27. "List of Suspected Nazi Criminals—Sweden List #2," SWCA.

28. Helene Lööw, "Swedish Policy towards Suspected War Criminals 1945-1987," *Scandinavian Journal of History,* Vol. XIV, Stockholm, 1989, pp. 135-45.

29. See the letters of Efraim Zuroff to Helene Lööw and her responses from March 26 - November 26, 1989, SWCA.

30. Helene Lööw, "Swedish Policy Towards Suspected War Criminals," *Scandinavian Journal of History,* Vol. XIV, Stockholm, 1989, p. 137.

31. Letter of Efraim Zuroff to Natalya Kolesnikova, November 29, 1989, SWCA.

32. See for example letter of Ruben Agnarrson to Efraim Zuroff, July 14, 1992, SWCA.

13

Is The Hunt for Nazis Over?

Besides our efforts in Australia, Great Britain, Canada, and Sweden, the Wiesenthal Center also submitted the names of hundreds of suspects to the United States[1] and Germany,[2] tens of suspects to New Zealand,[3] and fourteen to Belgium,[4] as well as lists with several suspects to Argentina[5] and Venezuela[6] and a single suspect to Iceland[7] and Brazil.[8] Both the United States and Germany have specialized agencies to handle such cases, which over the years have acquired considerable experience and achieved notable successes. In these countries, special legislation for the prosecution of Nazi war criminals was not enacted, and the material we submitted was dealt with by the existent agencies.

In New Zealand we succeeded in inducing the government to establish a special war crimes investigations unit, but failed in our efforts to convince them to pass legislation to enable prosecution. Although several of the cases we uncovered had considerable potential, New Zealand has chosen to ignore the presence (in Auckland) of a member of the 12th Lithuanian Auxiliary Police Battalion as well as several others whose wartime activities were highly questionable.[9]

In Belgium we were stymied by a statute of limitations,[10] while the South American countries we turned to have not taken any action regarding the suspects, with the exception of one unique case. But that particular exception and the case in Iceland are worthy of further scrutiny because they afford us excellent insight into what can still be achieved in the field of Nazi-hunting in the nineties.

On October 13, 1987, Rabbi Hier and I held a press conference in Jerusalem to direct attention to our efforts to obtain access to the files of the UN War Crimes Commission. At this point, access was still restricted to governments which were barred from releasing the information to private organizations and individuals. We decided, therefore, to issue a list of the ten most notorious Nazis still at large, each of whom had a file in the UN archives. At the same time I compiled a "shadow list" of Nazi war criminals living in Western countries who were currently under investigation thanks to our efforts but who did not have files in the UN. This was because they had committed their crimes in areas which were at one time part of the Soviet Union, which had not been a member of the UN War Crimes Commission. The reason we presented the additional list was to apply pressure on the governments in question, primarily England, which had still not made a decision on this issue, while simultaneously indicating that governments had not always fulfilled their function in this respect. In our minds, it was imperative therefore that private agencies such as the Wiesenthal Center be granted access to the documentation in the UN archives. We also wanted to indicate that the primary opportunities for the prosecution of Nazi war criminals were presently in the Western countries which had been the primary focus of our recent campaign.[11] In reality, we ourselves were doubtful whether any of the criminals on our first most wanted list would ever be apprehended, while we were almost certain that quite a few of the suspects on the shadow list would eventually be tried.

Reality, however, is known on occasion to surpass even the best fiction. One of the names on our most wanted list was that of Josef Schwammberger, an Austrian who had served as the commandant of three forced labor camps in Poland (Rozwadow, Przemysl and Mielec), was known for his cruelty and had played an active role in the murder of numerous Jews. He had been arrested after the war in Austria, but had escaped from jail and disappeared. There were rumors that Schwammberger was living in Argentina but they had never been confirmed nor had he been apprehended. Schwammberger was number five on our wanted list and we made his photograph, as well as those of the other suspects, available to the press. We also noted that he was rumored to be living in Argentina.[12] The next day Schwammberger's photograph appeared in the Argentinian media and our suspect made his first mistake. Fearful of being apprehended, he left his home and fled to Huerta Grande in Cordoba province about 780 kilometers northwest of Buenos Aires. There he was identified and arrested by the local police on November 13, 1987. The key factors in his apprehension were apparently the photograph which had appeared in the press and the substantial financial reward offered by the German government for information leading to his arrest.[13]

In the summer of 1988, the Argentinian government initiated proceedings in Buenos Aires to strip Schwammberger of his Argentinian citizenship, as a preliminary step to his extradition to Germany to stand trial for murder. (He could not be tried in Argentina because that country had a statute of limitations of 14 years on the crime of murder.) The Center, in the meantime, had located some two dozen survivors who could identify Schwammberger, three of whom testified at the citizenship hearings in Buenos Aires.[14] Each recalled how Schwammberger had personally committed murder. In the words of Abraham Secemski of Chicago who had been imprisoned in Rozwadow and whose uncle had been shot to death by Schwammberger, "He was the god, the judge, the jury, the executioner. He was everything." Edward Blonder of Miami who had been with Schwammberger in Przemysl described him as "a sadist an evil person. He played games of life with humans, with Jews."[15]

In December, Schwammberger was ordered stripped of his citizenship and nine months later a Federal Appeals Court in La Plata denied his appeal of that decision. Two months later, Schwammberger was hospitalized following an apparent attempted suicide, but that did not prevent his extradition to Germany which took place on May 2, 1990. Schwammberger was extradited despite the absence of an extradition treaty between the two countries, since his entry to Argentina was deemed illegal in view of the fact that he did not admit at the time that he was a fugitive.[16]

On June 26, 1991, Josef Schwammberger's trial opened in Stuttgart. He was charged with aiding in the murder of more than 3,000 individuals, mostly Jews, many of whom he personally murdered. According to the prosecution, Schwammberger had shot inmates in the neck, hanged them or watched them slowly bleed to death after they had been savaged by Prinz, his pet Alsatian dog. The first major Nazi war crimes trial to be held in unified Germany, the proceedings were attended by neo-Nazis who tried unsuccessfully to disturb the court.[17]

As the trial unfolded, more and more evidence was presented regarding Schwammberger's cruelty and sadism. According to the witnesses, Schwammberger had personally murdered children with his own hands,[18] had used children as live targets[19] and murdered a rabbi who refused to work on Yom Kippur.[20] These testimonies and others ultimately paved the way for Schwammberger's conviction. On May 18, 1992 the former camp commandant was found guilty of seven counts of murder and 32 counts of being an accessory to murder and was sentenced to life imprisonment. According to the court, Schwammberger had personally murdered at least 25 Jews and was an accessory in the deaths of more than 600 others in the Rozwadow and Przemysl camps. In the words of Judge Herbert Luippold; "You and others must pay for what happened in that cruel, unbelievable time . We regret the fate of those people. They were killed only because they were Jews; sent to certain death in a time of cold-blooded, rationalized genocide."[21] Thus at the age of eighty, some fifty years after he committed his crimes, Josef Schwammberger was finally punished for his role in the implementation of the Final Solution.

Another recent investigation in which the Center was able to present a convincing case for prosecution, despite the passage of more than five decades since the crimes were committed, was that of Evald Mikson, an Estonian presently living in Iceland. If anything, the Mikson case is conclusive proof that one should never close the book on a Nazi war criminal until he is no longer alive.

As often happens in this field, our involvement began as a result of a lucky circumstance. In the fall of 1991, Yaakov Kaplan, an Estonian Jew living in Israel, was reading an Estonian newspaper when he suddenly came across an interview with Mikson. An amateur historian who specializes in the history of Estonian Jewry, Kaplan was well aware that Mikson had played an active role in the persecution and murder of the Jews during the Holocaust, but prior to reading the newspaper had no idea that he was alive and living in Iceland. He immediately contacted Professor Dov Levin of the Hebrew University, the leading expert on the fate of the Jews of the Baltic Republics during the Holocaust, who advised him to contact me to see what could be done. On October 25, 1991 Kaplan wrote me that Mikson was living in Iceland under the name of Edvald Hinriksson and briefly outlined his crimes, mentioning the names of several of his victims, among them Ruth Rubin, the 14 year old niece of famous Zionist leader Chaim Arlosoroff, whom Mikson allegedly raped before he murdered her. According to the newspaper in Kaplan's possession, Mikson was reputedly a friend of Icelandic Foreign Minister Hannibalsson, but in Kaplan's words "It is unthinkable that the son of a bitch will continue to live in quiet and tranquility, especially since Israel maintains proper diplomatic relations with Iceland."[22]

Kaplan came to see me shortly thereafter and supplied additional details regarding the case. We also began our own research and discovered that there was considerable material in secondary sources regarding the crimes committed by Mikson. According to these publications,

Mikson had been the leader of the *Omakaitse*, an Estonian vigilante squad, in the Vonnu district which persecuted and murdered innocent civilians. Later he served as an investigator at the Tartu concentration camp and in the fall of 1941 was appointed Deputy Chief of the Estonian Political Police in the Tallinn-Harju district. In each of his posts, Mikson was actively involved, according to these sources, in the murder of civilians. To support these charges, documents bearing Mikson's signature were published which clearly indicated his role in the arrest, persecution, and murder of Jews in Tallinn.[23]

On Sunday February 16, 1992, I found out that David Oddsson, the Prime Minister of Iceland, was scheduled to arrive in Israel the next night for a three day trip. His visit was obviously a wonderful opportunity to raise the issue, but first we had to determine whether Mikson was still alive and well in Iceland, since more than four months had passed since the interview he gave to the Estonian newspaper. Kaplan therefore came to my office and called Mikson (whose phone number I obtained via the international telephone exchange), posing as an Estonian who was organizing a reunion in Estonia this coming summer for all those who had served in the Estonian Political Police during World War II. Mikson's response was extremely enthusiastic and he eagerly volunteered his address and pertinent details, little realizing that within less than 48 hours his tranquil existence in Iceland was about to end.

Having confirmed that Mikson was alive, sane and reasonably healthy, I immediately contacted Iceland's honorary consul in Tel-Aviv Gad Nashitz and asked him to give Prime Minister Oddsson a letter and material which we had prepared regarding Mikson, upon his arrival. Nashitz refused to do so, apparently for fear of ruining the visit, so we approached the Israeli Foreign Ministry with a similiar request. They agreed in principle but could not promise exactly when Oddsson would receive the material, so we decided to send the package directly to his suite at the King David Hotel and at the same time provided copies of the relevant portions for the local and foreign press. Our request was that Oddsson "take whatever steps are necessary to insure that Iceland does not continue to offer shelter to Hitler's henchman Evald Mikson" and that the government investigate whether any other Nazi war criminals entered the country and were still living there.[24] A similar package was also sent to Icelandic ambassador to Israel Ingvi Ingvarsson with a request for a meeting to discuss the issue prior to his return to Copenhagen[25] (he was a nonresident ambassador).

The revelations regarding Mikson received extensive coverage the next morning as Oddsson began his state visit.[26] His first stop was (how appropriate) Yad Vashem where, at my request, officials raised the Mikson issue with the visiting prime minister. His response was that although he knew Mikson personally he was not aware of the charges and would investigate upon his return home.[27]Oddsson's reply was fairly reasonable, but in Iceland there were those who were quite upset by the accusations. Mikson, needless to say, unequivocally denied the charges claiming that no Jews had been persecuted in Estonia.[28] Foreign Minister Jon Baldvin Hannibalsson was even more indignant. He accused Israel of ruining Prime Minister Oddsson's visit, claimed that the charges were KGB fabrications[29] and was quoted as saying that had he been in Oddsson's place he would have taken the first plane home. As a sign of protest, moreover, he cancelled his planned official visit to Israel.[30] It should be noted that although very few Icelandic journalists accompanied Oddsson on his trip, the story created enormous interest in Iceland and the Center was inundated with calls from the Icelandic media. As one Icelandic journalist put it, from their perspective this was "the story of the year."

In the wake of the extensive coverage in Iceland, several interesting facts emerged regarding Mikson and his postwar activities. We learned that towards the end of the war Mikson had initially escaped to Sweden, where his wartime exploits were investigated. Despite his protestations of innocence, the Swedes sought to expel him to Estonia. A sympathetic official let him escape, however , and he set out for Venezuela, only to be stranded in Iceland, when his ship broke down on the way. Since his arrival in Iceland, Mikson had been active on the local sports scene and was considered "the father of Icelandic basketball." In fact, several days after the Center publicized the charges against him, Mikson was the guest of honor at the All-Star game of the Icelandic Basketball Federation. In addition, both his sons, Johannes and Atli, were soccer stars who had played for the Icelandic national team (as well as for top European clubs in Germany and Scotland) and he apparently was well-connected politically as well.

Given the fact that Iceland was such a small country (260,000 inhabitants), whose population had an ingrained hostility to "foreign intervention" and almost automatically always sided with their own,[31] it obviously was not going to be easy to induce the government to take action against such a popular local celebrity who was already over eighty. Nonetheless, there was one encouraging sign from the very beginning, the attitude of two young and energetic Icelandic journalists, Karl Birgisson of the weekly news magazine *Pressan* and Thor Jonsson of Channel 2 of Icelandic Television. Both began serious investigative work on the case immediately following the revelation of the charges and were able to uncover extremely valuable information. Both were not afraid to publish the most incriminating material and to call for government action, even though such a position was extremely unpopular in Iceland and even among their professional colleagues.

During the initial months after Oddsson's visit to Israel, we tried to obtain as much original documentation on Mikson as possible. We immediately wrote to the Estonian Minister of Justice and the director of the Central Archives,[32] as well as to Sweden,[33] but Thor Jonsson obtained quite a few important documents in Tallinn and Stockholm before we received any replies. The documents in question were arrest orders and interrogation reports signed by Mikson which clearly implicated him in the persecution of civilians, primarily Jews, in Tallinn.[34] At about the same time, Karl Birgisson uncovered a report by Olavi Viherluoto, a Finnish police officer who had been sent to Estonia in October 1941 and had met Mikson who openly told him that the Jews were being murdered.[35]

In the meantime, the Cabinet decided on March 13 to refer the Mikson case to the Justice Ministry for examination, and recommended that experts in international law and criminal law be consulted before a formal reply was given.[36] This decision was officially implemented 10 days later when Justice Minister Thorsteinn Palsson announced the appointment of Gudmundur Eiriksson and Eirikur Tomasson to examine the legal aspects of the Mikson case.[37] During this period we also began our efforts to persuade Israel to put pressure on Iceland and Estonia[38] and wrote to OSI to have Mikson officially put on the U.S. "watch list".[39]

In June we sent Prime Minister Oddsson copies of the documents obtained in Tallinn regarding Mikson's service in the *Omakasitse* and Estonian Political Police as well as the report by Finnish police officer Olavi Viherluoto. At the same time, we urged him to submit a formal request to the Estonian government for additional documents which we believed were in the archives in Estonia but were not in our possession.[40] In this respect we were certain that the Icelandic government would be able to obtain far more documentation than we, a private

Jewish agency, had been able to collect. I later reiterated this point in a letter to Thorsteinn Geirsson, secretary-general of the Icelandic Justice Ministry[41] in response to his request for "any further documents or data, other than already forwarded to the Prime Minister, relevant to the [sic] Edvald Hinrikssen's case."[42]

On September 30, 1992, the legal experts appointed by Justice Minister Palsson submitted their report on the Mikson case. (In the meantime Stefan Stefansson had replaced Gudmundur Eiriksson of the Foreign Office as a member of the panel). According to their findings, Mikson, who had obtained Icelandic citizenship, could not be extradited, but could be tried in Iceland for crimes he committed abroad prior to his arrival in Iceland. Due to the passage of time, however, the only crime for which he could still be tried in Iceland was murder, since there was a statute of limitations on all other crimes. The members of the panel did not consider the material they reviewed to have proven that Mikson had committed murder and therefore "We consider it neither appropriate nor obligatory to begin a public inquiry in this case as it is at present."[43]

I was hardly in any position to argue with the conclusions of the lawyers panel regarding the status of this case in Icelandic law, but it was obvious that the government had not been entirely honest in dealing with this issue. In theory, the lawyers had been asked to determine the legal aspects of the Mikson case and not evaluate the evidence. The fact of the matter was that the government had never launched an official full-scale inquiry nor had it ever attempted to obtain all the pertinent historical documentation and witness testimony. The lawyers' conclusion was based, therefore, only on partial evidence which did not fully reflect the facts of the case. In addition, the report included numerous historical errors and suppositions regarding Nazi war crimes investigations which were simply not true, as I pointed out in a letter to Prime Minister Oddsson:

After reviewing the material, my initial reaction is one of shock and dismay. On what basis can these learned judicial experts decide that there is insufficient evidence to initiate criminal proceedings against Evald Mikson, when the government never made any serious attempt to obtain all the available documentation and interview potential witnesses? How can Messrs. Tomasson and Stefansson assume that "important evidence has been lost" and that "any witnesses there may have been of the events are now mostly dead and that the few who may still be alive *probably* [my emphasis] do not remember key facts with certainty" when in effect no serious effort was ever made by the Icelandic government to locate and question such individuals? These are unfounded assumptions which have no basis in fact and merely serve to support the government's reluctance to launch a full-scale investigation of Mr. Mikson's wartime activities. If these assumptions were indeed true, it would be impossible to conduct Nazi war crimes investigations anywhere in the world. Yet at this very moment such investigations are being carried out by the governments of the United States, Germany, Canada, Australia, Great Britain, and New Zealand.

With all due respect to the learned authors of the report, they are hardly experts on the history of Estonia during World War II, a fact clearly reflected by the numerous factual errors in their presentation of the events. There was no Estonian Army in July 1941, so Mikson could not have served in it at that time. As far as the Omakaitse are concerned, they were nationalist vigilante squads, not a "resistance movement." The authors fail to note, moreover, their active involvement in the persecution and murder of innocent civilians, a factor of no small significance in evaluating Mikson's wartime activities. Even more important, the authors seem to have accepted Mikson's blatantly false version of his employment at the Security Police. I don't think I have to explain why he prefers having them think that his job was merely "searching for information," when in effect he played a pivotal role in the murder of innocent civilians.

By making its decision in this case without launching a full scale historical and judicial investigation of the events, the Icelandic government has shirked its duty and paved the way for a scandalous decision, which will remain a blot on Iceland's record. At times like this, when neo-Nazi extremism is raising its ugly head in Germany and elsewhere in Europe and right-wing fanatics question whether the crimes of the Holocaust ever took place, the decision of the Icelandic government will be a source of joy and inspiration for the forces of evil the world over. It is true that prosecuting Mikson would not bring to life a single one of his victims, but the fact that he will never be held accountable for his crimes will only encourage those who view his criminal acts with respect and admiration.[44]

Under these circumstances, it was obvious that the only way to overturn this decision was to obtain additional evidence to prove that Mikson had indeed committed murder, while at the same time putting as much public pressure as possible on the Icelandic government. Some of the ideas we considered at this point were to conduct a public trial of Mikson in Iceland, to have the relatives of those harmed by him sue him for damages,[45] or taking out full ads in the Icelandic press.[46] The more I considered the various options the more convinced I became that the key to the case was the evidence, and that without new documents and/or witnesses we would never convince the Icelandic government to take any action. I therefore made arrangements to travel to Tallinn in late November to try and obtain access to the pertinent documentation and to attempt to find witnesses who could testify regarding Mikson's murderous activities. With the help of Shmuel Lazikin, an Estonian Jew living in Israel who accompanied me on the trip, I was able to meet with Estonian Minister of the Interior Lagle Parek and Justice Minister Kaido Kama on the day of my arrival. The former was officially in charge of the archives, but told me that she could not give me an answer until the day before my scheduled departure because the government, which was only in power for a month, had still not decided what to do. In the meantime, we attempted to find witnesses with the help of David Slomka and Evgeny Loov of the local Jewish community, but it rapidly became clear that without the Mikson file from the KGB archives our chances of success were exceedingly slim.

It was therefore with no small degree of trepidation that I came to my second meeting with Interior Minister Parek on November 30. My fears were unfounded, however, since the minister gave the Center full access to the pertinent documentation and the right to make whatever copies were necessary. We then were taken to the former KGB archives, where we were shown three thick files on Mikson, and we made the complicated technical arrangements (we had to provide the paper ourselves) for the reproduction of the material.

Our return visit to Parek was followed by a meeting with Prime Minister Mart Laar who asked to see me following an interview I did on Estonian television in which I advocated efforts to punish not only Nazi war criminals, but Communist criminals as well. Laar, a historian by profession, had perused the KGB files and was therefore interested in our efforts. He told me that his grandfather had been murdered by the Nazis and spoke of his desire to establish a commission to document the fate of all Estonians murdered by the Nazis and the Communists since 1940. Although he was willing to declare his readiness to try Nazi war criminals in Estonia, his skepticism regarding the value of the war crimes investigations carried out by the KGB in Estonia led me to doubt whether such trials would ever be held in independent Estonia.[47]

The material we obtained in Estonia regarding Mikson was a veritable gold mine. The three files of criminal case 15-61 contained tens of witness statements concerning the crimes committed by Mikson as the leader of the *Omakaitse* in the Vonnu district, including testimony from seven individuals who personally saw him commit murder. According to the investigators in the case, Mikson had personally murdered 30 people and was responsible for the deaths of an additional 150.[48] Thus, for example, Johannes Sooru related how Mikson had shot a young man from Piirsare and then decided that every third prisoner from among the men being held in Vonnu would be shot by the *Omakaitse*.[49] Raimund Punnar confirmed this execution and told how Mikson shot numerous men that same night.[50] Particularly horrifying was the testimony of Hilka Mootse who related how Mikson raped a Jewish mother and her daughter. In her words:

> While arrested in the Vonnu rural district I saw together with other prisoners through a window in the basement how Mikson with a group of other Omakaitse members, about 6 or 7 men, took two Jewish women out to the street, a mother aged about 40 and her daughter who was 17 to 19 years old, stripped them naked, put chains on their necks, tied their hands behind their backs and began to make fun of them. The guards dragged the women on the ground, forced them to bend down and eat grass then pushed them to the ground and raped them. I saw how Mikson raped the women first and after him all the other guards did so as well. The women suffered a breakdown, then they were dragged behind a shed and executed by shooting.[51]

With these documents in our possession, we knew that our chances of inducing the government to take legal action against Mikson were much better. We started to attempt to influence public opinion by selectively releasing portions of the testimony to Karl Birgisson and Thor Johnsson.[52] This was followed by a trip to Reykjavik at the end of January 1993 to meet with Icelandic officials, submit the documentation to the judicial authorities and engage in dialogue with the Icelandic public. Both Prime Minister Oddsson and Justice Minister Palsson refused to meet with me, claiming that the Mikson case had nothing to do with them, but the local media were more than eager to give me an opportunity to present my case. Accompanied by New York businessman Aryeh Rubin, who had become a major supporter of the Center's efforts to prosecute Nazi war criminals, I met with Hallvardur Einvardsson, the Director of Public Prosecutions, as well as other government officials. We also held a very well-attended press conference and I delivered a lecture to a packed hall at Iceland University under the auspices of the Institute of Ethical Studies.[53] Needless to say there was extensive coverage of all these events.[54] Throughout our stay, and in particular at our meetings with Einvardsson and Justice Ministry officials, we called for the appointment of a special prosecutor for this case due to its complexity and urgency.[55]

Upon my return to Israel and Aryeh's return to New York, we immediately began taking steps to build up the pressure on the Icelandic government to put Mikson on trial. Thus in the latter half of February 1993 we began a campaign to send letters of protest to Prime Minister David Oddsson calling on him to "take the necessary measures to ensure that Iceland ceases providing a haven for a Nazi murderer."[56] Within weeks tens of letters began pouring in to the Center's New York office which assumed the task of coordinating this project in the United States and on May 4, Aryeh Rubin, New York Wiesenthal Center director Rhonda Barad and myself delivered more than 800 letters to local Icelandic consul Kornelius Sigmundsson.[57]

In the meantime progress was being made, albeit slowly, in Iceland and Israel. In mid-April, Hallvardur Einvardsson, the Director of Public Prosecutions, informed me that he had hired Prof. Jonatan Thormundsson, a highly respected professor of criminal law at Iceland University, as a special expert on the case. Thormundsson had been a special prosecutor in a previous, particularly complex case, which was the precedent on which we based our request for such an appointment,[58] a sign that augured well for the investigation. In Israel, after much effort, we finally obtained the recommendation of the Justice Ministry for a request to be made through diplomatic channels to Estonia to determine whether enough evidence could be found to launch a prosecution, or to Iceland, alone or together with Estonia, to investigate the matter for the same reason.[59] Thus the way was now clear, at least in theory, for active Israeli involvement. At the same time we began to sign members of the Knesset, as well as other Israelis, on the letters of protest to Iceland.

In mid-July, Mart Laar came to Israel for a four day visit. In the course of his meetings at the Foreign Ministry, he was asked to conduct a full-scale investigation of the Mikson case, so that Estonia could ask for his extradition since his crimes were committed in that country. Laar replied that such an investigation had already begun and he cited his ties with the Wiesenthal Center which he hoped would continue.[60]

During the summer we continued our letters of protest campaign, primarily in Israel. On August 12, 1993 I sent David Oddsson the signatures of 85 members of Knesset who had signed our letter of protest.[61] They represented 83% of those who could sign, since Cabinet ministers and the Speaker of the Knesset are not allowed to sign such letters. (The Knesset has 120 members of whom 17 are ministers.) Members of every party in the Knesset with the exception of the Arab Democratic Party were among those signing and in several cases entire factions (Tzomet, National Religious Party) signed, as well as five non-Jewish members of the Knesset. This was perhaps the only initiative of its kind which could unite MK's with such diverse political views. Less than a week later, our office in Jerusalem sent Prime Minister Oddsson 6,410 letters of protest signed by Israelis from all over the country.[62] The letters of protest signed by the members of the Knesset obviously made an impact in Iceland, as on August 13, Hallvardur Einvardsson announced that he had given instructions to open an official criminal investigation against Evald Mikson which would be carried out by the State Criminal Investigation Police in close cooperation with his office.[63] In the following months, the Icelandic investigators began collecting the pertinent documentation in the archives in Estonia, Sweden and Finland and prepared to travel to Estonia to interview potential witnesses. The investigation was unfortunately halted, however, when Mikson died in Iceland on December 27, 1993. According to family members, his health had suddenly deteriorated over the past several months,[64] or, in other words, since his adopted homeland had decided to open a criminal investigation for murder against him.

Fifteen years ago, hardly anyone knew that thousands of Hitler's henchmen were living in Western democracies. At that time, very few people realized the extremely significant role played by the Nazis' local collaborators in the implementation of the Final Solution (particularly in Eastern Europe), let alone sought to bring them to trial. Over the course of the past decade and a half, however, Nazi war crimes units have been established in the United States, New Zealand, Canada, Australia and Great Britain and in the latter three special legislation has been passed to enable the prosecution of the perpetrators of the Holocaust.

Yet while these laws constitute a highly significant moral and judicial achievement, especially at a time when Holocaust denial has become increasingly dangerous, they have, in practical terms, yielded almost no concrete results. Stringent legal requirements, a lack of documents and/or witnesses, and the absence or loss of political will have plagued prosecution efforts throughout the world with the exception of the United States (where suspects are tried for immigration and/or naturalization violations rather than war crimes).[65] But the setbacks suffered in Canada and Australia, the failures in New Zealand and Sweden and the lack of progress in Great Britain do not tell the complete story.

The Schwammberger trial and the Mikson investigation are concrete proof that Nazis can still be hunted successfully more then fifty years after they committed their crimes. Although the task is getting increasingly harder, it should not be considered impossible, nor should these crimes be relegated to the history books as long as their perpetrators are still living in our midst. On the contrary, we owe it first and foremost to the victims, but to ourselves and our children as well, that every effort be made to see to it that those who committed the crimes of the Holocaust will be brought to the bar of justice.

I consider my participation over the course of the past thirteen years in the efforts to discover and help prosecute Nazi war criminals a unique privilege, albeit one that was more often than not extremely frustrating and exasperating. Allow me therefore to conclude with the hope that despite all the obstacles the efforts of the Wiesenthal Center and other agencies, groups and individuals engaged in this task will be as successful as possible. Beyond that, we, those who have undertaken to participate in this mission, can at least find consolation in knowing that, like Mr. Wiesenthal, we will one day be able to face the victims of the Holocaust and say proudly and with a clear conscience that, "We did not forget you."

Notes

1. Lists of suspects were submitted to OSI on February 12, 1987 (74 suspects); April 14, 1988 (47); May 2, 1989 (18); June 20, 1989 (6); April 26,

1990 (38); January 30, 1991 (113); April 12, 1992 (1); April 2, 1993 (209). In all, the names of 506 suspects were submitted to the U.S. Justice Department which has consistently refused to divulge any details regarding the cases under investigation. On June 15, 1992, Jonas Stelmokas of Philadelphia, who had served as an officer in the 3rd Lithuanian Auxiliary Police Battalion, was indicted for concealing his wartime activities when he applied to emigrate to the United States. His name and immigration data were submitted by the Wiesenthal Center to OSI on February 12, 1987. See USA files, SWCA.

2. Lists of suspects were submitted to the German authorities on December 29, 1986 (44 suspects); June 2, 1988 (52 suspects); November 10, 1988 (55); November 17, 1989 (51); April 22, 1990 (130); January 28, 1991 (102); April 2, 1993 (155). Unlike the situation in the other countries to which such lists were submitted, there was a strong likelihood that the individuals in question were no longer living in Germany. The information we uncovered indicated that they had been in Germany shortly after the end of World War II, but in many cases such people emigrated elsewhere. All the names were nonetheless submitted to the German authorities so that the appropriate investigations could be carried out. A few were indeed discovered living in Germany and are currently under investigation. In Germany today, however, only individuals who personally committed murder can be brought to trial. See Germany files, SWCA.

3. The first list of eight suspects was sent to Ann Hercus, New Zealand's ambassador to the United Nations on May 11, 1990. The name of a ninth suspect was sent to Solicitor-General J. McGrath on August 22, 1990 and 32 additional names were submitted to the New Zealand authorities on September 5, 1990. See New Zealand files, SWCA.

4. On December 13, 1990 European director Shimon Samuels submitted a list of 14 suspected Nazi war criminals to the Belgian Ministry of Justice. See Belgium file, SWCA.

5. An initial list of seven suspects was sent to the Argentinian government in February 1988. A second list with two names was sent to Argentinian Minister of the Interior Jose Luis Manzano by Rabbi Hier on February 14, 1992. Two additional names (along with six names previously submitted) were sent by Rabbi Cooper to Argentinian Foreign Minister Guido Di Tella on November 4, 1993. See Argentina file, SWCA.

6. On November 5, 1986 Rabbi Hier, accompanied by U.S. Congressman Bill Lehman, submitted a list of three suspected Nazi war criminals to the Venezuelan Consul-General in Miami Benjamin Ortega. Among the suspects was Vladas Dervojedaitis, who was a member of the infamous *Ypatingas burys*. We later learned that he had already passed away in Venezuela. See Venezuela file, SWCA.

7. On February 17, 1992 the Center wrote to Icelandic Prime Minister

David Oddsson, who was visiting Israel at the time, regarding Evald Mikson, an Estonian who had played an active role in the persecution and murder of numerous civilians during World War II and had been living in Iceland since 1946. See Iceland files, SWCA.

8. On November 5, 1986 Rabbi Hier sent the name of a Lithuanian alleged to have served as a guard at the Treblinka death camp to Brazilian ambassador to the United States Sergio Correa de Costa. See Brazil file, SWCA.

9. See for example Anthony Hubbard, "War crimes: Is It All Over?," *Listener*, February 6, 1993, pp. 20-25. Hubbard played a leading role in investigating and exposing the suspects in New Zealand, as well as explaining the importance of prosecuting Nazi war criminals to the New Zealand public. See for example Anthony Hubbard, "Viewpoint," *Listener*, April 8, 1991, p. 7.

10. Eric Silver, "Tracking a Death Squad," *Jerusalem Report*, December 27, 1990.

11. Glenn Frankel, "Group Seeks Access to Files on Nazis," *Washington Post*, October 14, 1987.

12. "Names of 10 Most Wanted Nazis Released by Wiesenthal Center," *Los Angeles Times*, October 14, 1987, p. 5.

13. "Argentinians Arrest Top Nazi Schwammberger," *Jerusalem Post*, November 15, 1987, p. 1.

14. "Three Testify at Argentine Hearing in Proceeding Against Ex-Nazi," *JTA Daily News Bulletin*, July 6, 1988, p. 3; Memo by Lydia Triantopoulos, July 1, 1988, SWCA.

15. Randall Hackley, "War Camp Survivors Complete Testimony in Nazi Deportation Case," Associated Press, July 6, 1988.

16. "Josef Schwammberger," Simon Wiesenthal Center Fact Sheet.

17. Richard Meares, "Neo-Nazis Protest at Mass Murder Trial of Death Camp Boss," Reuters, June 26, 1991.

18. "Ha-Nazi Yozef Shwamburger Harag Yeladim be-Mo Yadav," *Yated Ne'eman*, November 25, 1991.

19. Daniel Dagan, "Ed be-Mishpat Shwamburger: ha-Nazi Hishtamesh be Yeladim ke-Matarot Yeri," *Ha-Aretz*, December 19, 1991.

20. "Witnesses: Nazi Murdered Rabbi over Yom Kippur," *Jerusalem Post*, October 22, 1991, p. 16.

21. Steve James, "Ex-Nazi Camp Boss Gets Life for Murdering Jews," Reuters, May 18, 1992.

22. Letter of Yaakov Kaplan to Efraim Zuroff, October 25, 1991, SWCA.

23. See for example Raul Kruus, *People, Be Watchful!*, Tallinn, 1962, pp. 240-259; Leonid Barkov, *Morvarid Ei Paase Karistusest*, Tallinn, 1966, pp. 73-74.

24. Letter of Efraim Zuroff to David Oddsson, February 18, 1992, SWCA.

25. Letter of Efraim Zuroff to Ingvi Ingvarsson, February 17, 1992, SWCA.

26. David Makovsky, "Iceland's PM Arrives," *Jerusalem Post*, February 18,

1992, p. 2.

27. Alex Doron, "Evdok Keitzad hitzliach meratzeiach Nazi limtzo miklat be-artzi," *Ma'ariv*, February 19, 1992, p. 17.

28. "Eger Saklaus," *Althydublalid*, February 19, 1992, p.1.

29. "Likt og ad leida mann i gildru," *Morgunblalid*, February 19, 1992, p. 1.

30. Eliyahu Zehavi, "'Parashat ha-Nazi' Nimshechet: Sar ha-Chutz ha Islandi lo yavo le-bikur," *Ha-Aretz*, February 23, 1992, p. 8.

31. Letter of Thor Johnsson to Efraim Zuroff, February 19, 1992, SWCA; letter of Karl Birgisson to Efraim Zuroff, February 28, 1992, SWCA; "Enginn Syknudomur I Svip Jod," *Pressan*, February 27, 1992, p. 14; Karl Birgisson, "Nazi on Ice," *Jerusalem Report*, May 7, 1992, p. 5.

32. Letters of Efraim Zuroff to Mart Rusk (Estonian Minister of Justice) and Peep Pillak (Director of Estonian National Archives), March 2, 1992, SWCA.

33. Letter of Efraim Zuroff to Per Ahlmark, March 1, 1992, SWCA.

34. The documents in question were the originals of the ones published in *People Be Watchful!*, Tallinn, 1962, pp. 240-259.

35. "Matkekertomus," "About the Trip on official business made by me to Tallinn between the 1 and 12 days 1941 on Orders given me by the chief of the State Police," October 21, 1941, quoted in Hannu Rautkallio, *Finland and the Holocaust; The Rescue of Finland's Jews*, New York, 1987, p. 135.

36. Letter of David Oddsson to Thorsteinn Palsson, March 13, 1992, SWCA.

37. The Justice Ministry had actually already commissioned an investigation on March 1, 1992. See the final "Report," September 30, 1992, SWCA.

38. Letters of Efraim Zuroff to Justice Minister Dan Meridor, Gideon Ben-Ari and Dan Megido, March 15, 1992, SWCA.

39. Letters of Efraim Zuroff to Neal Sher, March 18, and 22, 1992, SWCA.

40. Letter of Efraim Zuroff to David Oddsson, June 10, 1992, SWCA.

41. Letter of Efraim Zuroff to Thorsteinn Geirsson, September 17, 1992, SWCA.

42. Letter of Thorsteinn Geirsson to Efraim Zuroff, September 7, 1992, SWCA.

43. "Report," Submitted by Eirikur Tomasson and Stefan Stefansson to Icelandic Justice Ministry, September 30, 1992, pp. 19 (English translation).

44. Letter of Efraim Zuroff to David Oddsson, October 4, 1992, SWCA.

45. Ihugum ad halda opinber rettarhold a Islandi, *Morgunblalid*, October 14, 1992.

46. Fax of Efraim Zuroff to Aryeh Rubin, October 25, 1992, SWCA.

47. Efraim Zuroff, "Report on European Trip, November 22–December 3, 1992," SWCA.

48. "Decision to file evidence," September 18, 1961, criminal case 15-61, former KGB Archives in Tallinn.

49. Testimony of Johannes Sooru, June 8, 1961, criminal case 15-61,

former KGB archives in Tallinn.

50. Testimony of Raimund Punnar, June 7, 1961, criminal case 15-61, former KGB archives in Tallinn.

51. Testimony of Hilka Mootsa, June 12, 1961, criminal case 15-61, former KGB archives in Tallinn.

52. See, for example, Thor Johnsson, "Vitnisburdur um fimm mandrap," *DV*, December 17, 1992, and the issues of *Pressan*, December 10, and 17, 1992.

53. For full details on the trip see Efraim Zuroff, "Report on Trip to Iceland January 31-February 2, 1993," SWCA.

54. See for example "Iceland Considering New Evidence in Alleged Nazi War Crimes," Associated Press, February 3, 1993. "Oskar eftir skipun serstaks saksoknara," *Morgunbladid*, February 2, 1993, p. 20; Hver Er Afstada Islendinga Til Stridsglaepa," *Althydubladid*, February 2, 1993, p. 1.

55. Efraim Zuroff, "Report on Trip to Iceland January 31–February 2, 1993," SWCA.

56. Text of protest letter originally formulated February 17, 1993, SWCA.

57. Sue Fishkoff, "Iceland Probes Nazi Suspect," *Jerusalem Post*, May 5, 1993.

58. "Conversation with Icelandic Public Prosecutor Hallvardur Einvardsson," April 13, 1993, SWCA.

59. Letter of Marvin Chankin (Justice Ministry) to Ehud Keynan (Foreign Ministry), May 20, 1993.

60. Letter of Tzvi Maz'el to Efraim Zuroff, July 21, 1993, SWCA.

61. Letter of Efraim Zuroff to David Oddsson, August 12, 1993 (sent by fax), SWCA.

62. Letter of Efraim Zuroff to David Oddsson, August 18, 1993, SWCA.

63. Letter of Hallvardur Einvardsson to Efraim Zuroff August 19, 1993, SWCA.

64. "Alleged Criminal Dies," *Baltic Independent*, January 7-13, 1994, p. 3.

65. As of November 1993, OSI has filed cases against 90 suspected Nazi war criminals living in the United States. Forty-seven have been denaturalized and 38 have been deported or have voluntarily left the country.

Bibliography and Sources

The material in this book reflects only a small portion of the research conducted over the course of more than thirteen years, initially for the Office of Special Investigations and later for the Simon Wiesenthal Center. The main source consulted was the Yad Vashem Archives, the premier repository of Holocaust documentation in the world. The collections which were most important were those directly related to Nazi war criminals (M-9) and (M-21). Others which proved particularly helpful were those consisting of survivors' testimony—(0-2), (0-3), (0-4), (0-33) (0-71), and (M-1), as well as the records relating to the trials of Nazi war criminals conducted in West Germany (TR-10 and 0-53). Other major Israeli collections of documents and testimony related to the annihilation of European Jewry exist at:

Wiener Library—Tel Aviv University;
Beit Lohamei ha-Gettaot (Ghetto Fighters' House) at the kibbutz with the same name;
Moreshet Archives—Givat Chaviva Seminar Center;
Bar-Ilan University—Institute for Holocaust Research;
Oral History Division—Institute of Contemporary Jewry, Hebrew University, Jerusalem.

The number of relevant works consulted during the course of the innumerable investigations could fill a separate volume. I have chosen therefore to list only those works which primarily focus on Nazi war criminals and their postwar escape to the West.

I. Books

Aarons, Mark. *Sanctuary; Nazi Fugitives in Australia.* Melbourne: Heinemann, 1989.
Abella, Irving and Troper, Harold. *None Is Too Many: Canada and the Jews of Europe 1933-1948.* Toronto: Lester & Orpen Dennys, 1982

Avotins, E., Dzirkalis, J. and Petersons, V. *Daugavas Vanagi; Who are they?* Riga: Latvian State Publishing House, 1963

Bar-Zohar, Michael. *Ha-Nokmim.* Tel Aviv: Levin-Epstein, n.d.

Bar-Zohar, Michael. *The Hunt for German Scientists.* London: Barker, 1967

Baranauskas, B. and Rozauskas, E. *Masines Zudynes Lietuvoje 1941-1944; Dokumentu Rinkys.* Vilnius: Mintis, 1965

Baranauskas, B. and Rusksenas, K. (eds) *Documents Accuse.* Vilnius: Gintaras, 1970

Baranauskas, B. and Rusksenas, K. *Nacionalistu talka hitlerininkams.* Vilnius: Mintis, 1970

Blum, Howard. *Wanted! The Search for Nazis in America.* New York: Quadrangle, 1977

Bower, Tom. *Blind Eye to Murder; Britain, America and the Purging of Nazi Germany—A Pledge Betrayed.* London: Granada, 1983

Bower, Tom. *Red Web; MI6 and KGB Master Coup.* London: Aurum, 1989.

Bower, Tom. *The Paperclip Conspiracy: The Battle for the Spoils and Secrets of Nazi Germany.* London: Michael Joseph, 1987

Browning, Christopher. *Ordinary Men: Reserve Police Battalion 101 and the Final Solution in Poland.* New York: Harper Collins, 1992

Cesarani, David. *Justice Delayed; How Britain became a Refuge for Nazi War Criminals.* London: Heinemann, 1992

Dinnerstein, Leonard. *America and the Survivors of the Holocaust.* New York: Columbia University Press, 1982

Ehrenburg, Ilya and Grossman, Vasily (eds) *The Black Book: The Ruthless Murder of Jews by German-Fascist Invaders Throughout the Temporarily Occupied Regions of the Soviet Union and in the Death Camps of Poland During the War of 1941-1945.* New York: Holocaust Library, 1981

Elkins, Michael. *Forged In Fury.* New York: Ballantine, 1971

Harel, Isser. *Ha-Bayit be-Rechov Garibaldi.* Tel Aviv: Ma'ariv, 1975

Knoop, Hans. *The Menten Affair.* New York: Macmillan, 1978

Kruus, Raul. *People, Be Watchful!* Tallinn: Estonian State Publishing House, 1962

Littman, Sol. *War Criminal On Trial: The Rauca Case.* Toronto: Lester & Orpen Dennys, 1983

Loftus, John. *The Belarus Secret.* New York: Alfred A. Knopf, 1982

Molochanov, Vladimir. *There Shall Be Retribution (Nazi War Criminals and Their Protectors).* Moscow: Progress, 1984

Posner, Gerald L. and Ware, John. *Mengele: The Complete Story.* New York: McGraw-Hill, 1986

Riwash, Joseph. *Resistance And Revenge 1939-1949.* Montreal: by the author, 1981

Rückerl, Adalbert. *The Investigation of Nazi Crimes 1945-1978: A Documentation.* Heidelberg and Karlsruhe: C.F. Muller, 1979

Ryan, Allan A. Jr. *Quiet Neighbors: Prosecuting Nazi War Criminals in America.* San Diego: Harcourt Brace Jovanovich, 1984

Saidel, Rochelle G. *The Outraged Conscience: Seekers of Justice for Nazi War Criminals in America.* Albany: State University of New York, 1984

Segev, Tom. *The Seventh Million; the Israelis and the Holocaust.* New York: Hill and Wang, 1992

Sereny, Gitta. *Into That Darkness: From Mercy Killing to Mass Murder.* New York: McGraw-Hill, 1974

Silabriedis, J. and Arklans, B. *Political Refugees Unmasked!* Riga: Latvian State Publishing House, 1965

Simpson, Christopher. *Blowback; America's Recruitment of Nazis and its Effect on the Cold War.* New York: Weidenfeld, 1988.

Styrkul, Valery. *We Accuse.* Kiev: Dnipro Publishers, 1984

Wiesenthal, Simon. *Justice Not Vengeance.* New York: Grove Weidenfeld, 1989

Wiesenthal, Simon. *The Murderers Among Us.* London: Heinemann, 1967

Yahadut Lita. Vol. IV, Ha-Shoa 1941-1945. Tel Aviv: Association of Lithuanian Immigrants in Israel, 1984

Zeimantas, Vytautas. *A Call for Justice.* Vilnius: Mintis, 1986

II. Published Reports

Deschenes, Jules. *Commission of Inquiry on War Criminals: Report,* Part 1: Public. Ottawa: Canadian Government Minister of Supply and Services, 1986

In the Matter of Josef Mengele; A Report to the Attorney General of the United States. Washington D.C.: U.S. Justice Department, 1992.

Matas, David, Nazi War Criminals in Canada: Five Years After. Downsview: Institute for International Affairs of B'nai B'rith of Canada, 1992.

Nazi War Criminals in the United Kingdom: The Law. London: The All-Party Parliamentary War Crimes Group, 1989

Report on the Entry of Nazi War Criminals and Collaborators into the UK, 1945-1950. London: The All-Party Parliamentary War Crimes Group, 1988.

Review of Material Relating to the Entry of Suspected War Criminals into Australia—submitted by Andrew C. Menzies to Australian government. Canberra, 1986

Rosenbaum, Eli. The Campaign Against the U.S. Justice Department's Prosecution of Suspected Nazi War Criminals. New York: Anti-Defamation League of Bnai Brith, 1985

War Crimes; Report of the War Crimes Inquiry. London: Her Majesty's Stationery Office, July, 1989

III. Articles and Lectures

Ezergailis, Andrew. "Who Killed the Jews of Latvia?" lecture delivered at conference on "Anti-Semitism in Times of Crisis," April 10, 1986, Cornell University, Ithaca, New York

Friedlander, Henry and McCarrick, Earlean M. "Nazi Criminals in the United States: Denaturalization after Federenko," *Simon Wiesenthal Center Annual*, 3 (1986), 47-85

Friedlander, Henry and McCarrick, Earlean M. "The Extradition of Nazi Criminals: Ryan, Artukovic and Demjanjuk," *Simon Wiesenthal Center Annual*, 4 (1987), 65-98

Levin, Dov. "Lithuanian Attitudes Toward the Jewish Minority in the Aftermath of the Holocaust: The Lithuanian Press, 1991-1992," *Holocaust and Genocide Studies*, Vol. 7, No. 2 (Fall 1993), 247-262

Lööw, Helene, "Swedish Policy Towards Suspected War Criminals," *Scandinavian Journal of History*, Vol. XIV, Stockholm, 1989, 135-153

Neshamit, Sara. "Bein Shituf Pe'ula le-Meri," *Dappim le-Cheker ha-Shoa ve-ha-Mered*, Sidra Shniya, Me'asef Aleph (1970), 152-77

Schochet, Azriel. "Chelkam shel ha-Lita'im be-Hashmadat Yehudei Lita," *Dappim le-Cheker Tekufat ha-Shoa*, Me'asef Aleph (1979), 77-95

Index of People

375

Index of Places